Social Power in International Politics

This text introduces and defines the concept of social power and considers how it works in international politics. It demonstrates how social power is a complex phenomenon that manifests itself in a wide variety of ways and circumstances, particularly in culture, institutions, law, and the media. Providing a global perspective on the role of social power from the EU, the US, the Middle East, and China, this book:

- Focuses on the key aspects of social power: centrality, complexity, and comprehensiveness.
- Examines the complex relationship between soft and hard power, the role of the media, and new communications technologies.
- Explores the interplay between state and non-state actors in framing the public discourse, setting the agenda, moulding identities, and ultimately determining the outcome of policy processes.
- Features a broad range of international case studies and addresses issues including: culture and pop culture, media, public diplomacy, and branding.

With particular focus on the social power of non-state actors, such as non-governmental organizations, the media, and consumers, *Social Power in International Politics* offers a thought-provoking new perspective on how power is exercised in the complex reality of the contemporary world. It will be of particular interest to students and scholars of international relations, political science, and media and communications studies.

Peter van Ham is Director of Global Governance Research at the Netherlands Institute of International Relations *Clingendael*, The Hague, and Professor at the College of Europe in Bruges, Belgium.

The New International Relations
Edited by Richard Little
University of Bristol
Iver B. Neumann
Norwegian Institute of International Affairs (NUPI), Norway
Jutta Weldes
University of Bristol

The field of international relations has changed dramatically in recent years. This new series will cover the major issues that have emerged and reflect the latest academic thinking in this particular dynamic area.

International Law, Rights and Politics
Developments in Eastern Europe and the CIS
Rein Mullerson

The Logic of Internationalism
Coercion and accommodation
Kjell Goldmann

Russia and the Idea of Europe
A study in identity and international relations
Iver B. Neumann

The Future of International Relations
Masters in the making?
Edited by Iver B. Neumann and Ole Wæver

Constructing the World Polity
Essays on international institutionalization
John Gerard Ruggie

Realism in International Relations and International Political Economy
The continuing story of a death foretold
Stefano Guzzini

International Relations, Political Theory and the Problem of Order
Beyond international relations theory?
N.J. Rengger

War, Peace and World Orders in European History
Edited by Anja V. Hartmann and Beatrice Heuser

European Integration and National Identity
The challenge of the Nordic states
Edited by Lene Hansen and Ole Wæver

Shadow Globalization, Ethnic Conflicts and New Wars
A political economy of intra-state war
Dietrich Jung

Contemporary Security Analysis and Copenhagen Peace Research
Edited by Stefano Guzzini and Dietrich Jung

Observing International Relations
Niklas Luhmann and world politics
Edited by Mathias Albert and Lena Hilkermeier

Does China Matter? A Reassessment
Essays in memory of Gerald Segal
Edited by Barry Buzan and Rosemary Foot

European Approaches to International Relations Theory
A house with many mansions
Jörg Friedrichs

The Post-Cold War International System
Strategies, institutions and reflexivity
Ewan Harrison

States of Political Discourse
Words, regimes, seditions
Costas M. Constantinou

The Politics of Regional Identity
Meddling with the Mediterranean
Michelle Pace

The Power of International Theory
Reforging the link to foreign policy-making through scientific enquiry
Fred Chernoff

Africa and the North
Between globalization and marginalization
Edited by Ulf Engel and Gorm Rye Olsen

Communitarian International Relations
The epistemic foundations of international relations
Emanuel Adler

Human Rights and World Trade
Hunger in international society
Ana Gonzalez-Pelaez

Liberalism and War
The victors and the vanquished
Andrew Williams

Constructivism and International Relations
Alexander Wendt and his critics
Edited by Stefano Guzzini and Anna Leander

Security as Practice
Discourse analysis and the Bosnian War
Lene Hansen

The Politics of Insecurity
Fear, migration and asylum in the EU
Jef Huysmans

State Sovereignty and Intervention
A discourse analysis of interventionary and non-interventionary practices in Kosovo and Algeria
Helle Malmvig

Culture and Security
Symbolic power and the politics of international security
Michael Williams

Hegemony and History
Adam Watson

Territorial Conflicts in World Society
Modern systems theory, international relations and conflict studies
Edited by Stephan Stetter

Ontological Security in International Relations
Self-identity and the IR state
Brent J. Steele

The International Politics of Judicial Intervention
Creating a more *just* order
Andrea Birdsall

Pragmatism in International Relations
Edited by Harry Bauer and Elisabetta Brighi

Civilization and Empire
China and Japan's encounter with European International Society
Shogo Suzuki

Transforming World Politics
From empire to multiple worlds
Anna M. Agathangelou and L.H.M. Ling

The Politics of Becoming European
A study of Polish and Baltic post-Cold War security imaginaries
Maria Mälksoo

Social Power in International Politics
Peter van Ham

Social Power in International Politics

Peter van Ham

Taylor & Francis Group

LONDON AND NEW YORK

First published 2010
by Routledge
2 Park Square, Milton Park, Abingdon, Oxon, OX14 4RN

Simultaneously published in the USA and Canada
by Routledge
270 Madison Ave, New York NY 10016

Routledge is an imprint of the Taylor & Francis Group,
an informa business.

Transferred to Digital Printing 2010

© 2010 Peter van Ham

Typeset in Times New Roman by
Sunrise Setting Ltd, Torquay, UK

All rights reserved. No part of this book may be reprinted or reproduced
or utilized in any form or by any electronic, mechanical, or other means,
now known or hereafter invented, including photocopying and recording,
or in any information storage or retrieval system, without permission in
writing from the publishers.

British Library Cataloguing in Publication Data
A catalogue record for this book is available from the British Library

Library of Congress Cataloging in Publication Data
Van Ham, Peter
  Social power in international politics/Peter van Ham.
      p. cm. – (The new international relations)
  Includes bibliographical references and index.
  1. Power (Social sciences).   2. World politics.
  3. International relations.   I. Title.
  JC330.V35 2010
  327.1 – dc22   2009033548

ISBN 10: 0-415-56421-2 (hbk)   ISBN 13: 978-0-415-56421-2 (hbk)
ISBN 10: 0-415-56422-0 (pbk)   ISBN 13: 978-0-415-56422-9 (pbk)
ISBN 10: 0-203-85784-4 (ebk)   ISBN 13: 978-0-203-85784-7 (ebk)

To Lidewij and Thomas

The Second Coming

Turning and turning in the widening gyre
The falcon cannot hear the falconer;
Things fall apart; the centre cannot hold;
Mere anarchy is loosed upon the world,

The blood-dimmed tide is loosed, and everywhere
The ceremony of innocence is drowned;
The best lack all conviction, while the worst
Are full of passionate intensity.
—W.B. Yeats (1920)

Contents

Series editor's preface   xi
Preface   xiii

1 Social power defined   1

    1.1 Introduction 1
    1.2 Soft, sticky, or social 6
    1.3 Common knowledge, framing, and policy congruence 10
    1.4 Legitimacy and governance 13
    1.5 The hard–social power predicament 17
    1.6 Conclusion 20

2 Geopolitics and hegemony   24

    2.1 Introduction 24
    2.2 Hegemony and lite powers 27
    2.3 Pax Americana 30
    2.4 Europe's normative power 34
    2.5 The new Asian hemisphere? 38
    2.6 Conclusion 43

3 Culture and constructivism   46

    3.1 Introduction 46
    3.2 Pop culture and Realpolitik 50
    3.3 Consuming American culture 55
    3.4 Europe's cultural Maginot Line 59
    3.5 Europe's culture of cooperation 62
    3.6 Conclusion 67

4 Institutions and law   69

    4.1 Introduction 69
    4.2 Norm entrepreneurs and regulation 72

    4.3 Transnational policy networks 76
    4.4 Private authority 81
    4.5 Embeddedness and symbolic power 84
    4.6 Conclusion 88

5 Media and globalization   91

    5.1 Introduction 91
    5.2 Blogs, wiki's, and social power 96
    5.3 New media meets old power 100
    5.4 Media, conflict, and war 105
    5.5 Sex, lies, and soft news 108
    5.6 Conclusion 111

6 Public diplomacy   114

    6.1 Introduction 114
    6.2 Wielding social power 118
    6.3 Winning the war of ideas 121
    6.4 Public diplomacy in practice 124
    6.5 Public diplomacy goes truly public 128
    6.6 Conclusion 132

7 Place branding   136

    7.1 Introduction 136
    7.2 Place branding's pedigree 141
    7.3 Branding Europe 145
    7.4 Brand USA 149
    7.5 Negative branding 153
    7.6 Conclusion 157

8 Conclusions   159

    8.1 Defining the situation 159
    8.2 Making it work 162
    8.3 Tilting the playing field 165

Notes   168
Bibliography   210
Index   247

Series editor's preface

Despite the historical importance of political realism and its obsession with "power politics," diverse International Relations (IR) scholars have long recognized that the (inter)discipline of IR has in fact systematically underestimated the amounts, sources, types, modalities, locales, and practices of power implicated in both the constitution and the conduct of international life. We know that politics is saturated with power: whether hard and sharp, whether soft, sweet or sticky, whether agentic or structural, power determines how political outcomes are produced and how the identities and actions of diverse actors, individuals, or institutions are enabled, produced, constrained, and transformed. That said, we also know that power as a concept is essentially contested. Both political and theoretical commitments influence our conceptualizations of power. Realists are committed to understandings of power that serve the national interests of states; liberals search for ways to check and limit the power of the always potentially totalitarian state; historical materialists investigate the power that resides in the structures of global capitalism and their exploitative class relations; feminists expose the gendered power relations that sustain the everyday practices of world politics; post-structuralists deconstruct the capillary practices of power that constitute the modern world and its subjects. Looking across these often competing but sometimes surprisingly complementary understandings of power, it seems that whatever "power" is, it works in such diverse ways that no single formulation can adequately capture it. So students of world politics rightly continue to search for ways to excavate and comprehend those varied practices we collectively consider somehow to be about "power."

Peter van Ham's *Social Power in International Politics* adds importantly to the debates about and the conceptualizations of power in international politics, arguing provocatively that "*social power is the key to understanding contemporary international politics.*" He sets his loosely constructivist, but wide-ranging and eclectic, analysis of power in the context of a rapidly changing and increasingly complex global system, one shifting from traditional forms of state-based authority towards structures and practices of global governance. In this increasingly global context, the establishment and, importantly, the legitimacy of rules and norms are of central importance, but sometimes of questionable robustness. In this context, van Ham is interested in how an assortment of actors – not just states but also NGOs, corporations, international organizations, and the media, among others – influence each other in setting and legitimizing norms and rules of global governance.

Van Ham offers us a constructivist notion of "social power," a "particular face of power" that captures "the ability to set standards, create norms and values that are deemed legitimate and desirable, without resorting to coercion or payment." Like soft power, which it subsumes, social power works by co-opting others, rather than coercing them. Social power is thus inherently relational – the locus of its operation is in reciprocal social interaction – as well as both intangible and versatile. Social power therefore resides in such diverse practices as agenda-setting, issue or problem framing, public diplomacy, norm advocacy, discursive power, and what van Ham calls "place branding." He examines all of these loci of power, and others, in this insightful volume.

Refreshingly, van Ham makes a modest epistemological claim for his book: it "will plausibilize, rather than test and prove new insights" about the nature and workings of social power. Moreover, rather than forcing the analysis of power in international politics into the straightjacket of rigid definitions and typologies, van Ham recognizes the "complexity and ambiguity" of social power. Rather than offering us a horse race – which conceptualization of power is better and thus wins? – this analysis opens up a terrain of research, investigating some of the complex relations between and among different forms of power. Van Ham urges us to "accept power's polymorphous character" and to recognize that different approaches to power may be rewarding when studying different facets of international life. Importantly, and in line with this assumption, he understands social power to interact in complex ways with hard power: rather than forcing a choice between definitions of power, van Ham's analysis recognizes that various forms of power can be, and often are, at play simultaneously. He investigates these complex interactions in a variety of contemporary settings, including the use by the United States, the EU and China of social power to sustain their hegemonic ambitions; an examination of how popular culture and consumer habits functioned as conduits of American cultural power and European resistance to it; the development and use of symbolic power embedded in institutions like NATO; the use of old and new media as conduits for social power; the practice of US, Chinese and European public diplomacy; and the "place branding," both positive and negative, of states like the United States, Kazakhstan, and Denmark.

Jutta Weldes, February 2010

Preface

It is the nature of politics that conflicts and scandals make headlines. Wars are visual spectacles that fit today's yearning for images. Pictures of rockets fired, cities destroyed, and people murdered grip the public imagination. But behind this visual tapestry of power and politics hides the complex world of global governance. Since hard power, coercion, and force play a less pronounced role in the management of the bulk of international politics, economics, and law, this vast area of global governance escapes the public eye. This is the area where states, International Organizations, non-governmental organizations, firms, and media shape the norms and rules that govern our societies, as well as our economic and financial system.

This book introduces the concept of social power to explain how this medley of actors influence each other and try to set the rules of global governance. It is often difficult to determine who influences whom, how, when, and why. Because it is so difficult, one is tempted to seek comfort in straightforward and simple explanations. This book offers no such soothing moorings. Instead, I have sought to systematically develop the concept of social power in international politics that I have previously only examined in a piecemeal fashion in other publications. Social power includes agenda-setting, framing, public diplomacy, as well as (place) branding. Social power is often used to advance policy issues not against the interests of others, but by co-opting other actors, rather than coercing them. Whereas Realists generally look for power in situations characterized by conflict, social power is frequently (but not exclusively) found in cases which seem harmonious, at least on the surface. By examining the intricacies of world politics through the prism of social power, we get into view the vast area of global governance and finally arrive at a better understanding of how interests are formulated and protected. Although we may still be confused about the complexity of contemporary power relationships, this book hopes to lift the reader's confusion to a higher level of sophistication.

I have benefitted greatly from the ten years that I have taught a course on global governance at the College of Europe, in Bruges (Belgium). I am also grateful to the anonymous reviewers whose critically constructive comments have made this a better book than it would otherwise have been.

Finally, I dedicate this book to my children, Lidewij and Thomas.

Peter van Ham, The Hague, July 2009

1 Social power defined

1.1 INTRODUCTION

When W.B. Yeats wrote his famous poem *The Second Coming*, in the revolutionary aftermath of World War I, it was generally assumed that the established rules and mores had been overtaken by events, and were ready for a major and radical overhaul. Indeed, anarchy was looming, things seemed to be falling apart, and traditional institutions of authority were no longer able to keep the center together. Although today's political tableau is less ominous and does not foreshadow a looming anarchy, it seems clear that we are equally witnessing a major reshuffling of economic, political, and social cards on the global stage. As Richard Haass has argued, the world is entering a new era "dominated not by one or two or even several states but rather by dozens of actors possessing and exercising various kinds of power."[1]

Although still dominant, the United States is no longer the unquestioned hegemon, setting and maintaining the guidelines of the world economy, international politics, and law.[2] Rising powers like China and India claim their rightful place in world politics, and want to get their voices heard and respected. Russia, which had its wings clipped after the end of the Cold War, is re-emerging, using military bullying and its abundant energy supplies as tools of statecraft.[3] On the other hand, globalization and the ongoing revolution in information technology (IT) continue to level the playing field between industrial and developing countries, making the world "flat", in Thomas L. Friedman's well-known phrase.[4] New Internet-based media are changing the global information environment, making it hard for classical gatekeepers (like the state) to control information, and easier for a multitude of social actors (especially firms and non-governmental organizations (NGOs)) to influence political agendas and priorities. This makes it questionable "whether any country can any longer consistently wield 'super' or even 'great' power, given the sheer pace and complexity of systemic changes, a global crisis of political authority, and the influence of so many polities of different types on a host of crucial issues."[5] The 2008 meltdown of the global financial system has further undermined the self-confidence of Western powers, whose role has been reduced to "impotent commentators."[6]

The sheer complexity and dynamics of global economic and political change requires a thorough reconsideration of one of the most fundamental concepts of

2 Social power defined

the social sciences: power. The debate about power is ongoing, and remains central to the study of international politics.[7] The godfathers of the discipline of international relations (IR), like E.H. Carr, Hans Morgenthau, Kenneth Waltz, and Karl W. Deutsch, were all primarily concerned with the working and distribution of power in the international system. Going further back in time, the philosophical roots of IR can be found in the classical works of Thucydides, Machiavelli, and Hobbes, whose tracts on war and conflict tried to answer the key questions: what is power and how can, or should it be used? Today, the debate about power is predicated on the understanding that the character of international politics is changing, and that we are moving away from classical state-based authority towards "global governance."[8] As David Held has it, "we must recognize that political power is being repositioned, recontextualized, and, to a degree, transformed by the growing importance of other less territorially based power systems."[9]

But radical change is not limited to the sphere of international politics. Social scientists remind us that power is all around us. No one can escape power relationships, since we all influence each other and are in turn influenced by others. Since the most common definition of power is the sense of someone getting someone else to do something they would otherwise not do, we are confronted with power within the family, as consumers, voters, lovers, and in all other social relationships.[10] Why we buy a certain product, support a certain presidential candidate, or accept a foreign country's political leadership, all boils down to the power of branding, spin-doctoring, or loyalty. As a result, power becomes ubiquitous, in the sense that it is in all arenas of social life, as well as complex, since it is often ambiguous who exercises power, and how.[11] Little surprise, therefore, that new facets and *loci* of authority, as well as new notions of power have come to the fore.[12]

This is reflected in today's political debate, which suggests that power comes in all shapes and sizes, catering to all tastes. Idealists with sanguine views about human nature may champion the notion of soft, smart, or sticky power, convinced as they are that persuasion and benchmarking will get the best out of Man, as well as out of states.[13] Skeptics and self-styled Realists who take anarchy for granted, continue to rely on hard, military power as the final judge of who is right, or at least who will get his right.[14] Since the Realist notion of power is the "meaning-in-use" in both the public and academic discourse of international politics, newer notions of power challenge and destabilize the debate. They give rise to several fundamental questions: How should we study power? Is it based on, or embedded in, resources or in relationships? Should we examine structures or focus on agency? Is power a potentiality or an actuality? Which actors are the most salient, deserving our attention?

Depending on one's theoretical and methodological choices, power is defined and measured differently. The study of power remains riddled with ontological dilemmas, turning it into an intellectual battleground whose outcome remains undecided.[15] In particular, making comparable judgments on the extent of power remains an intractable source of controversy. Who affects whom, and who has more influence over matters of central importance, ultimately seems to boil down to a value judgment. In this context, Friedrich Kratochwil has big-heartedly made

Social power defined 3

the case for pragmatism, calling upon scholars to continue their research despite uncertainties and unknowns, and in the absence of logically defensible warrants.[16] It is with this encouragement in mind that this book studies a particular face of power, which I label "social power." The term is not new, and has obviously been used more widely and more often in sociology than in the study of international relations.[17] This introductory chapter defines social power, relating it to other relevant notions of power and legitimacy. Although this opening chapter will set the theoretical stage, subsequent chapters will further clarify the notion of social power, explain its relevance and limits, and make clear why it is a key concept to understanding contemporary international politics.

There are many different ways to get one's arms around the concept of social power. To start with, the "social" in social power derives from the understanding that power is fluid and non-linear, and that it moves through relationships and communication. For example, merely looking at resources and objective capabilities is hardly useful without examining how they are used and perceived by other relevant actors. Realists generally examine power in terms of coercion, as something that is possessed and accumulated, measurable, visible, and working on the surface. The study of social power, however, takes a markedly different approach, looking for power beneath the surface, as permeating all social relationships, institutions, discourses, and media.[18] The notion of social power aims to offer a necessary alternative conceptualization of power since it acknowledges that the exercise of power always takes place in a specific social situation and is therefore inherently contextual. Just as a gun secretly hidden in a closet without anyone knowing about it does not result in a credible threat of force, social power is contingent upon interaction, communication, relationships, and institutions. Or, as Yale H. Ferguson has argued: "[p]ower is not like money in the bank, [but] rather a relative matter. The effective exercise of potential power is dependent on the actors being targeted, the issue involved, and prevailing circumstances."[19]

Power therefore comprises a dual ontology: one based on social interaction, and one as an essential condition and resource. This is obviously confusing. Social power's ontology, however, is much clearer, since (as the concept itself indicates) it is predicated upon the notion that this face of power derives from communication, social knowledge, and economic and political interaction. This implies that social power only works in relationships and is ultimately dependent upon the perception of others. David A. Baldwin has already recognized power to be situationally specific, mainly because power is exercised in a reciprocal relationship between two or more actors.[20] And, as Alain Touraine has claimed, "all social relations include power relations. There is no purely horizontal social relation."[21] For social power to become part of a strategic doctrine, policymakers must think carefully about how to *use* power. Policymakers realize that they can never take social power for granted, although they generally remain confused about how to use it. Moreover, since continuing relations give rise to social learning, social power is inevitably a long-term process, and should be studied as such.

What counts as power and being powerful remains controversial. Steven Lukes suggests that the study of power is fraud with two basic mistakes: first, the so-called "exercise fallacy", which assumes that "power can only mean the causing of an observable sequence of events"; and second, the "vehicle fallacy", which "equates power with power resources."[22] Often, the exercise of power suggests activity and agency to bring about certain intended consequences, whereas passivity and non-action may at times demonstrate an actor's power to resist change. More often than not, the assumption is made that power involves going *against* the interests of others, which excludes significant parts of the more novel (and as I will argue: more interesting) aspects of social power, which include agenda-setting, framing, public diplomacy, as well as (place) branding. Social power is often used to advance policy issues not against the interests of others, but by co-opting other actors, rather than coercing them. Whereas Realists generally look for power in situations characterized by conflict, social power is frequently (but not exclusively) found in cases which seem harmonious, at least on the surface.

R.P. Wolff's well-known example illuminates the subtle difference between power based on pure, often physical coercion, and social power: If I am forced at gunpoint to hand over my money, I am subject to coercive power, but if I pay my taxes (although I may dislike it and even occasionally cheat), I recognize legitimate authority, acknowledging the social power of the state.[23] Most European states have gone through the historical phase when tribute was paid to kings, which over centuries was transformed into paying taxes to governments. In this case, the difference is made by the new element of legitimacy, which transforms theft into a civic duty. It is therefore important to recognize that legitimacy may confer power, but should not be confused with power itself. From this perspective, legitimacy is just one method to socialize power.[24]

Social power is also at play when mothers are "not angry, but disappointed" by their children's behavior, by shoppers who buy Nike in order to fit in with their peers, or by European Union (EU) member states who reluctantly comply with EU regulations due to a complex mix of international legal constraints, political factors, and normative pressure. Social power is at work when the United States tries to touch the "hearts and minds" of the men and women on the "Arab street", trying to entice them to embark upon the thorny road towards liberal democracy. It is also at work when cities and states make efforts to lure tourists and students to spend time and money in their territory, or when US President George W. Bush takes tar and feathers to brand countries like Iran and North Korea as the Axis of Evil. In all these cases, power is embedded in complex, reciprocal relationships. At times it may not even be clear who *has* (let alone *exercises*) power. For example, it is uncertain whether social power is applied by consumers who buy Nike, or by Nike who gets consumers to buy their product. Generally, product branding suggests that Nike draws on social power. But when an organized consumer boycott pushes Nike to change social standards in Asian sweatshops, it is clearly the other way round.[25] Studying social power is therefore a highly contextual affair, which prohibits the drawing of general conclusions based on sweeping statements.

Admittedly, this complicates any study on the nature, *locus*, and scope of power in international politics, since it becomes problematical to distinguish between the hard power based on coercive measures (be they economic or military in nature), and the social power based on non-coercive mechanisms, structures, and processes. Whereas military power is visible and mediagenic (battleships are moved, and shots fired, oftentimes *live* on TV), social power generally lacks visibility and public attention. By their very nature, institutions and relationships are visually unappealing, and often elusive. The simplicity and straightforward quality of hard power stands in stark contrast to the complexity and ambiguity of social power.

Studying the Cold War's dying years offers us some good insights into the complex interplay between hard and social power. Obviously, the West "won" this Cold War, since its own societal model has prevailed.[26] But how did the West "win", and by which means? By outspending the Soviets through a military arms race? Or by the luring vistas of political and religious freedom, combined with affluence and consumerism? Soviet dictator Stalin famously asked: "The Pope? How many divisions has he got?" Stalin subscribed to an undiluted Realist worldview, seeing the globe like a chess game ultimately determined by sheer military force.[27] It was a twist of fate that the Polish Pope John Paul II may have been instrumental in undoing the Soviet "Evil Empire" not with military divisions, but by using the social power vested in his authority as leader of the Roman Catholic Church.[28] Others argue that it was globalization which gave the kiss of death to the Soviet system, since the image of an affluent Western society was just too enticing for ordinary people in Central and Eastern Europe to ignore.[29] As Benjamin Barber submits, the Communist revolutions of the late-1980s were less over the right to vote, than the right to shop.[30] This suggests that both explanations can hold true. Both the hard power of US President Reagan's Strategic Defense Initiative (SDI, or "Star Wars" as it was informally referred to), and the social power of a liberal democracy-*cum*-market economy have been at play.

But "the memory of the past is a prize worth struggling for", as Tina Rosenberg has rightfully argued.[31] By claiming that "NATO won the Cold War" under US leadership, the role of hard, military power has become privileged, offering American policymakers the discursive power to define economic, social, and political problems, and suggest policy solutions (*viz.* the 1999 Kosovo intervention, and the 2003 Iraq war). Those who argue that Western social power and globalization have been equally instrumental in undoing the Soviet system have a more complex story to tell since where hard power is visible, social power is intangible and versatile.[32] Moreover, and as we will discuss later on in this chapter, social power cannot be wielded easily, or deliberately and persistently applied by policymakers. Quite unlike hard power, it cannot be counted and measured, which makes it rather easy to dismiss and difficult to demonstrate.

This book makes up for these shortcomings by telling the story of how social power works in international politics, painting the big picture as well as offering the necessary vignettes and case studies. This book will not arrive at a final judgment about the role and place of social power in international politics. As we will see, the "how" and "how much" questions will continue to complicate any clear conclusion as to the impact of social power *vis-à-vis* other manifestations of power and influence. This book will plausibilize, rather than test and prove new insights. I will, however, argue that social power is a central part of contemporary international politics, that it is a complex phenomenon, and that it should be seen as a comprehensive feature of the power spectrum, and not as a side-show to hard power. These three C's—centrality, complexity, and comprehensiveness—are the fundamentals of social power this book will examine.

1.2 SOFT, STICKY, OR SOCIAL

The concept of soft power has emerged as the best-known challenger of hard power, famously defined by Joseph S. Nye as "the ability to get what you want through attraction rather than coercion or payments."[33] Nye claims that soft power derives from the attractiveness of the culture, political ideals, and policies of a country. In his view, soft power should be considered a significant asset to influence others, not by using force, but by "the ability to attract", which goes beyond influence, or persuasion. Moreover, he claims that when a country's foreign policy is widely regarded as legitimate in the eyes of others, that country's soft power is enhanced.[34] Nye sees legitimacy as a psychological lubricant within international politics, arguing that if "a state can make its power legitimate in the eyes of others, it will encounter less resistance to its wishes."[35]

Since Nye introduced soft power in the early 1990s, the concept has gained remarkable currency, even to the extent that Robert M. Gates stated in November 2007: "[B]ased on my experience and serving seven presidents, as a former Director of CIA and now as Secretary of Defense, I am here to make the case for strengthening our capacity to use 'soft' power and for better integrating it with 'hard' power. One of the most important lessons of the wars in Iraq and Afghanistan is that military success is not sufficient to win."[36] One could surely argue that when an American Secretary of Defense calls for more soft power—instead of more battleships, fighter aircraft, and "muddy boots on the ground"—this concept has become mainstream and conventional.

On the fringes of soft power, several other concepts have flourished. In particular, Walter Russell Mead has prolifically added different nuances by introducing notions like "sharp power", "sweet power", and "sticky power."[37] Sticky power is particularly relevant to our debate. Mead argues that the US has ample sharp (military) power as well as sticky (economic) power. Mead uses the carnivorous sundew plant as an example to illustrate the stickiness of power. This plant "attracts its prey with a kind of soft power; a pleasing scent that lures insects towards its sap. But once the victim has touched the sap, it is stuck; it can't get away."[38] Were it not for the somewhat creepy metaphor (doesn't the sundew plant ultimately digest its prey?), sticky power conjures up images of embeddedness, of the complex interdependence scholars like Robert Keohane and Joseph Nye introduced in the 1970s, taking a leaf out of a much older book by Norman Angell who in the early-twentieth century foresaw Kantian peace through economic connectedness.[39] The assumption behind all these different concepts and half- or fully-baked theories is that once an actor decides, often on the basis of hard-nosed Realist arguments, to join a framework of cooperation, that actor is "stuck", just like the insect on the sundew plant, and will not be able to free itself.

Sticky power therefore revisits liberal institutionalist thinking, which suggests that treaties and International Organizations (IOs) have a significant impact on state behavior in terms of formulating (and reformulating) state preferences and choices.[40] Sticky power is not limited to economic institutions, but applies to most—if not all—IOs and legal frameworks. Stephen D. Krasner's well-known definition of a regime as a set of explicit or implicit "principles, norms, rules, and decision-making procedures around which actor expectations converge in a given issue-area" is very relevant to our debate.[41] This was already recognized by E.H. Carr, who in his *The Twenty Years' Crisis* (1939) argued that the Anglo-Saxon control over ideas constitutes a major source of global power: "current theories of international morality have been designed to perpetuate their supremacy and expressed in the idiom peculiar to them."[42] The power of ideas and norms, as well as the dominance of discourse are therefore hardly new aspects in a new power game. Still, over the last few decades their importance has increased significantly.

John J. Mearsheimer still maintains that "power is based on the particular material capabilities that a state possesses (…) What money is to economics, power is to international relations."[43] Indeed, just as economists assume that people seek wealth, Realists assume that states seek power. Although this may be true at a very basic level, it is also an oversimplification, since power is hardly ever an end in itself and is almost always a means to achieve other goals (varying from survival to reputation, and everything in between). The study of power has therefore gone beyond Realism, and Realism's challengers have become more vocal, more sophisticated, as well as more credible. Apart from the dwindling pool of die-hard Realists, several schools of thought now acknowledge the relevance of norms and values as markers of the behavior of international actors. Over the decades, these challengers include the English school of IR, transnationalism, international regimes theory, and social constructivism, now analyzing the constraining and enabling effects of institutions, and the importance of framing and discourse (the so-called "linguistic turn").[44]

This is not the place to go into detail about the precise manner in which these schools consider norms to be relevant. Still, two aspects stand out (and are particularly relevant to our debate on social power). First, regime theory assumes that norms and rules guide actors' behavior, in the end even changing their notion of national interest and identity. Here, norms and values affect the strategic calculations of actors, and hence guide their actions and policies. Second, constructivist authors emphasize the *mutually* constitutive character of norms, changing and guiding preferences and identities by reciprocal interaction. Here, new actors, like NGOs and the media, are said to play an especially active and increasingly important role.

It is this second element which is of particular interest here, since it involves reciprocal social interaction as the *locus* of power. Despite the importance of non-state actors in a globalized economy and a mediatized international political environment, mainstream IR theory has remained deficient in assessing the political power of these "new" actors.[45] Both neoliberalism and constructivism tend to overlook questions of power, which are equally blindsided by most studies of global governance.[46] On the other hand, approaches examining contextualized and social aspects of power have offered useful conceptual tools which are awaiting to be used to gain insight into the sources and mechanisms of power and authority in an emerging global governance environment.

As this book argues, it is the capacity to establish the norms and rules around which other actors' actions converge that constitutes the core of social power. Social power can therefore be defined as the ability to set standards, and create norms and values that are deemed legitimate and desirable, without resorting to coercion or payment. Soft power's core components are attraction and persuasion; social power clearly goes beyond that. Nye's notion remains agent-centered, assuming that soft power remains largely based on resources, which can be used, applied, and wielded. Social power, on the other hand, also involves discursive power, drawing attention to the impact of framing, norm advocacy, agenda-setting, the impact of media and communications, as well as lesser-known practices like place branding and public diplomacy.

Like soft power, social power eschews the use of coercion and force, giving it a certain ethical appeal and making it morally superior to hard power. By reneging coercion, social power finds its basis on grounds other than territory, economic resources, and/or the capacity and willingness to threaten with violence. But how to define coercion remains debatable. As we will see, some scholars see coercion everywhere, making it nigh impossible to envisage a "coercion-free" social environment. Thomas Schelling has famously defined coercion as the "power to hurt" (or to threaten with "unbearable harm").[47] This implies that the threat of violence, rather than its actual application, is already coercive in nature. It also means that deterrence (dissuading an actor from doing something), as well as compellence (persuading an actor to do something) can never be qualified as social power, if the potential use of (military) force is implicitly exploited.[48] For this reason, the Cold War nuclear strategy of mutual assured destruction (MAD) involved the use of hard, rather than social power.

Still, the interplay between hard and social power remains intricate and perplexing. Given the difficulty to draw the line between coercive and voluntary, I will define "non-coercive" simply as the absence of military *force* and *threats* to use military force. Social power therefore deals with (international) norm-setting without using, or threatening to use, military force. As we will see, this definition of social power has conceptual links with sociological debates, as well as the study of public policy, public administration, media, and communications. This definition of social power also has the advantage that it incorporates the widely-used notion of soft power, but goes far beyond it, without being too all-inclusive and losing focus and significance.

The notion of social power obviously defies the Realist conjecture that norms and values mask underlying power realities, or are merely reflections of existing power structures. Walter Russell Mead, for example, maintains that sharp power forms the foundation of the American system and its power. Without military force, other forms of power lose much of their value. He suggests that the US built its post-World War II sticky power on two foundations: an international monetary system centered around the Bretton Woods institutions (the International Monetary Fund (IMF) and World Bank), and free trade. Today, almost all countries have a stake in this US-led global economic, financial, and trading system. But, since the US was able to set up the rules of this system, it still works to its advantage and assures that even if conflicts arise, "it helps the United States win."[49] Together, Mead claims, "sharp and sticky power sustain US hegemony and make something as artificial and historically arbitrary as the US-led global system appear desirable, inevitable, and permanent."[50]

The debate about the uses of hard and social power in international politics took central stage after 9/11, and has since become pertinent to all major crises, from hotspots like Afghanistan, Iraq, and Iran, to challenges such as climate change and energy security. How can the "international community"—the mythical, non-existing global authority that is often invoked—deal with these diverse and pressing security problems? Which power tools are most practical, and how and when should they be used? Although this book is concerned with the *nature* of social power, and less with the question of who draws on it and why, these last two questions are, of course, of great interest. Policymakers as well as academics remain undecided on the optimal mix between hard and social power, on when social power can be considered truly effective and on how much the use of social power still depends on hard power. Much of this book will try to shed light on these tough and essential questions. For example, Chapter 2 examines how the US, the EU, and China operate and try to optimize their influence by using social power in a geopolitical environment.

Social power does not use classical hard power tools, which are generally in the hands of public authorities. This means that the use of social power is open to most actors, and not restricted to the classical players in international politics. As we will see, the playing field for social power is broader and more diverse than that of hard power. Since the 1970s, non-state actors have frequently used social power processes by their active involvement in global governance and their participation in public debates, as they offer them the discursive power to define economic, social, and political problems, and suggest policy solutions. As a result, governance is provided by non-state actors who function above, beyond, as well as around the state. Traditionally, these non-state actors have had to limit themselves to non-material power resources, ranging from expertise, knowledge and information, credibility, respect and authenticity, to framing, representation, and discursive power. Given the relational nature of discursive power (based on the given that recipients listen to messages and are willing to place a basic level of trust in their validity), the role of media, public relations (PR), public diplomacy, and branding is particularly important. For our debate on social power, analyzing these discursive processes is essential, although we should acknowledge that measuring persuasion, perception, legitimacy, and (voluntary) compliance is inherently more difficult and complex than the more clear-cut use of instrumental power.

1.3 COMMON KNOWLEDGE, FRAMING, AND POLICY CONGRUENCE

The reluctance to understand and assess the nature of power in a globalized world economy and political system may be due to the fact that power is extremely difficult to locate and appraise, let alone quantify. This also applies to the study of social power, which is a bit like electricity and inherently Newtonian, since its effects are most often visible, whereas the source of power generally remains hidden. Social power is embedded in relationships, but these relationships are varied and can come in the shape of a sturdy IO like NATO, or a rather ephemeral bond like brand loyalty. It can be active and willfully used, or merely sat latently and discreetly in the background. Social power can be used by individuals, but cannot be shaped by it, since in the real world social power comes in big portions, molded by traditions, culture, and institutions, and by media, fads, and fashions. When social power deals with international norm-setting without using force, the next logical step towards conceptual clarity is specifying the processes through which this is actually done.

As Daniel Philpott argues in his *Revolutions in Sovereignty* (2001), what is "normal" in international society is not fixed, but dynamic, and changes with the geopolitical tide and fashion. Whereas till the sixteenth century it was common practice in Europe to legitimate political action by referring to religion and natural law, it is now required to refer to human rights and international law.[51] What is "normal" and common knowledge refers to socially agreed, intersubjective facts that cannot be wished away by individuals.[52] As we will see (in Chapter 5), media discourse is a primary source of common knowledge for average citizens, offering media a substantial influence on peoples' preferences and frame of reference. And, as Anna Holzscheiter suggests, the "construction of common knowledge or the creation of commonly agreed definitions and perspectives (…) are the dimensions of international politics upon which the notion of global governance heavily relies."[53] Still, this leaves unanswered the question why certain standards, norms, and values become privileged, accepted, and institutionalized, whereas others become (or remain) marginalized?

For our understanding of social power, norm advocacy obviously is of key concern. Martha Finnemore and Kathryn Sikkink define norm advocates (or norm entrepreneurs) as actors with "strong notions about appropriate or desirable behaviour in their community."[54] The literature on norm advocacy has cast its net widely, including studies on non-state actors such as transnational advocacy networks, individuals, and NGOs, as well as, of course, states and IOs. The emerging arena of global governance offers ample space for transnational actors to act as "honest brokers" or "meaning architects", oftentimes forming "discourse coalitions" amongst themselves to either shape or challenge the rules of the game of (global) politics. Since NGOs play such an important role in agenda-setting, opinion-building, and drafting of plans and policy proposals, they compel us to reconsider the understanding of power as a predominantly coercive process.

Finnemore and Sikkink have proposed a three-stage life-cycle explaining the steps by which norms become accepted as the appropriate behavior of states, starting with persuasive endeavors through cognitive framing (either by NGOs, or other norm entrepreneurs), and coming to an end when a certain "critical mass" of states creates a "tipping point" (or cross a "threshold").[55] For our study of social power, framing is a key concept. The discussion on framing takes place in a crowded conceptual field with overlapping terminology used by cognitive scientists, psychologists, and political scientists, who use notions like frame, image, script, and paradigm to refer to approximately similar processes of creating (social) meaning. Frames offer mental structures shaping the way we see the world, and therefore limit the range of interpretive possibilities; they tell us what is important, and what the range of options and solutions are to which problems.[56] Framing helps to place issues and problems within a broader social and historical context. All norm entrepreneurs using social power engage in frame competition, trying to persuade relevant audiences and actors to see things their way. Finnemore and Sikkink argue that framing is necessary because "the linkages between existing norms and emergent norms are not often obvious and must be actively constructed by proponents of new norms." Norm entrepreneurs must actively create new standards by "using language that names, interprets, and dramatizes them."[57] The concept of "grafting" is obviously closely related to framing, and can be defined as "incremental norm transplantation", usually by associating the new norm with a pre-existing norm in the same issue area.[58]

It is clear that social power can be as contested as hard power, since advocating and uploading new standards, norms, and values is a competitive, and at times even combative process, positing new notions of desirable and normal behavior *vis-à-vis* settled ways of doing things. Social power only very rarely takes place in a normative void, but has to compete in a normative, political space. Social power can be used conservatively, by maintaining existing standards and norms, or revolutionary, by uploading new ones. Often, paradigms shift due to shocking, or symbolic events which "recast or challenge prevailing definitions of the situation, thus changing perceptions of costs and benefits of policies and programs and the perception of injustice of the status quo."[59] Pepper D. Culpepper suggests that common knowledge *creation* occurs only after periods of institutional crisis, once most actors call into question old norms, values, and institutions.[60] Crisis undermines the taken-for-grantedness of these old rules and habits, destabilizing the cognitive basis of existing institutions. But, as Culpepper also points out, "[o]bserving how ideas become shared is much like watching grass grow: nothing seems to be happening in the short term, but after one day a former patch of mud is suddenly green."[61]

Paradigm shifting events—ranging from the fall of the Berlin Wall, to 9/11, and the current global financial and economic crisis—obviously constitute a crisis in common knowledge, offering opportunities to create new norms, and ultimately new socially agreed "facts." Major norm changes are always disruptive.[62] Most often, however, social power is used to introduce new standards and norms that fit rather coherently within the status quo, since new norms that "fit" are generally considered less threatening and therefore more legitimate.[63] As are all aspects of social power, framing is highly contextual, which implies that the "frame resonance" varies between different target audiences, as American public diplomacy has found out. The rhetorical framing of the Bush administration of the Iraq invasion as an effort to "spread freedom and democracy" has lost out to competing conceptual frames highlighting an on-going "civil war", or even the return of a Vietnam-like quagmire.[64] Robert M. Entman suggests that in the absence of an overwhelming Cold War frame of reference to analyze international politics, the competition over "news frames" has increased. Since foreign policy frames are more likely to be accepted when they "fit"—i.e., they are culturally congruent to existing values, norms, and interpretations—the Bush administration has depicted 9/11 as a terrorist plot of extremists "hating our freedoms."

It is therefore more than just a linguistic difference when European policymakers talk about the threat of terrorism as a police and management problem, whereas the US debate centers around a *war* on terror. As Donald A. Schön and Martin Rein have suggested, the struggles "over the naming and framing of a policy situation are symbolic contests over the social meaning of an issue domain, where meaning implies not only what is at issue but also what is to be done."[65] The Bush administration has sought to establish and strengthen norms in the global arena, claiming that the US seeks to "delegitimize terrorism and make clear that all acts of terrorism will be viewed in the same light as slavery, piracy, or genocide: behavior that no respectable government can condone or support and all must oppose."[66] Given that all policy debates boil down to competing frames and agendas, it is important to examine and understand why certain frames and agendas prevail over others.

Asking why and how frames change offers insight into the workings of social power. Two different methodologies can be identified: the actor representation approach (with a focus on the changing *distribution* of actors who participate in policy debates); and a frame adoption approach (with a focus of the *different frames* that actors attach to a policy issue).[67] Often, these two approaches can, and should, be linked since, when new political actors get their voices heard, new frames are generally introduced. Connecting policy frames to their sponsors indicates who has social power within a certain discursive field.[68]

One can also study social power from the angle of cross-national policy convergence, which examines the impact of European integration and globalization on the growing similarity of state policies over time. The causal factors for policy convergence are diverse, ranging from parallel domestic pressures, international legal constraints, international economic integration, and political factors, to elite networking, normative pressures, social isomorphism, and emulation.[69] This is a broad spectrum of factors, which generally involves different gradations of voluntary and compulsory transfer and adoption of norms and rules. At times, it is unclear whether any social power is at work at all. As Katharina Holzinger and Christoph Knill suggest, "[j]ust as individuals open their umbrellas simultaneously during a rainstorm, governments may decide to change their policies in the presence of tax evasion, environmental pressures, such as air pollution, or an aging population."[70] Where governments freely draw rational lessons from experience and adopt new rules, policy convergence is of course voluntary. But when regulatory competition takes place between actors, a certain measure of (overt or covert) pressure seems almost inevitable. Even institutionalized peer review, benchmarking, or scorecards ranking national policies in terms of performance have some intimidating quality to them. Erving Goffman, the sociologist who introduced the concept of framing in the 1970s, even argued that actors are consistently changing and manipulating (existing) frames.[71] Which begs the question: how can policies and frames become common practice without force and other forms of coercion?

Amitav Acharya suggests that the success of norm diffusion strategies depends primarily "on the extent to which they provide opportunities for localization", which involves "a complex process and outcome by which norm-takers build congruence between transnational norms (...) and local beliefs and practices."[72] Acharya therefore suggests that norm-takers have considerable agency through a process of dynamic congruence-building, implying that the "fit" between international and domestic norms is of key importance. Both Jeffrey W. Legro and Jeffrey T. Checkel point to the importance of a compatible "organizational culture" and "cultural match" between international and domestic norms, which explains why some norms are accepted swiftly, and others remain contested.[73] Acharya's emphasis on the role of norm-takers is especially appropriate since norm entrepreneurs are highly dependent on local elites "downloading" foreign norms. As Acharya argues, the prospect for localization depends on "its positive impact on the legitimacy and authority of key norm-takers, the strength of prior local norms, the credibility and prestige of local agents, indigenous cultural traits and traditions, and the scope for grafting and pruning presented by foreign norms."[74] As we will see in our debate on the role of place branding and public diplomacy as avenues of social power (Chapters 6 and 7), norm entrepreneurs may now also enter into relationships with foreign publics, approaching them both as consumers and citizens. Both elites and the general public may be instrumental in adopting new norms and rules, by recognizing their merit and legitimacy.

This process of normative change is especially relevant to our study on the role of social power in international politics, since much hinges upon the key concept of legitimacy.

1.4 LEGITIMACY AND GOVERNANCE

Being able to determine what is normal, the law-of-the-land, what is desirable, based on what model, constitutes the bulk of social power. In international politics, social power is the ability to push a preferred foreign policy frame. Central to social power is the element of legitimacy, the factor that changes paying tribute into paying taxes, and that alters hegemony into leadership. As mentioned earlier, legitimacy is one method to socialize power. As Ian Hurd argues, "[l]egitimacy refers to the belief by an actor that a rule or institution ought to be obeyed. Such a belief is necessarily normative and subjective, and not necessarily shared with any actor."[75] Morris Zelditch, in contrast, rather clinically defines legitimacy as "the acceptance of just about anything at all as 'right', provided acceptance does not depend simply on gain."[76]

In contemporary international politics, legitimacy is a powerful method to justify foreign policy actions and to gather support for them.[77] Legitimacy can derive from religious duties, like the Crusades in the early-Middle Ages and the *Jihad* amongst Islamists today, or be codified in international legal rules, such as UN Security Council resolutions. Few wars have been fought without the aggressor hiding behind the rhetorical shield of spreading religion, culture, or morality. Whether the ideology is Marxism-Leninism or liberal democracy, moral justifications have been instrumental in "rallying around the flag" at home, and in persuading foreign communities of the superiority of one's own dogma. This is why propaganda and today's public diplomacy efforts (see Chapter 6) remain important strategies to generate and use social power. What is considered legitimate, and which process generates legitimacy, has changed remarkably over time. But one constant remains: those who determine what is legitimate have social power.

So how does legitimacy come about today? Daniel C. Esty has argued that "[d]emocratic legitimacy depends on decision makers being seen as acting on behalf of a community. The prospect of successful delegated decision-making thus turns on the presence of social trust and a degree of community identity and civic engagement."[78] Social power derives from the fragile and often unverifiable psychological belief that certain actions and policies are necessary and legitimate. As Thomas M. Franck has argued in his study on the power of legitimacy, "[t]he real power of law to secure systematic compliance does not rest, primarily, on police-enforcement (…) but, rather, on the general belief of those to whom the law is addressed that they have a stake in the rule of law itself: that law is binding because it is the law."[79] Legitimacy therefore relates to a shared and mutual sense of trust, of a shared identity, and in some instances even the belief in a common destiny.

The debate about trust indicates that international politics is far removed from the cliché of Hobbesian anarchy. In the Realist worldview, "trust" is not even supposed to exist, which is quite odd since Realism does acknowledge other emotions like distrust and jealousy. This is so even though we can witness many examples of social learning amongst states,[80] reaching the phase where intra-European politics, for example, has become "domestic" politics. Arguably, the reason why Franco-German reconciliation could take place had as much more to do with the decades of Germany's *mea magna culpa*-policy after World War II, than with the development of institutions. Taking the full blame of the War and acknowledging the atrocities of the Nazi era helped to heal some of Europe's wounds, which ultimately made Germany one of the most appreciated Great Powers in Europe. The fact that Japan did not go through such a period of self-reflection at least partly explains why trust in Asian politics is a very scarce commodity indeed.

Legitimacy assumes tacit or explicit agreement on the rules-of-the-game, based on, or rooted in, shared norms and values. As we will see in Chapter 2, hegemony (as the foundation of empire) ultimately hinges upon cooperation and consent, requiring a shared understanding of norms and values that underpin the international system. This suggests that social power is derived from social capital, which is the lesser known cousin of physical capital (such as machines and infrastructure), and human capital (know-how). Social capital can be defined as the set of norms and values that are shared among members of a group that permits cooperation among them.[81] Such norms may include honesty and reliability, or reciprocity and fairness. Every society is based on social capital, which is the element that alters a *Gesellschaft*, based on the rational calculus of costs and benefits, into a *Gemeinschaft*, based on a shared identity and the belief in a common future.[82]

Trust and a sense of community are therefore basic underpinnings of social capital, in domestic politics as well as in relations between states and other international actors.[83] Francis Fukuyama argues that social capital is not only critical to a successful economy, but even a prerequisite for *all* forms of group endeavors within a civil, democratic society. Of course, social capital is difficult to accumulate and measure; it can also not be spent or exchanged. Social capital belongs to the category of atmospherics, the mood-music which sets the tone within a society. To understand legitimacy, the link between tradition, culture, and perhaps even religion on the one hand, and the requisite sense of community and connectedness on the other, is therefore crucial.

Esty argues that political legitimacy becomes more strained as the sense of community weakens and the physical distance between those in authority and the general public grows. His conclusion is commonsensical, but of central importance: "as the scale of governance expands and a sense of community becomes harder to establish, legitimacy issues become increasingly problematic."[84] As long as the perception exists that decisions are made on "our" behalf, based on a shared sense of community underpinned by shared norms and values, legitimacy is easily available and readily achieved. But an integral part of legitimacy is accountability, which ultimately depends on some sort of mechanism to "kick the bastards out", i.e., to translate public displeasure into a domestic or international regime change.[85]

Both legitimacy and accountability are problematic in international politics, since the further the process of policymaking is psychologically detached from its stakeholders, the less likely it is that legitimacy can be achieved. "Kicking the bastards out" remains a chimera in international politics, since no mechanism exists, for example, to fire the secretary-generals who head the International Monetary Fund (IMF), World Trade Organization (WTO), United Nations (UN), and all the other IOs who ostensibly hold the reigns of power across the globe. Since many of the rules are now shaped and formulated by private authorities and transnational policy networks (see Chapter 4), legitimacy wears thin and becomes a scarce, highly coveted resource. International legitimacy is rare since the shared normative basis which should sustain both the process of decision-making and its outcome, is usually lacking. Those who stand in the Rousseauian electoral tradition—like Robert Dahl—therefore doubt whether postnational decision-making and governance can ever be legitimate.[86] Direct electoral underpinnings of international decision-making are always contentious, reaching a shallow, quasi-democracy at best. Still, the lack of democratic legitimacy and accountability that elections provide may be substituted by two alternative processes.

First, Weberian legitimacy can be achieved if the decision-making process is based on expertise (i.e., rational analysis) employed within a clear legal structure.[87] As Esty argues, "Weberian legitimacy is especially important in the international realm: A demonstrated capacity to deliver good outcomes has been the main attraction for nation-states to delegate parts of their sovereignty and policymaking authority to supranational bodies."[88] Many IOs claim their legitimacy *à la* Weber, using external experts to underpin the often technical nature of their work. The WTO is a good case in point, since in this IO (which manages global free trade) the recommendations of an independent body of experts (the Dispute Panel) is *de facto* binding (after having been agreed by the Dispute Settlement Body) for all member states. Even the IO-averse US complies with the decisions of this unelected panel of experts, which is testimony to the legitimacy of the WTO. As we will see, firms, NGOs, as well as a wide variety of transnational policy networks equally claim a legitimate voice in framing policy debates on the basis of their expertise.

Second, Habermasian legitimacy can be achieved through robust dialogue, taking into account different perspectives which achieve a sense of collective ownership of the final policy outcome. The deliberative legitimacy that comes from a structured and inclusive dialogue, a thorough debate resulting in a transparent decision-making process, can do without the formal trappings of electoral democracy.[89] Here a good example can be found in the demand of countries like Germany to make more intensive use of the North Atlantic Council (NAC), the decision-making platform of NATO. German Chancellor Angela Merkel argued in February 2006 that if NATO wants to remains "the bond keeping together the transatlantic community of shared interests and values (…) we must discuss quite openly what NATO has to do. In my view it must be a body which constantly carries out and discusses joint threat analyses. It must be the place where political consultations take place on new conflicts arising around the world, and it should be the place where political and military actions are coordinated."[90] A NATO that is seen as an extension of American power is not legitimate, but an Alliance that reflects the collective will of 28 democracies has more prestige and may generate more support from other like-minded countries.

In the end, therefore, legitimacy is derived from formal democratic credentials (Dahl), expertise and legal structure (Weber), or the deliberative qualities of the policymaking process (Habermas). The main consequence of legitimacy is that compliant behavior is no longer based on rational calculations, but on the often internalized conviction that conformity is right and necessary. Legitimacy is therefore derived from the social interaction between states, rather than by a simple, one-off, cost–benefit analysis.

Legitimacy is especially relevant to the debate about global governance. The meaning of the concept of "governance" is not always clear. The body of academic literature that is based on "governance without government" tends to emphasize the role of international markets, international institutions and regimes, as well as formal and informal networks of cooperation.[91] But what does "governance" imply, if it does not mean traditional "government"?[92] James Rosenau argues that both government and governance refer to purposeful behavior, to goal-oriented activities, and systems of rule.[93] But whereas government is normally backed by formal authority, governance refers to activities that are backed by shared goals which are not necessarily embedded in a system of compliance. We could also argue that governing is not so much based on rationality and efficiency, as on reasonableness and eligibility.[94] In short: global governance centers around the goal of harmonizing the collective preferences of multiple actors. A short definition of global governance is therefore "the collective capacity to identify and solve problems on a global scale."[95]

Rosenau therefore claims that governance "embraces governmental institutions, but it also subsumes informal, non-governmental mechanisms whereby those persons and organizations within its purview move ahead, satisfy their needs, and fulfill their wants."[96] In other words, governance does not refer to hard power, but is the arena of choice where a wide variety of actors use their social power to frame debates, define the problem, set agendas, formulate policy options, identify and mobilize like-minded supporters, and build coalitions, all in the hope and expectation that "their" norm will become accepted as good and desirable. The capacity for direct control over factors and actors has now been replaced with a capacity to influence processes.[97] This explains why social power is rapidly growing in importance since it does not apply coercion and makes little use of the hierarchical mode of government which gradually loses its pivotal position in today's international politics.

1.5 THE HARD–SOCIAL POWER PREDICAMENT

Despite power's obvious intricacy, the debate about its use in international politics remains oversimplified, often stripped to a cartoonesque choice between the "hard ass" and "bleeding heart" approach. Ultimately, the difficulty of analyzing the intricacies of the hard power–social power mix comes down to the dynamic relationship between two ontological frameworks. Realism focuses on material power, assuming strategic and calculating actors, whereas constructivism emphasizes the role of norms and ideas within intersubjective processes, assuming interaction between agents and structures. Realism fails to explain the non-material aspects of power, whereas constructivism "has tended to operate within an oversocialized view of actors, treating them as near bearer of structures and, at the extreme, as cultural dupes."[98] Although this book makes the case for social power, it would be ridiculous to ignore Realism's continuous relevance in a significant part of the political domain, just as it would be ridiculous *not* to acknowledge that Realism has hardly anything to contribute to understanding and explaining the dynamics of (global) governance.

It is (all too) frequently argued that hard and social power are, and should be, juxtaposed, as if hardnosedness detracts from legitimacy and attractiveness. As we will see in the many case studies of this book, this penchant for simplicity and academic conceptual clarity is compounded by the complexity of political reality.

Still, if we want to make a convincing case that social power is a central and essential notion for understanding international politics, the hard–social power predicament has to be taken by the horns, scrutinized, and clarified. As we will see, hard power (i.e., the use or threat of military force) impacts upon social power in two major ways. First, the discreet ownership of hard power resources may give an actor a certain status and prestige, enhancing their voice, legitimacy, and credibility.[99] As Lukes has argued, social (or inactive) power is "often the residue of past uses of active power", and "derives from status, inducing deference."[100] Second, hard and social power can be applied simultaneously, whereby force may be used *vis-à-vis* some actors on certain policy areas, whereas social power is applied towards other actors on different issues.

To start with the first case in point, US foreign policy works on the assumption that its military might, and the guts to actually *use* it, offers it status and credibility. This understanding that imperial interventionism is an essential basis for American social power, rather than undercutting its cultural and ideological appeal, may well be considered counterintuitive. Much of global anti-Americanism feeds on the image of the US as a trigger-happy capitalist crusader. However, in the case of the *Pax Americana*, America's military and social power are dialectically related: American interventionism requires the cloak of legitimacy (morally, or under international law); without it, coercion would provoke too much resistance and be both too costly and ultimately untenable.[101] US foreign policy is therefore based on the assumption that without America's hard power and its superpower status its social power would ultimately shrink.

In Washington, this is considered not just an ideological hypothesis, but instead it is often framed as an "historical lesson" of recent American experiences in global politics. For example, America's prestige in Central Europe is closely related to the general consensus that US military superiority, steadfastness, and moral clarity have won the Cold War. This is put in stark contrast with Europe's wishy-washy *Ostpolitik*.[102] This was clearly illustrated by the depiction of America's Cold War President Reagan in the obituaries after his death in June 2004, as "the man who beat communism."[103] If social power thrives on the basis of social capital (be it trust, thankfulness, respect, or friendship), hard power may well stand at the basis of social power. Just as Western Europe has felt gratitude towards the US after World War II, Central Europe still has a living memory of the more recent American-led liberation from the Soviet yoke. It should be noted, however, that the subsequent *use* of social power takes place in a (always "more-or-less") coercion-free social environment, although the social capital itself may be derived from (or based on) violent precedents.

Renée De Nevers' study of piracy, the slave trade, and terrorism offers us insights into the second correlation between hard and social power. De Nevers concludes that, across history, Great Powers have used different power tools to influence different actors. When Great Powers promote (new) norms, they will coerce the weak, and persuade the strong. As De Nevers has it: "In norm promotion, great powers appear to 'speak softly' to those they regard as their peers, but they 'carry a big stick' to force others into line."[104] She concludes that: "[e]ven

Social power defined 19

though persuasion and socialization are clearly important tools for norm diffusion, force enters into the picture when great powers seek to influence the behavior of weak states as well as those whose international status is questionable or contested."[105] That force is used to impose new norms is hardly surprising since Great Powers tend to use all power tools available to them to set or bend the rules in their favor. What it is important to understand is that hard and social power may be used simultaneously to achieve similar goals, but within different frameworks, working upon different sets of actors.

As these examples reveal, it will always be difficult to prove beyond a reasonable doubt that social power is coercion-free. As Janice Bially Mattern suggests, soft (as well as social) power is rooted in hard power, since what "makes hard power 'hard' is its ability to threaten victims into compliance; that is, to coerce. Thus, where attraction rests upon coercion the logic of a distinction between soft and hard forms of power becomes unsustainable."[106] Or, as Linda Bishai suggests, concepts cannot be neutral, since "they have histories and so resist definition."[107] And Neta C. Crawford even goes as far as claiming that "norms established through coercion (…) lack legitimacy."[108] So where does social power end, and hard power (based on coercion and/or payment) begin?

Here the debate around policy framing and discursive power offers a good example of how and where to draw the line. Jürgen Habermas stresses the coercion-free force of the better argument, based upon a model using "persuasive talk" to reach agreement and encourage cooperation. Habermasian social power is based upon the reasoned exchange of evidence-based arguments among rational partners who are willing to seek the "truth." As I will argue in more detail later on (see Chapter 4), "wooing" willing partners into agreement by communication and argumentation is a central part of social power, since no coercion is used. Taking a strict stance, Habermas suggests that the strategy of framing implies manipulation, rather than persuasion, since framing does not imply a coercion-free discourse within an "ideal speech situation." Excluding framing from social power would, however, be overly purist, since the ultimate Habermasian model of communicative rationality within a 100 percent pressure-free environment, fully independent of material capabilities and considerations, may never be attained, and is especially difficult to imagine in the daily practice of international politics. Still, it is fair to say that if norm entrepreneurs distort existing communicative processes, then persuasion may well be perceived as coercion.

The Habermasian spirit of a truth-seeking, manipulation-free social environment is therefore illusory. But power can no longer be considered "social" when communication strategies spill over into what Mattern labels "verbal fighting" (or "representational force"). Mattern suggests that "verbal fighting is a communicative form through which an author attempts to bully the audience into agreement with his interpretation (…) It aims to close off its victims' options by promising them unthinkable harm unless they comply in word and in deed with the force-wielder's demands."[109] Where verbal fighting begins and the threat of coercion and the use of sanctions and force looms, social power gels into hard power. For example, the Bush administration's use of public diplomacy after 9/11 has oftentimes moved too far away from the Habermasian ideal and adopted verbal fighting and representational force to "communicate" with target audiences in the Muslim world. Against the backdrop of the Iraq war, Washington's message was less "let's argue!" (about democracy and freedom), as "listen to us, or else…!"[110]

Acknowledging the possibility of coercion in discursive and framing practices also offers non-state actors access to modest hard power tools. Academic studies about normative change indicate that norm entrepreneurs do not eschew using material leverage to persuade states, firms, or IOs to accept their views. As we will see, NGOs may use consumer boycotts (or threats thereof), naming-and-shaming, and other forms of pressure to influence policy outcomes. And, as Thomas Risse and Kathryn Sikkink argue, "countries most sensitive to pressure are not those that are economically weakest, but those that care about their international image."[111] Still, as we argued earlier, since violence and other forms of unbearable harm are excluded, these tactics should still be understood as demonstrations of social power.

1.6 CONCLUSION

Critics of the concept of social power maintain that it has too many inherent limitations. Barry M. Blechman argues, for example, that social power "may be influenced by governmental choices, but it is more an existential factor in the policy environment than something policy-makers can utilize to their advantage."[112] Blechman further claims that social power "will never be shaped fundamentally by the government, nor can it be tapped for use in particular situations."[113] This is a serious point of critique, since it is true that policymakers can wield hard power (from economic sanctions to military interventions), but may find it difficult to react in a concerted effort using tactics and methods based on social power.

As mentioned earlier, social power's indiscernible and subtle qualities raise the classical problem of how to link an abstract concept to a policy outcome, and how much weight should be given to a particular factor in explaining an empirical indicant.[114] Dissecting a policy process and examining how individual factors shape outcomes have proven extremely difficult. Assigning causal weight to the factors of social power remains basically unresolved. As Doris Fuchs admits, "the difficulty of attributing intent and agency to discursive governance provides serious obstacles to assessments of any given actor's respective efforts and influence."[115] Constructivist scholars may deny the relevance of these problems out of hand, just as Realist scholars may deny the impact of social power altogether. But given that both hard and social power are relevant in international politics, some middle ground has to be found.

Craig Parsons has formulated the challenge confronting ideational scholars as follows: "A growing literature points to actors' subjective beliefs as important causes of political outcomes. But if ideational theorists argue persuasively that ideas are often non-negligible factors in politics, they have trouble specifying *how much* ideas matter."[116] And, as Jeffrey Checkel argues: "norms are invoked as one of several causal variables with little or no insight given on how much of the outcome they explain."[117] Ideational scholars claim that it is ideas and identities that shape policy outcomes, against competing claims from political party theorists who posit that electoral or coalitional constraints are key, or bureaucratic theorists who trace interests to organizational rivalries, and Marxists who highlight that group interests derive from economic constraints. This constructivist predicament—to come up with proof, or make it at least extremely plausible that ideas do not just matter, but that ideas cause certain policy outcomes—is crucial, since it is probably the best way to convince Realist scholars that non-material power resources matter.

Still, telling stories about how ideas, identity, image and reputation, or brands somehow influence the murky process of policy-shaping may only convince those readers who are already intellectually receptive to notions such as social power.[118] Those who are not convinced can always claim that, in the end, not normative but economic and/or military pressures have been instrumental in achieving certain policy outcomes. Since this constructivist predicament persists, Realist scholars may continue to downplay social power factors by claiming that they are little more than a useful supplement to interest-based, rational actor models.

In his historical study of the role of ideas in the construction of the European Union, Parsons concludes that "[m]y answer to the 'how much' question is that leaders' ideas, as a cause irreducible to other factors, determined the outcome."[119] Parsons' story is indeed intriguing, but can hardly be considered real "proof", if such a notion has any validity in the humanities and social sciences. But his final claim, at the end of his study, is perhaps the most important, since he turns the tables on the critics of ideational scholars by arguing that the burden of proof should not fully and solely lay on them: "If we accord ideas basic credibility as distinct causes, not only must ideational theorists show that ideas do not reduce to objective factors, but also others must take seriously the possibility that apparently objective interests reduce to ideas."[120]

For our debate on social power, this implies that Realist scholars should prove, or make it likely, that the effect of military power or economic sanctions is solely due to their own qualities, and is not related to the credibility, legitimacy, and reputation of the actors involved. The result of such an exercise is that all IR scholars are confronted with the basic theoretical challenge of relatively weighing up the ideational, institutional, and structural causes of policy outcomes. The current game of Realists blaming constructivists for fuzziness, and Realists being blamed for arrogance, should come to an end. Who "wields" which power levers, and how, remains a fundamental question in the study of international politics.[121] It is also a question that remains unresolved. The challenge remains to arrive at a sub-optimal, still cloudy but better understanding of how global outcomes are produced and how power works in international politics.

The best way around the wielding problem is to accept power's polymorphous character as a given, and to bundle the multiple conceptions of power in international politics. A healthy dose of postmodern eclecticism is in order, accepting that different conceptual and theoretical approaches may be fruitful in the study of different cases. Realists should not be pitted against constructivists, and ideational scholars should accept that power is, and remains, a central notion within their theories as well. All too often, constructivist scholars overemphasize the underlying normative structures of international politics, by focusing on ideas and identities to the detriment of material power resources. Due to their focus on ideas and the desire to juxtapose their arguments to Realist notions of power, ideational theories often neglect the fact that normative structures are frequently, if not always, themselves infused by power. Liberal institutionalists, for example, are so keen to "prove" that IOs and regimes generate cooperation that no thinking space is left for the role and place of power, in all its different guises.

This book tries to make amends by combining the study of social and ideational factors and processes with a clear focus on power in international politics. It assumes that power has different faces, and that they are at work simultaneously in all key branches of (international) politics. This study (as Michael Barnett and Raymond Duvall inspiringly suggest) "incorporates both social relations of interaction and constitution, that is, both 'power over' and 'power to.' "[122] "Power over" involves the classical, Dahlian (or Baldwinian) notion of power, where A exercises influence over B. In contrast, "power to" is less actor-oriented, and examines the ways in which social relations and institutions are constituted, as well as the economic, political, and social structures and discourses that are imbued with (and themselves generate) power.[123] Obviously, the "power over" debate is seriously fraught by the wielding problem, since it assumes an apparent causal relationship between willfully applied non-material power resources and concrete policy outcomes. The "power to" debate, on the other hand, looks beyond the behavior of and interaction between actors, and examines "how social relations define who the actors are and what capacities and practices they are socially empowered to undertake."[124] Since it shifts the emphasis from control to the media, structures, and flows through which power is exercised, it is central to the topic of this book.

But how to connect the dots between, for example, place branding, prestige, legitimacy, and political impact? How to "prove" the three C's—centrality, complexity, and comprehensiveness—of social power factors in such a crowded field of competing claims? Those who want to see the dots may connect them quickly and effortlessly; skeptics, on the other hand, may deny any causal relationship. This book therefore uses a social ontology to underpin qualitative research. I will analyze the nature and role of social power by asking constitutive rather than causal questions, and I will look at intersubjective variables via an interpretive approach rather than by searching for measurable correlations. It may well be possible to apply quantitative research methods to provide a formal evaluation of the workings of social power in international politics, but this would go beyond both my own capabilities and the scope of this book.

Barnett and Duvall have argued that if IR scholars "have erred in their past attempts to understand power, it is by trying to identify and rely on a single conception. But no single conception can capture the forms of power in international politics."[125] They further warn against master theories that try to explain power across the board, as well as against gladiatorial competition between the different power-schools, since they overlook the many conceptual connections between them. This call for a kaleidoscopic approach will be followed in this book. As a result, no comprehensive and exhaustive taxonomy will be produced, and no attempt at an encyclopedic genealogy will be made. Instead, this book examines the social power embedded in culture, institutions, law, and the media, and studies how these structures and flows of power are relevant for public diplomacy and place branding. Needless to say, some aspects of social power will receive only scant attention. Still, this range of issues and examples should give an adequate understanding of the workings of social power, combining contemporary practices and fragments of its genealogy.

It is clear that political scientists should stick their necks out if they want to see things that others haven't discovered yet. But in being nuanced, I take a risk. It is well-known that scholars who study multi-causal explanations generally make little or no impact on the academic, let alone public, debate, whereas those who claim to have discovered the secrets of absolutely everything are assured to get followers, or are at least heavily attacked and never forgotten. Let me therefore make at least one claim that is feather-rufflingly straightforward and simple: *social power is the key to understanding contemporary international politics.* It is this statement, this thesis, that will be developed in this book.

2 Geopolitics and hegemony

2.1 INTRODUCTION

Our study of social power's role in international politics gets underway by probing its relationship with the classical Realist world of geopolitics and hegemony. For millennia, social power has played a key role in establishing and maintaining empires through hegemony, a practice which is now generally frowned upon. When European Commission President José Manuel Barroso admitted (in July 2007) that he likes "to compare the EU as a creation to the organization of empire. We have the dimension of [an] empire", his remark caused a stir. His rather innocuous comment was widely considered an unnecessary provocation, conjuring up the image of a European Superstate which sets many member states' teeth on edge.[1] Barroso's remark was followed by the soothing words that "[w]hat we have [in Europe] is the first *non*-imperial empire",[2] which is a paradox worth unraveling. Similarly, US Deputy Secretary of the Treasury Lawrence H. Summers famously described the US as the "first nonimperialist superpower."[3]

The reason why both the EU and US are in denial regarding their imperial qualities and missions is that the age of the traditional, modern empire is dead. Direct physical control of territories outside one's own—except as a temporary expedient in response to crisis, as in Afghanistan and Iraq, as well as in Kosovo—is nearly always a burden, rather than an asset. It might therefore be possible to recognize the US and its sphere of influence as an empire, but deny that it is imperialist. Still, the naked facts must be recognized. Just as the Roman Empire brought the *Pax Romana* to Europe, Asia Minor, and North Africa, and the British Empire controlled a quarter of the globe, the US currently maintains more than seven hundred bases in Europe, Asia, and the Middle East; its defense budget of US$711 billion (in 2008) dwarfs military spending in the rest of the world,[4] it guarantees the survival of several countries (from Israel to South Korea), drives the wheels of global trade and commerce, and fills the hearts and minds of an entire planet with its dreams and desires. If not a formal empire, this certainly resembles a *Pax Americana*.[5]

Empires traditionally involve a symbiotic mix of hard and social power, which is difficult to disentangle, but too important and interesting not to try it anyway.[6] David A. Lake defines an empire as "a particular authority relationship in which the rule of the dominant state over both economic and security policy is accepted as more or less legitimate by the members of the subordinate polity."[7] Imperial power is therefore based on a blend of military domination and the legitimacy offered by culture, ideology, and sometimes religion. Today, both the US and the EU are seen as the "New Rome", not just due to the similarities between Roman law and US and EU legal dominance (see Chapter 4), but since both Great Powers offer competing global governance models.[8] In today's global arena, the US is branded as the "empire of liberty", and the EU as the "postnational empire", each offering different flavors of modernity backed up by different combinations of hard and social power. These different appreciations of the utility of hard and social power set American and European imperial policy styles apart. China's emerging "Asian empire" adds to this crowded global governance menu.

The ideational fabric of empire was lucidly analyzed by Theo Farrell, who argued that empires are "supreme acts of human imagination. They are as much about social as material dominance (…) [I]deas about what works and is right define the instruments of empire—including, critically, the place and purpose of military force."[9] Farrell further argues that "popular culture and civil society are indispensable to the creation and evolution of empire", suggesting that, in the nineteenth century, missionary movements together with business entrepreneurs spread ideologies based on social progress that justified colonialism.[10] Rule based on force and control—like Nazi and Soviet rule—is expensive and inherently vulnerable to destabilization. Instead, empires that have based their hegemony on religious myths (like the Egyptians and Mayans), or cultural achievements (as the Chinese and British did), have made loyal subjects out of conquered, foreign peoples. As Richard Ned Lebow and Robert Kelly remind us, Rome ruled a massive empire with a mere 29 legions (of approximately 6,000 men each), just as Britain maintained colonies on six continents with an army of just 250,000 men (supplemented, of course, by local forces).[11] Arguably, both the British and the Soviet empires fell into decline because they lost legitimacy amongst their own people.[12] Within the British Empire, the idea of "white superiority" was no longer deemed credible (as Mahatma Ghandi demonstrated), and the erosion of Communist ideology led to its ultimate decay under Mikhail Gorbachev, who realized that no number of tanks could maintain Soviet control over the Central and East European "satellites."

As we will examine in more detail later on in this book, culture, law, and media are essential avenues of social power and play a crucial role in international politics, creating the ideational basis for legitimacy and authority. Ultimately, it boils down to the claim that the societal and/or economic model and the values that underpin it are superior and attractive, and hence worthy to be emulated. Major powers generally have different understandings of both domestic and international order. At times, ideologies have clashed, like the West vs. the Soviet Union, and, to a certain extent, the Chinese brand of communism. Now, a "clash of civilizations" may be emerging where religions stand at loggerheads.[13] In a sense, these societal models compete in a global beauty contest, showing off their curves to the critical global jury that is world opinion. The beauty pageant metaphor is not at all far-fetched, since the US in particular has used all possible ideological and cultural feathers to show off its advantages and good sides. Hollywood has, since its inception, sold the American Dream and the American Way of Life, followed by jazz and rock 'n' roll as expressions of America's freedom-loving spirit and pronounced sense of individualism. As we will discuss at length in Chapter 3, American popular culture has been instrumental in creating the social capital on which US geopolitical hegemony could thrive.

As Lebow explains in lucid detail in his book *A Cultural Theory of International Relations* (2008), the ancient Greeks' sophisticated view on the nature of power has great value for our understanding of contemporary international politics. Lebow argues that the Greeks distinguished two aspects of influence and persuasion: *dolos* (based on deceit and coercion), and *peitho* (achieved by common identities and friendship).[14] Even Thucydides, who is generally recognized as a Realist *avant la lettre*,[15] considered *peitho* more effective than *dolos*, "because it has the potential to foster cooperation that transcends discrete issues, builds and strengthens community and reshapes interests in ways that facilitate future cooperation."[16] *Dolos* is also generally costlier, since it is based upon threats and rewards, which have occasionally to be followed up and paid out. Lebow concludes that *peitho* "is only possible within a community whose members share core values, and is limited to activities that are understood to support common interests and identities. *Peitho* (…) is largely independent of material capabilities. However, it can help to sustain those capabilities because it does not require the constant exercise of *dunamis*" (i.e., resources).[17]

Lebow and Kelly claim that the US should take heed from the corrosion of Athenian democracy, and understand that *hegemonia* (legitimated authority) is preferable over *arkhe* (control).[18] Hegemony is ultimately based upon cooperation and consent, requiring a shared understanding of norms and values that underpin the international system. Without legitimacy, it becomes nigh impossible to exercise social power. And without social power, the only alternative is *dolos*, which remains costly and ultimately a dead-end street. Learning from the ancient Greeks, the US should have realized that, by being at odds with the accepted morality of the age, it increasingly has had to resort to threats and bribes to achieve its goals. As Lebow argues, "American hegemony during the Cold War was based on the sophisticated recognition that the most stable orders are those in which the returns to power are relatively low and the returns to institutions are relatively high. Influence depended as much on self-restraint as it did on power."[19] Once *peitho* no longer works, *dolos* comes into play, but only at tremendous costs to American social power.

This chapter examines the role of social power in the discourse and practice of contemporary "empires." The world's Great Powers all want to upload their own norms and values to the level of global governance, using *peitho*'s social power, with *dolos*'s hard power lurking in the background. Since all Great Powers have ample military capabilities, this raises the question of how social power and hard power are used (and mixed) in modern-day international politics.

2.2 HEGEMONY AND LITE POWERS

If we accept that the national interests and identities of states are socially constructed, that is to say that they are formed through continuous interaction with other states and embedded in a web of normative expectations, the logical question to ask is how do these dominant normative expectations and attitudes come about? Here the concept of "hegemonic socialization" is relevant,[20] intimating that the empire debate has clear neo-Gramscian overtones.[21]

Following Gramsci, critical approaches to world order emerged in IR in the 1980s, especially with the work of Robert Cox who suggested that hegemonic order is "based on a coherent conjunction or fit between a configuration of material power, the prevalent collective image of world order (including certain norms) and a set of institutions which administer the order with a certain semblance of universality."[22] Hegemony is unlike coercion, since it is a continuous process of opinion-shaping, the molding of norms and ideas, which boils down to the shaping of shared notions of social order and the "good society", both at home and abroad. When hegemony is indeed based on "persistent social practices, made by collective human activity and transformed through collective human activity",[23] this makes norm dissemination a key social power tool of hegemony. It also raises the question of how hegemons spread ideas and shape the belief systems, or identities, of others.[24]

Benjamin O. Fordham and Victor Asal have identified three reasons why Great Powers spread their norms: (1) their actions have serious consequences for other states; (2) they dominate important sources of information and ideas; and (3) their image as Great Powers encourages other states to emulate their behavior, their practices, as well as their institutions. Here, a distinction can be made between the impact of *prestige* and *promotion* on the spread of dominant ideas and practices. Morgenthau's notion of the "policy of prestige" follows the "hegemonic socialization" argument, assuming that "[e]lites in secondary states buy into and internalize norms that are articulated by the hegemon and therefore pursue policies that are consistent with the hegemon's notion of world order."[25] This is in line with Dennis Mumby's definition of hegemony as "noncoercive relations of domination in which subordinated groups actively consent to and support belief systems and structures of power relations that do not necessarily serve—indeed, may work against—those groups' interests."[26] In this case there is no direct, active involvement of the hegemon, whereas "promotion" obviously assumes that the hegemon is directly and actively involved. As we will see, postmodern empires are based on both elements, but with a notable emphasis on prestige and image. In particular, the practices of public diplomacy and place branding (Chapters 6 and 7) illustrate the complex workings of present-day hegemonic socialization.

Both prestige and active promotion buttress the dissemination of norms and social practices. Since the spread of norms is a central part of what is called "Europeanization" (i.e., the adoption of EU-based rules in domestic systems), the field of European Studies offers many a useful conceptual insight, and is particularly important to our understanding of the role of social power in international politics. Tanja Börzel, for example, suggests that EU member state governments both shape European policy outcomes and adapt to them. Börzel claims that member states have an incentive to upload their policies to the European level to minimize the costs in "downloading" them at the domestic level. Powerful states often set the pace in the uploading process, whereas less powerful states are "fence-sitting", waiting to see what the hegemons have in store for them.[27] The capacity to upload ideas, norms, and policies which others have to download, at times at considerable cost, constitutes a major element of social power. It is comparable to the "free" computer software Microsoft has spread across the globe, setting the standard and making it difficult for competitors like Apple or Linux to gain significant market share.

The notion of the hegemon as a norm entrepreneur has been further developed by Finnemore and Sikkink.[28] Both scholars argue that once new norms and practices have been accepted by a certain number of other influential states and social actors, they reach a tipping point after which we can expect a "norms cascade" in which these new norms and practices become the new standard of international behavior. The notion of a norms cascade assumes an ideational approach to the development of laws and conventions, suggesting that the origins of norms do not derive solely from statal and/or societal interests, but from principled ideas about right and wrong, good and bad.[29] It is important here that the role of military force remains modest, if not altogether minimal or absent. Threats, rewards, let alone coercion of a military kind, are all of lesser importance than the newly established legitimacy these new norms and practices have acquired. Since this supposes that states adapt their policies to changing models of appropriate behavior, we are basically looking at a world order perceived as an international society where state and non-state actors influence each other through social interaction. In this international society, it is international law and IOs that confer legitimacy to state actions, often codified, and usually expressed in approved practices.

Although this chapter takes a closer look at the norm-setting ambitions and capabilities of Great Powers, it is important to note that social power is put to good use by smaller states as well. For example, Annika Björkdahl's study on the influence of Sweden on the EU's foreign policy agenda shows the relevance of norm advocacy through framing, agenda-setting, and diplomatic tactics.[30] Sweden successfully uploaded its normative preference to include strategies of conflict prevention as an integral part of the EU's foreign and security policy, culminating in the adoption by the European Council of a *European Programme for the Prevention of Violent Conflict* (June 2001). Björkdahl concludes that the norm advocate has to suggest the morally persuasive aspects of the norm, linking it with the overall ambition and identity of the EU as an institution. Advocates have to frame the new norm as "the right thing to do", fitting it into the existing normative context.[31] She also claims that norm advocacy shuns coercive tactics, even moderate shaming and moral sanctions, or arm-twisting to ensure compliance. Björkdahl further suggests that norm advocates often spread nascent norms, using a variety of resources "such as diplomatic rhetoric and pedagogical skills, moral authority and legitimacy (derived from practicing what the norm advocate preaches, and thereby setting an example for others to follow)."[32] It is hardly surprising that, in a coercion-free environment, NGOs and other non-state actors (firms, media, as well as celebrities) are particularly interested in and suited to earning the respect of their interlocutors and appealing to their feelings and interests by offering arguments and making claims. In short: since *peitho* is today the preferred strategy to exert influence in a governance-based international society, the role of social power increases accordingly.

Both the US and the EU set standards in similar ways. Their ample social power and their frequent use of it distinguishes these postmodern empires from their modern predecessors. Barry Buzan and Gerald Segal refer to postmodern states as "Lite Powers", similar to the feeling one has after drinking Lite beer: a bit empty and unfulfilled.[33] Buzan and Segal suggest that "states are simply no longer the independent brewers of power that they used to be", since they no longer control the levers of power within their territory, as well as in international politics.[34] They were (in 1996) among the first scholars to suggest that the emerging postmodern state is incompatible with traditional Great Power politics. Their arguments are compelling, and are mainly based on the changed character of contemporary society, where civilian actors dominate the public debate, and where social cohesion and a single, solid national identity are difficult to find and individualism is rampant.[35] In societies where armed forces are professionalized and moral and legal debates dominate all foreign policy actions, support for an assertive, let alone expansionist, foreign policy is hard to generate. As Buzan and Segal put it: "Social Darwinist ideas about a hierarchy of nations clash with multicultural and democratic ideals and cannot be used to support aggressive foreign policies."[36]

This notion of introvert Lite Powers that are more interested in welfare (or, in the case of the EU, "lawfare") than warfare was obviously put to the test after 9/11. Robert Kagan's influential article *Power and Weakness* (2002) set the tone for the transatlantic debate on the nature of power.[37] Kagan argued that Europe's reluctance to use military force derives from the lack of it, and that America's preference for hard power can be explained from the fact that it has this tool in abundance. Kagan's depiction of Europe as a postmodern, Lite Power was not unjustified, but his conclusion that a more military capable Europe would close the transatlantic power-gap, and, hence, make US–European cooperation easier, remains controversial. In response, Robert Cooper (a former advisor to British Prime Minister Tony Blair and now Director General for External and Politico-Military Affairs at the EU Council) nuanced Kagan's point by claiming that "Europe may have chosen to neglect power politics because it is military weak; but it is also true that it is military weak because it has chosen to abandon power politics."[38] Ultimately, the post-9/11 transatlantic debate centered around the key questions of how, when, and where to use hard and social power to cut short international terrorism—a debate whose end is still not in sight.

Commentators have frequently summarized this chicken or the egg dilemma by quipping that "if all you have is a hammer, everything looks like a nail"; or, alternatively, "when all you have is a pen, every problem looks like a treaty." What may at first glance sound like a silly, somewhat trivial debate, is actually a profound and fundamental question about the relationship between capabilities and policy options on the one hand, and identity on the other. Whereas Kagan claims that a militarily stronger and more capable EU will, quasi-automatically, resemble the US in world outlook and threat perception, Cooper suggests that the EU has chosen to be "weak", privileging social power over military force. In the light of the EU's modest defense ambitions (especially the development of its European Security and Defence Policy, or ESDP), one could conclude that the EU is not a civilian power "by default" (making a virtue out of necessity), but rather a civilian power "by design."[39] Which begs the question why would the EU deliberately *chose* to be militarily weaker than it should be, and why would it renege on the option of becoming a military peer competitor to the US, as all Realist assumptions about the nature of power in international politics would suggest? In short, why cling to your diplomatic pen if you can go for the military hammer? Why stick with social power if you can have the hard-core version?

As we will see, Europe's choice for social power is deliberate, reflecting its identity as a normative, postnational actor. The remainder of this chapter outlines the different ways the US, EU, and China use social power to set global norms as an essential ingredient of their hegemonic ambitions. All major actors are keenly uploading their norms, values, and regulatory systems to the global level, and the strategies they use reveal as well as shape their identities, ambitions, and capabilities. For Great Powers, being passive and letting others decide what is standard, normal, and legitimate is hardly an option. But since the new game of global governance no longer privileges the direct use of hard, military power, these Great Powers have to strike a new and careful balance between *dolos* and *peitho*, between force and conviction. Whereas the EU and China have encountered few problems in finding their own, distinctive balance between hard and social power, the US faces a tougher challenge: with such a grand military hammer at its disposal, it has been tempting to reframe all foreign policy problems as nails. Which explains why it took the US almost a decade to acknowledge the limits of military force, and start thinking thoroughly about the role of social power, even within the traditionally Realist security paradigm.

2.3 PAX AMERICANA

The American neoconservative upswing in the late 1990s, resulting in the US-led invasion of Iraq and the toppling of Saddam Hussein's regime in March 2003, firmly placed the empire debate on the foreign policy agenda.[40] Andrew J. Bacevich suggested that the US was ruling over a global "empire of liberty", admitting that "Americans like being number one, and since the end of the Cold War have come to accept that status as their due. Besides, someone has to run the world. Who else can do the job"?[41] In a similar vein, political commentator Charles Krauthammer argued in an essay in *Time*: "America rules: Thank God. Who else should call the shots? China? Iran? The Russian mafia?"[42] Proponents of America's ascendancy argued that 9/11 had proven the risks of passivity and meekness, which led Krauthammer to claim that "after a decade of Prometheus playing pygmy", the US has to reinstate itself as an empire.[43]

Indeed, policymakers in Washington sold the idea of American leadership-cum-hegemony as a godsend and a guarantee for democracy, liberty, and prosperity not just for the US, but for the world as a whole. US President Bush argued in November 2003, that "[l]iberty is both the plan of Heaven for humanity, and the best hope for progress here on Earth (…) It is no accident that the rise of so many democracies took place in a time when the world's most influential nation was itself a democracy."[44] Despite the missionary zeal of US foreign policy, only few American policymakers went on record arguing that Washington has explicit imperial ambitions. In January 2004, Vice President Dick Cheney even claimed that the US is no empire, since "[i]f we were an empire, we would currently preside over a much greater piece of the Earth's surface than we do. That's not the way we operate."[45]

Still, the Bush administration faced a unique challenge after 9/11: How to frame this paradigm-shifting terrorist attack, and how to formulate an effective foreign policy response? As we discussed earlier, the choice of frames, concepts, and language impacts upon the frame of reference and the public discourse, which may ultimately alter political outcomes. The chosen frame of "global war on terror" (at times abbreviated as GWOT) did exactly that, implying that at times of war, "normal" political considerations no longer apply, and that new norms, standards, and rules are required due to exceptional circumstances.[46] One of these new rules, based on the Bush doctrine of pre-emptive (military) action, was put forward in the US National Security Strategy of 2002.[47] But the more far-reaching "new" norm was based on a new calibration of multilateralism and the role of IOs and international law (see also Chapter 4).

Heeding the Roman Empire's lessons, the US has traditionally pursued a strategy aimed at entrenching a set of institutions and rules favorable to its economic and security interest.[48] This explains why the US stood at the cradle of the UN, the IMF, World Bank, NATO, as well as the WTO. However, 9/11, globalization, and the end of the Cold War have proven a toxic mix eroding the hitherto strong multilateral pillars of this US empire. Under the influence of neoconservative thinking, multilateralism was framed as a sign of weakness, rather than strength. And, as US Secretary of Defense Donald Rumsfeld has warned, "weakness is provocative."[49]

America's dwindling trust in multilateralism has had major foreign policy implications, resulting in its withdrawal or estrangement from numerous treaties, such as the International Criminal Court (ICC), the Kyoto Protocol, the Anti-Ballistic Missile (ABM) Treaty, the Comprehensive Test Ban Treaty (CTBT), and the Biological Weapons Convention Protocol. Undersecretary of State John Bolton made it very clear that "[t]he idea that we could have a U.N. Security Council resolution or a nice international treaty is fine if you have unlimited time. We don't, not with the threats out there (…) We [don't] want to engage in an endless legal seminar."[50] And, as Bolton added, "[I]t is a big mistake for us to grant any validity to international law even when it may seem in the short-term interest to do so."[51] The rhetoric of threat which dominated the US discourse since 9/11 turned multilateralism into a good weather-option, a luxury that must be denied now that the going gets tough. This implied that existing global norms and rules should be altered, in order to fit America's need for security and flexibility.

The Bush administration has mainly used coercion and payment (i.e., hard power) to reframe post-9/11 international politics. This choice (privileging military force over social power) lies at the basis of America's post-9/11 foreign policy failures, a mistake which is now gradually acknowledged. US Secretary of Defense Robert Gates recognized in a speech in July 2008, "Over the long term, we cannot kill or capture our way to victory. Non-military efforts—these tools of persuasion and inspiration—were indispensable to the outcome of the defining ideological struggle of the 20th century. They are just as indispensable in the 21st century—and perhaps even more so."[52] A 2008 RAND report for the Pentagon similarly concluded that the US-led war on terror has failed, suggesting that it is time to replace the phrase with the more low-key, neutral term counter-terrorism. "Terrorists should be perceived and described as criminals, not holy warriors", the RAND report claimed.[53] Unfortunately, it took the US more than five years to adjust the hard–social power mix, proving Winston Churchill right when he quipped that "America can always be counted on to do the right thing, after it has exhausted all other possibilities."

This was the case even though the Bush administration was offered an unprecedented measure of goodwill, sympathy, and benevolence immediately after 9/11, even to the point that NATO member states invoked Article 5 ("collective self-defense") of the Washington Treaty. This was a very emotional period in which European allies declared their unrestricted solidarity and friendship with the US government and the American people. A headline in *Le Monde* famously stated: "nous sommes tous Américains."[54] This period of loyalty lasted a mere five months. American unilateralism quickly alienated European leaders, mainly since Washington was reluctant to make Europe and other allies stakeholders in their own foreign policies. Irwin Stelzer formulated this attitude as follows: "[T]hose who matter [in Washington] are convinced of two things: the important business of the world will be done by America, which will not let any coalition dictate its mission; and Europe is largely irrelevant to our efforts to make America safe from further harm."[55]

The trend of mounting anti-Americanism within Europe, Asia, and other parts of the world is an element of that same process.[56] Since 9/11, the US has wasted much of its goodwill due to the Manichean "us-versus-them" approach, the "you're-with-us-or-against-us" attitude, the denial of basic rights to prisoners in Guantanamo Bay, the torture pictures of Abu Ghraib, and the revelations about atrocities in villages like Haditha and others. Opinion polls conducted by the German Marshall Fund and The Pew Charitable Trusts indicated that America's image declined precipitously in most European countries due to Washington's foreign policy conduct after 9/11.[57] Even in countries who were long-standing allies, the popularity of the US has shown a dramatic decline. For example, in Britain, favorable opinions of the US dropped from 83 percent in 2001, to 56 percent in 2006; in France, the fall has been from 62 percent to 39 percent; in Germany from 78 percent to 37 percent. In Spain only 23 percent had favorable opinions of the US (in 2006); in Turkey the figure was as low as 12 percent.[58] As the Pew Report points out, "the bottom has fallen out of support for the U.S. in the Muslim world. Negative views of the U.S. in the Muslim world—which had been largely confined to the Middle East—are now echoed by Muslim populations in Indonesia and Nigeria (...) [F]avorable ratings for the U.S. have fallen from 61% to 15% in Indonesia and from 71% to 38% among Muslims in Nigeria." Furthermore, a CSIS Report (May 2003) indicated that Latin American attitudes towards the US followed a similar pattern of distrust and criticism towards the US and its foreign policies.[59]

The Bush administration's disregard (and repeated disdain) for social power has revealed the limits of (military) force in international politics, a lesson which the US has now learnt, but at considerable cost to itself and the rest of the world. As we mentioned earlier, social power derives from communication, social knowledge, and interaction, which implies that it ultimately depends on the perception of others. Unlike hard power, social power is therefore brittle and it has a rather short half-life. Much of it is based on social capital (i.e., legitimacy, trust, and friendship), which, as the US experienced after 9/11, is far easier to squander than to create. Rising anti-Americanism reflected the Bush administration's lack of legitimacy and respect in the eyes of global public opinion, and this proved to be a significant obstacle for the US as it tried to reframe international politics and change its standards and rules. Moreover, as we have already discussed, norm entrepreneurs generally require the support of local elites and the general populace, encouraging them to "download" foreign norms. Since using force is out of the question, this can only be accomplished if the new norms have merit, credibility, and prestige.[60]

The ancient Greeks realized that power may provoke resistance without the aura of "legitimacy through consultation, institutionalisation, soft words and self-restraint."[61] Without consultation and co-option, hegemony will be reduced to *dolos*. Or, as Isaiah Berlin once argued: "[T]o be the object of contempt or patronizing tolerance (...) is one of the most traumatic experiences that individuals or societies can suffer." They will respond, Berlin suggests, "like the bent twig of poet Schiller's theory lashing back and refusing to accept their alleged inferiority."[62] Without legitimacy and prestige, even hegemons will fail to change the global rulebook. On the other hand, when the legitimacy of norms and rules is more important than threats and rewards, and when particular institutions, practices, and norms are emulated because "they seem right", we can see social power at work.

As we will see, for contemporary non-imperial empires, it is a key challenge to gain the benefits of empire without being perceived as one. Mainly due to the wars in Afghanistan and Iraq, the US has not pulled this challenge off. Since 9/11, the analytical focus shifted from a debate of "US empire" as an objective category and empirical phenomenon to a second-order analysis of the power inherent in the representation of the emerging *Pax Americana*. As Dimitri Simes suggested, "whether or not the United States now views itself as an empire, for many foreigners it increasingly looks, walks and talks like one, and they respond to Washington accordingly."[63] As the opinion polls mentioned above indicate, for most political leaders in the world there is little popularity to be gained from supporting the US, which obviously detracts from America's social power. Many

Europeans and Asians have begun to question whether the emerging *Pax Americana* serves their interests now that the US fails to take their concerns into account. For example, European External Affairs Commissioner Chris Patten argued (in February 2002) that "however mighty you are, even if you're the greatest superpower in the world, you cannot do it all on your own." The European approach is quite different, Patten claimed, since in the fight against international terrorism "smart bombs have their place but smart development assistance seems to me even more significant (…) There is more to be said for trying to engage and to draw these societies into the international community than to cut them off."[64]

America now faces a unique challenge. Its hard, military power is unparalleled, but its credibility and prestige are in decline since it is not "winning" its self-proclaimed war on terror, and fails as a global norm entrepreneur. The Bush administration has not been able to upload new norms and rules to guide international politics, however hard it has tried. What is more, several fundamental American ideas that have dominated global thinking since the early 1980s imploded in 2008 with the onset of the financial and economic crisis. The US can no longer credibly preach the mantra of deregulation and small government, which seriously hampers its foreign policy objective of spreading liberal democracy.[65] This seems to have sunk in with the American people, who (according to a September 2008 Chicago Council on Global Affairs opinion poll) believe (with an 83 percent majority) that improving America's standing in the world should be a "very important foreign policy goal" of their new president.[66] Josef Joffe has therefore suggested that "[a]s long as the United States continues to provide international public goods while resisting the lure of unilateralism, envy and resentment will not escalate into fear and loathing." His advice to Washington is straightforward: "Pursue your interests by serving the interests of others. Transform dependents into stakeholders. Turn America the Ubiquitous into America the Indispensable."[67]

As we will discuss at greater length in the remainder of this book, the US still has inimitable opportunities to make good upon past mistakes. Not only does American popular culture continue to hold a remarkable sway over the global public imagination, the US also plays a key role in the development of new media (such as blogs), and IT. The resilience of America's political brand was also again shown by the election of President Barack Obama, which Joseph Nye probably rightly claims "will greatly help restore America's soft power as a nation that can recreate itself (…) [I]t is difficult to think of any single act that would do more to restore America's soft power than the election of Obama to the presidency."[68]

2.4 EUROPE'S NORMATIVE POWER

We left our debate on Europe's non-imperial empire by asking why the EU sticks with social power, whereas it could also pursue the hard-core version?[69] The answer to this question is twofold. First, the EU privileges social power since it reflects its own political identity. Second, and based on the first explanation, the EU believes it has a comparative advantage in the field of social power, and hence needs to capitalize on this, rather than try to close the nigh unbridgeable military gap with the US.

Like all identities, Europe's identity is socially constructed. It is not primarily derived from a clear codex of norms and values, but based on perceptions and performance. Here we may introduce Michel Foucault's notion of governmentality, which suggests that structures of domestic governance are an integral and important element of a society's culture and identity, and that the way a society is organized and citizens are governed are reflections of the state's views on global order and justice.[70] Since the domestic and international visions of what constitutes a good society are not separate compartments, and are not informed by different norms and values, the EU's experiences with postnational governance motivates and shapes its foreign policy. By privileging multilateralism at home, the EU is inclined to favor multilateralism abroad.

Ian Manners suggests that the EU exercises social (or what he labels "normative") power by way of example, arguing that "the most important factor shaping the international role of the EU is not what it does or what it says, but what it is."[71] As a unique postnational political entity, the EU radiates good governance and the proof that inter-state relations can go beyond Hobbesian anarchy, confirming the Kantian goal of perpetual peace. So, just as the US radiates the American Dream, the EU claims the Kantian paradise—and both do so by their very existence, functioning as models to be emulated. Euro-enthusiasts like Jeremy Rifkin therefore claim that "[t]he European dream emphasises community relationships over individual autonomy, cultural diversity over assimilation, quality of life over the accumulation of wealth, sustainable development over unlimited material growth, deep play over unrelenting toil, universal human rights and the rights of nature over property rights, and global cooperation over the unilateral exercise of power."[72] In this view, Europe's power base is its very socio-political model, which explains why the EU privileges social power over military power—at least for the time being.

Returning to the Kaganite debate on strategic culture, the EU challenges the US in the area of social power mainly by offering an alternative to America's governmentality. From history books to popular culture, Europe juxtaposes itself as an alternative to the American Way of Life, with important foreign policy ramifications. Colin S. Gray has remarked that "[f]or better or for worse, the United States is a society with a low tolerance for lengthy investment with distant payoffs (...) Americans do not resort to force quickly, but when they do, as citizens of the exceptional polity, they expect a thumping triumph."[73] Europe's strategic culture, meanwhile, has privileged compromise and appeasement since EU integration has undermined any illusion of absolute sovereignty and invulnerability. On a different level, Americans believe in self-help and small government at home, and project this image abroad. Europeans, on the other hand, stand for a strong welfare state based on strong social cohesion. Add to this the different geographical and historical peculiarities, and the dissimilar governmentalities become rather obvious, which at least partially explains the chicken or the egg dilemma.

The second part of the explanation suggests that the EU has a certain comparative advantage in the field of social power. This idea of Europe, and the EU in particular, as a normative power, setting standards for itself and the rest of the world which are morally superior, is a widespread notion. In his biography of the EU's Founding Father Jean Monnet, François Duchêne argues that Monnet saw European integration as a method to "civilianise, or turn into relations between people, the impersonal traditions and relations between states (...) Through partnership [Monnet] was seeking in the world the same effect as through the Community in Europe: to 'civilianise' international relations."[74] About half a century later, European Commission President Romano Prodi suggested that "Europe's destiny is not inherently Eurocentric, but one of universality. It should therefore reassert its role as the 'beacon for world civilization' (...) Such a role could eventually revive the Christian soul of Europe which is the basis for unity (...) It is precisely this dual consciousness of commitment to religious faith and full political responsibility, and having to aspire to a new cultural unity through a debate over ideals that gives us renewed vigour, and identity and a role to play."[75]

How does the EU bring this plethora of social power to use? The following chapters will study the EU's social power in the areas of culture, law, media, and public diplomacy, painting a diverse picture of the Union's norm-setting capabilities and record in international politics. But before we go into more detail, we need to examine the EU's particular role as a Lite Power, and clarify its approach towards social power in the context of geopolitics. Contrary to what might be expected, the EU is actively promoting the "European model" to achieve concrete geostrategic objectives. For example, Prodi argued (in February 2000) that "Europe needs to project its model of society into the wider world. We are not simply here to defend our own interests: we have a unique historic experience to offer. The experience of liberating people from poverty, war, oppression and intolerance. We have forged a model of development and continental integration based on the principles of democracy, freedom and solidarity and it is a model that works. A model of a consensual pooling of sovereignty in which every one of us accepts to belong to a minority."[76]

In its report *Shaping the New Europe* (of 2000), the European Commission argues that "Europe's model of integration, working successfully on a continental scale, is a quarry from which ideas for global governance can and should be drawn."[77] The EU takes some pride that the African Economic Community and the Organisation of African Unity remolded themselves into an EU-inspired African Union (AU), which was established in 2001. Similarly, French President Nicolas Sarkozy has been instrumental in establishing a new Union for the Mediterranean (launched in July 2008), taking a leaf out of the EU's book on postnational governance.[78] The EU does therefore not merely stand for "good governance" (encompassing the rule of law, transparency, democracy, etc.), but also for an alternative to the classical norms of Westphalian statehood. As Ben Rosamond argues: "the EU stands—self-consciously sometimes—as a beacon of what it might mean to engage in the post-Westphalian governance of globalization. It is in this sense a normative transmitter to the rest of the world."[79] And, as Manners suggests, the EU's "ability to define what passes for 'normal' in world politics is, ultimately, the greatest power of all."[80] It is therefore social power that has served Europe well, since (as Manners claims) the Cold War ended "by the collapse of norms rather than the power of force."[81]

Although we do not see other regions in the world taking carbon copies of the EU's model, it is clear that, as Ludger Kühnhardt claims, "European integration is perceived as a source of inspiration for other processes of regional cooperation and integration around the world."[82] The EU's social power is most evident in the transformations undertaken by governments in response to the lure of "joining Europe", i.e., joining the EU. For example, in February 2005, in a speech before the European Parliament, Ukrainian President Viktor Yushenko announced that his country has now "clearly defined the ingredients and forms for further decisions. These are the norms and standards of the European Union, its legislation, legal, political, economic, and social culture. European integration is the most effective and, in fact, the only programme of reforms for contemporary Ukraine."[83] For most Central European countries, the choice has been a stark one: it's either "Belarus" or "Brussels." It is a choice between isolation and marginalization on the one hand, and integration and globalization on the other. In reality, therefore, the EU's model is an offer no European country can refuse.[84] But the "price" EU aspirants have to pay is to accept not only the infamous 80,000 pages of *acquis communautaire*—the Byzantine collection of rules and regulations that govern the internal workings of the EU—but also the acknowledgment that the role of force and Realpolitik within the Union is minimal. Inside the EU, hard power counts for little (and only if it is deployed outside the EU), whereas social power is everything.

The EU is therefore constantly and actively advocating and uploading its norms, standards, and policy practices, whenever and wherever it can. EU enlargement has been a main vehicle for norm dissemination, and it still is *vis-à-vis* aspirant members like Croatia and Turkey.[85] The EU also persistently uses its so-called "conditionality clause" to spread its norms and rules, claiming that human rights, democracy, and the rule of law are essential elements for EU aid and political agreements with third countries.[86] Brussels also uses its Economic Partnership Agreements (EPAs) as a tool to spread good governance, especially towards the developing world. The European Commission itself makes no bones about it: "EPAs are part of the overall effort to build up the economic governance framework."[87] The EU's social power also derives from the central role it plays in humanitarian aid, where Europe is by far the global leader. Over the last few years, the EU has devoted substantial resources to famine relief for Ethiopia and Eritrea, drought relief for Afghanistan, and food aid for Niger and Mali. The EU has also actively supported regional economic integration in the Common Market for Eastern and Southern Africa. Moreover, in stark contrast to NATO, the EU has specialized in civilian crisis management and post-conflict reconstruction efforts. After the NATO-led intervention in Yugoslavia in 1999 came to an end, the EU again stepped in with a Stability Pact for South Eastern Europe, the EU's administration of the city of Mostar, as well as several police missions in Bosnia.[88]

Hovering over all these avenues of social power is the Realist question of whether or not the EU would be better off with a healthy dose of hard, military might. In short: does social power need hard power to be effective? On this question reasonable people have disagreed, and often fiercely. Manners, for example, claims that "[m]ilitarising the EU does not increase its power in inter-state politics, it decreases it (...) I have no doubt that militarization will dramatically undermine normative conceptions of the EU."[89] Robert Kagan, however, argues that the EU's credibility would improve if it had a more diverse toolbox of statecraft, including recourse to military force. It would, however, be overly simplistic (if not all-out wrong) to suggest that Europe's normative preference for social power conflicts with its "national" interests. As Finnemore and Sikkink maintain, "arguments about whether behavior is norm-based or interest-based miss the point that norm-conformance can often be self-interested, depending on how one specifies interests and the nature of the norm."[90] Normative frames and ideas cannot be analyzed without clarifying whose interests they serve, whereas all interests are ultimately motivated by normative considerations.

To illustrate this point, Zaki Laïdi has argued in his *La Norme Sans la Force* (2005) that "[t]he equation between soft power and 'nice power', hard power and bad guy power is partly misleading."[91] Laïdi makes the important link between normative power and social preferences. His bottom-line is that "Europe expresses, defends and promotes its social preferences through international or global norms."[92] Hence its penchant for social power over hard power.[93] Many studies have shown that Europe's social model reflects the preferences and often complex societal deals that have been struck over the last decades. The EU's Common Agricultural Policy (CAP) and the high social standards of Europe's welfare state are examples in point.[94] These European public policies now have to be legitimized and defended at the global level, and hence have become part of the EU's "foreign policy." If the EU pushes for the introduction of a social clause during WTO negotiations, it is therefore not merely the externalization of European social norms, but a strategy to *defend* Europe's own social standards against world-wide competition. This makes social power a key tool in managing globalization, not only for the EU, but also for other norm-setters in international politics.

2.5 THE NEW ASIAN HEMISPHERE?

In his influential book *The New Asian Hemisphere* (*without* a questionmark), the Singaporean diplomat Kishore Mahbubani makes the case for Asia's peaceful return to the world political stage.[95] Given the financial concussions which have shaken the global system in 2008, the rise of Asia—from Dubai, Mumbai to Shanghai—seems inevitable, with major unknown implications for the role of the West. Mahbubani foresees the dawn of a new Asian century, but is dismayed by the reluctance of Western leaders to applaud, or even accept this shift in the geopolitical balance. As Mahbubani argues, "[t]he universalization of the Western dream should represent a moment of triumph for the West (...) Most of the concepts we use [in Asia] to describe contemporary realities are Western. The willingness of the rest of the world to absorb and use Western concepts is one of the strongest foundations for global optimism."[96] In short, Mahbubani suggests that although the balance of hard power may well shift towards Asia, the West's social power—which is confirmed by the global dominance of its norms, values, ideas, and rules—persists regardless.

As we argued earlier, both the US and Europe are engaged in a global beauty contest where the effective use of social power plays an important, perhaps even decisive, role. But, as Mahbubani suggests, the avenues of social power are open to everyone. So what about the other contestants in the global model pageant? China consistently uses its "Asian values" to set itself up as a competitor to the West, and the US in particular. China uses Confucianism as an "imagined Asian identity" to construct and invent itself as the natural cultural leader of the region.[97] Confucianism's concern with ethics, the emphasis on groups rather than the individual, and the primacy of unity, harmony, order, education, and hard work, have a wide appeal, especially now that the "Western values" of individualism and liberalism are under pressure. For China, playing the "Asian values"-card offers opportunities to set competing norms and standards in international politics as well.[98] For example, Confucianism is said to inspire diplomatic principles like "harmonious world", and "live peacefully with neighbors", which are all promulgated by Beijing.

By playing the Asia-card, and stressing harmony and peace, China explicitly excludes coercion and hard power, and privileges the role of social power. In doing so, China tries to redeem itself from a long history shaped by its experiences of humiliation, victimhood, and racism. In the twentieth century, the rising influence of the West in Asia was accompanied by the simultaneous degeneration of Chinese society itself, with the Chinese Revolution killing off what had remained of the proud and immensely large Chinese empire. Even today, despite its growing economic and political weight, China claims the position of victim in international politics, where historical events—ranging from the Boxer Rebellion at the turn of the nineteenth century, to the NATO bombing of the Chinese Embassy in Belgrade in 1999—are all considered evidence of China's victimhood in international politics.[99] Given this historical context, it is hardly surprising that Chinese foreign policy discourse emphasizes international status and prestige as "the most desirable value."[100] In this context, the vital role of social power as a foreign policy process comes naturally.

Whereas the West is apprehensive about China's rise, most Chinese see this as a long-overdue resumption of their natural role and place in Asia and beyond. For them, China's weakness of the past century has been an anomaly, not the rule. Still, China's economic, political, and military awakening could easily result in a negative backlash, upsetting the US and Japan, and giving rise to counterbalancing coalitions. China's autocratic political system, its claim on Taiwan, and its record of human rights violations are all cause for concern, especially in the West. The Chinese authorities are well aware of this risk, and therefore stress that image management is required to confront and reduce suspicions. China also recognizes that, in order to become the cultural gyroscope of Asia, it requires social power to pull other countries within its economic and political reach.

Interestingly, there is a vivid academic and political debate in China itself concerning the nature and effectiveness of social power, based on the recognition that this novel approach to power is an important factor in explaining China's rising influence in the region and the world. In their study on this internal Chinese debate, Young Nam Cho and Jong Ho Jeong stress that top leaders in the Chinese Communist Party consider social power an important component of comprehensive national power. It is acknowledged that social power is required "to avoid following in the footsteps of the Soviet Union [which] collapsed because of the weakening of its soft power and resulting decrease of its international influence."[101] This Chinese debate on social (and soft) power also recognizes that this is predicated on good governance, which in China's case includes socialist democracy, a functioning economy, and resolving major imbalances in economic inequality.

In particular, public diplomacy is considered a useful strategy to achieve two closely interrelated goals: first, to oppose American cultural hegemony and the spread of Western values by strengthening a supposedly unique Chinese tradition based on ideology and history; second, to secure China's right to voice its own opinion within an emerging global society. As Cho and Jeong argue, China's "main objective [since 2005] is securing the right to speak in the process of making new international rules and conceiving major regional and global policies."[102] This confirms that using social power to advocate and upload new norms and rules is a competitive process, taking place in a competitive normative space.

China's efforts to frame the international debate about its economic rise as "peaceful" and "natural" offers a powerful and highly successful example of its discursive power. In the US, the public debate is mainly framed around the "China threat" and "China collapse" theories,[103] which stands in sharp contrast to China's soothing rhetoric of *heping jueqi* ("peaceful rise"), *heping fazhan* ("peaceful development"), in a *hexie shijie* ("harmonious world").[104] It seems clear that China is "winning" this geopolitical exercise of "verbal fighting", since opinion polls show that, since the late 1990s, perceptions of China's role in Southeast Asia have shifted. In most Asian countries, China is considered a pre-eminent regional power, playing a constructive role.[105] Almost without exception, Southeast Asian leaders accept China's economic and political rise as something that should be managed, rather than considered a security threat.

For China, uploading the norm of multipolarity is a vital geopolitical goal. It has understood that it cannot use hard power to get the notion of *heping jueqi* widely accepted, and has therefore used a variety of, overall successful, non-coercive approaches to alter perceptions, build trust and friendship, and develop relationships. In short: China is heavily betting on social power's impact to achieve distinctly geostrategic objectives. China has learnt the lesson that social power is an invaluable asset to manage its economic, political, and military ascent. It is the lubricant necessary to overcome obstacles of any kind, since it changes the frame in which China's foreign policy actions are being seen. What may have looked like aggressive behavior or hegemonic plans a few years back, now looks like the normal behavior of a rising power in search of a constructive role and place in the region and beyond.[106]

China has based its social power on a strategy of building connections and gaining goodwill, rooted in the understanding that it should develop the social capital of legitimacy, credibility, and respect which can thereafter be used to upload norms and rules. To start with, Beijing has begun to emphasize the cultural attractiveness of China. Chinese President Hu Jintao argued in 2003: "The Chinese culture belongs not only to the Chinese but also to the whole world (...) We stand ready to step up cultural exchanges with the rest of the world in a joint promotion of cultural prosperity."[107] China has therefore set up more than 325 Confucius Institutes (by April 2009) with the specific aim of promoting the study and knowledge of the Chinese language and culture, all around the world.[108] China Radio International is now broadcasting in English, 24 hours per day, and the number of foreign students enrolled in China's universities tripled from 39,000 (in 1997) to 197,000 (in 2007), with over 75 percent of students coming from Asia.[109] The Chinese government aims to quadruple the number of foreigners studying Chinese to around 100 million by 2010. This aim is made significantly easier to reach now that the US has introduced more stringent visa requirements on foreign students after 9/11. Due to China's economic growth, outbound tourism has grown dramatically, and in some European capitals Chinese tourists already outnumber those from Japan. The sight of affluent Chinese tourists crowding Amsterdam, Berlin, and San Francisco obviously conjures up images of wealth and self-confidence, which is exactly the role China is carving out for itself.

But most importantly, China is offering the world its own societal model as a serious competitor to Western-style liberal democracy and market economy. The so-called "Beijing Consensus" is founded on economic development based on each country's specific qualities and characteristics.[110] It rejects the US economic model (the so-called "Washington Consensus"), which is based on relatively low taxes and income redistribution, combined with equally low levels of health and social security, all within a system of little regulation. Needless to say, it implicitly suggests that authoritarian governments (like China) can successfully introduce and manage some elements of the market economy. The Beijing Consensus suggests a special Asian-style diplomacy, based on the reality that, unlike the US and most of Europe, "regime legitimacy and nation-building are an inherent part of security conception and are often placed at the top of security concerns."[111] China's live-and-let-live-model, rooted in old-style notions of national sovereignty and non-interference, fits well in this Asian appreciation of international politics. Moreover, Russia's disastrous experiment with so-called "cowboy capitalism" in the 1990s, and the subsequent clampdown of President Vladimir Putin, suggest that restricting democracy and managing the market economy may well become the preferred path for non-Western countries. China's governance model thereby gains attractiveness, whereas the American and European models are considered paternalistic, even dangerous.

Bates Gill and Yanzhong Huang suggest that China's charm offensive is particularly felt in the Middle East, Latin America, and Africa, and has worked miracles for this rising power's political fortunes.[112] Both authors refer to BBC polls in representative countries in these regions, who all increasingly favor China's growing influence in world affairs. Gill and Huang therefore conclude that the "existence of like-minded states in these regions and the attractiveness of China's development model have facilitated Beijing's quest for market, natural resources and political influence." They quote political leaders as diverse as Brazilian President Lula and Iranian leader Ayatollah Ali Khamenei, who all champion the "Chinese model" which combines economic growth with authoritarian political rule.[113] Gill and Huang further argue that the improvement of China's image in countries like Australia and France in the last decade "in part explains why some Western democracies seem less willing to get mixed up in US–China tensions, such as over Taiwan."[114]

Like the EU, China also uses trade and aid as political levers and PR instruments. China's emerging Africa strategy is the most obvious case of a remarkable attempt to gain status and influence, which are ultimately used to get China's voice heard and its norms and rules accepted and adopted. China's motives in Africa are clear: gain access to the continent's ample raw materials; gain market access for China's exports; get African support for Chinese foreign policy goals in IOs; and, to top it all off, counter both the US and EU, if possible.[115] The twenty-first century version of the "scramble for Africa" is mainly motivated by the growing need for energy resources and raw materials. China already imports around 30 percent of its gas and oil from sub-Saharan Africa, and purchases copper from the Congo, platinum from Zimbabwe, and ferrochrome and uranium from other African countries. This resource grab clearly follows the lines of classical imperialism, but like the empires of old, China cloaks its economic motives with the spread of its Beijing Consensus, based on a state-controlled market economy which offers little room for democracy and good governance.[116]

The fascinating side of China's Africa strategy is that it combines ordinary economic interests and Realpolitik goals with the smart use of social power. China's quest for resources is understandable and, of course, fully legitimate. But China also makes serious efforts to make friends across Africa. By boosting Chinese tourism to the continent, setting up training programs for Africa's future opinion leaders, and creating new structures for Sino-African business relations, China is trying to loosen the West's hold on Africa's elite. China is also keen to generate good-will by boosting its economic support to Africa (as well as to Latin America), increasing its development aid, and canceling the debt of some 30 African countries worth many billions of US$. It is little surprise that many African leaders now consider China as their main friend and a serious Great Power. All in all, Beijing is trying its utmost to make its social model as attractive as possible, offering generous aid programs to developing countries without the good governance strings the West attaches to its own aid. For China, the results on these investments have been huge. Joshua Kurlantzick claims that "China appears to be using its soft power to incrementally push Japan, Taiwan, and even the United States out of regional influence."[117] Mark Leonard even suggests that China's alternative political-economic model constitutes "the biggest ideological threat the West has felt since the end of the Cold War."[118]

Obviously, the 2008 Beijing Summer Olympics were planned as a showcase of China's peaceful development, conferring the prestige and respect that China thinks it deserves from the rest of the world. Giving in to its autocratic instincts, Chinese authorities went to enormous lengths to block "unreliable" Internet sites, imprisoning and intimidating dissidents, and tightening visa restrictions. Celebrity advocates like Steven Spielberg and Mia Farrow who openly criticized China for failing to use its influence on Sudan to stop the killings in the province of Darfur, were considered obnoxious spoilsports.[119] Western criticism of China's human rights record were equally ignored. Despite several blotches on its image, the Beijing Olympics offered athletes from 204 countries and the accompanying army of more than 30,000 journalists, as well as some 80 foreign leaders, an opportunity to see and experience "the new China", impressing a massive global TV audience with China's organizational skills and acumen. And this at a time when China's main geopolitical competitor, the US, was struggling with a botched Iraq war and a misfiring economic engine, while the EU lingered in a rather introspective mood pondering over its Constitution.

Interestingly, China's rise has hardly upset its delicate relationship with Taiwan, which it considers an integral part of its *One China*-policy. China uses the social power it has generated in Africa and Latin America to encourage these countries to take China's side, and several African states have already been lured into Beijing's camp (such as Sudan and Ethiopia). China also uses its leverage with these countries to limit any criticism against China's human rights record in international fora such as the UN Commission on Human Rights. Moreover, Beijing still frames its military modernization as an effort to develop "objective self-defense requirements",[120] which is a story it seems to be getting away with. Despite the massive build-up of China's military, obviously preparing for military contingencies in the Taiwan Straits, Beijing's relationship with Taiwan has improved noticeably over the years. This, of course, begs for an explanation. Realist analysis would suggest that China's rise would provoke a counter-reaction, most probably a balancing coalition of regional forces (perhaps under US leadership)—but this is obviously not happening.

These normative shifts in Asia, and, to some extent in Africa and Latin America, confirm China's success in hegemonic socialization. China's criticism of the US (and to a lesser extent the EU)[121] forms an integral part of this strategy to construct China as the legitimate alternative, or counterbalance, to a *Pax Americana*, or overall Western dominance of international politics. Chinese analysts and politicians see the US as a "neo-imperialist" power, which under the guise of its fight for human rights is actually aiming for American hegemonic control of the world. This fear, this distopia, is played up by Chinese policymakers in order to generate support for the "only credible alternative": China.[122]

2.6 CONCLUSION

Social power is not merely the patina for hard power, making the use of military force bearable and acceptable. As the American, European, and Chinese approaches to social power illustrate, one can no longer credibly claim that "ultimately" it is still raw coercion that counts, and that "real" power still comes from the barrel of a gun. Nevertheless, hard power obviously still counts for something, which explains why today's Lite Powers struggle to get the hard–social power mix right. The US has found it particularly testing to strike the right balance between using force and conviction, between making offers that should not be refused, and offers for dialogue and deliberation. Joseph Nye therefore suggests that the US needs a better social power strategy: "We will have to learn better how to combine hard and soft power if we wish to meet the new challenges."[123] This trade-off lies at the heart of America's foreign policy dilemma, and not just on security matters, but in principle on all policy issues ranging from trade and international law, to culture and media.

The EU and China are struggling with similar challenges, although their modest military capabilities and imperial ambitions limit the role of hard power in their preferred power-cocktail. As we have seen, Europe is particularly active as a norm entrepreneur, using its institutional appeal as an important avenue of social power. Its postnational model stands in stark contrast to China's old-style notions of national sovereignty and non-interference, which may better fit the priorities and interests of the non-Western, modern world. As we argued earlier, social power can be used conservatively, by maintaining existing standards and norms, or revolutionary, by uploading new ones. In today's geopolitical circumstances, all Great Powers aim at continuity *and* change: the US hangs on to its *Pax Americana*, but also pushes its Freedom Agenda of radical democratic reform;[124] the EU holds on to its economic and political privileges, but also advocates pervasive multilateralism; whereas China clings to Westphalian notions of sovereignty, but also aspires to a multipolar system. In order to keep what is desirable and change what is no longer needed, Great Powers use both hard and social power. As we have seen, untangling the jumble of coercive and non-coercive policies and tactics, and determining what has worked most effectively, remains a challenge.

So how should we appreciate the role of social power in today's geopolitical setting? As I argued earlier, much of today's global governance processes revolve around "power to"-issues, rather than using forms of coercion to get one's way. All Great Powers use social power to frame foreign policy in a way conducive to their strategic interests, pushing images and concepts that discursively legitimize their leadership. China, in particular, is striving for more voice on the international scene, using a wide variety of methods and practices to gain authority, credibility, and even friendship. By enhancing its social capital at a time when America's image is at an all-time low, China is smartly employing social power to turn the geopolitical table on the West.

As we have seen, even today's non-imperialist empires bring into play an amalgam of hard and social power, confirming power's polymorphous quality. Although the US is obviously most committed (and prepared) to use military force, even the EU and China realize that, in order to effectively upload their norms to the global level, hard power cannot be fully ignored. At the same time, American policy-makers have become more conscious of the fact that it is *not* better to be feared than to be loved; on the contrary, as President Obama argued in his Cairo speech of

June 2009: "I have come here to seek a new beginning between the United States and Muslims around the world; one based on mutual interests and mutual repsect."[125]

Issues such as the legitimacy of humanitarian interventions, the right to interfere in each other's domestic affairs, and the management of globalization are all highly politicized and sensitive debates on which all Great Powers cherish widely diverging opinions, reflecting their conflicting norms and interests, as well as their governmentalities. But despite the high level of media attention devoted to geopolitical questions (and conflicts and wars in particular), we should acknowledge that this is just the tip of the iceberg: the bulk of international politics is non-coercive and even non-conflictuous. Which means that, despite the relevance of hard power, the role and place of social power is inevitably growing. This was reflected in the words of US Undersecretary of State for Public Diplomacy and Public Affairs James K. Glassman, who argued (in June 2008) that America's Way of Life faces growing competition: "The Russian and Chinese ideological models, which suppress individual freedom while allowing market economics a good deal of breathing space, are growing disturbingly popular in some circles."[126] As Glassman acknowledged, despite the challenge to the US and Europe, it is still "a really good thing that around the world, countries such as China have adopted soft power means. It's a lot better than the alternative, that's for sure."[127]

3 Culture and constructivism

3.1 INTRODUCTION

Nazi potentate Hermann Göring famously remarked that "when I hear the word culture, I reach for my revolver."[1] To some extent, a similar animosity towards culture can be found in the mainstream of the discipline of IR. In his path-breaking edited volume on the role of culture in international politics, Peter J. Katzenstein argues that for Realists, "culture and identity are, at best, derivative of the distribution of capabilities and have no independent explanatory power. For rationalists, actors deploy culture and identity strategically, like any other resource, simply to further their own self-interest."[2] Given the silence within IR theory on culture, it has largely been left to sociological approaches to examine the state as a social actor, embedded in social rules and conventions that shape its identity and constitute the normative backdrop of the "national interests" that motivate its actions. Since the mid 1990s, culture has made a gradual, long-awaited entry in the realm of IR with the works of scholars such as Nicholas G. Onuf, Yosef Lapid, Friedrich Kratochwil, and Katzenstein.[3] Alexander Wendt's study *Social Theory of International Politics* (1999) has gone farthest in developing a constructivist ontology dealing with the role of culture in politics.[4]

For our study of social power, the constructivist predicament is essential: how to demonstrate that ideas do not just matter, but have "power over" other actors to shape concrete policy outcomes, and have the "power to" identify who these actors are and what capacities and practices they are socially empowered to undertake. As most ideational approaches, the constructivist study of culture and identity in international politics is ostensibly lacking "scientific rigor." For example, anthropologist Clifford Geertz suggests that cultural analysis in international politics is interpretative, and less about a search for causality between culture and state action, as about an interpretative search for meaning.[5] The postmodern, even antipositivist scent of cultural studies may further explain why culture has long been discredited as a soft, immeasurable, and (perhaps therefore) unscientific ingredient in IR theory. Obviously, this also colors our study of social power since it acknowledges the relevance of culture as a key facet of international society's normative environment.

Due to its sociological pedigree, constructivism has been able to bridge the disciplinary gap, making the study of culture and identity palatable to mainstream IR scholars.⁶ Constructivism famously argues that "ideas and discourse matter", and that norms, values, and identity heavily influence political life.⁷ Surely, international politics still offers numerous relatively unchangeable constraints to state behavior, such as the balance of military power or the global market. But constructivism suggests that "[m]eaningful behaviour, or action, is possible only within an inter-subjective social context."⁸ Ideas and discourse matter since they construct the socially agreed facts that cannot be wished away by individuals, and inform the common knowledge that sustains legitimacy and authority.

As Ted Hopf claims, identities play a crucial role in society, since "they tell you and others who you are and they tell you who others are."⁹ These identities, in turn, are the result of social practices whose power "lies in their capacity to reproduce the intersubjective meanings that constitute social structures and actors alike."¹⁰ This implies that normative factors shape the behavior of states and other actors, and that these factors may serve as road-maps or focal points for the expectations of others.¹¹ By analyzing how social collectives (i.e., states and other political actors) give meaning to their roles and actions, constructivism offers alternative understandings of several key themes in IR theory, ranging from the nature of power to the prospect of change in world politics.

The relevance of constructivism in clarifying the role of social power should be both self-evident and straightforward. Since the power of practice is the power to produce intersubjective meaning within social structures, *social* power involves the capacity to produce, shape, and influence the motives, attitudes, roles, and interests of actors in international politics (by non-coercive means). Social power first and foremost involves uploading norms and values, but these values may also inform relevant actors about their roles and interest in international politics. This is why international norms can be defined as "collective expectations about proper behavior for a given identity."¹²

In our study on social power, the question then arises as to how meaningful social action of states (and other political actors), based upon such "proper behavior", comes about. Michael S. Billig (in his study of Max Weber) suggests that states are at times value-oriented, tradition-oriented, and interest-oriented, and frequently oriented by a complex mixture of all three. And, as Billig concludes, human motivations exist within cultural, institutional, and symbolic contexts, "which themselves should be the central foci of any truly social science."¹³ This chapter follows Billig's (and Weber's) counsel, by examining the role of culture in the context of social power, followed by chapters on the role of institutions and law (as the institutional context), and media and globalization (as the symbolic context).

Probing social power through culture is a good point of departure, partly since Geertz has famously defined culture as "the webs of significance (man) himself has spun."¹⁴ This suggests that culture is the central prism through which "reality" acquires meaning.¹⁵ It also suggests that it is constructed, and hence is implicated with economic and political interest and motivations. As we have seen, the process of cognitive framing explains why certain (new) ideas resonate with relevant audiences, and others fail. Since norms only guide behavior within a given identity, the impact of culture to shape meaning is unmistakable. However, the problem with studying culture as a factor in social power is that it signifies anything from the most intangible lifestyle or the expression of individuals and groups, to electronically produced commodities and intellectual property emanating from the commercial sector. Moreover, today, consumption as a social practice has as much cultural meaning as the fine arts. To complicate matters even further, the very notion of ownership, let alone control, of these cultural manifestations is not only increasingly problematical, but also out of touch with consumers' actual experiences and expectations in the Internet era. In particular, *enforcing* ownership and control over culture becomes a major challenge of states (for political reasons) and commercial actors (mainly for legal and commercial reasons).

To talk about cultural power is therefore problematical.[16] As we will see, governments have tried to use, abuse, and manipulate culture (especially film, TV, and radio, as well as popular culture), but most often in vain. Culture has less "power over" other actors, but rather the "power to" establish frames that shape the way we see the world, telling us what is important, and informing us about options and solutions. Like social power, culture permeates social relationships, institutions, discourses, and media, and hence generally operates beneath the surface. In this way, culture has an immense impact on a society by setting, consolidating, and legitimizing standards and norms, using long-standing methods of social compliance, control, and discipline.[17]

As the scholarly product of different disciplines (including postmodern political theory and cultural and media studies), constructivism follows the footsteps of social theorists like Michel Foucault and Pierre Bourdieu, who argue that the most powerful form of compliance is social practice, which renders alternatives to compliance literally unthinkable. Setting the cultural standard and norm, making other standards and norms deviant or even unthinkable, surely qualifies as social power. With the postmodernization of global society, power moves away from territorial conquest to the annexation of imagination.[18] As Steven Lukes has asked, somewhat rhetorically, "is it not the supreme exercise of power to get another or others to have the desires you want them to have—that is, to secure their compliance by controlling their thoughts and desires"?[19] Obviously, the smoothest and least problematic use of power occurs when its application is not observable and is realized without friction and conflict.

This implies that the realm of popular (or "low") culture is social power's arena of choice. Since popular culture is uniquely capable of defining what is standard, normal, and legitimate, it constitutes an essential element of our understanding of social power. Gramsci has noted that popular culture plays a particularly central role since "a dominant ideology is symbolically mediated through cars, toys, advertising, food, news, and entertainment."[20] For Gramsci, the public and private sphere of domination interact, and are even complementary. Hegemony is no state-to-state affair, but uses more subtle, often less visible, channels through which social power flows, framing problems, suggesting solutions, and legitimizing policy options. In short, Gramsci is—rightly or wrongly—credited with undoing the orthodox Marxist notion of hegemony as coercive domination, and introducing the more subtle notion that the acceptance by the masses of the morality, norms, and rules of behavior of the society they live in is the most profound manifestation of dominance. Here, Gramsci clearly had a domestic society in mind, whereas this book argues that social power operates in similar ways in an emerging international society.

Following Gramsci, symbolic interaction theory sheds further light on the way meaning is socially constructed by applying familiar experiences and routines, such as consumer habits.[21] David L. Altheide therefore claims that our experiences and identities "are informed by mass-mediated images that are rapidly becoming key frames of reference for self and others."[22] This is also why popular culture should be understood as an institution, since (as Oran R. Young suggests) it comprises "rules of the game or codes of conduct that serve to define social practices, assign roles to participants in these practices, and guide the interaction among occupants of these roles."[23] Since popular culture is truly "popular" (i.e., beloved and widespread), it is also truly "embedded", which John G. Ruggie defines as the "fusion of power and legitimate social purpose."[24]

In their seminal work *Empire* (2000), Michael Hardt and Antonio Negri further suggest that "the creation of wealth tends ever more toward what we will call biopolitical production, the production of social life itself, in which the economic, the political, and the cultural increasingly overlap and invest one another."[25] Both authors thereby follow Foucault's notion of disciplinary power, which operates by setting cognitive parameters and defining normal (and deviant) behavior. Culture therefore plays a crucial role in producing the customs, habits, and norms that constitutes society itself. Where Foucault claims that life itself has become an object of power, Hardt and Negri suggest that biopolitical power "can achieve an effective command over the entire life of the population only when it becomes an integral, vital function that every individual embraces and reactivates of his and her own accord."[26]

Given the importance of culture as an avenue of social power, states have always been particularly keen both to export their culture and protect their cultural space against unwanted intruders and incursions. Media-scholar Monroe E. Price refers to this cultural space as a "bubble of identity", which the state shields "for the protection of domestic producers, sometimes creative and supportive of valuable aspects of national identity, territorial integrity, national security, and the strengthening of citizenship."[27] To equate this bubble of identity with "culture" itself may be somewhat too simple—but not that much. It is within this bubble that people interpret and make sense of their realities, which (following Geertz) is as good a working definition as any of what culture is all about.

But, as Friedrich Kratochwil has suggested, no theory of *culture* can substitute for a theory of *politics*.[28] Since the role of institutions, law, and media will be discussed in subsequent chapters, we will focus here on three pertinent questions, which taken together shed light on culture's role in the context of social power. First, this chapter examines how culture has been instrumentalized during the Cold War (and after) to reach traditional Realpolitik goals. Since the annexation of territory proved impossible during the Cold War, the "annexation of imagination" offered a worthy alternative. The US has consistently utilized its cultural attractiveness as an instrument of soft power, but also exploited its hegemonic popular culture as a means to achieve discursive and frame dominance, as well as political legitimacy. Since legitimacy is essential for the uploading of one's norms and rules, culture's soft power has been used as a mechanism to develop and bring to bear social power.

Second, this chapter appraises how popular culture and consumer habits have become major conduits of social power in international politics. Like public diplomacy and place branding—two phenomena discussed in greater depth in the following chapters—popular culture affects the values, preferences, and even identities of the wider public, going well beyond the usual foreign policy elites. By definition, popular culture reflects what is deemed "popular" in any given society, and what is perpetuated in daily life by sports, fashion, entertainment, and consumption. Popular culture has encroached upon every realm of our collective experience, initially only in the developed West, but due to globalization increasingly throughout the world. As Walter LaFeber has argued: "American popular culture (the jazz of Duke Ellington, the musical theatre of George Gershwin, the dance of Fred Astaire and Martha Graham, blue jeans, McDonald's fast food, Coca-Cola), has long been part of U.S. influence and profit overseas. The power of popular culture, however, multiplied with technological marvels that appeared in the 1960s and 1970s."[29] Popular culture thereby constitutes the biopolitical backdrop against which (international) politics takes place.

Finally, we will examine how Europe, and the EU in particular, has made efforts to defend and strengthen its bubble of identity, mainly against the perceived onslaught of globalization and Americanization. By studying the EU's efforts to exclude "cultural products" from the logic of free trade, we may come to appreciate how social power operates in a wider power framework where economic, political, and military rationales dominate. The approach of the EU is of particular importance here. Since the construction of "Europe" is not only an economic and political project, culture has played an important role during the five decades of European integration. According to modern myth, EU Founding Father Jean Monnet even argued that were he to begin again with the process of European integration, he would start with culture. In practice, the EU has continuously grappled with the application of culture's social power, offering us a better understanding of its limitations and opportunities.

3.2 POP CULTURE AND REALPOLITIK

It took the end of the Cold War and the easing of tensions between the West and its communist *alter ego* for constructivism to acquire academic thinking space and political appeal, putting culture firmly on the agenda. Samuel P. Huntington's thesis that "culture and cultural identities, which at the broadest level are civilization identities, are shaping the patterns of cohesion, disintegration, and conflict in the post-Cold War world",[30] received most attention, especially in its prediction that a "clash of civilizations" might be in the offing. But when Realist icons like Henry Kissinger praise Huntington's *Clash of Civilizations* as "one of the most important books to have emerged since the end of the Cold War",[31] you know that things have changed, and that culture has finally gone mainstream in IR.

That does not mean that culture was ignored as an important mode of power during the Cold War itself, just as it played a role in conflicts and wars throughout the ages. America's cultural power during the Cold War has been labeled Coca-Colonization, the Marilyn Monroe doctrine, or Rock 'n' Rollback.[32] These are puns with more than a kernel of truth in them. As Penny von Eschen has clarified in her book *Satchmo Blows Up the World* (2004), American policymakers after World War II made extensive use of all instruments of America's ample cultural power, which included sponsoring jazz musicians to tour Third World and Soviet-bloc countries like the GDR, Iraq, and the Congo. Duke Ellington toured the Middle East in the early 1960s, and Miles Davis played at the *Sala Kongresowa* in Warsaw, in October 1983, at the height of the clampdown of the *Solidarność* independence movement. Von Eschen suggests that American authorities saw jazz and rock 'n' roll as the "music of democracy", expressing the strong libertarian and egalitarian currents in American culture, constituting the most powerful antithesis of Soviet repression and Socialist Realism.[33]

Duke Ellington's efforts to spread the music of democracy to Europe's captive nations during the Cold War builds on a long tradition. In the 1940s, Hollywood was already dubbed the "little State Department."[34] During World War II, the US War Department used Hollywood to produce close to 2,500 war movies, supplying the manpower, equipment, as well as funding. For example, Frank Capra's *Why We Fight* documentaries traced the roots of fascism and were shown to soldiers before they headed overseas. Unlike any other movie, they helped to explain to the rest of the world who Americans were, and what they believed. America's post-war Marshall Aid included the use of these Hollywood films, which were either dumped or made mandatory as a political antidote to fascist and communist propaganda.[35] At the same time, the US Information Agency (USIA) carried the slogan "books follow the jeep", implying that pedagogical textbooks and the study of English would help changing post-war Europe's political landscape in America's favor.[36]

Monroe Price and Michael Nelson were among the first to argue that the Cold War was not won by the West's superior weaponry, but rather as a result of a media and information war. Nelson suggests that the "Soviet fortress fell not to the blows of the American army, but to a large extent to the subversive effects on its population of Western media such as Hollywood, Voice of America and MTV."[37] A new generation of historians has developed this thesis further, offering compelling case studies and arguments in its support.[38] Benjamin Barber, for example, quipped that "the most decisive battle in the Cold War may have been the one fought in a model kitchen at a consumer fair in Moscow in 1959, when vice President Nixon tried to parry Premier Khrushchev's rant about who would bury whom by talking about America's consumer magic."[39] More recently, US Undersecretary of State for Public Diplomacy and Public Affairs James K. Glassman argued (in June 2008) that "during the Cold War the Rolling Stones, the Beatles, the Yard Birds played a very significant role in Eastern Europe and they served as underground music and had a profound effect on liberalizing attitudes in Eastern Europe."[40]

During the Cold War, the impact of Western culture in the Soviet "bloc" was pervasive. Even in the GDR, with its excessive authoritarian regime, West German TV signals were relayed to the easternmost parts of the country (the Lausitz), since few East German citizens wanted to do without the TV programs from the West. Interestingly, it was not just objective news that East Germans longed for, but also high-quality entertainment, especially popular TV-*krimis* such as *Derrick* and *Der Alte*. During my own travels as a student in Poland in the mid 1980s, I was surprised to find all Polish families glued to their TV sets to watch *Dallas*, which was aired by state-television stations as soon as it was available in the US itself. *Dallas* (the 13-year soap-opera first aired in 1978) quickly reached a mass-audience in most Central European countries, who were spellbound by an irresistible executive lifestyle centered around booze and sex, and an archetypical anti-hero (JR) who they all loved to hate. Larry Hagman, who played JR, has even suggested that *Dallas* was "directly or indirectly responsible for the fall of the [Soviet] empire (...) They would see the wealthy Ewings and say, 'Hey, we don't have all this stuff.' I think it was good old-fashioned greed that got them to question their authority."[41]

The impact of Western popular culture during the Cold War remains hard to prove, and even harder to measure. Together with Larry Hagman, political scientists like Barry Buzan and Gerald Segal are convinced that "[b]ecause of the attitudes, morals, lifestyles, and cultural values it conveys, the primetime soft-porn television program *Baywatch* is much more subversive than CNN to authoritarian countries."[42] Still, claiming that shows like *Dallas* and *Baywatch* ended the Cold War would stretch it too far.[43] Even when we give credence to the constructivist thesis that ideas matter, it remains unclear which ideas had the most impact.

But it will be hard to deny that American popular culture, especially consumer brands and TV series, have been effective "colonizers" of the global imagination during the Cold War, portraying the US as a glittering consumer paradise. Its unspoken message is that the world wants to be like America, and that Americans are the righteous arbiters of freedom for all other countries.[44] US popular culture suggests that Americans believe that things will somehow work out well—and, of course, in Hollywood movies they generally do. The ideology of the happy ending, which was calculated to guarantee box office successes, is reflected in America's can-do foreign policy ideology. The steady drumbeat of the US entertainment and media industry frames America as a superhero who "reluctantly" steps in to rescue passive and usually incompetent communities and peoples. For example, in his exposé on America's empire, Robert Kagan suggests that "Americans can still sometimes see themselves in heroic terms—as Gary Cooper at high noon. They will defend the townspeople, whether the townspeople want them to or not."[45]

As Jennifer Sterling-Folker remarks, this image "stokes the American ego while tapping into its cultural and historical ideals about an anarchic and limitless frontier, the efficacy of violence for restoring order, and the ability to exclusively determine and mete out justice."[46] Eugene Secunda and Terence P. Moran have offered a long line of "American mythic characters" mediated by Hollywood and fiction, creating the image of US foreign policy along the lines of the "frontierman who brings law and order to the chaos of the wilderness."[47] This is a long-standing myth, starting with Captain America, the Lone Ranger, and Superman, continuing with Jack Bauer in *24*, framing the US as a redeemer nation. It is also an image which shapes and tickles the egos of US foreign policymakers. For example, when the influential German weekly *Der Spiegel* created a cover featuring President George W. Bush as Rambo, Vice President Dick Cheney as The Terminator, Condoleezza Rice as Xena Warrior Princess, and other officials as Batman and Conan the Barbarian, Washington did not express its indignation. Instead, the US ambassador to Germany ordered 33 poster-sized renditions of the cover, which were sent back to the White House.[48] American popular culture has therefore been instrumental in constructing roles and expectations in international politics, shaping identities of peoples as well as of states and governments.

During the many decades of the Cold War, culture played an important role in forging Western cohesion and undermining Soviet hegemony in Central Europe and beyond. But with the Western victory of the Cold War, US and European policymakers began to believe time was on their side, and that globalization would spread freedom and democracy, making additional guidance, support, and funding superfluous. During much of the 1990s, culture's social power was left untapped, culminating in the closure of the USIA, America's prime agency devoted to building support for US policies and spreading anti-communist propaganda.[49] It took the shock of 9/11 for Western policymakers to rediscover culture's value in uploading and solidifying norms and rules, as well as in winning the hearts and minds of an increasingly skeptical global audience. Immediately after 9/11, US entertainment executives offered their services to the Bush administration, discussing options to incorporate anti-terrorism themes into TV shows and movies.[50] Similarly, the US Ad Council initiated a country-wide "I'm an American"-campaign ("helping the country to unite in the wake of the terrorist attacks"), tracing its historical roots to advertisement campaigns such as "Loose Lips Sink Ships" and "Rosy the Riveter" during World War II. It obviously took an attack on America's territory and identity to rekindle available but dormant social power resources, indicating that culture's power to frame problems and shape meaning is in most demand during periods when America's (self-) image is challenged by others.

As the world's dream factory, Hollywood has played a particularly important role in framing issues and communicating political ideas. Hollywood's social power is best expressed by the remark that "at times Hollywood appears to be (…) no longer national cinema but *the* cinema."[51] Whereas in the past, national cinema was defined against Hollywood, the dominant Hollywood aesthetic has increasingly become the only visual language available. The normative mode of communication that underlies this aesthetic offers the world a golden mean of images, and hence succeeds in the international marketplace. The Hollywood aesthetic crosses boundaries easily because it is intelligible and appealing, and we can all recognize a part of ourselves in TV series like *Friends*, and movies such as *Titanic*. Cultural scholars Scott R. Olsen and Hans Blumenberg link the success of this aesthetic to what they call the "Hollywood mythotypos" designed to overcome the "existential dread that our lives might be short, meaningless, and ultimately ephemeral, the very things that myth and religion try to negate. This negation is most easily accomplished by appealing to those emotions that block out the absolutism of reality: wonder, awe, purpose, and participation."[52]

The easy conclusion would be that, by appealing to people's deepest emotions, Hollywood is more effective in drawing upon America's social power than the US army or any presidential speech. But this would underestimate the complexity of power and the dynamics of culture in international politics. American foreign policymakers have learned over the decades that popular culture is increasingly hard to control and manage. For example, US officials have found it difficult to accept that many foreigners simultaneously love American films, music, and fashion, and yet are prepared to harshly judge it, to the point that they believe that America got what it deserved on 9/11. As Margaret and Melvin DeFleur showed in a 2003 survey of teenagers from 12 countries, respondents associated "America" with sexual amorality, domination, warmongering, materialism, and violence. American popular culture is uniquely polyvalent, hedonistic as well as deeply religious, open as well as parochial. In this sense, Tony Soprano may be as much to blame for America's dwindling image as the bungled US-led invasion of Iraq.[53]

Moreover, as Conn Carroll argues: "Much of the anti-American disinformation that is eagerly consumed overseas comes not from governments but from Hollywood."[54] Popular movies like *Fahrenheit 9/11* and *Syriana* offer a picture of the US and its foreign policies that encourage (what Carroll calls) a "blame America first"-mentality. At the same time, Hollywood (and US media in general) continues to selectively frame Arabs, portraying them as potential terrorists. As Jack Shaheen argues in his book *Guilty—Hollywood's Verdict on Arabs After 9/11* (2008), these "images help enforce policy", and vilifying Arabs has "made it that much easier for us to go into Iraq."[55] Given this complex cultural environment, wielding culture's social power has become particularly problematic, as our investigation of public diplomacy and place branding further illustrates.

Cultural studies have debunked the notion of American cultural imperialism, arguing that hybrid cultural forms tend to mix Western and non-Western culture. Today, consumers deal creatively with the cultural expressions on offer, mixing them up themselves.[56] Katzenstein and Keohane suggest that Hollywood "is both in America and of the world. And so is America itself—a product of the rest of the world as well as of its own internal characteristics."[57] The infamous process of Americanization is therefore not an extension of American practices and products to the rest of the world, but rather a "selective appropriation of American symbols and values (...) a profoundly interactive process between America and all parts of the world."[58] Hollywood is not just an American aesthetic, but a specific way of engaging with audiences by presenting appealing images and familiar, attractive forms.

Latin American *telenovelas* are probably the best example of how the Hollywood aesthetic has gone global. These daytime soaps are familiar to a global audience, offering simple stories with a light-hearted cultural peculiarity on top of a text that is understandable to all.[59] Major centers of international television and film production such as Brazil and Hong Kong emulate the Hollywood approach by offering a microcosm of the international audience's taste. American culture represents the full spectrum of global culture, with hybrids of African, European, Asian, and Latin art, music, and norms and values. In a way, therefore, American culture is in a condensed form universal, which explains why it strikes a chord and is recognized by a wide variety of people, all over the world. This means that it has become both impossible and useless to throw up barricades against American culture, mainly since "Hollywood" has become "us"—and *vice versa*.

Katzenstein and Keohane consider America's polyvalence an expression of its social power, since individuals and groups in other societies can use and recast symbols associated with the US for their own purposes. Whether they use these symbols to associate themselves with the US, or as signs of resistance, the symbolic language of both anti- and pro-Americanism offers an idiom to express their opinions and debate their concerns. In this case, American popular culture has become the standard, the norm. Although this position hardly offers American policymakers possibilities to exercise social power, its disciplinary power is unmistakable. America's hegemonic pop culture does not offer Washington "power over" other actors, but it does offer opportunities to project America's social model and governmentality to the rest of the world, offering it the "power to" identify actors and fashion their roles.

3.3 CONSUMING AMERICAN CULTURE

Much of the West's attraction derives from its conspicuous wealth. During the Cold War, the tall building of Berlin's *Kaufhaus des Westens* (or *KaDeWe*, in common parlance) was the ultimate icon of capitalism and desire for GDR citizens, similar to the effect the exotic lifestyles of *Dallas*'s JR and Sue Ellen had on ordinary Poles. Benjamin Barber is therefore not far from the truth when he claims that the Central European revolutions of the late 1980s "had as their true goal not liberty and the right to vote but well-paying jobs and the right to shop (although the vote is proving easier to acquire than consumer goods)."[60] During the Cold War, the influence of affluence was considerable.

But, as argued earlier, it remains difficult to prove that the Berlin Wall was brought down by the popular desire to consume and emulate Western lifestyles. Most likely, the main reason for the Cold War's demise lies in the changed nature of the emerging post-industrial, knowledge and service-based economy which outpaced and outspent communism. The "new economy" was no longer plannable and no longer dependent upon the production of steel and brown coal. Instead, computers, IT, networks, and connectivity became key drivers of innovation and development. Nerds in garages dreaming up new computer-software and Internet solutions became the icons of this new era, an era in which Soviet leader Gorbachev realized he had to destroy his country (the USSR) in order to save it (by reinventing it again as Russia). This new era was based on Joseph Schumpeter's concept of creative destruction, the idea that innovation not only drives economic growth, but also obliterates established companies and production processes. Since it is frequently changing consumer patterns that drive this process of creative destruction, the power of consumption is substantial. It is this mode of social power that is of concern to us here.

Since the 1950s, the US has turned itself into the ultimate capitalist empire, the country that has brought us a new consumers' republic. Ever since sociologists studied the impact of mass production, or Fordism (named after the car company who introduced it), the concern for citizen-consumers has been present. The conflation of voters and consumers, of the political and commercial sphere, is therefore closely intertwined with America's economic history and its political ascent over the last century.[61] The notion that consumers are surrogate-citizens implies that the consumer marketplace is the sphere of political and civic action. Sociologists like Benjamin Barber, Lizabeth Cohen, and Victoria de Grazia have made in-depth studies into how citizenship and consumership have become entwined, and how shopping has become the guiding norm and ultimate social, if not political, yardstick.[62] In a sense, therefore, America is at the forefront of a global emporium, transforming citizens into shoppers whose power of the dollar, Euro, or yen assures a market response to their needs as citizens. Today, consumers have their very own Bill of Rights, acknowledging that they have become powerful political forces in Western democracies. Consumer choices, as well as occasional consumer boycotts, send clear political signals; and Industry Codes of Conduct (banning bribes, child labor, hazardous materials, and promising ecologically sound production methods) have set new standards under the pressure of citizens' demands. Consumer pressures against sweatshops and for social and environmental investment, in particular, are effective manifestations of the shoppers' power of the purse.

But consumption not only drives innovation, privileging fads and fashions, it also increasingly shapes the identity of people. Brands have become important manifestations of personality, lifestyle, and meaning, for some even replacing religious faith and nationalism. Commercial branding is based on the very notion that shopping has changed from a necessity to a leisure pursuit where meaning of life is sought and identity is construed.[63] Emerging consumption communities are based on the interconnectedness and communality of consuming the same brands, watching the same TV series, and listening to the same music. Since these consumption communities are becoming global in character, we are witnessing a consumer cosmology where brands replace traditional, more local cultural icons. With American styles, habits, and values firmly embedded in other cultures around the globe, the process of Americanization has become a victimless crime, where people and countries seem fully complicit, freely choosing to associate themselves with the norms and values that embody the idea of "America." This merger of the economic power of consumption with the social power of culture is an essential part of Hardt and Negri's concept of biopolitical production, where the economic, political, and cultural realms overlap and strengthen each other.[64]

The biopolitical aspects of consumption offer important insights into the nature of social power. Ordinary consumers can use their commercial clout to send political messages, uploading their norms and values through their purchasing decisions. Likewise, policymakers can call upon consumers to make choices on political grounds, and even for reasons of "national security." In 2002, for example, the US

Office of National Drug Control Policy (ONDCP) launched a campaign aimed at American youngsters where a direct link was made between drug abuse and the enrichment of terrorists threatening US security. President Bush unambiguously argued that "[i]f you quit drugs, you join the fight against terror in America."[65] To link public consumption patterns with foreign policy discourses is hardly new. For example, the now obligatory "made in"-label found on all products was first used by the British government after Word War I in order to "warn" consumers that they were buying German goods. Moreover, "Buy American"-campaigns were most powerful during World War II, but can today still be found to encourage "patriotic shopping", aimed against supporting "Middle East oil", or, more generally, to scold China. In all these cases, consumption is used as an avenue of social power, favoring certain norms and values over others.

What makes the social power of consumption unique is that it affects all of us: we are all consumers and although we may have widely differing purchasing powers, we all make consumer decisions on a daily basis. Two recent studies on the politics of consumption after 9/11 illustrate how "fear, consumption, and war were cast in the emerging and expanding meaning of terrorism."[66] Altheide examined how social power was taken up to keep Americans consuming and donating to 9/11-causes. Altheide suggests that this was "part of a symbolic healing act that fused individuals with a national identity", showing "how generous Americans were, how they always pulled together in times of crisis, and how a new resolve was merging."[67] By linking shopping to security, consumption was turned into a symbol through which citizens could show they cared, offering them an opportunity to literally buy the US *out* of a possible 9/11-induced economic recession by buying *into* the war on terror narrative. As Altheide argues (applying symbolic interaction theory), this "suggests that the economic realm reaches beyond the mere purchase of goods and services and into the marketplace of character and identity."[68] Post-9/11 America has offered a textbook example of the interplay of the mass media, popular culture, and advertisement in the symbolic construction of a "national experience" reaffirming the idea of a nation at war.

Another study, by David Campbell, examines how the sports utility vehicle (or SUV) became part of a discourse linking national identity with external danger.[69] Just as drug use was tied to terrorism by the ONDCP, the uneconomical but popular SUV became entangled in debates about the relationship between oil and security. These gas-guzzlers were often labeled "environmental vandals", who were also responsible for the increased revenues of Middle East oil producers. But America's lasting love-affair with SUVs, pick-up trucks, and full-size vans has also become a metaphor of America's identity and its role in the world. As Todd Gitlin has stated: "The SUV is the place where foreign policy meets the road."[70] Unlike any other means of transportation, the SUV communicates the feeling of ultimate security to people traveling crowded urban environments who often resemble militarized frontiers. As one 46-year-old mother of two driving a massive Toyota Land Cruiser suggested in 2003: "The world is becoming a harder and more violent place to live, so we wrap ourselves with these big vehicles."[71] SUV owners buy into the belief that they are invulnerable, and SUV advertisements convey the impression of the driver as a military figure, safe and sovereign in an insecure world. Obviously, the Hummer—based on the US military's High Mobility Multipurpose Wheeled Vehicle (or Humvee) that gained public fame during the first Gulf War in 1990–91—expresses this sense of superiority and safety most clearly.

The anti-SUV crusade of environmental pressure groups has hardly made a dent in the popularity of SUVs across the world, illustrating that this American icon of automobility is attractive to a global public. To many, SUVs express the American Way of Life, not only because these cars stand for freedom and a frontier-mentality, but also because they externalize danger. Tests indicate that the safety of SUV occupants comes at the cost of substantially higher death rates for those they collide with: "When SUVs hit a car from the side, the occupants of the car is 29 times more likely to be killed than those riding in the SUV."[72] The quest for personal safety at the detriment of the well-being of others is not only reflected in the concept of automobility, but also in America's behavior as a foreign policy actor. America's SUV-mentality manifests itself in the pursuit of sovereignty and security, the unwillingness to come to terms with (mutual) vulnerability, as well as the myth-driven notion of a divine destiny. As a 2002 Hummer advertisement claimed: "Excessive. In a Rome at the Height of Its Power Sort of Way." Obviously, people at Hummer forgot what happened to the Roman Empire, but the message remains all too clear: buying and driving the H2 makes you owner of the *Pax Americana*, which, just as the Hummer itself, is forceful, intimidating, and built on the belief that there is no "mission impossible."

The social impact of consumption is an increasingly important part of the power spectrum. People construct social and political meaning through their consumption decisions. By choosing eco-label food products they recognize the need to urgently deal with environmental problems; by choosing to drive SUVs they acknowledge the need and legitimacy for the US to maintain its global military reach underpinned by its dependence on imported oil. Policymakers, in turn, call upon consumers to keep spending, even if public confidence is undermined by 9/11 or the 2008 financial crisis. Since so much social and political meaning is generated through purchasing decisions, consumption has become a major platform and tool of social power. Consumers, brands, policymakers, and NGOs are all engaged in a reciprocal power relationship, since they all privilege certain norms and values (and occasionally rules) which they want to impress on others. Overlooking (or marginalizing) this arena of social power would create a vast black spot in our analysis of contemporary international politics. But since consumption is the focal point of identity, commercial interests, and foreign policy, the individual strands of power have become difficult to disentangle. Public discourses about the relationship between oil and security, or genetically modified food and safety, illustrate consumption's complexity.

As we will see in the chapter on place branding, commercial brands and political reputations interact. Since many companies remain associated with their countries of origin, the images and reputations of brands and states tend to merge in the minds of the global consumer. This explains why American commercial icons are usually the first targets of mass demonstrations venting discontent with US foreign policy. After 9/11 and the subsequent US-led invasion of Afghanistan and Iraq, Islamic groups not only burned American flags, but also looted and destroyed KFC's and McDonald's outlets. Nike stores and Pizza Huts were the obvious targets since they not only stand for American brands, but in a way they *are* the American brand.[73] As Walter LaFeber suggests, "not only are McDonald's and other American franchises global, but US troops are also positioned around the globe (…) These franchises and military units are overseas not primarily because of the attractiveness of American culture and military protection, but because of the needs of the United States."[74]

3.4 EUROPE'S CULTURAL MAGINOT LINE

Since culture's social power to define meaning, assign roles, and upload norms is of vital concern to states, the struggle for control over TV, film, and other modern media has triggered occasional "culture wars." Europe, in particular, has positioned itself as an outpost of resistance against America's cultural hegemony. This despite the fact that most European citizens have *de facto* already internalized the Hollywood aesthetic. Interestingly, "the American way of television" has been taken up more creatively in Europe than in the US itself. For example, the reality TV program *Big Brother* was a Dutch production which quickly spread around the globe.[75]

Still, concern about the Americanization of Europe's cultural space is widespread and deeply rooted amongst Europe's intelligentsia and EU policymakers. The notion that Europe should defend its cultural autonomy against the assault of Hollywood explains why the EU has thrown up a cultural Maginot Line, which will prove only temporarily successful. Given America's audiovisual dominance, the European governments' *Angst* to see their social power dissipate seems real. Europe has a US$7 billion deficit with the US in the audiovisual industry, and 80 percent of the export sales by the Hollywood film industry are now made in Europe. The European public obviously could not care less that their vision of "reality" is fashioned by American imagery, but Europe's cultural elite understand the far-ranging impact this may have on the collective consciousness of the European people. The president of the European Film Academy, Wim Wenders, has stridently noted that Europe will become a "Third World continent" mainly because it will "not have anything to say on the most important medium (…) There is a war going on and the Americans have been planning it for a long time. The most powerful tools are images and sound."[76] More recently, French President Nicolas Sarkozy suggested (in March 2008) that the digital world (and especially the Internet) is colonized by the English language: "What is at stake in the conquest of these new spaces is also the conquest of minds and the imagination."[77]

It is well-known that in the early 1920s, when 90 percent of the world's film exports were French, the US insisted on import quotas to protect its fledgling studios. But now that the situation is reversed, American studios are outraged that other countries try to protect their own creative industries. The European position that films and TV programs are cultural artifacts which should not simply be

60 *Culture and constructivism*

regarded as other tradable commodities is at odds with the US free-trade approach. But, as Barber has it, "with a few [American] global conglomerates controlling what is created, who distributes it, where it is shown, and how it is subsequently licensed for further use, the very idea of a genuinely competitive market in ideas or images disappears."[78] Unlike any other country, the US is largely immune to cultural expressions that do not project American values and sensibilities. It is also among the few countries that are able to indemnify the costs of producing expensive movies over its own populous and prosperous society. The US can therefore afford to have a so-called "cultural open-door policy", since it has little to fear from foreign competitors.[79]

It should, however, be acknowledged that part of Europe's current problems in developing a vibrant film and audiovisual industry is inherent to its fragmentary cultural landscape and the diversity of its languages. For example, whereas the US has eight distribution companies controlling 90 percent of the film market, Europe has around 700 of these companies competing for a small slice of film distribution.[80] At least half of the films that have recently won the European Film Academy Award (the so-called *Felix*) are known only in their country of origin.[81] It therefore seems that only the US generates the images able to catch the attention and stimulate the imagination of *all* European people.

This has not deterred Europe, and the EU in particular, from utilizing the discourse of "European culture" to call for a *de facto* mediatic Fortress Europe.[82] Since culture is largely outside the political remit of the EU, Brussels could only get involved when the US firmly placed culture on the *economic* agenda, which is, of course, a realm where the EU role is key. Protests became vocal with the massive demonstrations of thousands of European intellectuals and artists in the mid 1980s, calling for the exclusion of "cultural works" from the new General Agreement on Tariffs and Trade (GATT) arrangements that were then under negotiation. France called for measures to shield the European cultural market from American TV series and movies, asking for a 60 percent quota of "European content" of films shown on TV, as well as a tax on movie tickets to be used to subsidize innovative films, art-house cinema, and independent distributors. Interestingly enough, and probably to its own astonishment, the EU ultimately succeeded in excluding audiovisual services from the GATT accords (in October 1993), despite strong objections from Washington.[83]

This debate again flared up with the negotiations (1995–99) among OECD (Organization for Economic Co-operation and Development) countries to introduce the Multilateral Agreement on Investments (MAI). The MAI was designed to facilitate the movement of assets by individual and corporate investors across international borders. Opponents argued that this arrangement would undermine cultural diversity by treating culture as a mere "commodity" and "investment." The French cultural trade union SACD[84] referred to the MAI as an "economic war that American investors are waging on the European market, this time to win, and particularly to take its highly coveted plum: the audiovisual market."[85] Beatrice Clerc of the SACD even suggested that "creative artists refuse to see their works reduced to the status of merchandise and to see cultural identities disappear, little by little, throughout the world. It is high time to draw aside the veil masking one of the most serious attacks ever orchestrated by the United States against creative activity in Europe."[86] Former French Minister of Foreign Affairs Hervé de Charette further argued in 1997 that we now "live in a world threatened by the standardization of cultures and modes of thought. A single language has a very destabilizing effect. We French, are the first to become aware of this: The world cannot be based on images which are the same for everyone. If France wishes to take part in this contest, it will do so through its businesses and through the images it provides. *What is at stake here is vital for civilization.*"[87]

Ultimately, introduction of the MAI was blocked, mainly by European states, which was an important victory for the EU over Hollywood. This triumph was consolidated in October 2005, when UNESCO adopted the Convention on the Protection and Promotion of the Diversity of Cultural Expressions. This Convention exempts "cultural goods" from WTO regulations by granting states "the sovereign right to adopt measures and policies to protect and promote the diversity of cultural expressions within their territory." This implies that states will be free to regulate imports of foreign cultural products, including TV programs, films, as well as radio broadcasts. Of course, the very idea that culture justifies and requires protection is alien to WTO's free-trade credo. The Convention, ratified in December 2006, was therefore widely considered a resounding defeat for the US, which, as the world's primary exporter of cultural products, was fiercely opposed to the Convention.[88] The debate on the Convention soon turned into a referendum on American popular culture itself, between those who warned for American "cultural junk food", and those who feared that states could now control what its citizens hear and watch. To show its united stance on culture, EU member states voted *en bloc* during the formal approval in 2005.

Given the French penchant for protectionism, it has been relatively easy to reduce this French (and in a wider context: European) resistance as a rear-guard battle against the assumed logic and inevitability of globalization.[89] But for Europe, the dominance of the Hollywood aesthetic—based on the notion that culture is a "product" designed to circulate freely in a global economy—remains unacceptable. For almost all Europeans, culture is not to be considered a commodity devoid of political, social, and historical content and message. In many ways, Europe opposes the concept of a cosmopolitan culture, which is assumed to be universal and timeless, in essence superficial and devoid of any social or political "message." But since Europe's traditional definition of a rooted, "deep culture" hardly resonates *within* its own continent, let alone around the globe, there is little reason to assume that a European audiovisual sanctuary will survive.[90]

Despite the EU's resounding successes to kill the MAI and keep culture and commerce apart, these victories are bound to have a Pyrrhic quality to them. Europe's cultural Maginot Line is already trivialized by the digitalization of audiovisual "products" which are on offer as pay-per-view and digital-TV. The dawning global information society makes it possible to transmit any kind of service (voice, date, video) over any kind of network (fixed, wireless, satellite).[91] This convergence of telecommunications, computer, audiovisual, and publishing technologies, services, and industries, will further blur the line between traditional telecoms and computer-based communications and broadcasting.

These developments have turned the state into a theoretical, or hypothetical agent. Most states find it increasingly problematic to utilize culture's social power for political reasons. They no longer function as gatekeepers, deciding what "their" citizens watch, hear, and experience. Where in past centuries European states used high culture to mould society from a *Gesellschaft* into a *Gemeinschaft*,[92] this route is now firmly closed. Since popular culture and consumption have taken the place of the fine arts as conveyors of meaning and markers of identity, states have handed important social power tools over to outside actors, or have seen these tools simply disappear.

It would be comforting to assume that, with the triumph of popular culture, "the people" are now in the driving seat of social power, steering economic and political processes through conscious consumer decisions and lifestyle choices, using new technologies to shape their own cognitive environment. Without doubt, the information society has certain liberating qualities, offering consumers and citizens more freedom and flexibility. Still, since their choices remain bound by economic and political parameters that are largely beyond their control, even the most liberal information society remains imbued by social power, defined by a continuous tussle between citizens-consumers, states, and a plethora of other actors all engaged in agenda-setting, framing, and ultimately uploading their norms and values to the global level.

Consumers realize that their collective influence is huge, and therefore increasingly organize themselves in NGOs, pressure groups, and watchdogs. States also realize that they should do at least *something* to get more grip on the seemingly autonomous and anonymous processes that shape the identity of "their" people. But European states realize that even the EU's "victories" in its cultural campaign against Hollywood's hegemonic aesthetic are hollow and at best temporary. Europe, together with the rest of the world,[93] has internalized America's popular culture to such an extent that the concern of Americanization is generally shrugged off as being "so 1980s!" Still, this has not discouraged the EU from using culture as a process and platform to strengthen Europe's fledgling collective identity.

3.5 EUROPE'S CULTURE OF COOPERATION

As a global normative power, one would expect the EU to develop an active and assertive cultural policy. The EU is an avid norm entrepreneur, keen and experienced in uploading its norms and rules to the global level, as well as ensuring policy congruence between its member states. It is therefore surprising that the cultural dimension has long been neglected in the process of European integration. The main reason for the EU's constraint is the principle of subsidiarity, which protects member states' cultural policies and stops the union from having a possibly intrusive and harmonizing role. Only in 1977 did the European Commission propose to become involved with the economic and social aspects of culture. With the

Culture and constructivism   63

Adonnino Committee's report *A People's Europe* (1985), a flurry of initiatives towards strengthening and promoting the image of Europe came about, ranging from the development of European multilingual TV channels and European sports teams, to new school books and teaching materials emphasizing a stronger "European dimension." The idea behind many of these policies was to forge a European identity and a truly European cultural sector. Based on the Adonnino Report, the EU introduced many measures that have since become part of the EU's visual and cultural landscape: the European logo and flag, the harmonized European passport and driving license, European car number plates, the European anthem (Beethoven's *Ode to Joy*), European Culture Month, European Years dedicated to certain EU-chosen themes, May 9th as Europe Day, European Cities of Culture, etc.

As Cris Shore has argued, behind "these seemingly mundane cultural initiatives lay a more profound objective: to transform the symbolic ordering of time, space, education, information, and peoplehood in order to stamp upon them the 'European dimension.' In short, to reconfigure the public imagination by Europeanising some of the fundamental categories of thought."[94] For the EU to gain political legitimacy and authority, it has been considered essential to strengthen Europe's "imagined community", and to frame European integration as an inevitable, valuable, and beneficial process. Interestingly, the EU has therefore not only uploaded the European model to the international arena, but also *vis-à-vis* its own citizens. With the end of the Cold War, the enlargement towards Central Europe, and the membership application of Turkey to the Union, issues of legitimacy and identity have become even more important. For European policymakers, culture quickly became a source of legitimacy and a marker of identity. Without a culturally defined sense of Self, Europe's identity would not only become hollow and fragile, but would also make it more difficult for the EU to set standards and norms, and hence undermine its social power.

To study the EU's cultural *policies* goes to the roots of social power's wielding problem, since it assumes a certain rational and goal-oriented program using culture as a tool to reach economic, political, or strategic objectives. Today, the EU is surprisingly upfront about its ambitions to use the cultural dimension for political purposes. In a 1996 report on the role of culture, the European Commission concluded that Europe's "cultural policy must make a contribution to strengthening and to expanding the influence of the European model of society built on a set of values common to all European societies."[95] More recently, the European Commission's website proclaims that the "cultural 'soul' of Europe is becoming increasingly important as a means of bringing Europeans together and enhancing relations with neighboring states and the rest of the world."[96] The European Council therefore calls upon all member states and the European Commission to "regard culture as an essential component of European integration, particularly from the point of view of the enlargement of the Union."[97]

European Commission President José Manuel Barroso asked the obvious question most clearly in December 2005: "How can European culture promote European integration?" In other words: how can social power be used to strengthen the norm that further integration is both positive and necessary? A few years later, Barroso had obviously found the answer: "Culture and creativity are important drivers for personal development, social cohesion, and economic growth. Today's strategy promoting intercultural understanding confirms culture's place at the heart of our policies."[98] The European Commission's *European Agenda for Culture in a Globalizing World* (2007) offers the most comprehensive manifestation of the EU's appreciation of culture's innate social power.[99] Here, the Commission acknowledges three specific dimensions: culture as a tool to strengthen European identity; as a means to increase the EU's role and influence in the world; and as a dynamic trigger of economic activities and jobs in a knowledge-based society. The Commission's three-pronged approach nicely captures social power's versatility, applying culture as a sociological and psychological tool, as an instrument of foreign policy, as well as a means to optimalize the EU's role in the emerging game of global governance. All three are worth examining at some length.

Instrumentalizing culture as a tool to live out Jean Monnet's dream sounds simplistic. But Barroso's argument is actually subtle, even sophisticated. He suggests that, in order to bring Europe closer to "its" people, a fundamental change in perceptions, convictions, and actions is required, with the ultimate aim of developing a multi-layered sense of identity. European citizens should not look at the EU as a mere utilitarian project, offering wealth and security. And this is where the social power of culture comes in, which, as Barroso claims, "will help us to counter the growing imbalance between the rational and the emotional sides of European affairs (...) [A]rtists and intellectuals offer a novel way of looking at things. Because they involve all our senses and stir controversy. Because they arouse passions and make us think. For all these reasons, art and culture are the best antidotes to a purely functional view of the European Union."[100] In this view, culture is the normative content of Europe's bubble of identity, it is the current through which social power can be directed. European voices telling European stories, communicating European experiences, transmitting European values, are considered not only the best antidote to a functionalist, cold-hearted attitude towards European integration, but also as the best way to create the bubble itself, and shield it from outside (particularly American) incursions. In short, culture not only frames European integration as a worthy cause, it also uploads European norms to its own populace.

With Europe's non-imperial empire growing slowly but steadily, the political glue of culture has become increasingly important.[101] As Ernest Gellner has put it, "[m]odern man is not loyal to a monarch or a land or a faith, whatever he may say, but to a culture."[102] With as many as ten former communist countries joining the EU since 2004, each with its own recent history and peculiarities, the Union's social and cultural cohesion has been challenged. Cultural theorists such as Staffan Zetterholm have suggested that cultural heterogeneity will inevitably put a brake on European integration since it increases the risk that political decisions may be inconsistent with the core values of one or more groups.[103] As we argued earlier, international norms are collective expectations about proper behavior for a given identity. This implies that social power operates most effectively *within* an identity, since here frame resonance is at its highest, and even new norms tend to fit in well (especially through the process of grafting; see Chapter 1). With some, be it modest, success, the EU has tried to extend its cultural policies towards Central Europe, using the leverage of membership to apply EU media rules and regulations and introducing the plethora of EU signs, symbols, as well as Europe's ritual calendar (Day, Month, Year).

Arguably, the EU's official "high" cultural programs have been of minor importance, in stark contrast to the influx of popular cultural events such as the Eurovision Song Contest. As T.R. Reid, a former London correspondent from the *The Washington Post*, argued, the Eurovision Song Contest "is playing an historic role. Eurovision has become a celebration of Europeanness that strengthens the growing sense among 500m people that they all belong to a single space on the world map."[104] Surely, prize-winning songs with titles such as "Boom Bang-a-Bang", "La la la", and "Ding-a-Dong" belong to the lower echelons of popular culture. But, coincidence or not, since 2001 winners have come mainly from new or applicant EU countries: Finland, Estonia, Latvia, Turkey, Ukraine, and Serbia.[105] For them, organizing the Eurovision event has offered spectacular place branding opportunities, galvanizing their European credentials, and strengthening a sense of European belonging. Here, culture is not used in Durkheimian fashion in the quest for social cohesion. Instead, a unique element of European popular culture is spontaneously embraced by hundreds of millions of TV viewers, now using televoting to encourage symbolic interaction.

In this way, culture has become a key tool in EU foreign, and perhaps even security policy. The European Commission states that "culture is recognized as an important part of the EU's main cooperation programs and instruments, and in the Union's bilateral agreements with third countries."[106] The EU offers financial and technical assistance to developing countries across the world to preserve and restore cultural heritage sites and museums, or to assist artists, and organize major cultural events. By emphasizing the role of culture through conferences, exchange programs, and outreach projects, the EU positions itself as a valuable, constructive partner for third countries, willing to listen and engage on an equal footing. In this way, culture has become an important element of the EU's social power since it offers a means of communication on matters of difference, especially with Muslim countries in the Middle East and Northern Africa. By emphasizing culture as an important avenue of exchange, the EU creates a non-coercive platform of interaction where policy outcomes gain Habermasian legitimacy through robust dialogue. The European Commission deliberately uses cultural dialogue to upload its own "culture of cooperation", arguing that "intercultural dialogue [is] one of the main instruments of peace and conflict prevention," and a part of the EU's emerging public diplomacy (see Chapter 6).[107]

Culture has also become a branding tool for the EU (see Chapter 7). Declaring 2008 as the European Year of Intercultural Dialogue is not only an expression of the EU's self-proclaimed role as cultural interlocutor, but also a smart PR strategy to strengthen the Union's identity and image as a civilian power. The European Commission suggests that the EU's linguistic diversity will help promote knowledge of other cultures within Europe, and encourage links with all regions of the world. The EU is careful to avoid the impression of merely exporting its own culture to developing countries, but also aims to ensure market access for cultural goods and services by granting these countries preferential treatment or through trade-related assistance measures. Furthermore, by appointing cultural ambassadors, the EU tries to co-opt artists and intellectuals to gain credibility and extend its reach. For example, by taking on the Swedish crime fiction novelist Henning Mankell as the cultural ambassador for the European Year of Intercultural Dialogue, the EU taps into the trend of celebrity diplomacy.[108] The fact that Mankell is rather critical about Europe's asylum and immigration policies only adds to the credibility of the EU's overall cultural policy.[109]

The third facet of culture's social power is found in its ability to add to the economic dynamic of European society. The European Commission sees "culture as a catalyst for creativity in the framework of the Lisbon Strategy for growth and jobs."[110] The Lisbon Strategy, adopted in 2000, aims to make the EU "the most dynamic and competitive knowledge-based economy in the world capable of sustainable economic growth with more and better jobs and greater social cohesion, and respect for the environment by 2010." The EU suggests that creativity lies at the heart of social and technological innovation, and is therefore a key driver of growth, competitiveness, and, hence, jobs within the EU. This strategy is based on the fact that countries where cultural activity is highest—e.g., in the UK, the US, and Sweden—are also among the most competitive in the world. The European Commission estimates that at least 5.8 million people were working in the cultural sector in 2004, which was equivalent to 3.1 percent of total employment in the EU. The cultural sector contributed around 2.6 percent to EU GDP, with a turnover of 654 billion Euros in 2003.[111]

The power of culture as an economic factor is only gradually dawning upon the EU. Since it has been difficult to prove statistically that the cultural sector makes a huge economic contribution, policymakers have long marginalized culture, or even largely ignored it. However, numerous recent studies show that the cultural sector outperforms many other parts of the European economy, driving technological innovation and the IT revolution. Most modern culture is media-based and diffused by the Internet using the newest technologies. Even traditional art sectors (such as the performing and visual arts) can no longer escape this new technological environment. It has also become clear that culture and innovation may be used to attract investment, creative talent and students, as well as tourism in general. Moreover, for states, regions, and cities, culture has become a vital part in their emerging place branding strategies (see Chapter 7).

Taken together, the role of culture within the EU clearly illustrates the centrality, complexity, and comprehensiveness of social power. Culture, both traditional and popular, outlines the normative boundaries of social power, marking the space within which norms and values resonate. The EU has purposely used culture as a channel to create a process of interaction with the relevant public and counterparts, be they European citizens, applicant countries, or other important actors. Typically, the EU has tried to upload the norms and values underpinning its own social model based on postnational multilateralism to a still rather indisposed global level. Using culture to set norms and standards, the EU has therefore taken an indirect route, trying to establish a European public sphere as well as initiating a robust dialogue with neighboring countries, engaging culture as its preferred course of action.

3.6 CONCLUSION

Just as the EU finds it difficult to implement an effective cultural *policy*, the US faces wielding problems when it desires to use the ample social power which is invested in its cultural global hegemony. It is therefore hardly surprising that cultural studies have shown a remarkable lack of interest in the concept and question of power. Sociologists like Anthony Giddens and Roland Robertson, for example, prefer to speak in terms of the global flow of ideas, products, and techniques, rather than focusing on power. Indeed, it is difficult to collect evidence that consuming American and European brands, or watching Hollywood movies, results in psychological and attitudinal change. On the other hand, it is hard to deny that popular culture communicates important norms and values which affect our understanding of what constitutes "success" and "the good life." The social power of consumption should not be overlooked. As Barber has argued: "If sovereign power is in decline, and anarchy on the rise, the soft power of the West—its branding and commercial influence—flourishes. Washington is losing the propaganda war to fundamentalist adversaries, but American films and television programs continue to win the media war. The soft brands, however, distance themselves from sovereign America (…) Shrek and Spider-Man go where the First Cavalry Division no longer dares. America no longer wins real wars, but they dominate the video wargame market.[112]

Still, the cliché of America's cultural imperialism, especially strong in the 1980s, proved to be an oversimplified, Marxist notion of little relevance to the complex reality of globalization. Within today's global flow of culture, no easily identifiable core can be found which steers, determines, and dominates a dependent "periphery" which mainly consumes the cultural "products" on offer.[113] Selective borrowing and creative appropriation tend to result in cultural *bricolage*, where outside cultural influences are adapted and mimicked with surprising ease and equally surprising results. This does not, however, mean that cultures interact on a level playing field as equals. Obviously, Western culture, and popular culture in particular, plays a dominant role around the globe, feeding this rather old critique of inequality, disempowerment, and exploitation.[114] The English language helps the US media and its popular culture to take advantage of what has become in practice the global *lingua franca*. America's huge domestic market also offers economies of scale that smaller, less dominant cultures lack.

But the notion of culture should not be limited to the high arts, media, or popular music. To sociologists like Van Elteren and Barber, the real challenge is not so much the homogenization of cultures around the world based on an American model, but rather the "global spread of the institutions of capitalist modernity tied in with culturally impoverished social imagery (…), which crowd out the cultural space for alternatives."[115] America's cultural influence goes well beyond this more orthodox spectrum of culture, and also involves business and management culture, as well as social practices in the areas of finance, labor, IT, and communications. In most of these areas, the US, together with the EU, sets the standards, and creates the norms and values that are considered legitimate and desirable. For example, when we look at the way standards and rules are set that govern the Internet, or the accepted practices in the field of international accounting or management, it is in particular American *corporate* culture which dominates. As Van Elteren suggests, the US style of "corporate capitalism aimed at short-term interest of CEOs and shareholders that US companies epitomize tends to crowd out social market capitalism and other forms of associative, stakeholder capitalism."[116] Van Elteren further claims that this US "flavour of globalization stems from the culture of possessive individualism and consumerism that has its most radical embodiment in American society."[117]

Here too, American norms and values spread globally, traveling through social practices that others may ignore, but only at considerable cost to themselves. Assisted by non-state actors like multinational companies, consulting firms, and think tanks, this important element of American culture—corporate culture— spreads, offering channels through which American social power is managed, and sometimes wielded. The important point to stress is that even if most capital may come from non-US investors, and most top managers are European or Asian, all major multinational corporations are organized on an American management model, based on an American corporate style and culture.[118] As we will see in the following chapter, the process of hegemonic socialization through rules and practices is a key area of social power.

This leads us to a significant conclusion on how social power functions. If we assume that American societal preferences based on a profit-driven culture of consumerism are translated into dominant social practices that set the rules of economic, financial, and media globalization, these transnational regimes themselves embody America's hegemony. Combined with the US dominance in popular culture, this form of Americanization of corporate culture, based on the neoliberal values imbued in American society, explains how social power resources are generated and used. It is this comprehensive approach to culture which offers us a better understanding of social power's role in setting standards, norms, and values.

4 Institutions and law

4.1 INTRODUCTION

Institutions and law are the stable frameworks through which power is exercised. Institutions are congealed power realities and law constitutes their rulebook. Taken together, they constitute the political domain of society in which different groups decide upon the distribution of resources, rules, and meaning to shape their public life.[1] As Michael Mann argues at the very onset of his multi-volume work on the sources of social power, "[i]nstitutionalization is necessary to achieve routine collective goals; and thus distributive power, that is, stratification, also becomes an institutionalized feature of social life."[2] Mann suggests that studying institutions and their rules offers good insight into the role and place of social power, which is exactly what this chapter aims to do.

Institutions and law are socially constructed forms of political authority which are most successful if they are in line with the social foundations and cultural practices and expectations of their time.[3] As regime theory suggests, institutions and law are the moorings and points of reference around which expectations and actions converge. As Oran R. Young argues, institutions are "sets of rules of the game or codes of conduct that serve to define social practices, assign roles to participants in these practices, and guide the interaction among occupants of these roles."[4] This implies that international law can be seen as a multinational institution, which has been defined by Ruggie as formal and informal norms, regimes, and organizations.[5] Legitimate institutions and laws are normatively embedded in society, and social norms are in turn constructed and shaped by these very same frameworks and rules. Constructivist theory has contributed considerably to our understanding of the central role of socially constructed ideas and identities. By challenging Realist and rationalist assumptions about state behavior, constructivism claims that international society socializes actors to consider certain norms as normal, standard, and legitimate. As we argued earlier, legitimacy is a method to socialize power, which makes institutions and law central planks in any strategy to use social power in international politics.

The starting point of this chapter is that "international law itself is instrumental to, and shaped by, power."[6] In public discourse the dichotomy between law and (international) politics is upheld, where the former is the space of justice and reason, whereas the latter is the domain of power and the "law of the jungle." In reality, of course, law and politics feed on each other, and are often hard to distinguish.[7] As Javier Solana argued in 2003: "power is needed to establish law and law is the legitimate face of power."[8]

Historically, the Great Powers have used international law to solidify and justify their empires, whether it was Spain in the sixteenth, Britain in the nineteenth, or the US in the twenty-first century. Lisa L. Martin argues that Great Powers have made use of international law to establish, reinforce, and prolong their power.[9] Martin suggests that by creating predictability and avoiding continuous negotiations, institutions limit the costs of regulation. Moreover, by offering weaker states in the international system incentives to stick to the rules, quasi-voluntary compliance and pacification is encouraged. What is more, the multilateral norms embedded in these institutions assure stability, even when the hegemon's power eventually goes into decline. It is these three benefits of institutions and law—regulation, pacification, and stability—which constitute the social anchors of power.

As we have seen in previous chapters, Great Powers have been avid norm entrepreneurs, uploading their values and standards to regional and global levels of governance. The US has persistently used a strategy aimed at entrenching institutions and rules favorable to its economic and security interests, ranging from the UN and its Bretton Woods institutions, to NATO and the WTO. However, over the course of less than a decade, American criticism of established IOs (most notably the UN) has triggered a much-debated crisis of multilateralism, putting into question the three indispensable common goods of rule-based behavior, pacification, and stability. America's skepticism of multilateralist solutions has had major foreign policy implications, resulting in its withdrawal or estrangement from numerous treaties and their subsequent waning legitimacy. This has also eroded the status of international law as the ultimate, indisputable source of global justice. Since 9/11, the Bush administration has followed a policy of multilateralism "by invitation", asking others to work with the US, follow its leadership, and trust its judgment.

In the emerging cavities of established modalities of multilateralism, most notably classical treaties and alliances, there have been numerous attempts to form innovative, and usually more flexible, hybrid institutional arrangements. For example, when NATO declined to take on the Iraq mission in 2003, US Deputy Secretary of Defense Paul Wolfowitz famously stated that "the mission must determine the coalition, the coalition must not determine the mission (...) As a corollary, there will not be a single coalition, but rather different coalitions for different missions."[10] *The Wall Street Journal* aptly characterized these small-scale set-ups as follows: "There's no headquarters, no secretary-general, no talkfests—and, perhaps most important of all, no French or Russian veto."[11] Clearly, with the threat perception at red alert, flexibility and speedy action are preferred over cumbersome and sluggish cooperative efforts. Multilateralism is no longer valued as an essential force-multiplier, but as a brake on the kind of swift and flexible policy-making that is required in a changed post-9/11 security environment.

NATO is therefore gradually transforming from a classical collective defense organization into a glorified "security saloon", which offers the US sheriff a platform to round up his deputies who are able and willing to form America's posse and embark upon new missions. Since most conflicts are now wars of choice instead of wars of necessity, the shift from a traditional alliance to a more voluntarist coalition of the willing seems to be NATO's destiny. However, as the US has learned the hard way, this flexibility and voluntarism may boost speedy policymaking, but ultimately detracts from its legitimacy. But these dilemmas are certainly not unique to NATO, since all IOs are facing the challenge of finding the optimal balance between legitimacy and efficacy, and between inclusiveness and flexibility.[12]

America's move away from traditional IOs is therefore not only, or even mainly, given in by neoconservative and isolationist thinking, but a sign of our postmodern times, which privileges flexibility over solidity, and connectivity over exclusiveness.[13] As a result, it is not only NATO that is changing its *modus operandi*, but there is a noticeable trend towards *ad hoc*, small, often informal groups of like-minded actors working towards shared goals. Of course, history is replete with examples of small, flexible alignments, ranging from the Four Powers (the US, France, the UK, and USSR) in the post-war settlement in 1945, Sixes and Sevens in the late 1950s and early 1960s within the European Community, to the well-known 2 + 4 arrangement over German unification. But whereas these flexible arrangements were the exception to the general rule of open multilateralism, today's ad hocery seems to have become the new standard. For example, within the UN numerous "friends of"-groups have mushroomed over the past decade, often Friends of the UN Secretary-General, a specific country, or implementation and/or monitoring groups.[14] These small groups have come in different shapes and sizes, ranging from the Contact Group on the former Yugoslavia, and the Minsk Group within the OSCE on Nagorno-Karabakh, to groups of wise men (usually former statesmen) to broker a peace agreement. They may even involve NGOs, such as the Geneva-based Centre for Humanitarian Dialogue, which in 2002 negotiated a peace accord between the Indonesian government and the Free Aceh Movement, ending a 26-year long conflict.[15]

These new political arrangements lack the institutional fixity and transparency to be labeled IOs, and once in a while even the label "regime" would be too generous. Still, they bring with them the legitimacy of working under the auspices of the UN, the EU, or OSCE, or the authority that comes with the combined economic and political weight of its members, as is the case of the G8 and G20.[16] Their authority may also be derived from their effectiveness, which implies that legitimacy is less based on democratic credentials (*à la* Dahl), as on expertise and deliberative qualifications (following Weber and Habermas; see Chapter 1). These developments demonstrate that the crisis of multilateralism can hardly be blamed on America's political mood, and will most likely be continued well into the Obama administration. Rumsfeld's call for coalitions of the willing, the proliferation of Friends groupings, Troikas, Quartets, and Quints, are the tip of the iceberg of a major recalibration of the institutional foundation of global governance. The emphasis is on tackling projects, based on a work style that avoids fixity and rewards flexibility. But, as Richard Sennett reminds us (and as we will discuss later on), this "[r]evulsion against bureaucratic routine and pursuit of flexibility has produced new structures of power and control, rather than created the conditions which set us free."[17]

What concerns us in this chapter is the impact of our "liquid modern times" (as the sociologist Zygmunt Bauman labels it) on institutions and law, as well as the concomitant changes in the role, place, and quality of social power. Obviously, this is a broad field, too broad to cover fully, let alone in great depth. The study of social power may be most fruitful by paying less attention to established IOs such as NATO, the UN, and the IMF, and dealing instead with alternative multilateral arrangements, such as the emerging rules of global business, the setting of international standards, and the management of the Internet. Special emphasis will further be placed on the role of transgovernmental networks, as well as the rise of private authority and soft law. All these phenomena reflect the changing nature of institutions and law, and offer opportunities to see how new avenues of social power are emerging and developing. Hovering over this debate is Ruggie's claim that to say anything sensible about the character of institutions, "it is necessary to look how power and legitimate social purpose become fused to project authority in the international system."[18] The question is, therefore, whether contemporary institutions are truly embedded, which Ruggie defined as a "fusion of power and legitimate social purpose."[19]

4.2 NORM ENTREPRENEURS AND REGULATION

We have already remarked that the EU and US are active and successful norm entrepreneurs since they are both able and willing to shape structures and rules of global governance. In this new game of benchmarking, best practices, naming-and-shaming, scoreboards, and the like, one thing remains undisputed: those who set the rules, decide what is legitimate, and say who can upload their domestic laws and regulations toward the international level are in the advantage. Most powerful states (including the EU) have felt the urge to mold the rest of the world according to their own image, participating in a global competition to frame problems and solutions, trying to persuade relevant audiences and actors to see things their way. Apart from normative grounds, there have always been many practical, even mundane reasons to do so. Kal Raustiala argues that powerful states try to replicate their policy styles and structures in an effort to strengthen their autonomy, but also to create a compatible international environment in which their own policies can become more effective.[20]

The EU is well-versed in this process of (what Börzel has called) pace-setting, foot-dragging, and fence-sitting.[21] Börzel argues that, within the EU, member states employ these strategies to maximize the benefits and minimize the costs of EU policies by trying to upload their national policy arrangements and preferences to the European level. This would reduce the need for legal and administrative adaptation and prevent competitive disadvantages for their domestic economy. All EU member states are therefore trying to set the pace of EU-wide regulations. If that proves impossible, they adopt the opposite strategy (foot-dragging), by trying to stop, or at least impede, the attempts of other member states to upload their domestic policies to the EU level. Occasionally, member states neither set the pace nor put the brake on EU policies (fence-sitting). Obviously, being a so-called first mover implies that standards can be set for others, and that the laggards, or second movers, will inevitably have to pay the switching costs. Being able and willing to move first, to set the pace and direction of policies to which others have to adapt, is obviously what social power is all about.

It is little wonder that the EU feels comfortable in a global governance environment which privileges social power. To all EU member states, playing the two-level game of balancing domestic and European politics has become second nature.[22] The unique nature of EU policymaking, which comprises elements of intergovernmentalism, supranationalism, and comitology (i.e., the rule of committees and working groups), makes the European integration process a microcosm of the challenges facing global governance.[23] In a way, the EU itself is an elaborate network of supervisors. Over the decades, the European Commission has spun a dense network of advisory, regulatory, and management committees which provide channels for discussion and negotiations with relevant national officials and experts. These committees serve to set the agenda, prepare policy proposals, and implement agreed policies.[24] Obviously, these committees are the preferred entry points for advocacy groups and NGOs. It is the EU's intrinsic hybridity and its subsequent flexibility that makes it such an effective player in today's game of global governance.[25]

So how does the EU use its social power, and why is it, on average, more successful at this than other actors, including its main competitor, the US?

It is well-known that European and American ideas regarding the function of legal norms in society are markedly different. Americans prefer *ad hoc*, after-the-fact, corrective norms, which implies that most areas of social activity should remain open and free as long as possible and that regulations "should only be used as a means of last resort after free markets, understood in a broad and not only economic sense, have failed."[26] In a way, Americans seem to hope for the best and only impose laws when chaos and failure loom. Europeans, in contrast, "favor preventive rules aimed at averting crises and market failures before they occur. They try to anticipate future difficulties and establish norms in order to be prepared for problems in advance. Unlike Americans, Europeans are inclined to create a comprehensive legal order free of contradictions and lacunae. Moreover, stability and predictability are valued highly in Europe."[27] In short: the American model reflects a liberal constitutional tradition which allows everything unless it is forbidden, whereas the European approach may be brought back to the Napoleonic tradition that the state determines what is allowed, implying that everything else is in principle banned.

Europe's proscriptive legal vision is best illustrated by the EU's REACH program (the abbreviation of Registration, Evaluation, Authorisation and Restriction of Chemicals) which evaluates the safety of tens of thousands of chemicals using environmental and safety standards *before* they reach the market. Public interest groups and NGOs have jointly drafted a so-called REACH SIN list, containing some 270 substances of very high concern which should be substituted in priority—SIN standing for "substitute it now." The SIN list has a major impact on EU businesses and beyond, giving an "early warning" to downstream chemical users, such as companies making cars, electronics, consumer products, and toys. The EU's precautionary principle implies that scientists have to prove that new products are safe, whereas American companies enjoy a presumption of innocence for their products until proven otherwise (hereafter lawsuits usually follow). This is exactly the reason why *The Economist* suggested in September 2007 that "Brussels is becoming the world's regulatory capital",[28] mainly because the EU's approach "may better suit consumer and industry demands of certainty. If you manufacture globally, it is simpler to be bound by the toughest regulatory system in your supply chain."[29]

Walter Mattli and Tim Büthe confirm that Europe is particularly well-prepared to play a key role in international standardization due to its hierarchical and highly coordinated system.[30] Mattli and Büthe conclude that, in contrast to the American system of extreme pluralism, the EU system is centralized, coordinated, regulated, subsidized, as well as inclusive. The EU has developed an effective and efficient regional system of standardization, offering a "picture of hierarchy, with national standards organizations representing a broad-based domestic consensus with a single voice at the regional and international level."[31] This EU system, Mattli and Büthe suggest, usually constitutes a broad consensus which can be more "easily and authoritatively presented at the international level."[32] The EU makes effective use of the profound knowledge that exists in firms, and frequently asks a recognized private institution or representative association to examine a regulatory problem to arrive at appropriate solutions. For example, "co-regulatory" agreements between the EU and the European Automobile Manufacturers Association (ACEA) on the reduction of CO_2 emissions (of 2001) illustrate how the EU makes use of self-regulation as a means of quasi-public policy.

Mattli and Büthe further point out that European firms "possess much better information about international standardization opportunities and proposals and, thanks to this information advantage and more effective interest representation, to be more involved—*earlier and more effectively*—than their American counterparts."[33] American firms usually learn about developments of new international standards too late to affect their (technical) specifications. This ultimately means that many American firms often have to pay high switching costs since international standards differ from their current practices. As Raymond Kammer, director of the US National Institute of Standards and Technology (NIST), argued in 2003: "European governments and industries believe that they can create a competitive advantage in world markets by strongly influencing the content of international standards."[34] The European system of generating timely information and preference aggregation, based on the effective and legitimate representation of diverse national interests, obviously offers the EU unique opportunities to use social power in the global game of international standardization. The culture of cooperation within the EU creates an organizational mode that makes it easy to be flexible, and act swiftly and decisively.

The EU's importance as a norm entrepreneur is especially noticeable in areas where global regulation is in a stage of development, such as e-commerce and the management of biotech and genetically modified organisms (GMOs). The biotech debate, in particular, has gripped the public imagination, oscillating between fears of Frankenstein food to the dream of unlocking nature's secrets, between consumer safety and corporate power, between caution and recklessness. On this issue, EU Trade Commissioner Peter Mandelson has been quite outspoken: "I believe Europe should (…) shape a global system of clear rules that allows exporters and importers to trade GM crops and feed in confidence. Europe can and should play a leading role here."[35] Mandelson further suggests that it "is the rules of the single market which gives us the foundation to export our rules and standards around the world—an increasingly important part of my job as a trade commissioner. In short, no single market, no European project and no *Europe puissance*."[36]

Mandelson's approach is reflected in a 2007 European Commission Report on the impact of the EU's single market which sketches out the role of the Union as a global standard setter: "The EU cannot secure prosperity by looking inwards—it needs to exploit and build on its internal strengths in the world economy (…) It has spurred the development of rules and standards in areas such as product safety, the environment, securities and corporate governance which inspire global standard setting." It further concludes that this "gives the EU the potential to shape global norms and to ensure that fair rules are applied to worldwide trade and investment. The single market of the future should be the launch pad of an ambitious global agenda."[37]

The EU's internal market is considered a powerful economic base from which to upload Europe's norms, standards, and values to the global level. The EU's economic weight as a consumer market gives Brussels the opportunity to raise the bar for exporters to Europe in case they do not comply to the EU's rulebook. This is clearly reflected in the findings of Mark Schapiro, whose study on US and European approaches to market regulation concludes that American companies increasingly comply to the tougher EU standards, since otherwise their European market would disappear into thin air.[38] Compliance with European (as well as emerging international) standards is now an essential precondition for entry into globalized production networks.[39] Since the US realizes all too well that they cannot win this power contest by confronting the EU head-on, America's strategy has shifted to massive lobbying attempts to assure that EU regulations are compatible with the US approach. The EU has proven quite susceptible to these outside influences. The REACH program, for example, is based on the combined expertise and judgment of many actors, testifying to the EU's capability to engage with external influences, ranging from third states, NGOs, firms, experts, and lobby groups. As we will argue below, it is this eclectic combination of external influences that strengthens the EU's effectiveness and legitimacy as a global norm entrepreneur, mainly since it incorporates levels of societal expertise and private authority that would otherwise be ignored.

These conclusions are in line with the findings which John Braithwaite and Peter Drahos present in their book *Global Business Regulation* (2000).[40] Both authors define the globalization of business regulation as the international spread of the norms, standards, principles, and rules that govern commerce and the globalization

76 *Institutions and law*

of their enforcement.[41] In their detailed study of regulatory systems ranging from property to environmental controls, they conclude that these rules and principles "can be of consequence even if utterly detached from enforcement mechanisms."[42] They further suggest that the globalization of these norms and standards is a non-linear process set in motion by many different actors, and that there is no master mechanism explaining why some norms stick, and others don't. However, they do suggest that an actor's "influence has been greatest when it has captured the imagination of mass publics in powerful states", such as the environmental movement today, and the anti-slavery movement of the past.[43] This corroborates my earlier conclusion that power, and social power in particular, needs to be embedded in the Ruggiean sense, i.e., it requires a direct link with legitimate social purpose.

Importantly, both authors argue that this mechanism of globalization involves a multitude of actors using several key processes: "coercion, systems of reward, modeling, reciprocal adjustment, non-reciprocal coordination, and capacity building."[44] In particular, the concept of modeling, which carries some Gramscian overtones, is of interest here. Braithwaite and Drahos define modeling as the globalization of regulation "achieved by observational learning with a symbolic content; learning based on a conception of action portrayed in words and images. The latter cognitive content makes modeling more than mere imitation."[45] Modeling implies that norms, standards, principles, and rules become embedded into the practices and behaviors of key players. As we argued earlier, successful norm entrepreneurs make their own model attractive to others, not mainly (let alone only) by coercion or offering rewards, but by persuasion and making claims to a wide array of ostensibly legitimate social purposes. This so-called argumentative or cognitive turn in policy studies has shifted the focus away from questions of power, to issues such as trust, deliberation, complexity, and networks.[46] However, the negligence of power in the study of governance is mistaken, since power games are an essential part of the argumentation process, particularly since the capacity to argue is unevenly distributed among participants. As we will see, the power of argument transcends "simply agreeing", but involves elements of discursive power (knowledge, story lines, discourses, deliberation), and the social power to make norms stick.[47]

Uploading one's norms is made easier by being a first mover. But for new institutions and rules to emerge, norm entrepreneurs require authority based on reasoned arguments. These can range from claims to consumer protection (such as the EU's REACH program), to finding a delicate balance between privacy and flexibility (*viz.* the transatlantic Safe Harbor agreement on e-commerce governance).[48] Importantly, in all these cases social power plays a key role, ultimately determining which policy model norm entrepreneurs can get established and accepted.

4.3 TRANSNATIONAL POLICY NETWORKS

Global governance is increasingly based on so-called "soft law", which consists of "standards of good practices and codes of conduct endorsed at the international level but lacking legal standing, so that their implementation in the various countries is essentially left to the discretion of national authorities."[49] Self-regulation exists in a wide range of policy areas, from the Internet, insurance, accounting, and air transport, to environmental, social, and ethical concerns. Obviously, these non-treaty agreements offer more flexibility, simpler procedures, greater confidentiality, as well as opportunities to reach agreements with non-state parties and other groups governments may not be willing to recognize.

This rise of soft law indicates that matters requiring some kind of regulation increasingly bypass states as well as IOs.[50] Globalization is often moving too fast to be regulated by solid, fixed institutions, requiring more fluid arrangements that are fast-moving and unbureaucratic. Old-style institutions and traditional legal procedures are under pressure from transnational networks, soft law, and private authority. The state no longer monopolizes rule-making, and a wide variety of non-state actors now use their professional expertise and authority to legitimize their claim to set standards and rules. Non-state actors lack democratic legitimacy as well as access to traditional power tools (such as coercion or the use of force), which only leaves them the route of social power based on alternative sources of legitimacy, such as knowledge and the deliberative qualities of policymaking.

In this context, the advance of transgovernmental policy networks is particularly remarkable.[51] Within these networks, national regulators bring to bear a form of power that derives from their ability to convince others, mainly their peers and colleagues. As in all forms of social power, these regulators lack both capabilities to use force and the authority to compel.[52] But, as Anne-Marie Slaughter claims, "norms of professionalization (…) strengthen the socialization functions of these networks, through which regulatory agencies reproduce themselves in other countries."[53] In the end, members "are likely to try to meet agreed standards of professional behaviour and substantive commitments to one another because they know everyone is watching."[54]

Many examples can be given of these powerful transgovernmental policy networks. Among the most notable and influential is the Basle Committee on Banking Supervision, which was formed in 1974 and is composed of representatives of 12 central banks, which offers broad supervisory standards and guidelines and recommends statements of best practice in banking supervision. In the financial sector the International Organization of Securities Commissioners (IOSCO) and the International Association of Insurance Supervisors (IAIS) stand out. In most other sectors, ranging from the environment to intellectual property, the standard setting by the International Organization for Standardization (ISO) is prominent. Taken together, the codes and best practices established by these transgovernmental networks create a pattern of behavior within the private and public sectors around which the expectations of all relevant actors converge.

Slaughter goes one step further by claiming that these networks "are a direct outgrowth of the desegregation of [the] state—that is, of the ability of different political institutions to interact with their national and supranational counterparts on a quasi-autonomous basis."[55] She encourages us to think of the state less as a unitary actor, than as an aggregate of all its constituent parts which now have an opportunity to develop governance networks with their international equivalents. Being a lawyer, Slaughter emphasizes the accelerating process of judicial globalization, both at the level of private commercial law, and on international legal questions regarding human rights.[56] For example, she suggests that transnational bankruptcy disputes are now settled by national courts concluding cross-border insolvency cooperation protocols which "are essentially mini-treaties setting forth each side's role in resolving disputes."[57]

Slaughter's most controversial claim is that these global governance networks have the potential to overcome what she labels the "globalization paradox", namely that we need globalization as much as we fear it. She suggests that these emerging networks "open new institutional horizons for the possibility of global justice."[58] From this perspective, the growing number of regulators constitute a "new generation of diplomats", who use their collective social power to set norms, standards, and rules for their own communities, as well as for the world. For the management of globalization, Slaughter suggests, this is no minor matter, since the US has "an opportunity to lead through law, not against it, and to build a vastly strengthened international legal order that will protect and promote our interests. If we are willing to accept even minimal restraints, we can rally the rest of the world to adopt and enforce rules that will be effective in fighting scourges from terrorism to AIDS."[59]

These proliferating transgovernmental policy networks have become one of the main conduits for social power, flexible and authoritative as they are. Many of these transgovernmental arrangements are now gradually transmogrified into so-called "global public policy networks", which constitute loose alliances between governments, IOs, firms, NGOs, professional organizations, and cultural and religious groups, joining together in different configurations to achieve common goals.[60] The important novelty of these networks is that they are not driven by formal institutions and bureaucracies, and not managed in a modern, top-down hierarchical style. Instead, global public policy networks (or GPPNs) are "owned" by relevant slices of society, comprising as many stakeholders as is deemed necessary to be effective, efficient, and legitimate.

GPPNs try to overcome the trappings of modernity by ignoring national borders and by mixing up a wide variety of key players, whether they are state officials, firms, or academic experts. To manage globalization, timely and well-informed international action must be undertaken by relevant players and stakeholders. But, in order to get a complete picture, information and expertise has to be obtained from many different sources. GPPNs offer an opportunity to acquire and process information and knowledge more rapidly than traditional top-down hierarchies. Moreover, they are more effective in finding a consensus and translating this accord into concrete actions which all GPPN parties are inclined to support and implement. The experiences of such GPPNs as the Consultative Group on International Agricultural Research (one of the oldest, founded in 1971), the Global Water Partnership, or the World Commission on Dams are just a few within a broad array of these informal networks.[61]

One of the most remarkable and well-known GPPNs is the UN-sponsored Global Compact, which brings together business and civil society as key partners to achieve its goals of peace, poverty reduction, and human rights protection.[62] Launched in 2000, the Global Compact incorporates some 100 states, 3,000 firms (including 108 of the *Financial Times* global 500 firms), and around 800 civil society organizations, foundations, and academic partners. In the ten principles of the Global Compact, firms make a commitment to adopt a value-based approach to business and to reflect moral considerations (e.g., environmental responsibility, human rights, and labor standards) into their investment decisions. The Global Compact is a radical step for the UN towards promoting corporate social responsibility (CSR), which has already developed numerous guidance documents and practical tools to assist all participants (but of course primarily firms) in implementing these lofty principles. The UN has proclaimed that this learning-based approach is likely to raise the standards of environmental and social performance of all stakeholders. This is, of course, the central goal: co-opt all key actors, rather than confront them with legally binding codes of conduct.[63] Its main objective is to encourage the process of learning and engagement, rather than tricking firms into social and environmental standards they are uncomfortable with and unable and/or unwilling to implement.[64]

Clearly, such developments as GPPNs and CSR are linked, since governments as well as multinational corporations have a stake in shaping the rules of the globalization game.[65] Under pressure of loud protests from civil society and engaged activists who fear a so-called "race to the bottom", remedies have been proposed based on voluntary social responsibility, rather than relying on the classical instrument of top-down public regulation.[66] These societal pressures have raised social expectations about the place, role, and behavior of modern multinational corporations and have (most likely thereby) shaped the understanding of public responsibility that these firms have placed upon themselves.

Much of contemporary private-sector governance is therefore based on enlightened self-interest, since effective global governance structures and mechanisms may reduce transaction costs, ensure transparency and predictability, and strengthen the feel-good factor among customers and clients. The development of CSR has a major impact on the behavior of private actors, and multinational corporations in particular. It is important to note that the fact that the expected codes of corporate conduct do not carry the same legal weight as domestic (or international) law does not necessarily limit their normative power. Not only do these soft norms influence domestic laws enacted by national governments, they are also difficult to ignore since they are endorsed by powerful IOs (such as the EU and the OECD), as well as ordinary citizens who all wield the power of their purse through their consumer behavior.[67]

Transnational advocacy coalitions whose power derives from managing information and mobilizing public support have shown themselves remarkably adept to influence both formal government channels and GPPNs. Norms established within the Global Compact and CSR agreements encourage firms to act as good, responsible corporate citizens. The proliferation of CSR campaigns indicates the pervasiveness of "politics via markets." A vast array of NGOs now use market-based power to influence consumers and corporations to change their behavior, aiming to reduce negative environmental effects, improve labor conditions, or human rights. In particular, firms selling directly to consumers realize that their credibility and likeability are essential elements of their brand. This implies that NGOs, and the wider public of consumers, may steer business actors to comply with a wide range of social and environmental goals.

NGOs have become effective norm entrepreneurs in fields such as child soldiers, the ban on landmines, the stigmatization of small weapons, as well as HIV/Aids.[68] Using persuasion and normative claims, they frame policy debates, shape public perceptions of problems, and define (or redefine) issues through public statements, studies, and reports, as well as so-called "advertorials." Whether it is framing the nature of the Iraq war, climate change, or fighting poverty, NGOs mark out ideas by offering concepts such as "corporate environmental responsibility", "corporate citizenship", or the "greening of industry."[69]

Protests managed by Greenpeace over the disposal by Royal Dutch Shell of the Brent Spar oil rig in the North Sea in 1995 were the first indication of the power of NGOs to upload their norms and values to the global level. The shaming of sports equipment brands like Nike for their use of Asian sweatshops during the 1990s brought this message home to all multinational corporations.[70] Major NGOs still use this ability to stage public outrage as a discrete but crucial power tool within the collaborative processes of GPPNs. Since the brand, based on reputation, image, and emotional attachment, is such an important business resource, the social power of consumers and NGOs has taken many corporations by their Achilles heel, and is unlikely to let go anytime soon (see Chapter 7 for a more in-depth analysis of the importance of branding as an avenue of social power).

Sheldon Wolin has labeled this trend "fugitive democracy", since decision-making is now made by experts and through markets, rather than politics.[71] This explains why the impact of NGOs on many political processes has raised fundamental questions about their legitimacy. In general, the moral authority of NGOs derives from their capacity to provide expertise, their claim of being neutral and non-self-interested, as well as their claim of being socially progressive. The rise of NGOs and other configurations of non-state actors is most often explained as a "societal response to socio-economic factors, the new information revolution and/or the decline of the state."[72] But, as Kim D. Reimann has demonstrated, the growing role of NGOs in international politics has been actively promoted by states as well as IOs (and the EU in particular). NGOs are now "championed by numerous international actors as the voice of the people and vehicles of private initiative." The new pro-NGO norm is based on the liberal notion that a functioning free market and democracy require a flourishing civil society, giving rise to the notion of "consumer sovereignty", based upon the social power of consumption (see Chapter 3).[73]

The capability of NGOs to upload norms and set rules is unmistakable, since they are now engaged in the entire policy circle, from advocacy to active rule-making; from knowledge generation to monitoring treaty obligations. But, as former Brazilian President Fernando Henrique Cardoso has argued, "[t]he legitimacy of civil society organizations derives from what they do and not from whom they represent or from any kind of external mandate. In the final analysis, they are what they do. The power of civil society is a soft one. It is their capacity to argue, to propose, to experiment, to denounce, to be exemplary. It is not the power to decide."[74] This is, however, not as straightforward and clear as Cardoso makes it out to be. Since many NGOs shape the discursive environment of key political and economic actors, they may not make decisions, but they certainly shape them. The downside of GPPNs is, therefore, that it has become difficult to disentangle who pulls at which strings and, hence, who is responsible for which decision.[75] Dissecting these policy-shaping processes is often impracticable, which makes it hard to agree on the level of social power which individual actors can muster.

4.4 PRIVATE AUTHORITY

The rise of GPPNs and NGOs indicates that authority in the global economy as well as in global politics is slipping away from legitimate governments and is re-emerging in many an elusive shape and place. Over the last few decades, new forms of non-state authority have come forward, performing functions that were traditionally and exclusively associated with the state. New forms of private authority have emerged in all stages of policymaking, from agenda-setting, problem identification, decision-making, implementation, to evaluation. Of course, we have seen self-regulation in professions such as medicine and law, or stock exchange and international commercial arbitration in the past.[76] But today, several important sites of authority are neither state-based, nor state-created, which leads Rodney Bruce Hall and Thomas J. Biersteker to argue that "[t]he state is no longer the sole, or in some instances even the principal, source of authority, in either the domestic arena or in the international system."[77]

As our debate on GPPNs has indicated, private actors have contributed significantly to global governance by promoting common standards and advocating international regulatory convergence. Private regulatory agents exercise significant authority. In particular, professional service firms have over the decades developed mechanisms of governance amongst themselves, which have become so authoritative that they have a global reach and hence carry considerable economic and political weight. Little surprise, therefore, that private authority is increasingly considered a way to solve policy problems more effectively and even more legitimately than public, hierarchical regulation. Private authority is seen as a viable alternative to state control and liberal *laissez-faire*. Many non-state actors therefore now claim legitimacy, arguing that their power is authoritative, deserving not only obedience, but also respect and trust.

For our study on social power, the surge of private authority and self-regulation is of special importance.[78] Private rulemaking differs from public rulemaking because the former lacks clear institutions and legislative procedures that are constitutionally defined. Instead, private authority is usually organized within networks of actors who join voluntarily, and engage in a process of shared learning in order to arrive at common decisions. Historically, private authority was vested in gentlemen agreements, codes of conduct, ethical guidelines, voluntary agreements, standards, certification schemes, charters, syndicates, networks, alliances, and partnerships.[79] Since these arrangements are on the whole voluntary, they privilege management tools based on negotiation and persuasion, as well as collaboration and facilitation. This implies that, in most manifestations of private authority, discursive and argumentative power plays a central role alongside organizational power (rules and bargaining).[80] Forging cooperation through a common discourse and a shared understanding of problems and solutions is a key element in the development of self-regulation. Private authority thereby offers new challenges to public managers, indicating that practice is now leading theory, and that policy analysts still lack the conceptual tools to study the nature and consequences of the fragmentation and disarticulation of the modern state.

The question of how private authority emerges remains unclear as well: is it "delegated by the state, negotiated with the state, enabled by the state, allowed by the state, or seized from the state?"[81] Within the wide array of self-regulatory arrangements, we see authorities that are tolerated, encouraged, and recognized, and even those that are officially licensed by the state. Daniel W. Drezner argues that Great Powers remain the primary actors writing the rules that regulate the global economy, and that private authority is allowed to emerge since powerful states "will engage in forum-shopping within a complex of international regimes", or simply delegate regime management to non-state actors if this suits them.[82] Drezner suggests that the private sector always remains aware of the fact that states may intervene in case self-regulation goes against the national interest. On the other side of the spectrum, Hall and Biersteker claim that states are often "complicit in the creation of the market as authoritative. When state leaders proclaim that the 'forces of the global market' give them little room for manoeuvre or independent policy choice (...) [t]hey are not only ceding claims of authority to the market [but] are creating the authority of the market."[83] Other explanations are more mundane, based on practical and efficiency grounds. They explain private authority by the fact that it covers domains of novel economic activity where public authority may not (yet) be available, or that increased technological complexity may discourage public authority from stepping in.

The key difference with GPPNs is that private authority involves quasi-legislative processes (such as deliberative democracy, e-democracy, public conversations, participatory budgeting, and many other forms of deliberation and dialogue among groups of stakeholders), as well as quasi-judicial processes (such as mediation, facilitation, arbitration, and other forms of alternative dispute resolution).[84] Like public authority, private authority develops policies, practices, and rules, which require the normative consent or recognition on the part of the regulated and/or governed. But, as Hall argues, "authority is a social commodity that cannot be usurped or successfully claimed unilaterally. It must be publicly claimed and publicly acknowledged by the subjects of the exercise of power."[85] This implies that, in order to be effective, private authority not only requires the setting of rules and standards recognized and adhered to by others ("institutional market authority"), but also the moral authority of being accepted by a vast majority of the wider public, which increasingly acknowledges that private, market actors make decisions, instead of government officials ("normative market authority").[86]

Most states seem increasingly willing to make room for private governance. This reflects the broad support for neoliberal ideas which offer private actors more leeway and opportunities for private rule-making, self-regulation, and standards development. The discourse of downsizing government that dominated the 1980s and 1990s has been followed by the notion that globalization requires the transfer of authority upwards (to IOs) as well as downwards (to non-state actors, mainly firms). The emerging consensus that private authority is legitimate gradually turns these novel governance arrangements into embedded institutions, merging *de facto* power with legitimate social purpose. This neoliberal, normative move is based on the dual pillars of trust and apathy. Most Western states have become convinced that the delegation of authority to the private sector leads to efficiency gains, trusting the market rather than politics itself. But Western politicians also believe that by privatizing rulemaking they can renounce responsibility for the bleaker sides of globalization. This, in turn, requires non-state actors to legitimate their authority using convincing arguments, smart PR, and branding techniques. On top of this rhetoric, corporations are increasingly following their own CSR codes to boost their legitimacy within society. This combination of institutional and normative market authority offers firms and NGOs the social power to shape norms and set rules.[87]

As usual, the best examples of private authority are those which go unnoticed, and are considered normal, even natural. Whereas the authority of private military companies (PMCs) remains controversial, private companies setting global technical standards are widely accepted. Over the decades, setting these standards has shifted from a mainly domestic affair to a major source of global economic and even political power. What used to be mainly a technical specification—e.g., the thickness of a credit card (0.76 mm), or the sensitivity of photographic film (ISO ratings)—has, due to rapid technological change and economic integration, turned into a quest for setting rules, deciding upon winners and losers, and ultimately evoking the central question of economic and political power. Most standards emanate from private sector Standards Developing Organizations, so-called SDOs, of which the International Organization for Standardization (ISO) and the International Electrotechnical Commission (IEC) are the most important.

Both the ISO and the IEC are private sector organizations comprising hundreds of technical committees and involving many thousands of experts representing industry and academia from all over the world. States cannot be members of these SDOs, but obviously governments exert influence indirectly by adopting ISO standards as part of their national regulatory frameworks and using them as the technical basis of national legislation. ICANN (the abbreviation which stands for the Internet Corporation for Assigned Names and Numbers, set up in 1998), is another example of a private authority of great importance. This California-based non-profit corporation is a private entity designed to make rules for one of the most important global common goods: the Internet. ICANN is officially supervised by the US government, but with considerable input in its governing

84 *Institutions and law*

board by non-Americans.[88] It is one of the most effective hybrid private authority arrangements to date, offering global governance by bringing together actors from key states, the market, and civil society.[89]

But as we argued earlier, for social power to be effective, norm entrepreneurs require normative authority by linking their values and rules to legitimate social purpose. As Doris Fuchs claims, the "acceptance of a growing role for business in the end depends on the public perception of its legitimacy, and the appearance of failure to fulfill governance tasks can easily destroy this legitimacy."[90] This implies that the voice of business actors (as well as NGOs) in many policy debates, as well as their claim on legitimacy to set rules, is based on the widespread perception that these non-state actors have more expertise, superior information, and more flexibility to take on tasks previously belonging to the public sector. Since this public perception is volatile, non-state actors' social power is inherently vulnerable; ultimately, their legitimacy and voice depends upon the willingness of the wider public to accept neoliberal ideas.

The 2008 financial crisis has obviously offered this neoliberal consensus a serious blow. For example, the September 2008 Wall Street crash has undermined the credibility of credit ratings agencies such as Standard & Poor's, Moody's, and Fitch Ratings. Over decades, these private agencies provided issuer and bond ratings, researched banks, corporations, sovereigns, and structured and municipal finance, playing a pivotal role in global financial governance. But the failure of these credit ratings agencies to warn investors early enough about the risks of complex financial structures and securities has seriously dented their authority and legitimacy as global financial regulators.[91] Massive government rescue plans were required to salvage an obviously badly-managed financial sector, whose self-regulation was exposed as faulty and borderline illicit (if not immoral). If anything, the 2008 financial crisis has shown that social power requires legitimacy, confirming that social power is exercised in a reciprocal relationship between two or more actors.[92] Without legitimate social purpose and embeddedness, transnational policy networks will be unable to upload their norms. Without legitimacy, firms and NGOs will be unable to exercise public authority, losing any social power they might have had.

4.5 EMBEDDEDNESS AND SYMBOLIC POWER

As I argued earlier, the crisis of multilateralism can only be explained as a result of profound societal changes and the preference for flexible, network solutions. The fragmentation of global politics has resulted in a bazaar of norms and rules, where small groups of stakeholders join together for usually temporary joint efforts. Traditional IOs are gradually adapting to this new reality, and are thereby blamed for abdicating their responsibility to provide global public goods. For example, the global trend toward industry self-regulation has been referred to as the "global out-sourcing of regulation."[93] Critics claim that the on-going "privatization of world politics" will result in an eclectic, overly fragmented patchwork of transnational networks that lack the permanent authority, long-term financial backing, and subsequent continuity of old-style IOs. There is also a concomitant concern that these new policy arrangements will mainly serve business and sectoral interests, rather than the public good. Private rule-setting is now frequently used to prevent rule-setting by traditional, public actors. For example, the chemical industry's Responsible Care Program was created in response to numerous major scandals, and in the expectation that more stringent public regulation would otherwise be forthcoming.[94]

Traditionally, the legitimacy of global governance is measured by the inclusiveness, the accountability, and the deliberative nature of these networks.[95] Who is involved? How transparent is the process of policymaking? What is the quality of deliberation between stakeholders? This is closely related to what Fritz W. Scharpf has labeled input legitimacy.[96] But Scharpf also acknowledges the relevance of output legitimacy, which is generated by effective problem-solving. If a public good or problem is managed and/or solved effectively, legitimacy comes almost automatically. Interestingly, low input legitimacy can be compensated for by high output legitimacy, and, with a few caveats, low output legitimacy can be compensated for by high input legitimacy. The same flexibility and ephemeral quality which makes new (global) governance arrangements well-prepared to swiftly and effectively address new challenges also raises profound questions of legitimacy. But as we have seen with the demise of the neoliberal paradigm since the 2008 financial meltdown, it is nigh impossible to set standards and upload norms without legitimate social purpose. Lacking legitimacy, the avenues of social power become dead-end streets. For all actors involved in international politics, it is therefore crucial to become (and remain) socially embedded in the Ruggian sense, and fuse whatever power they can muster with legitimate social purpose.

In many cases, social power is generated by the dynamic between normative support and legal embeddedness. Since most (global) governance structures are relatively new and with a somewhat shaky claim on legitimacy, examining norm emergence is of special importance. To become embedded and considered a legitimate part of the (global) governance system, new policy arrangements will have to apply argumentative and deliberative power to make their claim and convince the general public. Overall, inclusiveness (measured by the scope and quality of participation), and accountability (especially to those affected by policies) is arranged quite well, since most prominent GPPNs and private authorities are both open and well-balanced in their membership. These new governance arrangements realize that maintaining legitimacy requires hard work, and depends upon "all actors who are affected by a decision [to] participate in a non-coercive and argumentative process and achieve a reasoned consensus instead of a bargained compromise that mainly reflects the bargaining power of the participating actors."[97]

Since the use (or threat) of force and coercion is out of the question, "arguing instead of bargaining" could well be the proper bumpersticker philosophy for social power. As the case of ICANN illustrates, non-hierarchical and network-like international arrangements offer structural conditions that allow these discursive and argumentative processes to be successful.[98] Coalitions of the able and willing,

Friends grouping, and stakeholder networks are small enough to favor arguing as a central mechanism to reach consensus. Within these relatively compact groups, norms are more easily generated and spread. As Kathryn Sikkink claims: "[T]he origins of many international norms lie not in preexisting state interests but in strongly held principled ideas (ideas about right and wrong) and the desire to convert others to those ideas."[99] She argues that in most cases of norm emergence—from the anti-slavery campaign and women's suffrage movement, to more recent campaigns for international human rights and the elimination of the use of landmines—networks of individuals and NGOs have tried to convince each other of the importance and value of their particular cause. Sikkink further suggests that this process is "one of almost pure persuasion",[100] since these groups and individuals usually lack any other means to exercise power. In the end, she argues, norms are followed because people as well as states "want others to think well of them, and because they want to think well of themselves."[101]

Since norms and rules are increasingly developed outside of the realm of state power, a new management model has to be devised which explains why states nevertheless promote compliance through an interactive process of justification, discourse, and persuasion.[102] Harold Hongju Koh suggests that the answer must be found in a "complex process of institutional *interaction* whereby global norms are not just debated and *interpreted*, but ultimately *internalized* by domestic legal systems."[103] Hongju Koh denies that states obey international law because it is convenient or in their national interest. Instead, many states follow the rules due to the "encouragement and prodding of other nations with whom [they are] engaged in a managerial, discursive legal process."[104] He concludes that states comply due to reasons of solidarity and in the spirit of a Grotian notion of international society. Within this international society, Hongju Koh claims, "nations comply with international law for essentially communitarian reasons: not solely because of cost–benefit calculations about particular transactions, but because particular rules are nested within a much broader fabric of ongoing communal relations."[105] The continuous cycles of interaction, interpretation, and internalization give law much of its "stickiness." This corroborates Louis Henkin's famous claim that "almost all nations observe almost all principles of international law and almost all of their obligations almost all of the time."[106]

The lack of hard power resources implies that all efforts to upload policies to (global) governance structures involve the power of persuasion. Non-state actors have to play it smart, since coercion is impossible, and payment does not come cheap. From the broad spectrum of power resources, only the social power segment is available to them, and it is obviously used with increasing skill and competence. Argumentative and deliberative qualities are significant social power resources, and can actually qualify as social capital. Becoming embedded implies that these new policy arrangements have to bring in and earn social capital, which is usually defined as "resources embedded in a social structure which are accessed and/or mobilised in purposive actions."[107] Social capital is generated in and by networks, facilitating the flow of information, creating opportunities to exert influence on others, establishing social credentials, as well as reinforcing identities, recognition,

Institutions and law 87

and status. Institutions generate a pool of social capital as a result of their development and role in international society. In the moral economy of international politics, the demand for social capital exceeds supply, which means that all institutions compete for it, and for good reason. The construction of legitimacy, credibility, and status is not mainly competitive or materialist in nature, but is essentially a symbolic accomplishment. All institutions have gone through historical struggles over the exercise of symbolic power. Modern states as well as major IOs such as the EU and UN are not just administrative institutions, but also pedagogical, corrective, and ideological organizations.[108]

In this process, a key role is played by symbolic power.[109] Pierre Bourdieu's perspective on the role of power in social action is of particular interest here. Bourdieu argues that symbolic power "is defined in and through a given relation between those who exercise power and those who submit to it, i.e., in the very structure of the field in which *belief* is produced and reproduced."[110] He claims that symbolic power is the capacity to constitute the given and the ability to make appear "natural, inevitable, and thus apolitical, that which is a product of historical struggle and human invention."[111]

In short, symbolic power defines and shapes the "reality" which makes the exercise of power (both material and social) possible and meaningful. The recognition of legitimacy and authority is the value-added of social power, of which symbolic power is an integral ingredient. Bourdieu, somewhat paradoxically, further suggests that "symbolic power produces its effects through *mis*recognition, that is, through the appearance that no power is being wielded at all."[112] The important bonus of symbolic power, according to Bourdieu, is that it "renders particular legitimizing claims superfluous, because the exercise of authority is no longer recognized as such."[113] Moreover, Bourdieu describes it as "that invisible power which can be exercised only with the complicity of those who do not want to know that they are subject to it, or even that they themselves exercise it."[114] The circular nature of symbolic power is invisible to the people involved in it, Bourdieu claims, despite the fact that these symbolic systems are structuring social action, as well as structured by human activity. Symbolic power, as an integral part of social power, is therefore not just about setting the rules, but about outlining the game of (global) governance, and establishing the cognitive schemes through which governance is experienced and understood. In short, symbolic power is exercised through that "which goes without saying", which does not need further explanation. This circularity and conscious concealment (or even complicity) may account for social power's three C's—centrality, complexity, and comprehensiveness—and may also explain the hard–social power predicament inherent to understanding contemporary international politics.

Of course, symbolic power also involves using symbols in the more concrete sense, which, as Sheldon Wolin has argued, may "serve to evoke the presence of authority despite the physical reality being far removed."[115] This goes beyond the classical symbols of power, such as flags and icons, but also incorporates more commercial visualizations such as logos and other facets of branding. Symbols are power, and, since symbols are socially constructed, they are part of the domain

88 *Institutions and law*

of social power. Which symbols do we trust, love, believe in, acknowledge, promote, copy, pay, and pray for? Which eco-label do we hold trust in when we shop? Which standard do we deem credible and trustworthy when we compare products? Which flag will we follow for new military missions? Which institution may claim our loyalty and taxes? In short: which message do we have faith in when we make decisions as economic and political beings?

In finding answers to these essential, and sometimes existential, questions, social power plays a central role. The power that institutions and law wield is a function of the esteem and trust in which they are held by the general public, that is to say: we, ourselves. Most of the novel governance arrangements that have emerged over the past decade lack coercive power and any authority they do have is derived from the legitimacy that is conferred to them. Without us, the "general public", all (global) governance arrangements would lack the social power they have now. This is the circular process of complicity that stands at the basis of Bourdieu's symbolic power, and is equally important to our study of social power in international politics.

4.6 CONCLUSION

The development of (global) governance associations and practices is evidence for the reconfiguration of authority under "liquid modernity." Policy dialogues, multi-stakeholder forums, cooperative management bodies, and partnerships of all kinds have evolved from the international to the local level, including participants from government, civil society, the private sector, and the general public. One could argue that these innovative modalities of policymaking are at least partially the responses to both state and market failures, since they try to provide the public goods that were until quite recently delivered primarily by states and traditional IOs. They also contribute to a new transnational legal order that is neither state-based, nor state-created, but is still authoritative in the sense that it can count on the normative and uncoerced consent on the part of the regulated and governed.[116]

Today, both Bono and the UN are "institutions", and norm-setting covers the broad spectrum from eco-labeling to human rights. Taking a giant postmodern leap,[117] it could be argued that in contemporary international politics everybody has the potential to set norms, and even take up the functions of an authentic diplomat.[118] In 2005, *Time* magazine named Irish rocker Bono and American philanthropists Bill and Melinda Gates "Persons of the Year", based on their efforts to raise public awareness for poverty in Africa and health care in developing countries. Andrew F. Cooper's study *Celebrity Diplomacy* (2008) shows how personalities (varying from rock and film stars, to sports and TV celebrities) have taken up advocacy roles that used to be the domain of either NGOs or mainstream diplomacy. Bono, the lead singer of U2, was the co-founder of DATA (Debt, Aids, Trade, Africa; now renamed ONE),[119] closing the divide between popular culture and diplomacy. Whereas Bill and Melinda Gates can aspire to change the rules of global health regulation through their Gates Foundation (which boasts a budget for health projects that, by some calculations, is bigger than that of the World Health Organization), Bono's efforts to frame international politics around the plight of Africa's poor is primarily explained by his personal credibility and celebrity.

In today's media-soaked political environment, celebrities obviously have access to the scarce resource of public attention, which they use to raise public awareness for issues close to their own hearts. Their intense presentness in the media and people's daily lives offers them opportunities to bring policy issues to the public agenda and to frame debates.[120] Most American celebrities now use the power of their brand to promote a "cause", varying from natural childbirth (Ricki Lake), refugees (Angelina Jolie), to saving Darfur (George Clooney) and aiding Africa (Bono). Celebrities, sponsors, and a cause are generally seen as the golden troika of branding, marketing, and PR. Since they also tend to have access to relevant policymakers, this offers celebrities the prospect of setting both the public and political agenda. As Donald Steinberg of the International Crisis Group (ICG) suggests, "[i]t's going to be hard for a foreign government to say no to Nicole Kidman."[121] Bono has most effectively used the political leverage of fame to get world-wide political attention for Africa's debt, the necessity of foreign aid, as well as trade reform, and the ongoing HIV/Aids crisis. As James Traud suggests, "Bono offered decision-makers an implicit bargain: do the right thing, and I'll say so in public. His currency was not just his fame but his credibility."[122]

The case of celebrity advocacy and diplomacy underlines the diversity of actors engaged in social power, all aiming to frame debates, set agendas, raise awareness, upload their norms, and shape rules and regulations. Celebrities have become acutely aware of the social power invested in their name and their brand. As Barber reminds us, when "President Hu Jintao of China came to visit President Bush in 2006, his first stop was not Washington DC, but in Seattle, Washington, where he met with Microsoft Chairman Bill Gates. The lesson (…) is that private power now trumps public power, because globalization has robbed sovereignty of its force."[123] As actress Natalie Portman admits, she is "not particularly proud that in our country I can get a meeting with a representative [of the US Government] more easily that the head of a nonprofit [organization] can."[124]

Be that as it may, any serious analysis of the role of power in institutions and law has to explain and understand new phenomena like GPPNs and private authority, as well as celebrity advocacy. In the end, this shift toward novel (global) governance arrangements has a sociological background, since public support for neo-liberal ideas remains broad and deeply rooted in the discourse of globalization and the market economy. The fact that Bono and other celebrities generate more "voice" than many traditional diplomatic initiatives, and that most consumers do not mind that private authorities label their food, cries out for a fresh look at classical political concepts such as legitimacy and power.

Although mainly a linguistic notion, Bourdieu's concept of symbolic power has particular heuristic value in the study of these new phenomena in global governance. The normative shift away from traditional IOs to smaller, *ad hoc* groupings, and away from the state to NGOs and other private actors, suggests that the transfer of power to more flexible policy arrangements has the implicit approval of key constituencies. Obviously, many people now consider NGOs, firms, as well as celebrities legitimate and credible, sometimes more so than elected politicians. Social power plays a central role in explaining the emergence of new norms and new norm-setting actors, especially since they require support to be effective and considered legitimate. In turn, new (global) governance arrangements, often in close cooperation with states and IOs within GPPNs, offer particularly effective vehicles to use this new configuration and conduit of social capital. Those arrangements whose power "goes without saying" and requires no further legitimating are socially embedded and hence belong to the policymaking establishment.

As with all power debates, social power also has to explain how and whether compliance to these (new) norms, rules, standards, and soft laws is fostered or even assured. Setting norms and rules, and framing questions and debates may be one thing, but assuring compliance is quite another. IR theory has developed three modes of social control that explains compliance: coercion, self-interest, and legitimacy.[125] Both coercion and self-interest are based on consequentialist mechanisms, where actors comply out of fear or because they expect rewards. Only legitimacy is based on shared understandings of both process and objectives, which are derived from shared learning and deliberation.[126] But as we have seen with the debate on CSR and the role of NGOs, it is difficult to disentangle the many, sometimes contradictory, reasons why firms comply with self-imposed norms and rules. Do they fear loss of reputation and strive to win the hearts and minds of their customers by complying to human rights, and social and environmental standards? Is it mainly a matter of calculating the costs and benefits of their strategic choices, or may firms be truly swayed by the power of arguments and deliberative persuasion? As in almost all debates on power, rational choice arguments and constructivist explanations compete with each other, with the social power argument striving against all odds to prove its case.[127]

My claim is that, within the multitude of new policymaking arrangements, social learning takes place and that deliberation changes the behavior of actors. The norms and rules that emerge from these new mixtures of public and private authority are internalized and gradually considered normal, as is always the case when the standards of our daily operations shift. The compliance pull of standards and norms is based on their perceived legality and effectiveness, which in turn evokes a compliance push by national governments adopting new rules within domestic settings. It is this dynamic between normative support and legal embeddedness which brings the role of social power to the fore.

5 Media and globalization

5.1 INTRODUCTION

The social power of the media obviously goes well beyond films and TV programs. It is less about what people watch as it is about the impact media have on the shaping of common narratives, ideologies, and loyalties. Since these narratives and identities are a vital element in the social power equation, the role of media in international politics is key. As Monroe E. Price has argued, media today are the "arena where imagery becomes a supplement or substitute for force."[1]

The role of media as an avenue of social power is manifested in two ways. The *first* can be seen in the efforts of the state to manage its own information space against undesired external influences and pressures. As we have seen in Chapter 3, states have gone to great lengths to protect domestic producers of culture and sources of information and knowledge. For reasons of national identity, national security, or commercial interest, protecting the national (or at times: European)[2] bubble of identity is often considered a top priority. Media have been instrumental in "bringing the nation together", offering government officials and elites a unique political tool to imbue a sense of community in an otherwise fragmented society. As Neil Postman suggested long ago, watching television is the most commonly shared cultural experience in the US, as well as throughout the Western world.[3] Where culture is the glue keeping societies together, media offer the required infrastructure through which these social attachments are made and solidified. Here, social power is used to frame the nation by setting its policy agenda and suggesting common solutions. As Robert M. Entman argues, national media offer a particular national frame by selecting aspects of a perceived reality and making "them more salient in a communicating context, in a way to support a specific problem definition, interpretation, and 'treatment recommendation' for the problems portrayed."[4]

This process has existed for centuries. For example, Benedict Anderson claims that the printing press was essential in the development of nationalism and that the newspaper was a "technical means for 'representing' the kind of imagined community that is the nation."[5] This remains the case today: mainstream media (TV, radio, newspapers) are still for and of their own country, focusing on national issues for a national (or linguistically defined) audience. Since mass media are the dominant source of information on political matters, their news coverage and commentaries even *create* the symbolic environment in which politics is being conducted.[6] As Susan J. Douglas suggests, radio has been key in the construction of the American nation, mainly through "national entertainment programs that attracted [millions of American] listeners, Roosevelt's fireside chats, sporting events, and coverage of the war."[7] Similarly, the media environment is shaping society's understanding of what constitutes "Europe", and what place the emerging Euro-polity will come to play in the political discourse.[8]

Over the centuries, all media revolutions have provoked their own expectations, fears, and reactions. From the printing press to the Internet, "new media" have challenged established power structures and have often been heralded as "technologies of freedom."[9] Martin Luther used the novelty of the printing press to multiply the famous 95 theses he nailed to the door of the Castle Church in Wittenberg in 1517, paving the way for Protestantism's challenge to the Holy Roman Empire. More recently, Ayatollah Khomeini circulated audiocassettes of his sermons through clandestine networks after he had been exiled by the Shah of Iran in 1964. Through these audiocassettes, who were copied by his followers, he could take immediate control over the opposition upon his return to Iran in 1979. Chinese Tiananmen Square demonstrators and opponents of the Russian coup of 1991 used the fax machine to mobilize support, and email was used effectively by students and other opposition protesters to bring down Indonesia's Suharto government in 1998.[10] Today, Osama bin Laden uses (or abuses) the Qatar-based Al Jazeera satellite channel as a platform to communicate his messages to the world.[11] And Twitter, a free social networking and micro-blogging service, has been instrumental in organising massive street protests after alleged election fraud in Moldova (April 2009), as well as in Iran (June 2009).

Even the once media-shy Taliban have gone high-tech, using the full range of media—from mobile phones, email, DVDs, to websites—to communicate and publicize their views and actions. Ayman al-Zawahiri, Al Qaeda's deputy leader, proclaimed in 2005: "More than half of this battle is taking place in the battlefield of the media. We are in a media battle, a race for the hearts and minds of our *Umma* [i.e., religious community]."[12] Moreover, Internet technology is used by virtual communities who successfully counter government controlled mainstream media, bringing their cases to the international court of public opinion, whose influence over states has grown rapidly over the last two decades. Examples can be found from threatened Indian tribes in the Amazon jungle to demonstrators in Bosnia, and from rebels in Chiapas to monks in Tibet. The Internet therefore poses particular challenges for the state to maintain its bubble of identity, and control its foreign policy agenda.[13]

The *second* face of media's social power in international politics involves policies to influence, or at least affect, the media space of other actors. Efforts of this kind range from orchestrated propaganda and public diplomacy strategies such as Radio Free Europe/Radio Liberty and the Voice of America, to more subtle media incursions such as CNN and Al Jazeera. The following two chapters on public diplomacy and place branding offer many examples of such policies. But what concerns us most in this chapter is how media, and the so-called "new media" in particular, are used as conduits of social power. Globalization and the new media have made it increasingly difficult and costly to territorialize information, images, and knowledge, mainly due to the evanescence of national borders. Obviously, states remain engaged in negotiations to protect and manage their information space, at times quite successfully. Still, the intricacies of classical information gatekeepers defending their national bubble confound existing modes of political authority and organization.[14]

The new media environment therefore affects the balance, as well as the nature, of power amongst key actors in international politics. Like culture, media play a central role in shaping discourses, policy agendas, and social and political policy hierarchies. Mainstream media still have an important agenda-setting influence, including that on international politics,[15] since the amount of coverage given to a foreign policy issue offers the general public clues about its relative importance. In this sense, news is a socially conditioned system producing both knowledge and reality. In general, official authorities still determine the sphere of legitimate controversy, setting the frame within which mainstream media define and debate foreign policy matters. But the possibilities for states to use national media to communicate and upload norms and values to their own populace as well as the world has diminished.[16]

During the 1980s, foreign policy debates in the US were framed by political elites through the so-called Big Three news networks (ABC, NBC, and CBS). Similarly, Europe's public broadcasting system was firmly controlled by governments, which is still largely the case in Russia, China, and most other parts of the world. But the new global media system now challenges state control by making data and, hence, news and information ubiquitous. Although there remain inequities in the global pattern of IT connectivity—for example, in 2005, less than 4 percent of all Africans used the Internet—new media have the capacity to distribute everywhere, with little to no extra costs. New mobile services, including mobile voice, Internet, messaging, and content services, make it possible to have news in the palm of our hands, using cell phones. This is widely seen as the start of a dramatic transformation of global news and media, with the potential to change "the international political climate and the way in which governments and officials respond to natural disasters, security emergencies, foreign policy changes, and social developments."[17]

Media transformations are arising ever faster. Thirty years ago, cable television brought us 24/7 news, helped by communications satellites. Over the last two decades, the Internet sparked an even more fundamental information revolution, not "just" shrinking time and space, but deeply affecting the market for loyalties and allegiances, which is such a crucial part of (international) politics.[18] The new media have been heralded as revolutionary, transforming politics into e-democracy, and business into e-commerce. Now blogs and wiki's are again reshaping the media and information environment (see below). For example, as Andrew Sullivan argues, blogging is "the most significant media revolution since the arrival of television."[19] These new media deliver their messages ever faster, adding to mainstream media's travails. News is increasingly defined as what is happening "here and now." As a result, rather than setting the foreign policy agenda, government officials now find themselves forced to react to a continuous stream of "news", generally beyond their control. Walter Cronkite, anchorman of *CBS Evening News*, could for decades end his newscasts with the catchphrase "And that's the way it is." Clearly, this surety and authority is no longer warranted, or considered socially acceptable.

Western governments do not only see domestic media control slipping away, but also worry about the erosion of their social power to frame the global international agenda. As Kishore Mahbubani argues, Western media are still "filled with an incestuous discourse among minds who believe that the 12 percent of the world's population who live in the West can continue to dominate the remaining 88 percent who live outside the West."[20] But this is changing. Martin Walker, for example, claims that "[t]hanks to al-Jazeera and al-Arabiya and China's English-language news channel CCTV, and to the rapid spread of the Internet in India and China, plus the growth of India's Bollywood, Nigeria's Nollywood, and the soap opera powerhouses of Mexico and Brazil, the West no longer dominates the world's media."[21]

Since social power involves setting standards and determining normality, declining media control is of great concern to Western governments. The media revolution based on satellite communications and the Internet "is not simply an increase in the volume of information (...) It is also qualitative, as information of all kinds becomes cheaper, its structure ever more complex and nonlinear, and its distribution far more symmetric than at any time in the past."[22] As a result, it has become more difficult for political elites and government officials to control the nature, timing, and content of foreign policy debates. In particular, the battle for control over the framing of international politics and the foreign policy agenda has acquired many new, and often powerful, competitors. Although it is a myth that blogging will transplant existing mainstream media (see below),[23] the digital revolution has surely diversified the media landscape, increased frame competition, and further complicated agenda-setting. As Joseph Nye and William Owens have argued: "[J]ust as nuclear dominance was the key to coalition leadership in the old era, information dominance will be the key in the Information Age."[24]

One of the most influential new players in the global media arena is the satellite channel Al Jazeera, launched in 1996 by former Arabic BBC employees and financed by Qatar's "liberal" Sheik Hamad bin Khalifa al-Thani. The network offers an eclectic mix of Arab and non-Arab sources, often presented by fashionable female anchors. Interestingly, Al Jazeera's impact partly derives from the fact that it has adopted many of the practices and structure of American news media. Al Jazeera's motto is "the opinion, and the other opinion", which, although commonplace in the West, is exceptional in the Arab media world. Offering daring news programs and political debates between guests with widely divergent opinions, combined with viewer call-in sessions, Al Jazeera changed the Middle Eastern media overnight.[25]

Most Arab countries have at times issued complaints against Al Jazeera's regular and fierce political attacks on Middle Eastern political elites. But the fact that Al Jazeera has been labeled Islamist-oriented, pro-Iraqi, as well as pro-American and pro-Israeli indicates that its news coverage is criticized by all political camps, which strengthens its credibility. Thomas L. Friedman therefore argues that "in a region where the evening news for decades has been endless footage of Arab leaders greeting each other at the airport, and singing each other's praises, it is no wonder that Al-Jazeera, with its real news and opinions, has every Arab with a satellite dish trying to bring in its signal and every Arab leader gnashing his teeth. Libya, Tunisia, and Morocco have all broken diplomatic relations with Qatar at times after being criticized by Al-Jazeera."[26]

Al Jazeera considers itself independent, and not even controlled by Qatar itself. Together with Al Arabiya, the second most popular TV network in the region, it reflects and feels the mood of the so-called "Arab street", which is hostile to Israel and the West. It has shown rather unsettling images of injured Iraqis, and dead US soldiers, footage generally eschewed by the US and Western media. Al Jazeera caused considerable concern to US officials by broadcasting videotapes of Osama bin Laden during the wars in Afghanistan and Iraq. The Bush administration subsequently asked US (and implicitly Western) television networks not to air bin Laden's remarks, claiming that they might contain hidden messages to terrorist cells in the US and beyond. Although the US successfully disciplined Western media, bin Laden's words and images were readily available on Al Jazeera's website, and hence accessible to everyone. As Philip Seib concludes: "In years past, the US government could count on being able to deliver its message to the world through US news organizations (…) The first Gulf War was the high point for this method of influencing world opinion. Slightly more than a decade later, the balance of information power has changed drastically. During the Iraq War, American media voices no longer held the world's attention by default. And, indeed, those who made the case for US policy encountered opposition that was loud, persistent, and far reaching."[27]

For Western Great Powers in particular, one question is key: Do technology and media drive foreign policy? If media are indeed conduits of social power, how should the surge of new media, which seem to spread out news and information beyond the hands of the state, be understood? Although tempting, the path of technological determinism leads us astray. For example, Marshall McLuhan's notion of an emerging "global village" (coined in 1964) suggested that the free flow of information would inevitably bring about a greater, more empathetic global awareness of, and responsibility for, other cultures and people.[28] Technological determinism has, however, been proven wrong, since the same technology that enables us to look beyond our borders also offers us unparalleled opportunities for ethnocentrism and narcissism.

As Susan J. Douglas has shown, after 9/11, US entertainment programming brought American viewers *less* foreign news than before. Instead, both US and European TV channels flooded audiences with non-scripted reality television focusing on individuals in "confined and controlled spaces hermetically sealed from foreign peoples and cultures."[29] US media, with other Western media following suit, seem to accept the triumph of youth demographics insisting that entertainment and celebrity gossip is more important than anything else. Douglas therefore suggests that media has telescopic properties (McLuhan's thesis), as well as microscopic features, which is what we see today.

Although new media are often cast as the prime movers and shakers of public opinion, and even foreign policy decisions, technology is rarely the primary agent of change, and media hardly ever wag the dog. In general, three drivers of social change can be distinguished: technological progress, human agency, and political economy. Obviously, the new media and the digital revolutions have offered opportunities to realize McLuhan's vision, but human agency has often led in the opposite direction. The "objective" laws of political economy and globalization have equally proven less predictable and sturdy, since today's media conglomerates are seriously challenged by blogs and so-called "me-media."

5.2 BLOGS, WIKI'S, AND SOCIAL POWER

New media are widely celebrated, based on the expectation that before too long all content, knowledge, information, and news will be digital, interactive, shared, and free. Developments such as video-on-command, peer-to-peer file sharing networks, and iPods have all contributed to the convergence of computer and TV, changing the way we receive our (visual) information. Google, YouTube, and Wikipedia have changed and accelerated spectatorial consumption, offering unprecedented immediate gratification not only of text, but also of images and video. Together with the Internet as a whole, and Google in particular, YouTube has changed the expectations of the general public and developed a widely shared sense of access entitlement.

New media and digital technology have made the production and distribution of news and culture easier and cheaper, adding to the decentralization of information and the erosion of central authorities. New media also add to the postmodern process of decontextualization. The continuous and growing stream of information and emotional stimulation is generally presented without context, leaving it up to each individual viewer to create personal meanings that were often unintended by the original creator.[30] The new media environment offers people the opportunity to negotiate and participate in the creation of their own, personal mediated experiences, without too much external interference.

As a result, mainstream media have become questionable gatekeepers, no longer able to control the flow of information to Western audiences. Since the deregularization of the Internet in 1995, and its subsequent spread across the world, new media technology formed the basis of a wave of democratization. Traditionally, ordinary citizens had little to no influence on mass media. Apart from writing an op-ed piece or a letter to the editor of a newspaper, individuals were recipients and receivers of news, which generally came filtered and pre-packaged by mainstream (or more often: liberal) journalists. But the Internet has leveled the playing field by promulgating revolutionary search engines, message boards, and especially blogs. In a way, the Internet and the blogging phenomenon stand for the self-regulatory paradigm of global governance.

Media and globalization

Blogs, short for weblogs, are characterized by reverse chronological journals of personal opinions and voices, using archives and hyperlinks to other news stories and postings elsewhere online. Blogs allow information and opinions to be disseminated quickly, making claims public much faster than mainstream media. They are an interconnected, collective enterprise, without editorial oversight and without the professional requirement to provide accurate and unbiased information. As a mainly amateur phenomenon, blogging offers bottom-up comments, turning news from a "lecture" into something akin to a true "conversation." In a way, blogs have become the e-equivalent of the proverbial soap boxes, but this time on a myriad of sometimes highly specific topics, such as cats, knitting, illnesses, and, yes: politics and international affairs. There are now approximately 80 million of these websites—and counting.

In general, blogs are openly partisan, which also offers them the opportunity to create a community of like-minded bloggers and their audiences. Within this blogosphere, trust and credibility are not based on the traditional notions of neutrality and objective validations of information and news (as newspapers still do), but on the shared cultural and political beliefs of their audience.[31] As Lev Grossman has argued, "[w]hen you read [a blog], you feel as if you're part of a community, a like-minded righteous few. It's as if you've stumbled on a sympathetic haven in a lonely trackless wilderness on the Internet."[32] Indeed, the term "blogosphere" conjures up the idea of a new, Internet-based public sphere. This virtual agora has disrupted the top-down character of political communication. As *Instapundit* blogger Glenn Reynolds argues, the impact of blogs on mainstream media "is akin to what happened to the Church during the reformation."[33] News and reporting used to be something produced and communicated by others, offering politicians, journalists, and other elites the chance to define the hierarchy of political and social issues. Potentially, "news" is something we can now all do ourselves. Not too long ago one could quip that the freedom of the press only applied to those that owned one—today, everyone with a laptop and an Internet connection really and truly does.

Blogging was made easy and free after new software became available in 1999, and the phenomenon took off. Blogs, also called the "fifth estate", have since burgeoned all over the world, symbolizing the main difference between "old" and "new" media. Although the blogosphere looks chaotic and flat, it has developed a distinct hierarchic structure since only a small number of blogs attract the most attention. These elite blogs (like *jihadwatch*, *littlegreenfootballs*, or the *dailykos*) attract the bulk of Internet traffic, whereas almost 90 percent of the remaining millions of blogs receive fewer than 100 hits per day.[34] These elite blogs take great pride in their role as the thorn in the side of the MSM (aka "mainstream media"), routinely checking facts and stories, pointing out their errors, and spotlighting issues and stories they feel are underreported. Widely cited examples of the impact of political blogs have been littlegreenfootballs' (or LGF's) so-called "Rathergate." When mainstream US media ignored a seemingly racist remark made by the Republican Senate Majority Leader Trent Lott in December 2002, blogs turned it into a full-blown scandal, eventually forcing Lott's resignation. Afterwards, mainstream media paid homage to bloggers for refusing to let Lott's *faux pas* go. Another widely quoted blog revelation occurred during the 2004 US presidential election campaign, when blogs proved that the documents leaked by CBS news anchorman Dan Rather to discredit George W. Bush were forgeries. Here too, Rather had to resign (or go into "early retirement"). Such "war stories" indicate the potential political influence of blogs, although they remain few and far between.

Blogs are also used by firms to strengthen ties and emotional bonds between their own company, opinion leaders, and government officials. Cisco Systems, for example, set up its own public policy blog in February 2005, arguing that this "was the easiest way to connect with others out there with similar viewpoints." Cisco successfully used its blog to confront Washington-based policymakers with novel ideas, managing to reach 45,000 page views a month, and more than 136,000 regular users in 2007.[35] In the world of non-profit advocacy organizations, blogs are also used to influence the general audience, opinion-makers, as well as policymakers, opening up new routes of social power. Blogs are also enabling US service members fighting in Afghanistan and Iraq to communicate with the home-front (and thereby potentially with the rest of the world), by posting their stories, photos, and videos on blogs.[36] Whereas the US military was initially reluctant to allow soldiers' blogs, popular blogs such as *companycommander.com* and *platooncommander.com* have offered valuable, real-time insights and information which would otherwise not be available to US planners. The blogosphere is used here as a space where issues can be discussed freely, and the gulf between specialists, public opinion, and officials may be narrowed, or even overcome.

As a result, blogging is acquiring qualities of a nascent, mature publishing industry, particularly in the US. It was during the 2004 presidential elections that liberal and conservative activists started using their blogs for fundraising, political organization, and mobilization. The successful Obama 2008 presidential campaign has been lauded as a political watershed, proving the political effects of new media in raising awareness, funding, and public support. In general, blogs are mainly used to bypass traditional media and to build grassroots political support for a wide variety of causes. With their own Media Bloggers Association (MBA), elite bloggers now frequently obtain press credentials to major news events, even in the White House. As a result, the thin line between "Big Journalism" and political bloggers is fading quickly.

But blogs are only a part of a much broader media revolution. Internet technology has also given rise to the now well-known "wiki"-phenomenon. A wiki is a software that allows users to collaboratively create, edit, link, and organize the content of a website, usually for reference material. It is an online resource, allowing users to add content without restrictions. It is also a mass communications tool of a decidedly democratic, even somewhat anarchic, nature. Wiki's are often used to create collaborative websites and to power community websites. A wiki is even more cooperative than a blog, and thrives on collaboration and the willingness to engage. Wiki's are also used in many businesses to provide affordable and effective Intranets and for Knowledge Management. The Wikipedia, online, editable encyclopedia, which started the wiki craze, has become immensely popular and used more often than Amazon, or even eBay. As Nicholson Baker has suggested,

Wikipedia "worked and grew because it tapped into the heretofore unmarshalled energies of the uncredentialed. The thesis procrastinators, the history buffs, the passionate fans of the alternate universes of Garth Nix, *Robotech*, Half-Life, P.G. Wodehouse, *Battlestar Galactica*, *Buffy the Vampire Slayer*, Charles Dickens, or *Ultraman*—all those people who hoped that their years of collecting comics or reading novels or staring at TV screens hadn't been a waste of time—would pour the fruits of their brains into Wikipedia, because Wikipedia added up to something."[37]

Together with blogs and wiki's, the remarkable rise of YouTube and social network sites completes the upsurge of me-media, at least for the moment. YouTube, which was launched in December 2005, reached tens of millions of visitors world-wide, within only a few months. Offering easy-to-use opportunities to view, post, and share streaming video, YouTube became popular by word of mouth, through blogs and social-networking websites like MySpace, Facebook, Orkut, Friendster, Skyrock, and Hyves, whose members log on at least once every 24 hours, enabling them to connect with friends and acquaintances, at times at the detriment of real, human relationships.[38] To celebrate the rise and impact of me-media, *Time* magazine even named "you" (referring to YouTube), the "Person of the Year" for 2006.[39]

The political and sociological impact of these media revolutions is diffuse; it is clearly too early to tell. Blogging guru Glenn Reynolds is rather modest about the social power of blogs to frame debates and upload norms and values: "I think it's easy to exaggerate bloggers' importance. We have 'influence', sometimes, but not real power. Blogs—usually working together—can put things on the agenda, but that's not always the same as making practical things happen."[40] Reynolds is certainly right that framing and agenda-setting should not be confused with political change. But since public awareness and attention are valuable, because scarce, new media continue to upset established media environments. As we will examine in the following section, governments have been keen to regain some level of control over blogs, search engines, and other powerful Internet-based communications tools. A 2008 World Information Access (WIA) report announced that more than half of the arrests of bloggers since 2003 have been made in China, Egypt, and Iran. Although this may indicate the hold of autocratic states on the Internet, it also is testament to the growing political importance of blogging.[41] In addition, new media have already had a remarkable impact on our understanding of international politics and war, and governments have in turn used them to influence public opinion, both in public diplomacy and place branding efforts.

The *potential* shift in social power due to new media should be obvious. Although technological determinism is usually wrong, and human agency frequently misdirects time's arrow, the latent, prospective political impact of blogs, YouTube, and me-media is significant. Internet-based technology offers opportunities to democratize the spread of information and news on an unprecedented scale. However, as we have seen, information abundance does not necessarily result in more knowledge and understanding; at times it results in narcissism and cynicism. The fading role of traditional news and information gatekeepers has great democratic potential, but also results in uncertainty and disquiet. Whereas the impressive tomes of the *Encyclopaedia Britannica* spell authority and confidence, how can we be confident that Wikipedia offers us trustworthy, let alone respected information if truly anyone can write, edit, and add?

The social power of new media therefore resides in novel mechanisms to build confidence, and ultimately trust and authority. For example, Google applies a sophisticated way to order its search results on the basis of mutual linkages, and eBay offers both sellers and buyers the opportunity to give feedback, which provides valuable information on reliability and service. Using Google, Internet users know that search results are based on relevance; using eBay, users can make decisions on the basis of records of buyers and sellers. Equally, links and hits on YouTube and me-media offer users valuable clues to judge the popularity, relevance, and credibility of websites, blogs, and videos. Classical gatekeepers may still exist, but their role and power has diminished markedly. Increasingly, political agendas and priorities are set by a multitude of social actors, without too much interference from government officials and traditional elites. This implies that new, media-based avenues of social power are opening up, offering opportunities to an unprecedented number of new actors, all engaged in uploading their norms and values to different political levels. Elite blogs have become influential, if not powerful; YouTube gives everyone with a camcorder a potential global audience; and Wikipedia truly democratizes information and knowledge. As a result, the question of who *has* and *wields* the social power embedded in new media remains a hard question to answer conclusively.

5.3 NEW MEDIA MEETS OLD POWER

Most Western governments subscribe to Thomas Friedman's notion of an emerging "flat world", based on the new realities of new media, where "more people in more places now have the power to access the flat world platform—to connect, compete, collaborate, and, unfortunately, destroy—than ever before."[42] As we have seen, media globalization and the new media indeed lower national information barriers, making them porous and transient. Although Western governments engage in lukewarm efforts to manage their information space and bubble of identity, they do so with little commitment and perseverance. Both the US and EU oversee "their" media space, but know that taking control is illusory. They obviously concur with Price's dictum that "[t]he market is so powerful, technology so ubiquitous, that we are often reminded that the process of law making, especially in the field of media regulation, is like building castles in the sand where complex structures will be forcefully erased by an overwhelming cascade of waves."[43]

But Price further suggests that political borders not only affect media borders, but also *vice versa*: the changed media map will ultimately affect the physical, political map on which (international) politics is based. New entrants to national media landscapes pose a challenge, or even a threat, to the social power of elites. Using media to establish norms and create the rules of the game is a vital element of politics, and one that few politicians, if they were given the choice, would want to do without. This makes the rise of new media disconcerting to *all* governments, but especially to authoritarian countries (like China, Saudi Arabia, and Iran). By their very nature, non-democratic regimes are keen to maintain their monopoly on the framing of political narratives and policy options, and make great efforts to maintain control over their information space. For example, China as well as most Arab governments see the Internet as a tool of Western cultural domination, provoking political dissent and supporting local unrest. These countries are quickly installing new boundary technologies to manage the ideas that float through their societies, ranging from low-tech to high-tech countermeasures, from banning satellite dishes to blocking websites. More than anything, the political center's desperate efforts to hold on to its information monopoly confirms the significance of social power.

Rehabilitating borders in a digital era seems impracticable and costly, running counter to the "flattening" of boundaries in a globalizing world. In the West, these efforts are generally considered to be self-defeating strategies from retrograde regimes. Although the Internet was initially designed to resist centralized control, authoritarian governments now have power over the Internet (or at least a relevant subset of Internet users within their borders) by regulating national gateways, which are the national computer networks connected to the world-wide Internet. China has established an effective architecture of control over the Internet, proving that the Internet is not inherently control-frustrating.[44] China's infamous "Great Firewall" functions as a huge national intranet, linked to the world-wide web through carefully filtered portals. China's Internet censorship is based on the so-called Golden Shield Project, managed by China's Ministry of Public Security.[45] This system is based on IP blocking, DNS filtering and redirection, and URL filtering, and successfully blocks undesired political and pornographic content. Moreover, the same software designed to keep our PCs free from spam and pornography is well-suited to assist China's censorship efforts.

In advance of the 2008 Beijing Summer Olympics, the NGO *Reporters Without Borders* revealed that more than 50 online dissidents were jailed, and more than 2,500 websites were blocked.[46] China also blocked YouTube for China-based websurfers, as well as other new media portals (e.g., *Sina.com* and *Sohu.com*), during the political unrests in Tibet, just a few months before the Olympics. YouTube in particular was considered a challenge to Chinese authorities, since videos footage of police atrocities in Lhasa were posted there, making them freely available for a Chinese and global audience. News reports from CNN and BBC were also blacked out by China's censors, and the Tibetan Autonomous Region, as Tibet is officially known, became off-limits to foreign journalists.[47] This leads Shanthi Kalathil and Taylor C. Boas to conclude that "the Internet is not necessarily a threat to authoritarian regimes."[48]

As China's economic growth figures attest, the Chinese economy is also not hindered or penalized for stifling political freedom. To break into the attractive, burgeoning Chinese (Internet) market, Western companies like Microsoft, Cisco, Yahoo!, and more recently Google have been ready to sacrifice principles of free speech for market share. These companies have "voluntarily" signed up to a "Public Pledge on Self-Discipline for the China Internet Industry", making them complicit in China's censorship strategies. Western news organizations are not prepared to defy powerful governments, since this is bad for business. Google, for example, has created a Chinese version of its search engine (*Google.cn*), which filters out websites that Chinese authorities find politically objectionable. For search engines it is important to maintain a server network in China, since outside servers connecting to the Chinese Internet are slow and cumbersome. Western companies are obviously willing to accept political scrutiny in exchange for a slice of China's e-commerce market, which reached US$6.5 billion in 2007.[49]

Still, Beijing's censorship has a hard time managing the blogging phenomenon, which has also hit China. In China, around 210 million people use the Internet (at year-end 2007), among them around 75 million bloggers. Also, with some 560 million subscriptions, China is home to the world's largest mobile communications user base.[50] Internet enthusiasts and pro-democracy advocates expect that the new media revolution will ultimately also undermine China's control over the Internet. Liberal thinking is based on the dogma that it is impossible to manage an effective, decentralized, modern economy without at least a basic level of open, democratic discourse. There are indeed concrete signs that the new media have had some impact on China's political climate, sometimes with notable success. For example, when a 27-year-old Chinese college graduate was detained by Chinese police for not having proper identity papers, and subsequently died in jail, the story was picked up by Chinese bloggers and quickly spread through cyberspace. Within three months, China's Custody and Repatriation system, an outdated and arbitrary form of administrative detention under which the graduate student was held in custody, was abolished.[51]

These glimmers of hope suggest that China's emerging blogging community is developing in an *ersatz*-public opinion, or what is now frequently called *Wangluo Yulun*, or "Internet opinion." Lacking a systematic and democratic way for the general public to be politically vocal and active, the *Wangluo Yulun* system is developing as a new way to influence the political and social agenda in modern China.[52] As Xiao Qiang argues: "This means that when an issue resonates with millions of Chinese netizens, it is expressed not only on BBS's [Bulletin Board Systems], but also through the 'implicit' Internet communication channels and within the growing Weblogging community. Instead of being produced by official media, these online uprising events, powered by the internet (...), now drive the agenda of official media."[53] This suggests that the rise of "Internet opinion" is blurring the boundaries between new, online media and traditional, state-controlled news and information. Despite the fact that, overall, Chinese censorship is effective, the Internet still transforms China's political life, creating social change. It has proven extremely difficult to combine an organization built on policing the Internet, whilst simultaneously keeping China's national IT sector internationally competitive. In the end, technological control is no longer possible, and only self-censorship based on fear and discipline has a chance to keep a semblance of political control over news, opinion, and information in Chinese society.

A similar, liberating effect of new media has also been long awaited in the Middle East. New ideas are percolating in the Arab world, empowering Arab democrats as well as anti-democratic and radical countertrends. NGOs use the Internet to gain access to Arab societies, and to get global public attention for violations of human rights throughout the Middle East. But extremist religious organizations and political opposition groups have taken to the Internet as well; Lebanon's Hezbollah maintains a popular website, as does the UK-based Saudi reform movement, the Movement for Islamic Reform in Arabia.

One notable effect of the digital communications revolution has been that many Arabs know more about each other. Like in the case of China's *Wangluo Yulun*, this has sparked hope for the creation of a new, Arab public opinion, not necessarily based on a shared ideology or religion, but on a new sense of common interest and belonging.[54] Al Jazeera has turned itself into an international channel, and its real success is based on its pan-Arab character. Arab émigrés in particular, mostly from the US and Europe, have brought their cultural, political, social, and Islamic religious issues to cyberspace, influencing the Middle Eastern agenda. Although the Arab online community is rather small, it is still argued that the "new media are encouraging increasing cultural unity among the Arabs even by acknowledging their diversity, by helping to reflect and mobilize public opinion on issues of common concern, and by overcoming some narrow regional loyalties."[55]

In the Arab world, where 22 nations use approximately the same language, there is an obvious potential for the development of a more cohesive public sphere. The spread of satellite dishes (which have become smaller and cheaper), in particular, has reached broad segments of the region's population. Internet access and computers, however, remain expensive in the Middle East, and beyond most people's budget. The UN's 2003 Arab Human Developments Report pointed out that the Middle East is dragged down by government censorship and state-ownership of most media institutions. The Middle East lags behind other regions, with only 1.6 percent of the Arab population having Internet access. This much-quoted report indicated that, in a region of 284 million people, a book that sells 5,000 copies is considered a bestseller. Interestingly, most major Arab newspapers are published outside the Arab world. *Al-Hayat, al-Sharq al-Awsat, al-Zaman*, and *al-'Arab*, are all published out of London. These dailies are published simultaneously by satellite in most Arab countries, and read widely. They have a broad regional influence in the Arab world due to their Western-style standards of journalism, offering an open, and free debate on social and political issues relevant to a Middle Eastern audience.

As Jon Alterman has argued, these Western-based Arab news outlets contribute to a "broadening of the bounds of debate, a subtle integration of Western ideas with Arab ideas, and a general bridging of gaps between the Arab world and the West (…) [T]he information revolution has already arrived in the Middle East, and it poses significant challenges for the status quo."[56] Although the Internet is not widely available, it still offers revolutionary possibilities for instant and cheap distribution of ideas. The Internet offers Arab liberals a unique platform, as well as relative anonymity and security, to open up their closed societies. As Pierre Akel, the Lebanese host of an Arab-language blog argues: "The Internet is a historical opportunity for Arab liberalism. In the Arab world, much more than in the West, we can genuinely talk of a blog revolution."[57] Despite all controls and restrictions, the Internet is having a profound impact on closed Arab societies, offering a unique and unprecedented forum for minority and dissident views.[58] As Jonathan Rauch concludes: "The suffocating duopoly of state-controlled media and Islamist pulpits is cracking—only a little bit so far, but keep watching. In the Arab world, the Enlightenment is going online."[59]

From a Western viewpoint, the rise of new media has made it increasingly difficult to reach out to the world's 1.5 billion Muslims. Before the Gulf Wars of the 1990s, there was no credible Arab TV news. Until Al Jazeera's launch in 1996, most Arabs were exposed to CNN's coverage of the Gulf Wars, whose gloating over the superiority of Western weaponry and technology, combined with the lack of interest in Iraqi civilian casualties, set Arabs' teeth on edge. Today, the Internet and Al Jazeera offer tough competition to Western news and views. Al Jazeera's continuous airing of violence in Gaza and Falluja strengthens Arabs' suspicions and anger against the West, rather than bridging political and cultural divides.

This reality stands in stark contrast to the widely shared Western assumption that connectivity and flatter borders are desirable, since linkage to the global economy supposedly results in free markets and democracy. But, as Charles M. McLean has argued, the Internet is also a "rage enabler", providing "instant, persistent, real-time stimuli [which] takes anger to a higher level."[60] The Internet offers enraged people an opportunity to gather and organize themselves. Indeed, one could qualify the Internet "at its ugliest, [as] just an open sewer: an electronic conduit for untreated, unfiltered information."[61] As Roger Cohen suggests, "Al Qaeda is (…) a child of the Internet age bouncing its murderous ideas around the globe."[62] Indeed, Al Qaeda operatives use the Internet as their main mode of global communication and propaganda, proving that the social power of new media is an important factor in international politics, and is at times malignant.

Social power involves the ability (and willingness) to set standards and upload norms and values that are deemed legitimate and desirable, without resorting to coercion or payment. Clearly, Al Qaeda's norms are widely questioned and generally considered illegitimate. The explicit threat of terror also disqualifies Al Qaeda's "soft power." However, as the continued popularity of Osama bin Laden in the wider Middle East testifies, challenging Western-dominated news frames and Western values generates legitimacy within certain Muslim communities, creating opportunities to use the ensuing public support to reach political goals, including terrorism. In closed societies like China and the Middle East, new media and new actors challenge the establishment's social power to set frames and agendas, and make decisions. But as the examples of Al Qaeda and the rage-enabling qualities of the Internet illustrate, the democratization of social power is a mixed blessing. Zaki Laïdi has rightfully claimed that normative power does not equal nice power.[63] Although social power excludes the use of force and payments, it remains agnostic about the moral value of the proposed norms and standards. Even if

Media and globalization   105

social power requires legitimacy and social embeddedness, this obviously differs markedly between societies, religions, and cultures. As we will see (in Chapter 6), this has major implications for public diplomacy, which aims to effectively engage foreign audiences.

5.4 MEDIA, CONFLICT, AND WAR

It is well-known that "wars can be won on the world's television screens as well as on the battlefield."[64] During war, whether it was the Cold War or America's war on terror during the Bush administration, the military has used the media to serve as an information conduit to national and international audiences, to rally support, and to defuse enemy propaganda. Military leaders have many opportunities to leverage the media, using it as a strategic tool, an enabler, and a multiplier. This does not mean that the military "uses" the media in a sinister, manipulative way (although this does surely happen as well), but mainly as a channel to convey messages and information, to frame problems, and to suggest policy solutions.[65] Pentagon war-games now also include the "CNN factor", which is shorthand for being alert to the impact of real-time, 24/7 press coverage.[66] For the military, the "CNN battlefield" is the virtual reality running parallel to the real conflict on the ground. In order to be successful and win, one must prevail in both arenas.[67]

The CNN effect became a major force in international politics when US President Bush decided to send troops to Somalia in 1992, to end the refugee crisis there. The US mission was widely seen as a response to the non-stop coverage of starving children by the Western media, and CNN in particular. When, one year later, US President Clinton decided to withdraw these same troops after Western media televised scenes of a dead American soldier dragged through the streets of Mogadishu, the CNN effect was deemed undeniable.[68]

In the 1990s, America's Operation Desert Storm (1991) and NATO's "humanitarian intervention" in Kosovo (1999) have been called CNN wars, where new communication technologies offered audiences a distant and sanitized "show", sometimes live on the evening news, complete with smart bombs, cross hairs, and infrared shots from the pilot's cockpit. Around the clock news media coverage became an integral part of the battlefield, offering new challenges and opportunities for all parties to win the information war. As a result, the (mainly Western) audience was turned into armchair imperialists, becoming both complacent and complicit with the daily show of violence on their TV screens and PCs. To some extent, this also applied to TV journalists, who were flying from one international crisis to another, using satellite and video technology to report (*live!*, of course), from Baghdad, Kabul, Gaza, and Darfur.[69]

The Lebanon war of summer 2006 became the first major conflict where new media, and the Internet in particular, played a key role in shaping both news and public opinion across the world. During the 34 days of bloody conflict between Israel and the Hezbollah (or "Party of God"), a global audience could follow the war as it unfolded from their sofas, watching the grim reality of the battlefield through live reports from two American networks and Internet journalism. Even though Israeli forces tried to apply censorship, journalists could still cover the war without much intrusion. The 2006 Lebanon war was unique in that a global audience could actually watch Israeli troops invading southern Lebanon, destroying villages, responding to Hezbollah rockets striking northern Israel and Haifa, and follow the movements of the many thousands of fleeing civilians—all live. Obviously, this turned the camera and computers into important "weapons of war", shaping the opinions and attitudes of governments and their actions.

Blogs also played an important role during the Lebanon war. Pro-Israeli and pro-Hezbollah blogs bombarded traditional media with their well-organized and angry opinions, putting pressure on mainstream journalists to double-check their facts, and balance their opinions to assure that they remained objective. Internet bloggers and regional call-in radio and TV stations all tended to expose and stress the vulnerability of the Israeli forces, which was subsequently picked up by mainstream international media. As Malvin Kalb argues, during the Lebanon war, "the bloggers had more influence over the flow of the story than they had had during any other war (…) The Lebanon War produced a bumper crop of stories both good and bad, growing out of a new kind of asymmetrical warfare waged by a state on the one side and a religious, nationalistic guerrilla force on the other side."[70] Clearly, new media came of age during the Lebanon war, playing a major part in competitive framing, uploading a wide variety of images, norms, and values to an already saturated global public opinion.

In several cases, blogs and amateur journalists also exposed mistakes and fabrications of major news stories, of which the photoshopped picture of a burning city, published by Reuters in August 2006, was most prominent.[71] Since photos and videos have a more direct, emotional impact on an audience than text, a war of images was conducted in all parts of the global media. As David Friend of *Variety* magazine argued, images "succinctly capture so many layers of meaning in a confined space, it's the artistic equivalent of atomic power, where you have so much energy in a small space that it has to explode."[72] Military experts already use the term "information battlefield" to highlight the vital role and place of images and information during wars and conflicts. Steve Fondacaro, an American military expert, argues that "[t]he new element of power that has emerged in the last 30 to 40 years and has subsumed the rest is information. A revolution happened without us knowing or paying attention. Perception truly is reality, and our enemies know it."[73] As US troops in Iraq have experienced, several ambushes on American convoys were specifically planned to get spectacular video footage of burning US humvees. These pictures and videos are subsequently circulated on CD-ROMs and the Internet to a vast audience across the Middle East, visualizing—and thereby "proving"—the vulnerability of American forces.

Obviously, watching war and conflict unfold live on TV is a very different experience than reading about them in a newspaper. As M. Rex Miller suggests, printed communication "created more analytic, rational minds that see the world as parts assembled in an orderly whole, like the words in a sentence." Print, which has dominated communication for centuries, did away with the "irrational" thought of the preceding oral world, based on stories and myths. Miller suggests that print has made reason king, stimulating reflective thinking. Today, however, TV and other new media have elevated "desire and emotion and encouraged *reflexive* thinking—the kind of thinking we do while driving a car."[74] The power of images is not based on rationally debated truth claims, but rather works on emotional, physiological, and symbolic levels. Visual power is based on emotional engagement, fulfilling our desire for symbolic meaning and cultural conditioning.

TV only demands our scant attention, but does not require our active participation, let alone our own analysis. Today's media is bent on the continuous, and preferably entertaining drama of "breaking news", which usually leaves little time for reflection. Since the newsworthiness of news is defined primarily by the visualization of conflicts and disasters, Western media focus on wars and terrorist attacks, military coups and genocides, as well as floods and famines. As is frequently remarked, "the very definition of news may continue to shift to 'that which is happening now and can be seen in pictures.' This is news voyeurism (…) News will tend to come from the streets and frontlines of battle, rather than from the traditional venues of institutionally-situated reporting of official pronouncements and descriptions."[75]

The best recent example of this kind of "voyeurism" has been the Abu Ghraib torture scandal, which hit the news in early 2004. The scandalous pictures of Abu Ghraib are well-known, and have quickly become icons carrying vast emotional power.[76] The photograph of US Private First Class Lynndie R. England captured the public imagination in particular. Here we saw a petite American female soldier holding a leash, looking down dispassionately at the body of a naked Iraqi man with a leash around his neck on the floor of the infamous Iraqi Abu Ghraib prison. This image was distributed widely in Western and global media, symbolizing the inhumane treatment (since leashes are commonly used for animals) of Iraqis by Americans, and conjuring up images of lynching and enslavement based on racial and imperial narratives.[77]

US mainstream media put the spotlight on the soldiers committing these crimes—focusing on their working-class backgrounds, for example—rather than on the political context which made this possible in the first place. Later, US media transformed "Abu Ghraib" into a serial forensic drama, with a huge infotainment potential. But, in the rest of the world, the icons of Abu Ghraib, together with the orange-clad "enemy combatants" of Guantanamo Bay detention camp, stood for America's cruelty, and lack of concern for human rights. Here too, the role of new media in highlighting America's duplicity has been huge, with blogs and websites beating the drum of US "imperialist war crimes", even if Western mainstream media had already shifted towards other, newer news.[78]

As we concluded earlier, news organizations have generally left policy framing and agenda setting to government officials and political elites. But with the rise of new media, this dynamic has changed fundamentally. Empowered by the Internet and other digital and satellite-based information gathering capabilities, new media are challenging the premises of government officials, scrutinizing their objectives. This quality has turned new media into a major factor in international politics, particularly during conflicts and war. But as the story of Lynndie England illustrates, Western media construct "hard news" as a continuous stream of victims and combatants, dehumanized and sanitized, which is duly compensated by "soft news" based on lifestyle and human-interest stories, celebrity journalism, and mayhem news.[79] These episodes have clearly proven wrong McLuhan's vision of media technology driving an empathetic global awareness, at least for now. Media's social and political impact works in mysterious ways, and if history teaches us anything it is that audiences rarely adopt and use media and communications technologies in the ways they were originally envisioned.

Now that old and new media are merging, and "news" can be produced and delivered globally by bloggers as well as governments, it is hardly surprising that media and entertainment are mixing as well. News only constitutes a small part of media content, and in order to compete for the viewer's attention news must be attractive, both in content and style. As a result, today's "hard" news of conflicts and wars is often delivered by embedded journalists, showing off their shaky-cam images and low-definition videophone transmissions, indicating that they are personally at risk in the dangerous, premodern periphery of the civilized world.[80] The journalists themselves have become enmeshed in human-interest stories based on patriotism and heroism, where military officers appear on staged Hollywood-style briefing sets, following made-for-TV captivity narratives.[81]

Nothing illustrates this odd mixture of war and entertainment better than the following vignette: During the Gulf War, General Colin Powell was in charge of media relations, making sure that Operation Desert Storm was sold to a wide international audience. In his memoirs, Powell recalled: "We auditioned spokespersons (…) We picked Lieutenant General Tom Kelly as our Pentagon briefer because Kelly not only was deeply knowledgeable, but came across like Norm in the sitcom *Cheers*, a regular guy whom people could relate to and trust."[82]

5.5 SEX, LIES, AND SOFT NEWS

As General Powell's deliberate choice for an utterly normal, Norm-like spokesman testifies, the symbiotic relationship between US media, the military, and the war on terror is remarkable, and widely recognized.[83] This symbiosis goes beyond vignettes, and has become structural, influencing not only the US military itself, but also the media, both old and new. For example, immediately after 9/11, the US Army convened an *ad hoc* working group at the University of Southern California in Los Angeles, bringing together Hollywood screenwriters, directors, and media moguls. The goal was straightforward: "to brainstorm about possible terrorist targets and schemes in America and to offer solutions to those threats."[84] Two years earlier, in 1999, the US Army had already rewarded a five-year contract to the USC's Institute for Creative Technologies (ICT), trying to enlist Hollywood's best and brightest, including videogame makers and computer specialists, to advance immersive environment and virtual reality training simulations for their soldiers. In 2004, ICT received another US$100 million grant from the US Army to develop its Experience Learning System, used by the US Army to develop case studies and interactive learning systems supporting soldiers' leadership skills.[85]

Hollywood's entertainment industry obviously has the expertise to develop stories, visual effects, and production know-how, which is required to prepare the US military for action on the battlefield. But this symbiotic relationship is also of great value to Hollywood's movie industry, which has gained access to the Pentagon's facilities and equipment. For example, during the filming of the 2001 blockbuster *Pearl Harbour*, the US military contributed Pearl Harbour facilities as well as its aircraft carrier *USS Constellation*. In return, the Pentagon gave historical advice, and gained some access to Hollywood's scripts, influencing storylines and characters to assure maximum patriotic effect. This is standing practice in US commercial filmmaking. The main aim for any Hollywood film with Pentagon assistance is that it "aids in the retention and recruitment of military personnel", and, of course, depicts the US military in an overall positive way.[86] Portraying this relationship as a "military-industrial-media-entertainment-network", may be overdoing it; Hollywood remains independent enough to also fiercely criticize US foreign policy, even during wartime.[87] Still, as Jack Valenti, the head of the Motion Picture Association of America, argued in November 2001: "We are not limited to domestic measures. The American entertainment industry has a unique capability to reach audiences worldwide with important messages."[88] Hollywood's social power to upload norms and shape ideas has been of particular value to America's post-9/11 public diplomacy efforts, as we will examine in the next chapter.

Occasionally, one is tempted to see a symbiotic relationship between hard news and entertainment as well. Fox Cable Network, for example, passed CNN in the ratings after it unashamedly offered patriotic news after 9/11. At the same time, Fox Television produced the highly successful series *24*, where its hero Jack Bauer (played by Kiefer Sutherland) frequently battles Al Qaeda-like terrorists, rationalizing and even promising an endless, total war. *24* is broadcast world-wide, not only in traditional markets like Europe and Asia, but also in Africa and the Middle East. The first six series of this Golden Globe award-winning drama were all centered around a fictional Los Angeles branch of a US government counterterrorist unit. Because of *24*'s "real-time" storytelling approach, Bauer, the main character, is under continuous time pressure and "therefore" occasionally "obliged" to use torture to acquire information, ignoring laws, and misusing government authority to save humanity (on an almost daily basis).[89] Given the immense popularity of *24* in the US and beyond, its impact as an allegory of America's war on terror is undeniable since it offers a discursive and performative rationalization and justification of American (and Western) post-9/11 policies.

The popularity of *24* and similar series are part of a Western infotainment boom and a foreign-news bust, which even the post-9/11 hard news boomlet could not turn around. America's large urban daily newspapers are slowly spiraling downward, resulting in reductions in news staff. Similarly, US TV network news divisions see their budgets slashed and foreign bureaus closed. A 2004 Pew survey revealed that more young people (aged between 18–24) get their news from *The Daily Show* than from mainstream news sources, like newspapers. US TV has been captured by soft news, which includes TV programs like Dateline NBC, Late Night with David Letterman, or MTV News; most European channels are dominated by clones of these shows.

With the rise of cable and the fall of major networks, commercial media corporations seek to maximize their profits, and are hence led by the preferences of audiences. These media are particularly bending over backwards to get the attention of 18–49 year-old women, who are generally drawn to softer interests, such as health and celebrity stories. News reporting has therefore shifted to real-life, human-interest drama, which can be produced at far lower cost than either fictional drama or hard news. Focusing on social and lifestyle trends, personal interest stories, and personal service journalism (how to become happy, healthy, and wealthy), soft news is more interested in the comments of celebrities than of governmental dignitaries. This has certainly contributed to the rise of celebrity diplomacy, and the blurring of news, opinion, emotion, and drama.

As Matthew A. Baum has argued, "for many individuals who are not interested in politics or foreign policy, soft news increasingly serves as an alternative to the traditional news media as a source of information about a select few political issues, including foreign policy crises."[90] Western TV tends to package human drama as entertainment, which has over the years resulted in the framing of foreign policy issues in terms of scandals, violence, heroism, and other forms of human drama. Soft news is generally set as a story with recognizable characters, devoid of a public policy component, and wrapped in a sensationalized presentation. Soft news performs the role of today's postmodern storyteller, using the route of popular culture for political socialization.[91] For example, at the height of the Bosnia war, US media "devoted most of their coverage to a single dramatic story: the travails of U.S. fighter pilot Scott O'Grady, who was shot down over enemy territory on June 2, 1995. Captain O'Grady's heroic story of surviving behind enemy lines for five days on a diet of insects and grass, before being rescued by NATO forces, represented an ideal made-for-soft news human drama."[92]

In Western (and especially US) media, soft news is gradually crowding out hard news. François Debrix suggests in his book *Tabloid Terror* (2008) that "tabloidization of everyday culture takes place when the media and their programming and factional realities become an all-encompassing dimension of a vast majority of people's daily life."[93] In short: in order to be relevant and effective in US foreign policy debates, any argument needs to be presented in a tabloid framework. More than ever before, Western audiences have a choice between hard and soft news, and a substantial part of that audience now chooses, if not exclusively, for entertainment-oriented news programs presented in tabloid style. It is easier to focus on Captain O'Grady's ordeal than on NATO's role of stabilizing and rebuilding a far-away and unknown Balkan country; it is also more appealing to focus on the Appalachian hell-raiser Private Lynndie England than on the legal and political background of the Abu Ghraib debacle. Soft news offers a generally disinterested public a perspective lacking context and an oversimplification of complex issues as stories that are framed in ways

Media and globalization   111

that highlight entertainment over information. In doing so, soft news has the capability to shape the political understanding of a mass audience, giving it the largely unrecognized social power to frame political issues, determine legitimate options, and suggest solutions.

Akin to the CNN effect, soft news has its own "Oprah effect", since Oprah Winfrey is generally acknowledged as the most influential woman in US entertainment. When soft news programs pick up a foreign policy issue, it becomes what Baum labels a "watercooler event": an event everyone talks about at the workplace across the nation.[94] The Oprah effect of soft news therefore not only involves the crucial function of agenda setting in international politics, but also the framing of the discourse as a human drama, rather than a contextualized political event, worthy of critical analysis. This may explain why, for most governments, soft news is preferable to hard news: it entertains the general public, but it hardly ever results in harsh criticism and major popular discontent.

The shift from hard to soft news, and from old to new media, is part of a wider societal transformation. The shift to commercial broadcasting has resulted in more advertising messages, persuading viewers to assume the role of consumer as their primary social identity. The victory of free and independent media over public broadcasting symbolizes the victory of consumerism over citizenship. And although advertising has freed most media from state control and may therefore be overall laudable, the dominance of advertising in the daily menu of signs and images is culturally as well as politically significant. For media to be "free", they have to subscribe to the logic of Western consumer society, and stick to its rules. The content industry (TV and film in particular) has been at the forefront of opening new markets, preparing new audiences for a lifestyle of consumerism in which entertainment is usually pre-packaged, and bite-size. The rise of soft news therefore reflects the victory of commerce and entertainment over the traditional role of the media: scrutinizing the government and educating and informing the general public. This is the main reason why new media, and idiosyncratic and anarchic blogs in particular, have become better watchdogs than (what is often referred to as) the "lamestream media."

5.6 CONCLUSION

Mass media do not only produce the content of politics, they also help to determine the hierarchies of political issues. This is not to say that news media determine what political *opinions* people may come to hold, but they certainly play a role in deciding what *issues* people start thinking about in the first place.[95] Governments have, at least until recently, functioned as powerful gatekeepers, using sovereignty and territoriality as control instruments. Even the altruistic goal of preserving a country's national identity can be considered as a thinly disguised effort of ruling elites to maintain and strengthen the political and cultural attitudes that help them uphold existing power structures. Indeed, media, like culture, have the special capacity to produce "us." By offering the means through which people interact with each other, media form communities based on a sense of belonging. Identity is mediated through media, although many certainties are now eroding due to the process of decentralization and decontextualization. The rise of the Internet, the growth of cable communication, and satellite TV have contributed to the fragmentation of what used to be a rather cohesive national audience.[96]

Because of this splintering of audiences, it has become hard to use media for traditional identity-shaping experiences. Only major, paradigm-shifting conflagrations form the exception. For example, by watching the daily news (hard and soft) in combination with patriotic movies and TV series, media and popular culture have imbued a Western audience with the notion that 9/11 is an assault on American culture and civilization. The iconic images of the burning and crumbling Twin Towers have had a political impact akin to Pearl Harbour, offering the world a new frame of analysis with the war on terror at its core. Like all paradigm-shifting events, the visual impact of 9/11 has been dramatically amplified by the incantations of the Western media, who have repeated the images *ad nauseam*, commemorating and mystifying the event in the process. At the same time, these media-generated symbolic constructions of terrorism and fear have contributed to a reaffirmation of classical American narratives and communal values.

Since new media have always affected the size and quality of the public domain, new publishing platforms like blogs are expected to set new standards for political reporting, and hence affect the public and political agenda. Blogs are changing the face of global media, ushering in a new paradigm based on assumed access to information and knowledge, on immediacy and speed, and on the presumption of cross-border (regional as well as global) blogospheres. Today's communications technology has inherent capabilities to privilege some cognitive and behavioral processes over others. Technology is constructed by society, but in turn it also has a significant social impact. M. Rex Miller suggests that the new media, due to their interactive nature, may well end the couch-potato passivity of today's TV audience: "This experience [of new media] is quite different from the intellectually passive experience of watching television or the emotionally distant experience of reading. Consequently, our minds and bodies will undergo a rewiring to support this different sensory experience."[97]

Whether this will really happen remains rather speculative. But that new media is changing our frames of reference and conceptual background can hardly be denied. Inevitably, this will impact on the nature and dynamics of international politics. As David J. Rothkopf suggests: "The *realpolitik* of the new era is *cyberpolitik*, in which the actors are no longer just states, and raw power can be countered or fortified by information power."[98] The problem is, however, that "the international system may represent more voices but be unable to advance any of them."[99] As a result, the emerging media environment, like a black hole, fragments, crumbles, and sucks up the much-heralded information power that ostensibly is the way of the future. Obviously, the growing fragmentation of new media does not sit well with visions of a concentrated and well-orchestrated global political–military–media "unholy trinity", aimed at managing consent. Like culture, law, and institutions, media is deeply embedded in society and politics, which makes it unavailable as a strategic tool. The very notion of cyberpolitik assumes that a struggle for information dominance is emerging, where states strive to get the information edge as a multiplier of their diplomacy and social power.[100] Nye and Owens, for example, suggest that "the information advantage can strengthen the intellectual link between U.S. foreign policy and military power and offer new ways of maintaining leadership in alliances and ad hoc coalitions."[101] They further argue that the US has to adjust its foreign and defense strategies to make better use of this information edge, since "information about what is occurring becomes a central commodity of international relations."[102]

However, neither information nor knowledge is a commodity, just as culture and media are too ephemeral to be tied down as political real estate that can be managed, bought, or sold. This hardly detracts from the social power that is embodied by and derived from the media. But just as Adam Smith's invisible hand plays a central role in the management of economic and financial markets, media's social power plays a central role in shaping the dynamics of domestic as well as international politics—not always visible and readily usable, but always present and relevant.

6 Public diplomacy

6.1 INTRODUCTION

Just as contemporary Defense Ministries used to be less euphemistically called Ministries of War, efforts to influence other people's political beliefs used to be labeled propaganda, or (in the Soviet case) even *disinformatia*.[1] These terms conjure up images of secrecy and dishonesty, of deceit and betrayal, which explains why today's efforts to manage the international environment through engagement with foreign audiences is still looked upon with suspicion. This means that when terms like public diplomacy are used in order to describe activities that were previously called psychological warfare, caution and even a healthy dose of skepticism are in order. Still, in the US, Europe, as well as China and Israel, public diplomacy has become an increasingly important avenue to apply social power in international politics.[2] As a 2002 report by the German Foreign Ministry noted: "In Europe, public diplomacy is viewed as the number one priority over the whole spectrum of issues."[3] British Minister for Europe Jim Murphy commissioned a detailed study on the relevance of "new" public diplomacy, in 2008,[4] based on the argument that the "nature of influence has altered irreversibly in many countries and our diplomacy has to take account of that. How do we best conduct diplomacy in an internet-enabled, increasingly democratised world?"[5]

As we have seen in previous chapters, touching the hearts and minds of foreign publics is hardly original. As Hans J. Morgenthau argued in his *Politics Among Nations* (1948), a "government must (…) gain the support of the public opinion of other nations for its foreign and domestic policies."[6] What is new, however, is what Minister Murphy described as the "internet-enabled, increasingly democratised world", which has opened up new opportunities to use social power, and make it work. So, what makes public diplomacy innovative, and how does it inform our analysis of social power in international politics?

Diplomacy used to be the domain of a rather small and exclusive elite of experienced experts of the Foreign Services establishment. Traditional diplomacy is a process with fixed players and rules, with clearly delineated responsibilities for only a limited number of actors. Mainstream diplomacy is often defined as international actors attempting to manage the international environment through engagement with other international actors, usually governments and IOs. Today, these diplomatic rules and mores no longer apply. Celebrity advocacy upsets diplomacy's ontology, and since NGOs and other non-state actors are actively engaged in molding public support for their preferred policies, diplomacy seems to be truly and irrevocably democratized.[7] Within this global pandemonium of norm entrepreneurs, the concept of public diplomacy has acquired its special place, and for good reasons.[8]

Public diplomacy tries to reach classical diplomatic goals through engagement with foreign publics.[9] Common definitions of public diplomacy are (by Paul Sharp): "the process by which direct relations with people in a country are pursued to advance the interests and extend the values of those being represented", or (by Hans Tuch): "a government's process of communicating with foreign publics in an attempt to bring about understanding for its nation's ideas and ideals, its institutions and culture, as well as its national goals and policies."[10] Both Sharp and Tuch assume that public diplomacy involves the use of social power by states and diplomats. Bruce Gregory's definition of public diplomacy goes beyond state policies, and includes "the means by which states, associates of states, *and non-state actors* understand cultures, attitudes and behavior; build and manage relationships; and influence opinions and actions to advance their interests and values."[11] Since public diplomacy is based on communication and aims to build non-coercive relationships, it constitutes a central avenue of social power.[12]

Obviously, influencing opinions and actions of other actors stands at the core of international politics, and goes back to the ancient Greeks and Rome, as well as the Byzantium and the Italian Renaissance. As Nicholas Cull has argued: "Ancient examples [of public diplomacy] include the Greek construction of the great library at Alexandria, the Roman Republic's policy of inviting the sons of 'friendly kings' from their borders to be educated in Rome, and the Byzantine Empire's sponsorship of Orthodox evangelism across the Slavic lands."[13] The battle of ideas has obviously been of all ages.[14] The exact term "public diplomacy" can be traced back to a retired American diplomat Edmund Gullion. When Gullion became dean of the Fletcher School of Diplomacy at Tufts University in Boston, in the mid 1960s, he suggested that the US needed a more benign alternative to terms like propaganda and psychological warfare, mainly to stress the contrast with the manipulative practices and totalitarian nature of the USSR. The term was thereafter widely used by the USIA, and was applied to a wide scope of activities ranging from cultural diplomacy, exchange diplomacy, to international broadcasting.

Cultural diplomacy attempts to manage a country's cultural resources and achievements, including its language, as we have seen in Chapter 3.[15] Given its long pedigree, cultural diplomacy remains at the core of what public diplomacy aims to achieve: to touch the general public and elites of other countries in a way that generates more understanding and support for one's own interests, ideas, and values.[16] To these ends, exchange diplomacy has also played a significant role. Sending one's citizens (oftentimes students) abroad and accepting foreign citizens to work and/or study has been the staple of public diplomacy programs such as the Fulbright and Rhodes Scholarships since World War II.[17] Over the decades, Washington has been especially effective in attracting foreign students so that they can become familiar with the US, which has generated a wide international network of support and sympathy for things American, including its foreign policies. As we have seen, Beijing is combining all these strands of public diplomacy in an assertive policy to massage away the apprehensions about China's economic, political, and military rise.[18]

Today's public diplomacy fits well in a world where networks and fluid relationships among multiple actors with fuzzy roles abound. Where classical diplomacy centers around high-level talks and conferences, public diplomacy is about direct interaction, for example through blogs and music festivals. It is argued that this shift is due to the fact that, in a globalized, networked international environment, ordinary people have become increasingly important. In politics, state sovereignty is challenged by people power generated by the global triumph of democracy.[19] In economics, wealth is created more by weightless assets like knowledge and skills (which belong to individuals), than by physical assets and resources (which belong to states). Even in the area of security, human security and identity questions are crowding out classical inter-state rivalry as the key concern and dominant paradigm.[20] As Mark Leonard and Vidhya Alakeson argue in their study *Going Public* (2000), "with an unprecedented spread of democracy, our ability to win over other governments will depend in part on how we are perceived by the populations they serve."[21]

Public diplomacy depends on, and is rooted in, communication. The social power derived from this strategy hinges on other actors knowing of one's positive and alluring policies and qualities. It is key to spread the social knowledge about one's attractiveness—or, in the case of new public diplomacy: the importance of certain policy issues[22]—otherwise little social power can de derived and used. This explains why the importance of social power has increased with the onset of a new media era, since, in a world where IT is cheap, wide-spread, and evasive, communication has become simpler. The mechanisms used to communicate with foreign audiences, often across the world, have moved to new, real-time and global technologies, especially the Internet. Radio, TV, and printed media are still important, but satellite, YouTube, and Twitter are now considered more effective, and certainly quicker and more economical. As a result, these new technologies blur the once rigid lines between domestic and international news spheres. What is said in Berlin for a specific German audience is heard in Beijing, Baghdad, and beyond.

What is more, public diplomacy increasingly uses, even mimics, the concepts that are developed for commercial marketing and branding. As we will see in the next chapter, place branding—which deals with managing the emotional ties between territory and people—is now integrated into the best practices of public diplomacy. Those who study and exercise public diplomacy find notions of social power and brand management of great relevance, moving away from the classical terminology of (national) image and prestige management. Concepts like honor belong to a medieval mindset, it is argued, whereas legitimacy and branding are deemed more relevant to understanding the challenges of globalization. Public diplomacy is the use of social power *par excellence*, since it explicitly rescinds from the use of coercion (as well as payment), whilst pushing norms and values and influencing the beliefs and identities of foreign audiences.[23]

But today's public diplomacy is not only focused on bringing out a targeted message, it also strives to build relationships with others. It is therefore less about authority, telling others what to do, as it is about showing others what we consider to be desirable, in the hope (and expectation) that it will be emulated. This relationship does not need to be between a government and a foreign audience, but could well be between two audiences, foreign to each other, whose communication and interaction a specific government wishes to facilitate. For example, in 2008, British diplomats started a public diplomacy campaign to appeal to public opinion in 20 countries across the globe to get support for a plan to deal with climate change. Interestingly, British public diplomacy includes engagement with American public opinion as well as key public officials in those American states that have agreed to cut carbon emissions regardless of the Bush administration's refusal to commit itself to binding targets at a national level. By successfully engaging American and European publics, public diplomacy is considered a useful way to shape a cooperative transatlantic foreign policy agenda.[24] Unlike propaganda, public diplomacy is therefore less about "getting the message out", as it is about creating a wider, perhaps even global community, which is susceptible to a way of thinking that is considered desirable. As a consequence, it is less about telling than about listening; it is less about spreading information than about facilitating and networking.[25]

Today, few international actors do without a consolidated public diplomacy program, whether they are Great Powers like the US, the EU, and China, or international actors like Amnesty International, Shell, and the Roman Catholic Church.[26] Public diplomacy's aim of a balanced partnership is attractive since, by using social power, it rejects the classical paradigm of military power projection and information dominance. Several recent cases illustrate how these postmodern, public diplomacy efforts work. For example, former US vice-president Al Gore's efforts to place climate change on top of the global agenda have been effective since he made use of modern media and technology (mainly the Internet and a movie called *An Inconvenient Truth*). Gore did not receive official backing from the US Bush administration, which made him more, not less, credible to both the general public and relevant policy elites. Similarly, British prime minister Tony Blair's efforts to get attention focused on the economic and humanitarian plight of Africa made him align to popstars such as Bob Geldof and Bono (who had both campaigned for Africa before), and aid agencies like the Jubilee Debt Campaign and Make Poverty History to gain global support for what was ultimately British government policy. This led up to 2005, the Year of Africa, when the UK chaired both the G8 and held the EU Presidency, putting Africa successfully at the top of the agendas of both IOs.[27]

Public diplomacy efforts like these aim to unleash the energy of other societies, creating wider, often global communities that support foreign policy goals whose achievement requires consorted action by many players. Looking at the list of political challenges that confront all societies (from demographic pressures and fatal diseases, to organized crime, terrorism, and environmental threats), it is evident that broad international cooperation and a multilateral approach are key elements to any credible and sustainable solution. The problem is, however, that countries with mature democracies and functioning economies who support the idea of multilateralism are by far the minority. In terms of population, underdeveloped autocracies may outnumber democracies five to one.[28] As Leonard and Alakeson rightfully argue, "the greatest challenge will be to win over the publics of countries that are excluded. Most peoples around the world do aspire to join the club of developed democracies but the leaders of China, India, Pakistan, Russia and many smaller countries are—to varying degrees—still thinking in terms of the old balance of power game."[29] Public diplomacy, akin to the famous Heineken slogan, aims to touch parts of the global body politic other strategies cannot reach, namely international public opinion. Winning the hearts and minds of these foreign audiences, and setting the foreign policy agenda, constitutes the bulk of all public diplomacy. Public diplomacy frames debates, sets the (global) agenda, and establishes the parameters of legitimate policy solutions.[30] By challenging accepted notions of what is good, normal, and legitimate, public diplomacy confronts the hard power paradigm of Realpolitik with the alternative of social power.

This chapter examines the place of contemporary public diplomacy in the expanding topography of social power. Since the US experience has shaped the academic debate as well as the practice of public diplomacy, it will be most useful to start our examination there. In the US, public diplomacy is widely seen as a strategy to win over the hearts and minds of foreign communities, and convince them that their values, goals, and desires are similar to America's. Since 9/11, the Bush administration has therefore initiated a flurry of initiatives to open a dialogue with the Muslim world, and tried to alter America's image from a global bully to a compassionate hegemon. The argument has been that "millions of ordinary people (…) have greatly distorted, but carefully cultivated images of [the US]—images so negative, so weird, so hostile that a young generation of terrorists is being created."[31] US policy towards the Muslim world is based on the assumption that these negative ideas should be neutralized and, in the end, changed, by a focused effort of public diplomacy. This approach has quickly become a central plank of America's war on terror.[32]

Much of this chapter offers a case study of the wielding problem which bedevils the study of social power. The modest success of a communication giant such as the US in its efforts to use social power after 9/11 indicates that the size and material resources of an actor are by no means a guarantee for success in this new postmodern power game. As Richard Holbrooke argued, immediately after 9/11: "How could a mass murderer who publicly praised the terrorists of Sept. 11 be winning the hearts and minds of anyone? How can a man in a cave outcommunicate the world's leading communications society?"[33] America's experiences with public diplomacy therefore shed light on the promise (and limits) of social power in international politics.

6.2 WIELDING SOCIAL POWER

It is, of course, a cliché to argue that 9/11 has changed the world. But this is only partially true. In many respects, not much has changed at all: most people continue to face the same every day problems as before. Moreover, the vast majority of the world's population has never seen a Boeing 767 or a skyscraper, much less one flying into the other. For the world's poor, the American fear of terrorism seems overdone compared to their daily struggle for survival. This adds to the image of an aggressive and militant US, and feeds into the anti-Americanism that already finds a fertile soil in most of the Muslim world.[34] Still, the terrorist attacks of 9/11 have challenged—even provoked—America's identity as a superpower. Many Americans were shocked to be confronted with such a violent hatred against their country and everything it stands for: its foreign policies as well as its values. Could anyone dislike the country that offers Harvard *and* Hollywood, McDonald's *and* Microsoft?[35] "Why do people hate us so much?" soon became a key question, not only for ordinary Americans, but for policymakers in Washington as well.

From the outset it was therefore clear that the US is not only fighting a war on international terrorism by classical, military means, but is also engaged in efforts to get the moral and political support of the Muslim world. The gritty videotapes of Osama bin Laden that emerged from a cave in Tora Bora directly after 9/11 were shown to a global TV audience, indicating that the media were both the weapons and the battlefield of choice for this war. In America's new quest for sympathy and support across the globe, media, PR, and marketing specialists would no longer be a sideshow to traditional, government-to-government diplomacy. No surprise, therefore, that US Secretary of State Colin Powell defined American diplomacy as follows: "We're selling a product. That product we are selling is democracy."[36] An indication of this approach was the appointment of Charlotte Beers, former chairman of advertising agencies J. Walter Thompson and Ogilvy & Mather, to Under Secretary of State for Public Diplomacy and Public Affairs, in October 2001.[37] Just as the Pentagon has enlisted the help of Hollywood's creative thinkers to brainstorm possible terror events and solutions (see Chapter 5), Beers asked her former Madison Avenue colleagues to help sell Uncle Sam to an unreceptive Muslim world.[38]

All this was not new, since the US had been confronted with similar challenges over the last century and each time invented new means and mechanisms to communicate its message, and establish a long-term relationship with new foreign communities.[39] For example, a Committee on Public Information was set up during World War I, followed by the Office of War Information and the Advertising Council (whose official aim was to "out-Goebbels Goebbels") to win over hearts and minds (both at home and abroad) during World War II. During the Cold War, the USIA was engaged in a wide range of activities, from managing information and exchange programs, to cultural events.[40] In the 1980s, President Reagan established the Office of Public Diplomacy mainly to manage the media and encourage support for America's covert wars in Central America. More recently, the Clinton administration set up a special office to address the Serbian people, encouraging them to overthrow their dictator Slobodan Milosevic.[41] This is, of course, a mixed bag of public diplomacy efforts, with equally mixed results.

Elaborate public opinion research showed an "Arab world that fears the United States as a threat to its way of life, a Europe that largely does not trust the United States and wants to pull further away, and a dwindling support for the U.S.-led war on terror."[42] Following Nye's argument that "soft-power resources are slower, more diffuse, and more cumbersome to wield than hard-power resources",[43] governmental Advisory Committees, Task Forces, and Hearings concluded that this anti-Americanism could not be solved by a quick and easy fix.[44] Instead, Washington should take the political, cultural, and religious beliefs of others into account while formulating and communicating its own policies in order to make American actions better understood, accepted, and hence more effective. It was realized that this was a crucial time for getting the hard–social power mix right, and the mistakes made in Vietnam must not be repeated, where lack of domestic and international support ultimately eroded the political basis of America's military engagement.

Despite these wise counsels, the Bush administration's public diplomacy initially focused on "selling" the war against Iraq, claiming that this was not just a war, but a "just war" which could not (and should not) be avoided. Almost inevitably, some of the selling of the Iraqi war could also easily be labeled propaganda, information warfare, and most certainly perception management.[45] It was used to put pressure on foreign governments to toe the US-line and accept its concept of preventive war. American foreign policymakers worked on the mistaken assumption that Saddam Hussein's regime change and the democratization of Iraq (and the rest of the Middle East) would convince doubters and silence critics. Under the optimistic motto that "nothing succeeds like success", the social power factor of legitimacy was ignored, expecting that the smoking gun of Iraqi weapons of mass destruction (WMD) capabilities and facilities would offer ample *post hoc* compensation. The (then) dominant neoconservative mood in Washington gladly ignored words of advice and caution, convinced as it was that America's victory was historically inevitable. What is more, neoconservatives seemed to imply that the very lack of a UN mandate signaled the dawn of a new era of American supremacy, officially constituting the *Pax Americana* they longed for. This approach assumed that the US "is strong enough to do as it wishes with or without the world's approval and should simply accept that others will envy and resent it."[46]

However, the lack of legitimacy quickly turned into one of the main obstacles for the US (and its coalition partners) to stabilize Iraq. The vast majority of European and Muslim public opinion already seriously questioned the rationale for a preventive war on Iraq in the first place. In particular, since no Iraqi WMD program was found, the argument for intervention became flimsy and unconvincing. After the speedy collapse of Saddam Hussein's regime, the aim has therefore been to gain international support and legitimacy to make a democratic Iraq a showcase of reform in the Middle East. President Bush made it clear that "Iraqi freedom will succeed, and that success will send forth the news, from Damascus to Tehran—that freedom can be the future of every nation (…) America has put its power at the service of principle. We believe that liberty is the design of nature; we believe that liberty is the direction of history."[47] It is, however, risky to bet on output legitimacy if the desired output (a stable and democratic Iraq) requires international cooperation.

To some extent, this shambles of post-9/11 US public diplomacy comes as a surprise. American policymakers should have learned from their experiences in the Balkan and Gulf wars of the 1990s, that a political mandate of the "international community" (preferably the UN Security Council) normally comes with the handy permission to use foreign bases, allied troops, financial means to fund the operation, and—most importantly—the credibility and status of legitimacy. As mentioned in Chapter 1, legitimacy is a crucial factor to socialize power, and essential to mold public opinion, determining what is normal, desirable, and justified. If anything, America's war in Iraq illustrated the limits of hard power, and the centrality of social power.

Over the years, and with the stabilization effort in Iraq facing serious problems, Washington has come to acknowledge these limits, and put more emphasis on the opportunities for a renewed and intensified democratic dialogue between the US and the Muslim world. Washington's intensified public diplomacy efforts after 9/11 therefore follow a well-established tradition of using America's social power resources as a means to communicate with foreign publics, and shape their norms and beliefs. As I mentioned in an earlier chapter, after having won the Cold War, the US largely neglected public diplomacy for a decade in the belief that its own societal model was no longer seriously challenged by an ideological competitor.[48] This implied that international broadcasting (e.g., through the Voice of America) and international exchange programs (e.g., through the USIA) were scaled down in the expectation that, once liberated, the "captive nations" of Central and Eastern Europe would spontaneously opt for the Western model of liberal democracy and an open economy. This proved to be a costly mistake. Republican Senator John McCain even labeled the abolishment of the USIA as "unilateral disarmament in the war of ideas."[49] The events of 9/11 have been a rude awakening that America's societal model remains vulnerable and that continued efforts are required to neutralize critics and sway skeptics. Public diplomacy is now seen as the key to make up for this decade of complacency by reinvigorating America's unique and underutilized social power.

6.3 WINNING THE WAR OF IDEAS

America's public diplomacy aspires, at least for now, to *enter* into a dialogue with the Muslim world, a dialogue which hardly exists at the moment. US public diplomacy should therefore be differentiated from information warfare since it is less focused on the domination of communication flows, as it is on creating a Habermasian practice of democratic discourse aimed at finding shared assumptions and values. This quest for deliberative legitimacy based on structured and inclusive dialogue sets it apart from the old-style public diplomacy of past decades, when dialogue was practically impossible and communication had a one-way character. It has, however, proven difficult to develop such a balanced public diplomacy approach towards the Middle East in the face of the stark realities of war and violence in Afghanistan and Iraq.[50] As we argued earlier, Washington's message was less "let's argue!" (about democracy and freedom), as "listen to us, or else…!" The US has often engaged in "verbal fighting" (or "representational force"), since its public diplomacy efforts have been *perceived* as attempts to bully another audience into agreement with America's norms and policies.[51] The temptation has remained huge for US administrations to use public diplomacy as a weapon on the information battlefield, rather than to engage in democratic, non-coercive communications with the Muslim world.[52]

Within this broader context, there are three basic concepts that underpin current US public diplomacy. *First*, it rejects the Huntingtonian vision of a pending clash of civilizations and instead clings to Fukuyama's end of history thesis.[53] For example, the US National Security Strategy (2002) argues that it should be clear that there is only one "single sustainable model for national success: freedom, democracy, and free enterprise."[54] We may safely assume that the White House here has had the American model in mind. This implies that Islam is not seen as a credible, let alone viable, political program offering an alternative to Western modernity. This assumption has major implications for US public diplomacy, since Islamic culture and Muslim society are considered compatible with Western values and institutions. President Bush has therefore continuously argued that the US is fighting a war against "evil", and not against Islam.

US public diplomacy seems to take for granted that Islamic culture accepts the constituent elements of modernity, and that all Muslims have an innate, be it somewhat repressed, desire to support both liberal democracy and capitalism. This implies that, despite the obvious political differences between the US and (at least some) Muslim countries, American and Islamic culture do not clash, but are in agreement. It further assumes that although ordinary Muslims may be opposed to US policies in the Middle East, they continue to be drawn to American values like individual choice and freedom. This distinction between hostile, extremist Islamic governments and political groupings, and the "silent majority" of a wider and larger Muslim community around the world is a central tenet of America's public diplomacy, based on the claim that "the peoples of the world, especially those ruled by unelected regimes, comprise our true allies. We are allies because we share common aspirations—freedom, security, prosperity—and because we often face common enemies, namely the regimes that rule over them."[55]

A *second* concept underlying US public diplomacy is the inclusion of a wide variety of non-state actors to reach out to foreign communities to achieve strategic objectives. Much of America's social power derives from its economic and cultural hegemony, where commercial and ideational normalcy is set by brands and cultural icons. America's popular culture is appreciated as a valuable and pervasive avenue of social power, infusing the world with the same values and norms that underpin US foreign policy. As one proponent argued, "we must draw upon the talents in the private sector who have acquired practical experience in the creation and promotion of compelling images and ideas here and around the world."[56] Instruments of public diplomacy include media, education and exchanges, culture, sports as well as more classical diplomatic avenues. A report of the US Advisory Commission on Public Diplomacy acknowledges that "[b]rands, products, popular entertainment, higher education, corporations, and Web sites all may reinforce or undermine U.S. foreign policy objectives."[57] One could therefore argue that public diplomacy utilizes all modes of social power discussed in this book, from culture, law, and media, to the most recent opportunities offered by place branding.

Public diplomacy's task is to appeal to the core values of foreign communities, often by using new techniques which are frequently directly derived from commercial practice. Since these efforts go beyond spreading information, a natural relationship has evolved with professionals in the (place) branding sector.[58] In order to be successful, public diplomacy officials need to identify target audiences in each country and/or region, and tailor strategies and tools to reach these communities in a variety of different ways. Linguistic barriers and cultural nuances obviously hinder the effectiveness of generic, one-size-fits-all public diplomacy efforts. Specialized knowledge is required to develop a better, more detailed, understanding of audiences in the Muslim world. In general, two-way communication and interaction with such target audiences are preferred, although it still remains the exception rather than the rule. The aim is to breach the culturally and politically determined sphere of mediated images of the "world out there" within Muslim societies. Public diplomacy seeks to challenge the world views of foreign communities and to bridge the gap between areas of cultural apartheid.

As we discussed in Chapter 5, the emotional power of America's media industry is considered an especially valuable ally in this new approach. Commercial TV programs, Hollywood movies, and other cultural products (from poetry and other art, to cuisine and folklore) are all supposed to communicate a better and more durable understanding of the country's essence. Mainstream American TV programs and movies are expected to reinvigorate America's reputation by projecting images of individual freedom and endless opportunity.[59] As we concluded earlier, communities in the Middle East, Asia, and elsewhere take much of their ideas of what the US is all about from American TV series and movies. The social power imbued in these images and narratives may well be greater than any description of the US and its values offered through governmental channels. We have also seen that, despite the rise of satellite TV and access to the Internet, much of Arab society remains closed to America's voice.[60] What is more, depending upon mass media to communicate with the Arab world remains problematic, since "[i]n the Arab world, more people get their news from their neighbours or people whom they know (…) If America relies primarily on mass media to get its message out, it may find its message further distorted on a mass media scale."[61] In addition, one could hardly expect that watching *The Sopranos* or *Weeds* will instill values and norms that sit well with America's strategic vision for the Middle East and beyond.[62]

The *third* concept upon which public diplomacy is based is its inherent two-pronged character: it does not only open a dialogue with others, but also assumes that this dialogue and interaction has a certain effect on one's own beliefs, even one's identity. David Baldwin has argued that all power is exercised in a reciprocal relationship between two or more actors.[63] Although social power involves the ability to set legitimate standards, norms, and values, it is just to be expected that all norm entrepreneurs are themselves susceptible to other norms and values. The events of 9/11 have therefore not only triggered renewed efforts to strengthen and reinvigorate America's image, but also generated a process of reflection on what America

124 *Public diplomacy*

actually stands for (or, perhaps better, *should* stand for). However, the margins for such a review of America's identity have proven limited. In order to be effective, public diplomacy should open communications between communities, not based on a line of command, but aimed at facilitating and networking. Although the US has certainly made serious efforts in that direction (see below for examples), this has proven extremely difficult, mainly since the aspired openness of public diplomacy stands in sharp contrast with the emotional retrenchment that goes with "war."

Rather than holding America's identity to the light, post-9/11 public diplomacy has strengthened already strong feelings of patriotism, spilling over into jingoism. Directly after 9/11, Beers' Office requested the Ad Council—which specializes in so-called Public Service Announcements (PSAs)—to develop messages capturing the essence and value of American freedom and democracy. One such commercial ("I am an American") shows American citizens of different races and religions expressing their patriotism. Another shows a typical American suburban street with the caption "9/11 has changed the USA for ever", where after the picture fades the same street is shown with American flags flying from every house. It is important to stress that these ads were aimed at the *American* people, but were of course also part of a broader exercise to reposition and recharge America's image abroad. These efforts to affect Americans' self-perception also impact upon the way outsiders—in this case the Muslim world—see US policy objectives and weigh up Washington's determination to pursue them.

6.4 PUBLIC DIPLOMACY IN PRACTICE

So how has American public diplomacy worked in practice? One of the key recommendations coming out of the Advisory Committees and Task Forces has been to immediately develop a coherent strategy, making public diplomacy a genuine priority. This has proven to be difficult enough, given the multitude of agencies, offices, and working groups who all feel responsible for communicating America's message to foreign audiences. Shortly after 9/11, the Office of Strategic Information (OSI) was created to "sell" American policies in the Middle East, Asia, and Europe, and to generate as much support as possible for the US-led war on terror. However, the OSI came under scrutiny in February 2002, because it was suggested that the Pentagon misused it to deceive the public and media on the reasons and realities of the war on terror. Within a week, the Pentagon closed down OSI, mainly because its reputation (and hence credibility) was seriously damaged.[64]

In July 2002, a new start was made to reinvigorate America's public diplomacy. After years of cutbacks, the US Congress passed a bill allocating significantly more funds to public diplomacy efforts, and authorized funding for several new programs, such as a 24-hour TV network aimed to compete with Al Jazeera. At the same time, the White House set up a new Office of Global Communications (OGC), taking over the initiative from Mrs Beers and giving the public diplomacy effort both more exposure and political weight. As its name indicates, this Office was intended to coordinate the administration's foreign policy messages and supervise its image around the globe. A few months later, it was announced that the OGC would oversee a US$200 million PR blitz against Iraq using advanced marketing techniques to persuade crucial target groups that Saddam Hussein should be ousted. The OGC has focused on winning the daily soundbite battle and dominating every news cycle. It has worked closely together with the Coalition Information Center (CIC), with offices in Washington DC, London, and Islamabad. These were the so-called "instant response forces" who were ready 24/7 to neutralize negative information and news. On top of that, the Iraq Public Diplomacy Group—an Inter-Agency Taskforce—has targeted newspaper editors, foreign policy think-tanks, and media in Europe and the Middle East to convince them of the war's necessity.[65]

Since public diplomacy obviously goes way beyond printed books and aims to apply the most up-to-date communications techniques and methods, specialized agencies and consultancies have been signed up to generate new ideas and projects which the US government hesitates to undertake itself. Since public diplomacy oftentimes involves intercultural communication, serious efforts were made to adapt the US political message to reflect the cultural sensitivities of foreign (usually Muslim) publics. New marketing and PR methods were introduced to communicate with this target audience. This requires skills which diplomats cannot be expected to master, at least not instantly and with the requisite practical expertise. It is therefore little wonder that much of America's public diplomacy activities have been outsourced to private communications agencies. This indicates Washington's policy to embrace the social power potential of a wide range of NGOs, commercial firms, and public figures.[66]

This decision to outsource major parts of US public diplomacy to PR firms has introduced market-oriented research to get a better appreciation of how America's image and message should be positioned more effectively. Only a few initiatives have been developed to open the much-heralded free communicative space in which US and Muslim communities might find each other (see below). Since cultural sensitivity is especially required to package political messages, it may be less important *what* you say, as to how others *hear* and *understand* it. In the world of PR and marketing, this has been pointed out *ad nauseam*, but it has remained largely unheeded in the rushed daily practice of diplomacy and politics. This implies that US public diplomacy, in order to be effective, should be more sensitive to these cultural differences and identify the norms and values which are shared by the Western and the Islamic world. This requires careful research and analysis.

Some research outcomes indicate that many of the core values of American society are fundamentally opposed by significant parts of the Islamic world, and that although the cultures do share many of the same values, they also obviously set different priorities from amongst them. Zogby International—an opinion research group which regularly surveys Middle Eastern attitudes—suggests that the top five Muslim values are faith, family, justice, ambition, and knowledge. In the US the priority is freedom, family, honesty, self-esteem, and justice. American public diplomacy efforts therefore focused on *shared* cultural priorities, namely family and children.[67] These cultural differences also affect the method and style of communication. It has, for example, been argued that "[i]n the Arab world, emotional neutrality, in an emotionally charged context, can be perceived as deception. If one hides one's emotions, what else is being hidden?"[68] This implies that the typically American direct and rational approach often does not work and may even be counterproductive. American public diplomacy has therefore taken a leaf from the book of commercial branding, which assumes that an emotional relationship based on trust must be built gradually, rather than through one-off, outspoken messages which may well be viewed as offensive and culturally alien.

Strategic communications firms have been used to cover the whole gamut of technology and media to reach the Islamic world in order to achieve these objectives.[69] These firms are also engaged in classical propaganda, ranging from leaflet bombs (picturing women beaten by the Taliban, with the message "Is this the future you want for your children and your women?"), to actions like dropping wind-up radios that can only tune into a single channel: Voice of America.[70] Other initiatives include setting up "Radio Sawa" ("Radio Together"), and airing programs like "Good Morning Egypt", and "Next Chapter." Radio Sawa is an Arab-language broadcasting service aimed at younger people, mixing Western pop music, sports, and weather, sandwiched by twice-an-hour newscasts. Shows like "Good Morning Egypt" screen interviews with ordinary Americans to counterbalance some of the stereotypes US TV programs and movies tend to offer. "Next Chapter" is a hip, MTV-inspired show broadcast in Farsi to Iran (and simulcast on the radio and over the Internet).[71] These are shows portraying the US as an open, tolerant society where all religions are practiced on the basis of equality. Arab language websites and print publications are also part of this effort.[72] In 2008, US-funded international broadcasts such as Voice of America, Radio Sawa, and Radio Free Asia topped a 175 million audience weekly, which is a 75 percent increase from 2001. US funding for educational programs has more than doubled since 2003, to US$500 million. The State Department has increased spending on public diplomacy to US$1.6 billion, up from about US$600 million between 2001 and 2007.[73]

The biggest problem with America's public diplomacy has been its reluctance to accept the inherent reciprocal nature of social power. For example, the US government (in close cooperation with the communications firms it employs) has put pressure on national and foreign media to spin the news and stick to the privileged White House scripts. Western media are, in general, independent enough to overcome official pressure to follow any party-line. However, the atmosphere of being under siege and engaged in war (against Al Qaeda, Iraq, and still unknown other terrorists and rogue states) encourage both self-censorship and official censorship.[74] A few weeks after 9/11, CNN's standards and practices department sent out a memo that read: "We must remain careful not to focus excessively on the casualties and hardships in Afghanistan that will inevitably be a part of this war, or to forget that it is the Taliban leadership that is responsible for the situation Afghanistan is now in." The memo went on to suggest that reporters might also want to tell viewers that the war is in response to a terrorist attack "that killed close to 5,000 innocent people in the U.S."[75] Another example has been that both President Bush and British Prime Minister Tony Blair have summoned their national media to censor any tapes by Osama bin Laden. Downing Street press officers even coined the nickname "Spin Laden" to illustrate the point that these videotapes could not just contain "secret messages" to sleeping terrorist cells across the globe, but are a part of Al Qaeda's propaganda efforts.[76]

Based upon the experiences of two Bush administrations, Bruce Gregory has offered three key lessons for America's public diplomacy.[77] First, abandon message influence dominance. Since public diplomacy occurs in a complex media environment, the message that is actually received by the target audience is the most important. This implies that message control is an illusion, since much of it is lost in the white noise of reality.[78] Second, Gregory suggests that framing the narrative is key. The war on terror framework has been counterproductive, and a new frame should be found which offers a more forward-looking, constructive context. Third, new actors should be involved in public diplomacy, bringing a new dynamic in communication, and achieving more interaction with target audiences, encouraging a so-called "diplomacy of deeds." Providing health care, education, and humanitarian assistance, Gregory argues, is more effective than empty words.[79]

US Undersecretary of State for Public Diplomacy and Public Affairs James K. Glassman (who accepted his post in summer 2008) has heeded Gregory's advice, understanding that the US should change its public diplomacy-course. Glassman has introduced a "public diplomacy for the 21st century", aimed at "understanding, informing, engaging, and influencing foreign publics", based on the assumption that the "threats that America faces and the goals that we want to achieve are profoundly dependent on influencing foreign publics—not with arms, not even with arm-twisting, but with the softer power of ideas."[80] He acknowledges that "[o]ur aim is not to preach, but to encourage interaction that will lead to the understanding of principles and policies of the United States."[81] This involves more student and cultural exchanges, especially with the Arab world, introducing Web 2.0 to the Middle East and beyond, as well as giving access to social networks (like Facebook) in regions where communication remains difficult.

Glassman suggests that "the aim of the war of ideas is not to persuade foreign populations to adopt more favorable views of America and its policies. Instead, the war of ideas tries to ensure that negative sentiments and day-to-day grievances toward America and its allies do not manifest themselves in the form of violent extremism."[82] Glassman therefore claims that "[o]ur priority is not to promote our brand but to help destroy theirs."[83] US public diplomacy toward the Muslim world therefore aims to reframe terrorism from an act of *jihad* into one of shame and hostility towards life itself. The main goal is less making Muslims like (let alone love) the US and all it stands for, as to point at and offer alternatives, especially to impressionable segments of the population who might be susceptible to recruitment into terrorism. Glassman claims some success of this approach, since support for suicide bombing throughout the Muslim world has dropped sharply.[84] US public diplomacy, Glassman suggests, is to achieve "a world in which the use of violence to achieve political, religious, or social objectives is no longer considered acceptable."[85] The main objective is therefore to delegitimize terrorism, and not necessarily to "love the US."[86] This is, of course, a remarkable change of heart compared with the "old" public diplomacy after 9/11.

But public diplomacy has obviously also become an integral part of the foreign policies of other major actors in international politics. Although this chapter has focused on the American example, the picture would hardly be complete without briefly examining the experiences of other key players on today's stage: China, the EU, and NATO.

6.5 PUBLIC DIPLOMACY GOES TRULY PUBLIC

It comes as little surprise that China, in particular, has discovered public diplomacy as a useful tool to manage its image as a cooperative, peace-loving, developing country, keen to play a constructive role in international politics. As we have seen in previous chapters, Beijing fully understands that it has to overcome, or at least neutralize, the suspicions in Asia as well as in the West about the economic, political, and strategic consequences of China's rise. As a one-party state with a centralist, even authoritarian regime, China obviously has direct control over the usual instruments of public diplomacy.[87] It can also fall back on a tradition of public diplomacy, which started in the early 1970s with the famous ping-pong diplomacy (using sport to open the world to China, and *vice versa*), and the famous Chinese pandas, which were used to give the country a less stern, and more cuddly image. Today, strengthening the notion of China's peaceful rise is the main objective of China's public diplomacy. Obviously, China's public diplomacy efforts are often based on the soft power of attraction. But public diplomacy also aims to influence foreign publics (especially in democracies) as part of a wider strategy to set norms and values which look favorably upon China's aim of rapid domestic growth and modernization.

China has lived through several recent PR disasters, most notably the Tiananmen crisis of 1989, which severely damaged China's political image, as well as the continuous tussles and skirmishes with Taiwan and over Tibet. Lurking in the background are the yearly Amnesty International and Freedom House reports on China's appalling human rights record. In order to neutralize opposition to China's peaceful rise, public diplomacy has been actively, and rather successfully, used to win the hearts and minds of relevant policy elites and communities around the world. The advantages of China's centralist approach to public diplomacy have become obvious, since the whole gamut of instruments has been used, ranging from China's global Voice of China (officially called China Radio International), broadcasting in all of the major world languages, active use of the Internet, to major cultural and sports events (with the 2008 Olympic Games as the obvious flagship). China has become extremely active in its cultural diplomacy, regularly organizing major cultural and trade events on all continents to showcase its long history and ancient culture, as well as its spirit of innovation. China is also making active use of the enormous overseas Chinese emigrant communities, who are called upon to be their (former) country's ambassadors abroad. In the US alone, 3.6 million Americans with a Chinese heritage are considered by their very presence to promote Chinese culture, and hence to be potential lobbyists for their homeland.

Public diplomacy 129

China has established numerous pro-China associations among these overseas communities, in an effort to get some grip on the image of China which they emanate. But even if central control from Beijing on the Chinese diaspora is illusory, Chinese emigrants play a useful role since they diversify and democratize China's public diplomacy.

Looking at China's public diplomacy today, the impression one gets is that of hyperactivity, even nervousness. This hyperactivity is orchestrated from China's State Council Foreign Publicity Office, whose official task is "to promote China as a stable country in the process of reform, a China that takes good care of its population, including the minorities, and works hard to reduce poverty."[88] China's state-centric approach to public diplomacy is not only a strength, but also a weakness. This came to the fore during the SARS crisis of summer 2003. As a direct result of China's misinformation campaign, this dangerous new disease was given time to develop from a largely controllable problem that could be stopped by quarantine into an almost inescapable global pandemic. As Ingrid d'Hooghe argues: "This is when China gets into the old Communist cramp of maintaining full control of society and concealing unfavorable information from the public, thus not only hampering the growth of China's soft power but also damaging cautious international impressions that China is moving towards a more open society."[89] According to d'Hooghe, China's current public diplomacy still carries with it the burdens of the country's state-controlled propaganda, which means that it "hampers the development of a modern model of public diplomacy that is based on an open dialogue and the policy networks of independent action."[90]

Given its network-oriented structure, the EU may be well-placed to develop a less centralized, but equally effective public diplomacy strategy.[91] Just as the EU has not dealt with cultural policy until quite recently (see Chapter 3), it has also kept its distance from managing its own reputation and image, and has been slow to use public diplomacy as an avenue of social power in its still nascent foreign and security policies. Still, as we have seen throughout this book, the EU is an effective norm entrepreneur, setting standards, and uploading rules and regulations to the global level. The EU's normative appeal, combined with its institutional flexibility and permeability, further explain its public diplomacy potential. As Vice-President of the European Commission Margot Wallström argued in October 2008: "We Europeans believe that public diplomacy plays a special role in the external relations of the European Union (…) The EU can be surprisingly robust on certain issues, even in its use of public diplomacy."[92] Be that as it may, the EU faces structural and political obstacles standing in the way of unlocking the Union's possibilities to reach out to foreign audiences, one of them being (as Wallström observed) that "the EU is in a curious position: for many citizens, the other 26 member states are still 'abroad'."

The EU's Directorate General (DG) Communication (headed by Wallström) is responsible within the European Commission for coordinating public diplomacy. Its 2005 Action Plan to Improve Communicating Europe by the Commission offers the usual wide range of public diplomacy initiatives and tools, from integrating public diplomacy in all the EU's external endeavors, to audiovisual services, active use of the Internet, dealing with journalists, and special events. But the EU goes well

130 *Public diplomacy*

beyond these classical public diplomacy tools, and realizes that "[c]ommunication is more than information: it establishes a relationship and initiates a dialogue with European citizens, it listens carefully and it connects to people. It is not a neutral exercise devoid of value, it is an essential part of the political process (...) [C]ommunication is a dialogue, not a one-way street. It is not just about EU institutions informing EU citizens but also about citizens expressing their opinions so that the Commission can understand their perceptions and concerns. Europe's citizens want to make their voices in Europe heard and their democratic participation should have a direct bearing on EU policy formulation and output."[93]

The subsequent White Paper on a European Communication Policy (2006) goes into great detail on how the EU can communicate with its own people, empowering its own citizens, and creating a European public sphere. Here, new technologies and media are especially privileged, and the EU has taken significant steps to bridge the gap between "Brussels" and "its" citizens. The European Commission published its new Internet strategy in December 2007, aimed at engaging citizens by communicating over the Web. More attention is to be paid to online videos, blogs, and RSS feeds.[94] In April 2008, the Commission also launched a Europe-wide multilingual radio broadcasting service (in 13 countries, using ten languages), bringing EU news to its citizens.

For our discussion, the use of public diplomacy as a social power channel is most relevant. The EU has taken numerous initiatives to reach out to its immediate neighborhood, mainly through its European Neighbourhood Policy (ENP), and the Euro-Mediterranean Partnership (Euromed). The ENP reaches out to countries to the EU's east who do not have a direct prospect of joining the Union, whereas the Euromed obviously connects with the EU's southern vicinity. Euromed, in particular, has developed into an effective public diplomacy tool, with projects such as the Audiovisual Program which supports regional TV and cinema projects, but also aims to preserve valuable archives. The Cinema Med project has sponsored many film festivals of Arabic cinema within the EU, and has helped with the distribution of Arabic films throughout the EU. The Euromed Youth Action Program organizes youth exchanges, training, and voluntary (NGO) service between the EU and its Mediterranean partners. The list of these programs can be continued at some length, indicating that the EU is less interested in sending its message in undiluted form towards its eastern and southern neighbors than it is in aiming to establish long-term, fruitful relationships based on mutual cooperation and understanding.

The main reason why the EU follows the path of *new* public diplomacy (rather than old-time neo-propaganda) may well be that it is difficult, if not impossible, for the Union to arrive at one, clearly-formulated foreign policy in the first place. Since it is hard for all EU member states to arrive at a unified message, the preferred route for public diplomacy is to establish networks and platforms which can be used for two-way communication. This leaves the ultimate message which is to be communicated ambiguous, but it effectively initiates an open dialogue as a prerequisite to using any social power at all.

But the EU's public diplomacy also takes a more direct route, most notably by the Commission's DG Development which provides generous amounts of foreign aid to developing countries. The EU is gradually learning the lesson from humanitarian NGOs that it is not only important to *do* good, but also to be *seen* doing good. To make amends, the Commission has started an information campaign (in 2006) with the slogan "Europe Cares." The overall purpose of this campaign is to "address wide-spread ignorance about the EU's position as the world's most significant aid donor with activities promoting development objectives across the globe."[95] The Europe Cares campaign has made active use of the Internet and other media for its promotion campaign, launching its own website, combined with audiovisual commercials on major European airlines and on the TV news channel EuroNews.

Similar promotion campaigns have been developed for DG ECHO (European Community Humanitarian Aid Office), which annually spends around €43 billion, and together with its member states is the largest aid donor in the world. Despite these impressive figures and achievements, ECHO's case is similar to that of DG Development since its public diplomacy potential hasn't been fully utilized due to under-funding, under-staffing, and poor communications. Philip Fiske de Gouveia and Hester Plumridge give several examples illustrating the poor branding of ECHO's operations: it did not receive enough public credit for its role as the first institution to reach the Asian tsunami (in 2004); it endures serious competition for aid visibility from USAID, as a much more centralized, experienced, and better funded institution; and it has trouble enforcing aid visibility clauses in aid-receiving countries. They also cite an official at the DG who reveals that ECHO recruited only two information officers for communication work covering the entire continent of Africa (in 2005).[96]

This brings me to the third case where public diplomacy has gone truly public: NATO. The Atlantic Alliance has only recently moved from thinking in terms of information to public diplomacy. It has learned the hard way that the war of ideas can be lost on the TV screen. During the 1999 NATO-led Kosovo war (or, in NATO's own nomenclature, "humanitarian intervention"), the Alliance conducted its first 24/7 media campaign led by spokesman Jamie Shea. Today, NATO not only has to win the hearts and minds of people in Afghanistan, but also within its own home base. It is clear that, without the support and trust of the Afghani people, Al Qaeda and the Taliban cannot be defeated. Equally, without the continued support of people at home, NATO will not be able to draw together sufficient troops and funds to maintain a long and expensive military operation. In this new security environment, member states have the luxury of choosing whether they commit troops to a NATO operation. Today's wars of choice encourage coalitions of the willing, turning troop contributions to NATO-led missions into a voluntary venture. This implies that the Alliance has to engage in public diplomacy to assure the support of its own member states, and their people. As an organization, NATO has to use its social power to strengthen the norm of transatlantic security cooperation, a standard which is eroding since the Cold War came to an end and liquid modernity crept in.[97]

Although most of these lessons were already learned in the 1990s, it took NATO until 2006 before it became truly active in the field of public diplomacy. After setting up a Public Diplomacy Division, it has made serious efforts to integrate communications and reputation management in all of NATO's activities, including its military operations. NATO Secretary General Jaap de Hoop Scheffer has argued that the Alliance is "not doing nearly well enough at communicating in this new information environment. And we are paying a price for it, not least in Afghanistan."[98] De Hoop Scheffer argues that NATO has to embrace the new media environment, including blogs, YouTube, and Facebook: "Information gathering has been democratized. Every soldier in the field has a videophone and a webpage (...) When there is an incident in Afghanistan, the Taliban are quick to say there have been a high number of civilian casualties. The wires pick it up—then the TV stations—then the web. This goes around the world in minutes. By the time we [i.e., NATO] have sent a team to investigate, checked the results, and put them through the approval system, our response comes days later—if we are lucky. By that time, we have totally lost the media battle."[99] NATO's Public Diplomacy Division has therefore introduced a specific Action Plan to give the Alliance the capability to take the lead in the field of video and the web, and has introduced *natochannel.tv* in April 2008 (at its Bucharest Summit), offering the general public and journalists a wide variety of video footage on NATO policies and operations.

To some extent, NATO encounters similar structural and political problems as the EU (and arguably most, if not all, other IOs) in sending its message out. Since member states disagree amongst themselves what message NATO should communicate (for example, is the International Security Assistance Force a reconstruction or a fighting mission? Or both?), public diplomacy becomes unfocused and generic. As we have seen in the case of the EU, this may be advantageous, since it allows for a non-hegemonic discourse, offering opportunities for foreign communities to engage in a useful debate about the nature of the problem and possible policy solutions. Still, the problems facing both the EU and NATO getting their public diplomacy act together illustrate the difficulty of communicating with target audiences in media-soaked societies. It has proven extremely difficult to "get the message out", particularly since the multilateral nature of these IOs has made it hard to arrive at a convincing and cohesive message in the first place. This is why both the EU and NATO have focused on opening channels of communication and building relationships, based on the assumption that verbal fighting and message control are futile efforts, whereas showing others what is considered desirable may strengthen the cherished norms of postnational governance and transatlantic security cooperation.

6.6 CONCLUSION

The problem with public diplomacy as a social power phenomenon is that we still lack detailed knowledge and a thorough understanding of how it works. How do certain fringe ideas become received wisdoms? What is the most effective way to change minds and win over hearts? What are the triggers that encourage the general public and elites to reframe the issues and think (as well as feel) differently? Knowledge is still very patchy on both the psychological and sociological aspects of these questions. What we do know, however, is that influencing the way people think, what they consider normal and desirable, is a key goal of any foreign policy, and touches upon the very roots of our debate on social power.

The examples offered in this chapter have brought the challenges of public diplomacy to the fore. The pull to drift from establishing channels of open communication into attempts at information dominance has proven real. It remains tempting to slide back into modern notions of control and hierarchy, and difficult to accept the postmodern requirements of flexibility in a new information age. However, to be successful in contemporary diplomacy implies openness and the capability and willingness to engage in multi-level cooperation with various types of actors. In this multi-actor international environment, effective public diplomacy requires different skills, attitudes, and management techniques compared to the mainstream diplomacy of the past. To set these new approaches apart from cultural and exchange diplomacy, Jan Melissen has introduced the label "new public diplomacy," which is "much more than a technical instrument of foreign policy. It has in fact become part of the changing fabric of international relations."[100] In the emerging, but still rather modest, literature on new public diplomacy, two features stand out illustrating how social power is both generated and used in contemporary international politics.[101]

First, new public diplomacy aims to create partnerships and platforms, which embodies the shift from the standard practice of advocacy to a so-called "ideas-based" public diplomacy strategy. Advocacy has been central to diplomatic practice, using communication tools to actively promote a particular policy or cause. The style of an ideas-based public diplomacy is not to use the megaphone and make claims, but to shape an idea or argument that will eventually be taken up and reproduced by others, and hence get a life of its own. It effectively applies social power and shapes (new) norms and values, but using different tactics. This is why the new public diplomacy may well try to boost the credibility of an idea by dissociating itself from it. For example, given America's limited credibility in the Muslim world, Washington often uses other, more neutral channels to spread its ideas and arguments. It also implies that an ideas-based public diplomacy may adopt an even broader approach by promoting an international environment that makes the spread of ideas possible in the first place. Here examples can be found in the United Kingdom, where the British Council worked together with the consultancy agency River Path Associates. River Path set up several blogs (e.g., during the World Summit on Sustainable Development in Johannesburg, in 2002, and around the debate on the new president of the World Bank, in 2005), which were actively used and provided a valuable opportunity for international dialogue on matters high on London's foreign policy agenda. Similarly, the EU sponsored the launch of a joint Israeli–Palestinian web-based dialogue project (called *bitterlemons.org*, set up in 2006), which soon reached more than 100,000 active participants in the region.[102] The new public diplomacy therefore goes beyond spreading ideas, but aims to facilitate and generate an international public platform that did not exist before.

There are good reasons why states have given leeway to NGOs in the public diplomacy process. States should perhaps acknowledge that NGOs may be better equipped, both mentally and in organizational set-up, to make optimal use of the new dynamic and rules of the social power game. States may still be good in mass media-driven, one-way communication, supported by cultural and educational exchanges. But over the last decade, NGOs have clearly demonstrated their power to set the international political agenda by framing debates on dealing with global poverty and global warming, as well as by campaigning to ban landmines. The success of the International Campaign to Ban Landmines (ICBL) illustrates how an informal network communication approach has made excellent use of social power's potential to shape policy outcomes. The story of the so-called "Ottawa process" is well-known.[103] Six prominent NGOs formed the ICBL in the early 1990s, and had attracted more than 1,000 NGOs from over 60 countries by 1996. The ICBL was a typical loose network, without a clear hierarchical structure, but made the most of its social power through network synergy. Relationships, coalitions, and trust were built up over the years, while its many members all over the world communicated via the Internet to coordinate events, distribute petitions, raise money, and, perhaps most importantly, educate the public media. This loose network of NGOs used their collective social power by gradually changing the attitude of key players towards banning anti-personnel landmines, effectively altering the standard and norm of responsible behavior in international politics. This did not occur through the classical negotiating pattern of conventional arms treaties where states would often take a decade to bargain behind closed doors, but in the astonishingly short period of less than two years, using an open, public debate where everyone could join in.

A *second* element of the new public diplomacy involves the practices of cultural, exchange, and broadcasting diplomacy which makes optimal use of the opportunities offered by today's new media. As we discussed in Chapter 5, the days that an exhibition or opera company could transgress the international cultural boundary and win hearts and minds are long gone. With increased technological connectivity, the porosity of borders, and the reality of mass migration, cultural exchange has acquired a truly new meaning. The US and Europe host, oftentimes involuntarily, millions of migrants from all over the world, whose impressions of their new "home" country turn them into unpretentious, yet important opinion-formers. Diasporic populations have always communicated with their kin at home through mail. But with the increase of new and cheap mass communication, these millions of (legal or illegal) ex-pats play an important role in how host countries, especially Western ones, are perceived around the world. Increasingly, the role of immigrants as a mechanism of international cultural communication is taken into account as an integral part of the new public diplomacy. In a way, it reflects the democratization of diplomacy, which implies that ordinary people become the main focus of diplomacy, rather than traditional elites.

But the development of new technological opportunities has even further widened the horizons of public diplomacy, beyond the real into the virtual. Several on-line virtual worlds have sprung up over the last few years, from the role playing game World of Warcraft (which claimed over 11.5 million monthly subscribers in 2009), to Second Life (which had just over 15 million accounts in 2008). Famously, Sweden opened the first "embassy" in Second Life, and many traditional diplomatic actors have considered following suit (and some of them actually did) towards the yet unknown vistas of cyberdiplomacy.[104] The advantage of opening a presence in these virtual environments is to enter into new debates, shaping new environments, from which new ideas and arguments may ultimately arise. Even online gaming is considered a (potentially) useful avenue for the new public diplomats. For example, a game like Peace Maker has allowed Israeli and Palestinian players to take a new and fresh look at their age-old dispute. The University of Southern California's Center for Public Diplomacy received a US$550,000 grant by the John D. and Catherine T. MacArthur Foundation in June 2007 to study how philanthropy might function in virtual worlds such as Second Life and There.com.[105] In a similar way, YouTube challenges the standards of classical broadcasting and is encouraging truly interactive programming where all people with minimal computer skills can play a role. This so-called peer-to-peer (P2P) revolution in the digital media has transformed the relationship between audiences, and has undermined the classical hierarchy on which traditional diplomacy used to be based.

These new developments suggest that the very nature of public diplomacy is changing rapidly. Traditional diplomatic actors (like states and IOs) have lost their monopoly and have to run very fast just to stay in the same place. Since gate-keepers, be they diplomats or other government officials, no longer control the flow of information on any issue of public relevance, citizens around the globe can react in any way they want using global media at negligible cost. It also means that diplomacy now increasingly takes shape in global public policy networks (see Chapter 4), which bring together actors from government, private business, and civil society, all aimed at finding common solutions to policy problems. Proponents of these new networks expect both more effectiveness and democratic legitimacy from governance that goes "beyond the nation-state."[106]

As we have seen in previous chapters, these changes and challenges require a recalibration of the relevance of hard and social power in international politics. All these new approaches clustered under the heading of public diplomacy suggest that social power is of growing importance, not just for states but for IOs and sub-state actors (like regions and cities) as well. The bottom-line for all actors in international politics is that the new realities of complex interdependence, globalization, the empowerment of public opinion, and the IT and media revolutions create opportunities as well as pressures to develop new methods and ways to get heard and achieve policy objectives. Whether one would like to call this a new era of Mediapolitik, Cyberpolitik, or Noopolitik,[107] all these new approaches are grappling with the challenge of how to get the ordinary citizen's attention, his/her loyalty, and even affection.

Surely, international diplomacy and politics have not changed completely—Realpolitik still plays a role of major importance. But "c'est le ton qui fait la musique", and the tone has truly changed over the past decade, giving priority to social power concerns, and privileging public diplomacy approaches as well as new strategies of place branding, which are discussed in the next chapter.

7 Place branding

7.1 INTRODUCTION

In the academic discourse on social power, the concept of place branding has acquired its proper, be it still somewhat awkward, place. In our study on the role of culture and media, and particularly the impact of public diplomacy, we have already come across the notion of branding, and place branding in particular. We are used to seeing brands all around us, bombarded as we are with commercial messages, signs, and appeals for our money, attention, commitment, and even devotion. From experience, we know that anything can be branded: Perrier branded water; American Express branded credit; and Intel branded computer components. But what exactly is *place* branding, how does it work, and why is it rapidly becoming such a hotly debated, because still controversial, concept, both amongst policymakers and academics? And, more particularly, how does place branding fit into our examination of social power's role in international politics?[1]

Let's start with a definition: Place branding can be considered an effort to manage, if not necessarily wield, the social power of a geographical location by using strategies developed in the commercial sector.[2] It is closely linked to public diplomacy since place branding tries to affect the image and perception of foreign as well as domestic communities regarding territorial entities, be they states, regions, or cities. Both place branding and public diplomacy use social power by uploading (new) norms and values, and occasionally pushing for (new) standards and rules.[3] Today, even IOs such as the EU, UN, and NATO are conscious of their brand, as are NGOs, universities, and media.[4] Place branding is inherently part of the constructivist paradigm, since it builds on the understanding that territorial actors have considerable agency in shaping their place and role in international politics. As this chapter will point out, states use place branding to affect, even modify, their reputation by similar means and processes to commercial brands. Since social power is the ability to set standards and determine what is normal and desirable, the relevance of place branding as a phenomenon in international politics should be evident.[5]

As the link with social power suggests, place branding goes beyond mere slogans or old-fashioned ad campaigns. It goes beyond placing territory on the map as an attractive tourist destination, and it is certainly not mere gloss or spin. In today's overcrowded marketplace of ideas, the image and reputation of a state have become essential parts of its strategic equity. For example, we have seen that legitimacy and credibility are key elements in socializing power, and precious assets that can only be built over the long term through relationships. But once legitimacy and credibility are attained and possessed, they constitute the backbone of all other policy actions of a state and a key to success. This is why Keohane and Nye argue that "[c]redibility is the crucial resource, and asymmetrical credibility is a key source of power."[6] They suggest that credibility is the "centre of gravity" of soft power, just as I argue that place branding is important to understand the nature of social power in contemporary politics.

All territorial actors already *have* a brand. They may not always realize this, but it is most certainly true. A place brand comprises "the totality of the thoughts, feelings, associations and expectations that come to mind when a prospect or consumer is exposed to an entity's name, logo, products, services, events, or any design or symbol representing them."[7] A place brand is (amongst others) determined by its culture, its political ideals, and its policies. In today's globalized and mediatized commercial marketplace, the corporate brand has become an essential part of a business identity which helps consumers to identify with the company, and—lest we forget—encourage them to buy its products and services. In a similar way, branding has become essential to create value in the relationship between territorial entities and individuals. Just as commercial brands invest a major part of their budget to establish and solidify the credibility of their image, today's territorial actors do the same. For students of international politics, one of the interesting questions is whether place branding entices people to "buy" the "products" of brand states, in other words: do they support a state's ideas and foreign policies?[8] As this chapter points out, states indeed use place branding to gain legitimacy, credibility, and trust, which have become major assets to realize their foreign policy goals.

The practice of place branding has taken off at a time when the role and power of states (and other territorial actors) is changing. States as well as IOs vie for authority, legitimacy, and loyalty in a dense and highly competitive political arena. Just as religious faith no longer has a monopoly in giving purpose to people's lives, the state can no longer claim the loyalty of "its" citizens. Patriotism, let alone nationalism, can no longer be taken for granted. States have therefore embarked upon a renewed quest for the hearts and minds of people, at home as well as around the world.[9] As we have seen, states have always used the best and newest technologies in their pursuit of legitimacy and power. For example, without the printing press, today's modern state would not even have come into existence.[10] It is therefore logical that states now add branding strategies to their arsenal of statecraft. Place branding therefore stands in a long tradition of innovations in statecraft and advances in the application of social power. Against this historical backdrop it becomes clear that the emerging brand state is not a brand new state, but a political player promoting itself more assertively than before ("Now even more efficient/clean/democratic/liberal…"), using the latest avenues of social power available to them.

Since place branding takes a leaf out of the book of commerce and marketing, it is clearly not only a political phenomenon; it also has an important economic motivation. States as well as regions and cities realize that they all offer the same product: territory, infrastructure, educated people, and an almost identical system of governance. And like Coke and Pepsi, states realize that they have to do a little extra, not just gaining the fleeting attention of potential consumers, but engaging in a long-term relationship built on trust, amity, and preferably loyalty.

The harmonizing effects of globalization and European integration put further pressure on territorial actors to develop, manage, and leverage their brand equity. Territorial actors compete with each other for investment, tourism, and political power, often on a global scale. As we have seen in previous chapters, Great Powers like the US and China, IOs like the EU, global firms like Microsoft, NGOs like Amnesty International, as well as new transnational networks and public–private partnerships all vie for the same "business", blissfully disregarding their unequal legal status and political weight. The state has become just one player amongst many, jockeying for position in search of authority and credibility; in short: in search of the social power to set standards and determine what is normal and desirable. Without a strong brand, norm entrepreneurs will find it hard to be successful. In order to stand out from the crowd and capture significant mind share and market share, place branding has become essential.

This means that having a good brand is more important than ever. For example, now that the market has moved manufacturing to the developing world where labor is cheap, what distinguishes the West from the rest is the simple fact that "we" have the respectable brands; many other states don't. The West has everything that counts, it has all the right labels, from "market economy" and "stability", to "democracy" and "security"; most other states don't. States also realize that their political and commercial images and reputations interact. This is most notable in the so-called country-of-origin effect which plays an important role in consumers' purchase decisions (*viz.* "German cars" and "Japanese cameras"). Since many companies remain associated with their countries of origin, the images and reputations of brands and states tend to merge in the minds of the global consumer. For example, for a global consumer public, it is not Korean history or culture that defines Korea itself, but rather Samsung's or LG's latest product line. As Choi Jung-wha, director of the Corea Image Communication Institute (CICI), argued in 2008: "The Samsung image equals the Korean image."[11] In many ways, Microsoft and Coca-Cola *are* America, just as Nokia *is* Finland (and *vice versa*).

As these cases indicate, place branding is no static game—quite the contrary. Although all states have an image and hence a brand, whether they like it or not, place branding has become an active endeavor for many territorial actors, offering numerous possibilities to finally take the levers of social power in their own hands.[12] In order to do their job right, policymakers all over the world have to carve out a brand niche for their state; to engage in competitive framing and marketing; to assure customer satisfaction; and, most of all, to create brand loyalty. The art of politics no longer centers around old-style diplomacy, but now also involves the art of brand-building and reputation management. This applies to all economic and political actors around the world, with no exceptions. Whether it is the US trying to "sell" democracy around the globe, or China convincing others of its "peaceful rise", place branding has become a central plank of their foreign policy strategies. And since place branding may generate authority, NGOs and transgovernmental policy networks, who generally lack Weberian legitimacy, especially consider place branding a good, and rather cheap, solution to their predicament.

Like public diplomacy, much of today's place branding is outsourced to professional branding consultants, and for good reasons. Most policymakers still lack the mindset and hands-on knowledge and experience to effectively construe and implement place branding strategies. These specialists offer their services to a wide variety of territorial actors, based on the claim that anything for which one can construct a mental inventory is, in principle, a brand. Brand managers offer four arguments for why branding is both necessary and beneficial for commercial and political actors alike: (1) Products, services, and locations have become so alike that they can no longer differentiate themselves by their quality, reliability, and other basic traits. Branding adds emotion and trust to these products, thereby offering clues that make consumers' choice somewhat easier; (2) This emotional relationship between brand and consumer ensures loyalty to the brand; (3) By creating an aspiration lifestyle, branding offers a kind of *ersatz* for ideologies and political programs that are losing their relevance; and (4) the combination of emotions, relationships, and lifestyle (values) allows a brand to charge a price premium for their products, services, and locations, which would otherwise hardly be distinguishable from generics.[13]

Although these four branding qualities apply most directly to commercial products and services, political actors find themselves in an environment dominated by similar pressures and parameters. Commercial brands compete with states for the allegiance, loyalty, as well as money of the customer-*cum*-citizen. In particular, now that public authorities adopt business-speak when addressing citizens (who are often called, if not often treated as, clients), and some companies take on tasks that traditionally fell within the domain of states (like education, health care, and even police), commercial and place brands become harder to distinguish.[14] As one branding consultant argues: "One simple truth is that governments don't want to run things any more—whether it's the railways, the Bank of England or the Health Service. The role of Government today is to inspire rather than control."[15]

These developments also play an increasingly important role in an area where the very idea of branding remains alien: the high politics of security.[16] Like commercial brands, we talk about a state's "personality", describing it as "friendly" (i.e., "Western-oriented") and "credible" ("ally"), or, in contrast, as "unreliable" ("rogue state"). Commercial branding gives consumers information and clues to make choices and judgments, relying on the brand to guarantee certain standards, quality, and service, and thereby reducing the risk of failures in purchase. Brands are a guide for consumers and citizens facing complexity and information-overload. It has become common knowledge that in a turbulent market brands are key to customer loyalty, a company's growth, and, ultimately, its long-term survival. Commercial brands realize that it is not factories that make profits, but relationships with customers; and it is the brand which assures those relationships. Major brands now calculate their "brand equity" in billions of dollars, based on the level of consumer loyalty, name awareness, perceived quality, and strong product associations. Brand equity also includes other intangible assets such as patents, trademarks, and channel relationships.

Since these are the received wisdoms and canons of the commercial branding community, similar assumptions now inform the practice of place branding. Today, most territorial actors are aware of their own brand, which, like commercial brands, offers important information and clues about their role and place in international politics. Their political brands are shaped by their capabilities and policies, and constitute a major part of their identity as foreign policy actors. All territorial actors therefore have a certain brand equity, which they try to manage and wield to the best of their abilities.

As we will see later in this chapter, states can also find themselves on the receiving end of a branding process. One could, for example, argue that states like Iran and North Korea have a "bad" image, especially since US President Bush has been able to cluster them together in an Axis of Evil. America's successful effort of negative branding of these rogue states brings to mind the origins of the word "brand", which derives from the Texan practice of working cattle on a roundup ground, branding and marking them with the decorations employed by their owners. In a similar way, the marker Axis of Evil brands Iran and North Korea as the "gangsters" of the world community. Whereas such an image has brought instant stardom for gangsta-rappers like Snoop Dogg and 2Pac, it is much more difficult to sell on the political market. As a rule, being "bad" is not cool in international politics, does not reap economic benefits, and is politically detrimental.[17] The Axis of Evil has framed several rogue regimes as dangerous and even illegitimate, illustrating America's social power as well as its relevance in international politics.[18]

On the opposite side, the *un*branded state has a difficult time attracting economic and political attention.[19] Why would we visit or invest in a country we don't know, and why would we pay attention to its political and strategic needs and demands if we have no clue as to what the country is all about, and why we should care? All this implies that assertive brand asset management is central to keeping a competitive economic *and* political edge. States, regions, and cities now adopt place branding strategies in the knowledge that, as a strong, attractive brand, they acquire voice, legitimacy, credibility, respect, and trust. These elements of social power are scarce resources and difficult to come by, and of increasing importance in contemporary international politics.

As we indicated above, place branding has also become a key strategy to strengthen the internal legitimacy of the state (and, as we will discuss later, of IOs like the EU). With nationalism on the wane, states have adopted place branding as a preferred route to charge citizens' batteries of loyalty, turning branding into a postmodern process of identity formation. In his book *Trading Identities: Why Countries and Companies are Taking on Each Others' Roles* (1999), British branding guru Wally Olins suggests that global companies are led in the direction of "internal marketing", a process that is better known under the political label of nation-building.[20] He argues that traditionally nation-based companies (like Philips and Toyota) have mutated into multi-national, multi-cultural organizations without clear national roots and mores. These centrifugal companies require branding as a means of suggesting coherence, cohesion, and unity. Olins therefore claims that today one of the key targets of the branding process is internal. Branding gives a sense of direction and purpose to the organization's own staff all over the world, rather than reaching out to the traditional customer audience. Branding, therefore, is not only about "selling" products, services, ideas, and foreign policies, it is not only about gaining market share and attention, it is also all about managing identity, loyalty, and reputation. In a sense, branding helps to frame the nation (or city, or region), setting new norms and standards of belonging and identity.

This chapter examines the relevance of place branding as a salient component of international politics. After setting place branding in its proper historical and conceptual context, I will map out the connections between branding and international politics by looking at three examples. The first case examines the challenges facing the EU to strengthen its image as a global player. The EU is still perceived as a civilian, normative power, a notion that forms the core of its institutional identity. But, over the past decade, the EU has increasingly branched out into the area of security and defense, and hence has made significant efforts to reframe itself as a "global actor." As we will see, Brussels considers social power a key route to change the public's expectations of the EU.

Secondly, this chapter examines Washington's efforts to deal with its collapsing image in the aftermath of its war on terror and the botched military intervention in Iraq. Opinion polls indicate that America's credibility has suffered, making it harder for the US administration to be successful as a norm entrepreneur. In the end, America's social capital has diminished, since it is no longer taken for granted that the US and its traditional allies share similar norms and values which permit cooperation among them. During the Bush era, America's brand changed, closing off numerous avenues of social power which the Obama administration now attempts to re-open. Both examples confirm the hard–social power predicament we identified earlier (Chapter 1).

Thirdly, I will examine two cases of negative place branding by focusing on the *Borat* movie which upset Kazakhstan in 2006, and the cartoon crisis which erupted in Denmark in September 2005. These two, rather distinct examples of negative branding confronted both countries with surprisingly new challenges to manage their reputation and image. These cases also illustrate that branding is not limited to state actors, but is part of the social power repertoire of societal groups and, in odd cases, even individuals. Taken together, these three examples offer a good foundation to evaluate the social power potential of place branding, making it possible to assess its possibilities and limits.

7.2 PLACE BRANDING'S PEDIGREE

One of the ironies of place branding is that the concept itself has a bad reputation. The very idea that states are, let alone should be, considered brandable entities sets many people's teeth on edge. "Our beloved nation" should be beyond branding, it is argued, since it carries specific dignity quite unlike a marketed product. But also less emotional observers, such as IR scholars, often remain reluctant to study place branding as a serious political phenomenon. Still, most political analysts have begun to appreciate that if states as diverse as the US, Finland, and Qatar are all actively engaged in place branding, it must be for good reasons; it is difficult to believe that so many policymakers are collectively blinded by the glitz and schmooze of branding guru's.

Pointing out place branding's long pedigree merely underlines the obvious fact that images and reputation have been important throughout history. The dynamics and immediacy of these images were more predictable and controllable in the pre-CNN, pre-Internet era, when radio (and later TV) were still mainly in state hands. As we saw earlier in this book, states have always used new media to manage their bubble of identity and to control the flow of information. States still try, of course, but they have found it increasingly difficult given the rise of new media and the surge of new economic and political actors. But we have also seen that the free flow of information has hardly given rise to the global village which McLuhan predicted in the 1960s. Although we can within a few minutes find massive amounts of information about any economic and political actor around the world by using Google or other search engines, it is still true that human beings jump to conclusions based on knowing only a few things about a person, or a place. Even in today's age of information overload, most people thrive on stereotypes and clichés.[21] It is this unalterable mental phenomenon underlying the process of branding which assures that it is not a fad.

Until quite recently, it was the *lack* of information that shaped people's image of other places, rather than information overload. Throughout history, this lack of information and communication has given rise to skewed and wrong images, which have often solidified and proved nigh irresistible to change. For example, Germany's perceptions of Russia were shaped decisively in the sixteenth century by diplomatic reports and travel stories about the despotic rule of Czar Ivan IV ("the Terrible").[22] Since then, Russia's image in Germany has long been that of a cruel and servile people. Russian perceptions of Europe have been equally skewed. As Iver B. Neumann has argued, Europe has functioned as a mirror for Russians, reflecting their desires and hopes, as well as their anxieties and fears.[23] This stereotyping (and occasional wishful thinking) has influenced Cold War politics, and to some extent still influences Europe's policies towards Russia and Central Europe (and *vice versa*).[24]

It has taken Central European countries more than a decade to shed the image of communism and ideological antagonism, which has had a negative impact on their economic development and their chances of joining Europe's main political and security institutions. In his book *Inventing Eastern Europe* (1994), the historian Larry Wolff describes how West Europeans have historically ascribed barbaric qualities to the peoples living in the East.[25] For Voltaire and Diderot, Europe's East was a space dominated by poverty, gloom, and backwardness. In 1945, the British historian Hugh Seton-Watson observed that the peoples of Eastern Europe "have unpronounceable names and live in plains and forests, on mountains and by rivers which might be in another world."[26] The Cold War has further deepened this European divide. The military conflicts in Chechnya and Kosovo have certainly not helped to make "the East" more reputable. For example, although Bulgarians, Serbs, and Albanians see themselves as living in south-eastern Europe, most people in the West refer to that region simply as "the Balkans", a label that still evokes associations with ethnic conflict, crime, and instability. These historical frames have a major economic and political impact since they shape the way we see the world, and therefore limit the range of interpretive possibilities.[27] Brands tell us what is important, and what the range of options and solutions are to which problems.

History is replete with vignettes of place branding, indicating that political leaders have taken their brand seriously, and often actively and successfully tried to change their image and reputation. Olins has argued that the French state has undergone regular rebranding exercises, from Louis XIV to the Republic, from the Republic to the French Empire under General Bonaparte, on to the Bourbons and the restored monarchy, into Vichy France and the contemporary Fifth Republic.[28] As Olins claims, "[t]he Tricolour replaced the Fleur de Lys, the Marseillaise became the new anthem, the traditional weights and measures were replaced by the metric system, a new calendar was introduced, God was replaced by the Supreme Being and the whole lot was exported through military triumphs all over Europe. In other words the entire French package was changed. You may not like the term, you may prefer to talk about a new or reinvented nation or state, but if revolutionary France wasn't a new brand I don't know what is."[29] France has changed its colors so often, Olins argues, that "by the time the Third Republic emerged from the ashes of the Second Empire, French politicians had become the world's specialists at branding and rebranding the nation."[30]

History shows that other countries have, although with less regularity and less enthusiasm than France, rebranded themselves as well. Examples vary from Ceylon which reinvented itself as Sri Lanka, colonial Gold Coast which became independent Ghana, similarly Southern Rhodesia which changed into Zimbabwe, to the remarkable transformation of the Ottoman Empire into Atatürk's modern Turkey, and the USSR into the Russian Federation. In all these cases, the change of political system was accompanied by a change of name, flag, and other symbols, as well as basic matters such as clothing style (Atatürk abolished the *fez* in 1925), or even language. It was not called (re)branding at the time, but the link with place branding is obvious.

Stretching the concept a bit further, one can also argue that Nazi Germany and the Soviet Union, with their strong logos (swastika, hammer and sickle), slogans, emotive identities, and ideological manifestos, were successful examples of place branding. In both cases, Nazi Germany and Soviet leaders used the available communication means to establish a new identity, both at home and abroad. This use of social power has effectively redefined expectations, set new standards, and hence rationalized a new role for these two states in the international arena. Calling to mind the Nazi and Soviet examples of place branding obviously raises questions about the risks and drawbacks of these practices. For example, Leni Riefenstahl's movies glorifying Nazism remain so powerful that their distribution is restricted in some countries out of fear that they still touch people's souls (strangely enough, most Soviet emblems have quickly disappeared, also from our collective minds and sensitivities). The conceptual and historical link between propaganda and place branding still undermines the latter's credibility, especially with a wider public. This explains why the concept of branding has a rather wishy-washy image itself.

Due to this blotted track record and image, place branding consultants are, almost without exception, subjected to much opprobrium. Most notably, Naomi Klein (herself a remarkable anti-branding brand) has warned of the emergence of "a fascist state where we all salute the logo and have little opportunity for criticism because our newspapers, television stations, Internet servers, streets and retail spaces are all controlled by multinational corporate interests."[31] The place branding specialist Simon Anholt realizes that the public's suspicion towards his line of work is not new, and that since the publication of Vance Packard's *The Hidden Persuaders* (in 1957)[32] "the population has always been ready to believe that there is something innately corrupt or even sinister about an industry that panders so effectively to people's vanity, aspirations and simple desire to better themselves. Somehow, when these fiendish tricks are applied to something as sacred as the nation-state, all hell breaks loose. Insults are heaped on the head of brands, marketers and policy-makers alike—'spin', 'gloss' and 'lies' are the most commonly heard in this country. In my own work, helping to improve the prospects of emerging markets through better branding of the country and its products, I am often accused of 'rewriting history', 'social engineering', 'exploitation', 'condescension', 'neoimperialism' and worse."[33]

Since the world may be understood as a massive and complex communication network with multiple transaction streams (e.g., tourism, business, media, and immigration), strategies to influence images and reputations are both difficult to accomplish and measure. Still, over the centuries, a great many events at the international level have had an indisputable symbolic communicative character, and states have done their utmost to manage their image and reputation, both at home and abroad. In a world where the state functions as the gatekeeper of the flow of information as well as the flow of people, propaganda has been standard practice, especially in times of conflict and war. This is the reason why China, with its centralist, even authoritarian regime, has taken direct control over its public diplomacy and place branding policies. It also explains why after 9/11 the US has used its social power primarily to send government-controlled messages out to the Muslim world. But just as merely selling a product through advertising differs from contemporary commercial branding practices, traditional propaganda is a world apart from today's place branding strategies. As we will see, the media-genic creation of emotional ties between the citizen-*cum*-consumer and the place brand has unique qualities that makes any comparison with past efforts of image management problematic.

The following case studies examine two examples of place branding. The opposing foreign policy styles of the EU and the US will tease out the different approaches that can be employed. These cases show that the brands of these two key players in international politics are framed by history, images, as well as their foreign policy agendas and actions. They also illustrate that these brands may change, and should be managed. Whereas the EU lacks ownership of its own brand (mainly due to the diffidence and reluctance of member states), the US seems more aware of the need for reputation management and better prepared to incorporate place branding in its foreign policy strategies.

7.3 BRANDING EUROPE

Like states, IOs have their own reputation and brand, and compete with states for legitimacy and credibility. As we have seen in the previous chapter, NATO became, be it somewhat belatedly, conscious of its brand, and developed a consorted public diplomacy program to communicate its policies to a variety of communities in a search of authority and loyalty. With dwindling public support for NATO, the Alliance even decided to give "the green light to think about a branding policy for NATO", as Assistant Secretary-General Jean-François Bureau acknowledged in July 2008.[34] NATO therefore hired Michael Stopford, an executive from the Coca-Cola company, to guard and manage the image of the Alliance.[35] Whereas NATO's brand is based on military security, the EU is the ultimate affluence-brand, radiating material comfort and family values.[36] Central European applicant countries keen to join the West after the end of communism knew exactly where Europe's key institutions stood for: NATO offered them an American security guarantee against Russian domination, and the EU assured jobs and prosperity. To some extent, this division of labor lingers on in the collective consciousness of Europe, and beyond.

As we have seen in earlier chapters, the EU's normative power constitutes its identity and image, just as America's can-do mentality and unilateralist nature and policies shape its brand. The EU's social model, based on postnational cooperation and continuous compromises, has turned it into a powerful brand competing with the hard-nosed Realist Brand USA, as well as with the emerging alternative of "Asianism."[37] Although Europe's norms are not always considered "nice" (at least not always by all), the EU's brand is based on the assumption that it offers the public good of good governance. For example, within the EU's Partnership and Cooperation Agreements (PCAs), the EU makes compliance with internationally recognized fundamental rights and standards a prerequisite to trade; and within the International Labour Organisation (ILO), the EU promotes the agenda for "Decent Work", based on collective labor laws and gender equality. Moreover, the EU is actively pushing sustainable development and responsible climate policies, turning itself into the champion of Green Leadership, and possibly even a Green Civilian Power Europe.[38] These examples of the EU's normative policies confirm that brands are not only, perhaps not even mainly, based on logos and visual attributes, but on actions and narratives. The EU, like commercial brands, has to deliver upon its promises to establish and confirm its reputation. But it also has to use all of the other tricks in the place branding toolbox to communicate and frame its policies effectively to relevant communities.

Obviously, the EU is a master brand, offering its name, style, and character to all the policies, events, and ideas it generates. It has a highly visible identity offering many possibilities to position itself in the competitive market place of ideas. As a place brand, the EU stands for the idea of "Europe", which is associated with a wide variety of concepts and notions, ranging from Christendom and the Enlightenment, to the Holocaust and football hooliganism. Historically, the story of *Europa* has been an inspiration for politicians, artists, and entrepreneurs. After summarizing the Greek myth of the captured and raped Europa, the historian John Hale exclaims, "what a subject this was! Sex, and violence, seascape, landscape, beauty and the beast, gestures of alarm and affection. In every medium, from painting to pottery, relief sculpture to enamel, the story soared on."[39]

As a visual brand, the EU has much going for it. Like NATO, the EU has a powerful logo (a blue flag with a circle of 12, yellow five-pointed stars), which is inconspicuously omnipresent across Europe. The EU flag can be seen in all public spaces, buildings, ceremonies, and important events.[40] It has a currency named after it, which makes it one of the most frequently used names across the continent. ("That will be 2 Euros and 50 cents, please"). The numerable Euro-prefixed products and events, ranging from the Eurostar train, the Euro 2008 soccer championships, to the annual Eurovision Song Contest, make Europe one of the most competitive global place brands.[41] The EU is recognized all over the world, which confirms its legitimacy and adds to its credibility as a global norm entrepreneur and policy actor. This is a major achievement, given that the EU has only recently begun to alter its profile from a mainly trade-oriented player into an all-round policymaker dealing with the broad gamut of issues (ranging from culture to WMD proliferation, and everything in between).

Since the 1950s, the European integration project has progressed steadily. But, like the Tower of Babel, every advance in Europe's architecture seems to further escalate the controversy and cacophony among member states about the EU's prospects and future identity. Since the EU has long functioned as the scapegoat of first resort for its member states, an often rather wretched image has been the unfortunate, but inevitable result. Until quire recently, the EU has clung to its founding myth that "European integration brings peace." But today, another Franco–German war (or basically *any* intra-EU war) no longer serves as Damocles' sword, begetting discipline and respect; for most Europeans, any attempt to resuscitate the story of the EU as the zone of Kantian peace is futile.[42]

Now that peace has become so apparent and normal within the EU, it has lost its narrative appeal. The EU's brand as a peacemaker has lost traction, at least with its own citizens, which partially explains why the Union has been grappling with the need to find a new, postmodern *raison d'être* which inspires its own populace and appeals to the wider world as well. But whereas the EU's consociational model is taken for granted by a somewhat decadent Europe, the Union's model of "peace and prosperity" remains emotionally vibrant and strong for most non-Europeans. This is the main reason why the European Commission makes no bones about its role as a model which others might, perhaps even should, emulate. In its report *Shaping the New Europe* (2000), the Commission argues that "Europe's model of integration, working successfully on a continental scale, is a quarry from which ideas for global governance can and should be drawn."[43] The EU does not merely stand for good governance (encompassing the rule of law, transparency, and sustainable development), but also for an alternative to the classical norms of Westphalian statehood. As Ben Rosamond argues: "The EU stands—self-consciously sometimes—as a beacon of what it might mean to engage in the post-Westphalian governance of globalization. It is in this sense a normative transmitter to the rest of the world."[44]

The EU's 2009 Lisbon Treaty illustrates that the Union hesitates to formulate clear-cut "European interests." Instead, the EU prides itself on the normative foundations of its foreign policy. The EU promulgates and defends its basic *principles* (like peace, democracy, and the rule of law); *ideas* (sustainable development and the social market economy); and *norms* (good governance and institution-building). The Lisbon Treaty summarizes the EU's global mission as a fighter for and contributor to "peace, security, the sustainable development of the Earth, solidarity and mutual respect among peoples, free and fair trade, eradication of poverty and the protection of human rights, in particular the rights of the child, as well as to the strict observance and development of international law, including respect for the principles of the United Nations Charter" (Art. 2.5). Europe's normative power is derived from its ability to shape the notions of what is to be considered normal behavior in international politics. Intra-European politics now more resembles domestic politics (where order and solidarity are feasible), than classical international politics (where anarchy and mistrust are said to roam). In summary, the European Dream is to domesticate global politics, and the EU makes active and purposeful use of the social power inherent in its brand to upload these norms and rules to the much more anarchic, global level.

The EU is the only international political space in the world where Realpolitik has been assuaged by a dense network of law, civility, and a commensurate high level of mutual trust. It is the EU's policy *style* that is considered its best asset—its Unique Selling Point (USP)—at home, but now especially abroad. Surely, European political life is not perfect, but for Arabs, Asians, and Africans alike, emulating the EU model in their own region may only figure in their wildest dreams.[45] But if Germany and France can become friends after fighting three bloody wars within one century, why could India and Pakistan, or Israel and the Arab world, not follow this remarkable success story? The EU's history and practice therefore add to its attraction and credibility as a normative actor, both in Europe's direct vicinity and beyond. The EU's brand is that of a beacon of civilization and prosperity in an otherwise disorderly and disoriented world (see Chapters 2 and 3).

Although the EU's political brand is mainly determined by what it is and does, place branding also has an active component, which assumes that the social power inherent in the brand can be deliberately applied to reach specific foreign policy goals. Both elements are crucial for the EU's brand since they determine Europe's legitimacy and credibility as a norm entrepreneur and foreign policy actor. Why would the world listen to what the EU has to say? Why would others endorse European policy proposals and accept its norms and standards? These questions have become particularly pertinent now that the EU is morphing from a regional

148 *Place branding*

Zivilmacht into a more fully-fledged Great Power with growing responsibilities for coordinating Europe's foreign, security, and defense policies. But how can this transition be made if both EU citizens and outsiders still associate the Union more with subsidies and good governance, than with Battle Groups and military operations all around the globe?[46]

Geopolitically, Europe is reaching adolescence and is rethinking its role as a mature, global actor.[47] The EU is already a superpower in areas such as trade, finance, agriculture, and humanitarian aid. As a security actor, the EU is testing the waters with military missions in the Balkans, the Democratic Republic of Congo, as well as Aceh (Indonesia), Georgia, and the Palestine Authorities.[48] But since it always takes time for perceptions to catch up with reality, it is hardly surprising that the EU's old brand lingers on. This also means that the EU is facing the difficult challenge of combining its current brand as a global normative actor and entrepreneur with its burgeoning Great Power ambitions. Since all (place) branding works on the premise that actions speak louder than words, the EU's military operations will ultimately alter the Union's image and identity, both at home and abroad.[49] Once the EU starts to act as the US does today, rebranding will come automatically, affecting the EU's social power as a norm entrepreneur.[50]

But in order to minimize inertia and speed up the EU's transformation into a Great Power, a rebranding exercise would be required. The European Commission (as well as the Council Secretariat) is well aware of this challenge, but is faced with reluctant member states who refuse to give the go-ahead for such a consolidated rebranding strategy. In May 2006, Vice-President of the European Commission (and European Commissioner for Communications) Margot Wallström briefly considered asking the input of brand consultants to evaluate the EU's image and brand identity. British brand specialist Anholt was asked to chair a panel of experts to deconstruct Europe's identity and to think through the possibilities of devising a branding strategy for improvement.[51] But when the story hit the news that the EU was engaged in rebranding, the Commission spokesman immediately denied this idea, calling it "fantastic" (i.e., in the realm of fantasy, rather than great!).[52]

Rolf Annerberg, Mrs Wallström's head of cabinet, made it clear that "the EU is a brand but it is competing with 25 national brands. It is very seldom you use them as a unit. The Ryder Cup [where the EU plays golf] against the US is about the only case."[53] Given the reluctance to think in terms of place branding, it is already remarkable that a senior EU official acknowledges that the EU *is* a major brand, and that place branding is a serious option, if not a necessity, for the EU. Still, place branding continues to play second fiddle to conventional communications strategies within the European Commission. In 2006, following the European Constitution fiasco, Commissioner Wallström launched a so-called *Plan D – Debate, Democracy, Dialogue*, which aims to reconnect the EU with its citizens, using the Internet, new media (including chat sessions), as well as the recruitment of sports and music celebrities as EU ambassadors. The European Commission has also expressed interest in setting itself up in the Second Life virtual community (see Chapter 6), in an attempt to bring the EU closer to young people and make them more aware of its policies and objectives.[54] As we have seen in Chapter 3, the EU also uses culture to strengthen its image as a consensus-oriented actor (e.g., with initiatives such as the 2008 European Year of Intercultural Dialogue).

For the moment, however, the EU resembles the proverbial rabbit blinded by approaching headlights: numb and immobile. Member states remain apprehensive about branding the EU. They are afraid of being criticized for spin-doctoring, and concerned that a truly effective EU place branding exercise will ultimately result in a strong and vibrant European identity and image. Member states realize all too well that, with such a strong brand, the EU will be a powerful competitor for scarce social capital, such as legitimacy and credibility. And, at the end of the day, the EU will also vie for the taxes and loyalty of its own citizens. These identity games between the EU and member states are played all the time. For example, member states have been skeptical about the Commission's plans to introduce the label "Made in the EU", which Brussels believes will add to its visibility and image abroad. However, member states (who are backed up by most commercial branding specialists) suggest that the EU is too generic and bland, offering consumers little information and emotional clues as to what the product is really about. For similar reasons, member states remain reluctant to brand the EU as an authoritative Great Power—at least for the time being.[55]

For member states, the EU oscillates between the role of closest ally and harshest competitor. This explains why the European Commission has yet to get the green light to enter into a consorted place branding strategy, which would be a long-overdue process to tap the EU's social power resources. Until then, the EU will continue to brand itself through its policies, policy documents, and speeches. These performative and narrative modes of branding generate their own social power by shaping expectations, determining standards for EU policy behavior, and legitimizing the scope of its actions. Still, for the EU, the main wielding problem related to place branding is that it lacks member states' authorization to open up new and attractive avenues of social power. The lack of place branding therefore remains a missing ingredient in an overall EU-led strategy to develop not only the capabilities, but also the legitimacy and credibility, to act as a Great Power. Both in the case of public diplomacy and place branding, the EU is unable to optimize its social power, tied up by the caveats of its member states, similar to a Gulliver held down by a multitude of Lilliputians.

7.4 BRAND USA

Anholt labels Brand America the "mother of all brands", and for good reasons.[56] Anholt suggests that not only do people all over the world think about, talk about, and relate to America as if it were a great, global brand, but the US also has "quite deliberately and quite consciously built and managed itself as a brand right from the very start."[57] For centuries, the US has been the ultimate promise of liberty and opportunity for millions of emigrants. From the onset, America has positioned itself as the ultimate aspirational brand, strengthening the emotional pull on the world's tired and poor, who were welcomed by the Statue of Liberty upon arrival. As we have discussed in detail in previous chapters, America's cultural appeal, Hollywood's global visual hegemony, and Washington's activist and interventionist foreign policies reinforce each other and are integral parts of the overall Brand USA.

Like the EU (and most other place brands), the US therefore already *has* a strong brand, regardless of the place branding strategies it puts together. As the annual reports of brand consultancy Interbrand and *Business Week* indicate, American brands dominate the table of the world's top commercial brands, and, out of the hundred most valuable global brands, around two-thirds are American owned. America's policies and actions have shaped its image, which is remarkably strong and resilient. As Anholt suggests: "Putting a man on the moon may not have been intended as an advertisement for American technology, but it certainly worked as one, and Brand America was credited with the achievement. NASA isn't, strictly speaking, a sales promotion agency for American technology, any more than Hollywood is the advertising agency for American values, culture, and tourism, but both have always performed these roles with vigour and effectiveness."[58]

But unlike many states, the US has effectively managed its own brand. Brand management involves the process of cautious, often measured supervision of existing perceptions. In this sense, the US is considered a corporate brand, since the United States (or "America") is not *itself* the primary brand, but the manager of a series of related sub-brands which are embodied in the arts, sports, media, technology, as well as its foreign policy actions. Just like the EU, America's place brand is embedded in a strong visual presence, from its eagles and Great Seal, to the Stars and Stripes, the dollar, and its buildings (as diverse as the Empire State building, to the White House, and the Pentagon). But America's master-brand is based on freedom (or liberty), not only within the US itself, but also in international politics.

Following the concept of governmentality, America's national and international brands are basically similar. Both at home and abroad, Brand USA is based on individual responsibility in a self-help setting. This organic link between America's domestic reality and its foreign policy actions is self-evident, strengthening its overall brand. For example, just as American entrepreneurs can create huge fortunes from humble beginnings in a free environment, US foreign policy has been markedly anti-colonial, assuming that every state can prosper as long as it is free and independent. In this way, America has successfully embedded its values and norms into the rulebook of global politics. As Suzanne Nossel remarked on the role of the US after World War II: "International institutions helped spread American values, which in turn fuelled an appetite for American products. Trade enhanced political influence, and political influence helped further extend American values."[59] This suggests that America's social model generates social power. Like in the case of the EU, this mode of social power is of a passive nature. Clark S. Judge, for example, argues that the US "example is the hope of those who are striving and rising. We cannot escape this conflict by changing what we do in foreign policy or other arenas of action, because in this arena *our power derives not from what we do but from who we are*."[60] Obviously, snags such as the Abu Ghraib torture scandal seriously challenge, and even undermine, America's freedom-brand—but Brand

USA seems (at least for the moment) sufficiently flexible and resilient to deal with these anomalies.

As we have seen in earlier chapters, the US neglected its public diplomacy and place branding efforts during the 1990s, in the belief that its own societal model was no longer seriously challenged by an ideological competitor. But after 9/11, America's "unilateral disarmament in the weapons of advocacy"[61] was halted, bringing an end to a period of complacency. Winning the war of ideas obviously requires different tools and strategies, which has offered ample policy space for place branding. As Richard Holbrooke argued in October 2001: "[C]all it public diplomacy, or public affairs, or psychological warfare, or—if you really want to be blunt—propaganda. But whatever it is called, defining what this war is really about in the minds of the 1 billion Muslims in the world will be of decisive and historical importance."[62]

Much of America's brand management has gone under the heading of public diplomacy. Both avenues of social power overlap, conceptually as well as in their practical application.[63] Both emphasize visual symbols to conjure up images and emotions in the minds of certain people; both want to create and maintain a positive relationship with certain communities; and both favor the use of new media tools and PR campaigns, copying the example of commercial marketing. What is more, public diplomacy and place branding rely heavily on market research in the formulation of their campaigns and strategies. But there are, of course, some differences. Most notably, place branding privileges one-way communication and aims to take control of the message without too much interaction with consumers and citizens. This stands in stark contrast to the phenomenon of new public diplomacy, which aspires to connect communities, and listens to what is said without always pushing specific interests and opinions.

Since the appointment of Charlotte Beers to Under Secretary of State for Public Diplomacy and Public Affairs, in October 2001, using branding as a relevant strategy has become halfway *salonfähig* in Washington DC.[64] Mrs Beers argued, upon accepting her job, that this is the "most sophisticated brand assignment I have ever had. It is almost as though we have to redefine what America is."[65] Obviously, this proved neither possible not necessary; Brand USA has been strong enough to weather the post-9/11 fall-out of Washington's botched war in Iraq, and other policy failures. But place branding has certainly not lived up to its expectations, and has failed to affect both the course and the packaging of America's foreign policies. Two reasons stand out. First, place branding has lacked credibility among foreign policy analysts and policymakers by using marketing terminology. By framing foreign policy in marketing terms (like "selling" the war on terror), place branding has become conceptually incompatible with the gravity of fighting an actual war.[66] Second, place branding (as well as public diplomacy) has found it hard to prove, and hence justify, its plans and policies, since its impact is so difficult to measure. Social power's wielding problem is a serious handicap when policies are evaluated, and institutional priorities and budgets set.

But regardless of its attitude to branding, the Bush administration has followed Machiavelli's dictum that it is far better to be feared than to be loved, and better to compel than to attract. But how valid is the claim that the (successful) use of military (hard) power generates the requisite (social) power of legitimacy? Looking at today's Iraq and the dismal standing of the US in public opinion polls across the Middle East, the opposite argument seems more likely, namely that ostentatious (hard) power play simply eclipses low-profile place branding and public diplomacy. For the US, it has proven impossible to conduct a deliberate branding exercise based on liberty and opportunity with stories about torture and human rights abuses dominating the media, all over the world. From marketing experience we learn that it is more important to *show* than to *tell*. For US place branding, this implies that America's performance on the global stage speaks louder than any smooth words it may voice simultaneously. Or, as Anholt argues: "You can't smash them with your left hand and caress them with your right. If you're going to war you should suspend [public] diplomacy because if you're attacking a nation that's all there is to it."[67]

Although rebranding America is futile given its long pedigree and stable emotional basis, managing Brand USA remains an absolute necessity. Since performative branding trumps its narrative variant, only visible and structural changes in America's foreign policies could make a notable difference. The election of Barack Obama to become the first black American president certainly falls into that category. President Obama is every brand manager's dream: young, smart, black, smooth, and, best of all, a visual testimony to America's clean break with the Bush era. Where President Bush radiates the image of a trigger-happy cowboy, President Obama embodies JFK-meets-Martin Luther King. President Obama's positive image of change offers a unique opportunity for the US to recast itself from global baddie to a responsible superpower. There is little doubt that the Obama administration will use its regained social power to set a new agenda and ask old and new partners to support its policy initiatives. As Senator Obama already argued in October 2007: "If you believe that we've got to heal America and we've got to repair our standing in the world, then I think my supporters believe that I am the messenger who can deliver that message."[68] Indeed, as French foreign policy analyst Dominique Moïsi claims: "The very moment [Obama] appears on the world's television screens, victorious and smiling, America's image and soft power would experience something like a Copernican revolution."[69] Indeed, President Obama offers a dollop of new policies: shut down Guantanamo, reduce carbon emissions, open talks with Iran, and so on. Such a change obviously goes beyond window-dressing, consolidating the positive effect of such a "fresh start" in the White House, and constituting the basis for a more even-handed Brand USA.

As the EU and American cases illustrate, place branding, especially in conjunction with public diplomacy, is a valuable, but still largely unfamiliar and untested avenue of social power. Policymakers still have to get their bearings on how to apply it to best effect in international politics. For the moment, place branding has already proven effective for cities and regions; relatively small players have little problem "staying on message", and organizing and coordinating campaigns and strategies following well-known marketing paradigms.[70] In contrast, Great Powers usually already *have* a strong brand, and since all their foreign policy actions are recognized and visible, they find it hard to engage in effective brand management. This, again, touches upon the relevance of social power's wielding problem, since both the EU and Brand USA spread their values and norms, setting standards, and raising expectations. Obviously, their brand offers them legitimacy and credibility, strengthening their roles as norm entrepreneurs. But, both in war and peace, the road of social power has proven slippery, and tricky to navigate.[71]

7.5 NEGATIVE BRANDING

As we mentioned earlier, the notion of branding derives from the practice of marking cattle with the decorations of their owners. Since a brand, like legitimacy and credibility, only exists in the mind of others, it may therefore also be applied as a negative strategy, which has at times been done rather successfully, *viz.* Reagan's Evil Empire, and Bush's Axis of Evil. Being aware of, and sensitive to, the reality of negative branding has become an important element of responsible reputation management within commercial firms, who have become aware that PR fiascos can seriously harm their relationship with consumers, and damage their image. Debacles such as the Brent Spar oil rig imbroglio of 1995, gave Greenpeace the opportunity to brand Shell as an irresponsible multinational, polluting the North Sea. Public consumer pressure has also changed major sports gear brands, such as Nike and Adidas, to take responsibility for labor standards in "their" factories in Asia. Similarly, major commercial brands have fallen victim to culture jammers and adbusters, who, in their desire to reclaim the streets, alter well-known logos and slogans into anti-commercial messages.[72]

These examples underline the fact that, due to the new media environment and the absence of political gatekeepers able to filter information, a host of new players have acquired sufficient social power to shape images and reputations. Just as states compete with many other norm entrepreneurs in uploading rules and regulations to the next (global) governance level, place branding has become an arena open to many a new player. And since it is easier to burn a house down than to build one, it has proven easier for brand-hackers to attack and damage existing reputations than to do the opposite (i.e., improve or enrich). Two vignettes illustrate this new, very level playing field of image and reputation. In both cases (Kazakhstan and Denmark), governments have been confronted with the fall-out of negative branding, waking them up to fact that the use and abuse of social power has become a matter of serious concern, mainly since it can be wielded by irresponsible actors to reach dubious policy goals.

In November 2006, the movie *Borat, Cultural Learnings of America for Make Benefit Glorious Nation of Kazakhstan* hit American cinemas. The film was distributed by 20th Century Fox, and topped the Box Office charts in the US, taking in US$26.4 million on a limited release of 837 screens in its first weekend. Due to the major controversies it raised, however, the release was widened to 2,566 screens the following weekend, becoming a major blockbuster in the US and Western Europe. The controversy centered around the main character of the

154 *Place branding*

movie, the British comedian Sacha Baron Cohen who specializes in prank interviews, this time posing as a fictional Kazakh journalist traveling across the US to make a documentary in order to bring back findings for "benefit of glorious nation of Kazakhstan." The movie makes the audience believe that Kazakhstan is a backward and anti-Semitic country. Although the main goal of the movie is to show how easily ordinary Americans go along with his racist, homophobic, and sexist jokes, the country of Kazakhstan comes across as a boorish place, the armpit of the world, so to speak.

It may be hard to believe that this is actually an amusing (be it rather banal) movie, and since explanations kill the joke I won't even try to prove it. It may be enough to say that *Borat* was widely acclaimed, and Cohen received the 2007 Golden Globe for "Best Performance by an Actor in a Motion Picture – Musical or Comedy." However, for a country like Kazakhstan, bearing the brunt of all the hilarity, *Borat* was everything but funny. Kazakhstan, although the size of Western Europe, was basically unknown to most people in the West, who now received their first "information" about the country by watching *Borat*. How does a country react when others are made to believe that their people are addicted to drinking horse urine, enjoy shooting dogs, view rape and incest as respectable hobbies, and take pleasure in pursuits like "running of the Jew" festivals.

Kazakh officials reacted nervously and took serious offence. Kazakhstan's Foreign Ministry spokesmen Yerzhan Ashykbayev told a news conference that Cohen's behavior was deemed "utterly unacceptable, being a concoction of bad taste and ill manner which is completely incompatible with the ethics and civilised behaviour of Kazakhstan's people—We reserve the right to any legal action to prevent new pranks of this kind." Ominously, the spokesman further claimed that "we do not rule out that Mr. Cohen is serving someone's political order designed to present Kazakhstan and its people in a derogatory way."[73] Interestingly, Russia's Federal Agency of Culture and Cinematography banned *Borat*, allegedly due to the risk that it might stir religious and ethnic disputes.

This episode also immediately started a debate among place branding specialists about the impact of *Borat* on Kazakhstan's image and reputation, as well as, of course, the country's edgy and less-than-amused reaction to the movie. Does *Borat* prove that "there is no such thing as bad publicity?"[74] Was it wise of the Kazakh authorities to block the website borat.kz (obviously registered under Kazakhstan's two-letter national domain to feign authenticity—the site is now running under boratdvd.com)?[75] But most specialists acknowledged that for Kazakhstan it was a lose–lose situation: not reacting would look complacent, whereas reacting would look very silly, especially since they were followed by Cohen/Borat's official response: "I'd like to state I have no connection with Mr. Cohen and fully support my Government's decision to sue this Jew."[76]

So how can you win this one? Kazakhstan hired two PR firms to counter *Borat*'s claims, and also ran a four-page advertisement in The *New York Times* and the *International Herald Tribune* for the same reason. Furthermore, Kazakhstan ran a campaign on CNN to show the world the country's "real face."[77] But since most people have not visited Kazakhstan, know no Kazakh brands, artists, or sports personalities, or have no other forms of contact with the country, *Borat* lingers on in the background as their main frame of reference. A few pages of ads in eastcoast broadsheets and CNN does little to alter this. It also means that conclusions are hard to draw from this case. But the irony is that Cohen could have easily taken other unknown countries (like Turkmenistan and Uzbekistan) to make a fool of, showing all unbranded countries the risk of not being in charge of their image and reputation.[78] To some extent, it shows that it is not possible at all to be in full control of one's own brand.[79] In the end (but with a few years delay), Kazakhstan has thrown *Borat* a counterpunch by launching the film *Mongol*, which earned the country its first nomination for a foreign-language Academy Award, in 2008. *Mongol* is a big-budget Genghis Khan biopic which deliberately aims to bolster the self-respect of the Kazakh people, and tries to reframe the country by placing it in its proper historical and cultural context.[80]

"Humor" of a totally different nature hit a small, European country's image in September 2005, when the Danish newspaper *Jyllands-Posten* published an article entitled "Muhammeds ansigt" ("The face of Muhammad"), which, amongst others, showed cartoons of the prophet wearing a bomb as headgear. After an angry reaction from Danish imams, eleven ambassadors from Muslim-majority countries (including Turkey) asked for a meeting with Danish Prime Minister Anders Fogh Rasmussen in October 2005, to discuss what they perceived as an "on-going smearing campaign in Danish public circles and media against Islam and Muslims."[81] What could have remained a modest controversy quickly escalated into a worldwide row. Consumer boycotts against Danish products were organized in Saudi Arabia, Kuwait, and other Middle Eastern countries, and demonstrations against Denmark took place world-wide. In February 2006, the Danish (and, remarkably, also Norwegian) embassy in Syria was attacked; in Beirut, the Danish embassy was set on fire. The protests cost the lives of an estimated 150 people, mainly in Nigeria, Libya, Pakistan, and Afghanistan. The whole cartoon crisis (also called the "cartoon intifada") escalated further when US Secretary of State Condoleezza Rice accused Iran and Syria of organizing anti-Danish and anti-Western protests in their own countries as well as in Lebanon.

The Danish people and their government were flabbergasted that a rather innocuous page of cartoons in *Jyllands-Posten* could cause serious damage to their image as a tolerant, open, thoroughly liberal society. Seeing Danish flags burnt by angry crowds on CNN caused a stir in Copenhagen, and the Danish government did not know how to react to such a sudden attack on their reputation, in the Muslim world and beyond. Prime Minister Rasmussen even called the cartoon crisis "Denmark's worst international relations incident since the Second World War."[82] Obviously, being branded as anti-Islam by an outraged Muslim world opinion was the mirror-image of President Bush's Axis of Evil label stuck on Iran & co, with similar political and economic costs involved.

In September 2006, Danish export figures showed that the Muslim boycott of Danish goods had led to a 15.5 percent drop in total exports between February and June 2006. Danish trade to the Middle East fell by half—exports to Saudi Arabia fell by 40 percent, and those to Iran by 47 percent. The cost to Danish businesses was estimated at 134 million Euros (US$170 million).[83] Interestingly, the cartoon crisis also evoked opposite reactions from consumers showing their support for Denmark by buying Danish brands. The "Support Denmark Movement", for example, encouraged a world-wide audience to buy Danish produce and display stickers and web banners with supportive slogans and Danish flags. Numerous websites and blogs sprung up, listing Danish products that people could buy. As *The Guardian* noted in 2006: "While Danish milk products were dumped in the Middle East, fervent rightwing Americans started buying Bang & Olufsen stereos and Lego. In the first quarter of this year Denmark's exports to the US soared 17 percent."[84]

As one blogger remarked during the crisis: "A week ago when one thought of Denmark one would likely conjure an image of a breakfast pastry or Shakespeare's Hamlet. Now Denmark is in the midst of a real life epic tragedy but its people are holding steadfast."[85] This change in Denmark's reputation, both in the Muslim world and beyond, has been mapped by place branding experts who came to the unsurprising conclusion that Denmark's national image weakened significantly in 2006. The country's image as "democratic, strongly oriented towards human rights" had suffered severely.[86] The 2006 *Anholt Nation Brand Index* (which regularly measures the image of states) also showed that Denmark dragged other Nordic countries with it, since Norway and Sweden were all put in the same "Scandinavian" basket by Muslims around the world. Interestingly, some Danish brands replaced (be it just temporarily) their "Made in Denmark" label with that of "Made in the EU", obviously using this decoy to hide their true identity behind Europe's broad and protective back.

Like *Borat*, the Mohammed cartoon crisis took a country by surprise.[87] Like Kazakhstan, the Danish government has become more conscious about the vulnerability of its image and the frailty of its brand. The Danish government has also started an internal debate about the management of its place brand, and the lessons that could be learnt from this episode. Uffe Andreasen, the Danish diplomat responsible for his country's public diplomacy, argued that the "moment that a country is looking for support and alliances—one of public diplomacy's most important *raisons d'être*—it is not the man in the street that it is dealing with, but (...) politicians; editors and journalists; business executives; university people and teachers, etc."[88] Copenhagen's concern with place branding has also spilled over into NATO, since Denmark took the lead to re-energize the Alliance's public diplomacy and branding strategy, in 2007 (see Chapter 6).

Both cases indicate the impact of globalization and new media on a country's brand. As *Borat* proves, place branding is not always high politics, and state officials are not in full control of their own brand. Since social power involves reciprocal relationships, reputations and images may be vulnerable and challenged by competing frames, narratives, and actions. Muslims all over the world used their collective social power to challenge Denmark's image as a liberal country, an image that proved strong enough to endure, but still fragile enough to be shocked. The rise of me-media and blogs adds to the scattering of social power. For better or for

Place branding 157

worse, social power has dispersed in international politics, making it hard, but not impossible, to manage elusive qualities such as image and reputation.

7.6 CONCLUSION

The new technological environment has significantly leveled the economic and political playing field, offering opportunities for new players to compete for scarce social capital, such as legitimacy and credibility. This puts pressure on all established actors to manage their image and reputation. As we have seen, both the EU and NATO have become metaphors for the "West", pulling off what the General Electric Company (GE) wanted to do in the mid 1920s: to transform itself from a faceless institution to "the initials of a friend."[89] Many a place brand is aspirational, and a really strong brand makes the public overlook, or rationalize, the negative sides of the brand. But even in these times of spin there are limitations. Perhaps one should try branding China as the "Home of the Free", or try to sell Bratwurst with that "typical German" *joie de vivre*, to experience the limits history sets to the contemporary brand state. Established roles limit the room for maneuver for place branding.[90] History and patterns of expectation frame a state and its foreign policy actions. Only major upsets and paradigm-shifting events can radically alter these patterns, offering opportunities to states (and other territorial actors) to reinvent themselves.

The growing importance of place branding implies a shift in political paradigms, away from the modern world of geopolitics and force, to the postmodern world of images and reputation. The phenomenon of place branding suggests that the preference of form over function is increasingly shaping Europe's political landscape, even affecting the process of EU and NATO enlargement. With the existential Soviet threat now long gone, security and prosperity have turned from ultimate survival tools to luxury items which are branded with a high premium. Like other elite brands, the EU and NATO wear their logos like Armani and Chanel labels, telling their clientele that buying their "product" implies that they are sophisticated and safe. These branding efforts follow the same logic, since both Armani and NATO aspire to reinforce the "customer's" sense of self, offering a feeling of security and belonging. Little surprise, therefore, that new members like Poland, Bulgaria, and the Baltic states wear their NATO badges as signs of achievement and chosenness. For these countries, the rationale of their Alliance membership is quite simple: "Because I'm worth it!"

Although no doubt unsettling to conservative thinkers, this is a positive development, since place branding is gradually taking over the role of nationalism as the emotional glue keeping society together. In our secular age, the brand has become an *ersatz* religion and a new way of working and living. Peter York even argued that Nike's "swoosh/tick logo means precisely what the crucifix meant to an earlier generation in ghettos—it promises redemption, vindication and a way out."[91] Although primordialists cherish a romanticized picture of every nation's deep and sacred roots, modern nations are based on invented traditions and the continuous mobilization and adaptation of history. Ernest Renan famously argued that France was merely "une ensemble d'idées",[92] which has never been more true than today.

One could say that, with its flag, anthem, and constitution, the modern state is nothing more than a brand with a logo and a mission statement. Although this would be too simplistic for comfort, place branding forces us to revisit the debate on identity, and the prevailing postmodern condition of international politics. By capriciously using its history, geography, and its ethnic and folk motifs, place branding constructs a distinct image without the deep-rooted, and often antagonistic, sense of national identity and uniqueness. Culture and history are now used as rather superficial decorations festooning what are in essence indistinguishable patches on Europe's colorful quilt of semi-sovereign states. By forgetting nationalism, the process of place branding makes a major contribution to the further pacification of the European continent. By doing so, it strengthens the credibility of the EU's social model and adds to Europe's social power.

As our examination of public diplomacy and place branding suggests, a new Great Game of politics is emerging, this time not about oil and trading routes, but about image and reputation. Looking at the number of IOs, states, regions, cities, and NGOs engaged in both public diplomacy and place branding, it is clear that this new game is becoming increasingly popular. All these actors realize that they have to compete for legitimacy and credibility, as well as loyalty and trust, which help them to successfully upload their norms and standards to the next (global) governance level.

In international politics it remains hard to quantify brand equity, even of established actors like the US and EU. But in the commercial sector, the value of a brand is measured meticulously, since marketing researchers have come to the conclusion that the brand is one of the most valuable assets a company has. For example, Interbrand estimates Coca-Cola's brand equity at US$66.7 billion, and Intel's at US$31.3 billion (in 2008).[93] In fact, a successful place brand may ultimately do without any territory whatsoever. Do we really care whether the "Rive gauche" exists at all, as long as one can sell fashion and perfume under that name? The time may not be far away when states will resemble these ephemeral brands, and De Gaulle will finally be right that there is "une certaine idée de la France", but nothing more tangible than that.

8 Conclusions

8.1 DEFINING THE SITUATION

This book has examined the role and relevance of social power in international politics. Social power, a concept not frequently used in IR, has been defined as the ability to set standards, create norms and values that are deemed legitimate, desirable, and, best of all: normal. More commonly used notions such as soft power, but also smart, sticky, and sweet power, can all be accommodated under the generous umbrella definition of social power as the ability to define the situation. In order to set standards and define a situation in international politics, hard power may be used, and has at times proved expedient. Military power has obviously been exercised for millennia to "define a situation" in international affairs, with mixed results. Even in today's postmodern Europe, one could argue that Kosovo has used terrorism and guerrilla warfare to gain sovereignty, with marked success, as its independence since February 2008 testifies. Military power remains relevant, but requires the legal and/or moral basis of legitimacy to sustain its triumphs.[1] Since social power ultimately depends upon legitimacy and credibility, military force alone is of marginal use. Today's Iraq is a clear illustration of the results of military power without legitimacy. And even Kosovo now has to wait until the international community recognizes its independence, illustrating that neither legitimacy nor credibility can be owned, but are conferred by others.[2]

Social power includes, but goes beyond soft power. Nye's definition involves the ability to get one's way through attraction, rather than coercion or payments. A substantial part of this book has dealt with the attraction of a state's culture, the TV programs and films it produces and offers to a global audience, as well as the political ideals it subscribes to and propagates through its foreign policy actions, its public diplomacy, and place branding strategies. But although soft power is a valuable concept which has widened the debate about the foundations of contemporary power, its scope has become too limited. In order to be successful in international politics, attraction and persuasion are valuable resources. Being popular and admired is important also for political actors; it makes it easier to sway others, and influence policy decisions. But in order to successfully compete in today's economic, political, and security pageants, we have to go beyond attraction and persuasion, and study the mechanisms of (global) governance. And we have to do this in quite some detail.

All major powers aspire to upload their values and norms to the global level. As we have seen, this particularly applies to the US and the EU, with China as a relative newcomer, offerings its Beijing Consensus as a competing development model to the West's market-based liberalism.[3] Traditionally, Great Powers have used empires, or at least the idea of empire, to expand their normative reach and ideational range. But since the notion of empire is now frowned upon, conjuring up images of oppression and exploitation, different rationales are offered and different narratives developed. It is no longer *comme il faut* to admit that both the US and EU are engaged in a *mission civilisatrice*, since this immediately raises the specter of neo-colonialism, if not full-fledged imperialism. Against this backdrop, the modest aspiration of uploading one's values and norms and influencing the rulebook of global governance sounds innocuous—and it probably is.

Since social power centers around being able to determine what is normal, desirable, and the law-of-the-land, legitimacy and credibility are important, if not essential requirements to successfully upload one's norms and values. In contemporary international politics, legitimacy and credibility have become powerful resources and tools to justify and gather support for foreign policy actions. The ability and capability to legitimate foreign policy *in the eyes of others* is the staple of social power. Legitimacy assumes the tacit or explicit agreement on the rules-of-the-game, based on or rooted in a shared set of norms. Credibility is based on trust that policies will be conducted effectively. The ability to acquire and sustain both legitimacy and credibility requires social capital, which can be defined as the set of norms and values that are shared among members of a group permitting cooperation among them. Every community is based on social capital, based on norms such as honesty and reliability, or freedom and justice.

How, and even whether, social capital can be accumulated in international politics remains somewhat elusive. But it has become obvious that political legitimacy becomes more strained as the sense of community weakens, and the physical distance between those in authority and the general public grows. As the scale of governance expands, legitimacy becomes increasingly problematic. Since global governance functions without a formal system of authority, the capacity for direct control over actors has been replaced with a capacity to influence processes. Today, global governance centers around the goal of harmonizing the collective preferences of multiple actors. In these efforts to solve problems on a global scale, social power is rapidly growing in importance since it does not apply coercion and makes little use of the hierarchical modes of government. Since legitimacy is rare and the normative basis (i.e., social capital) usually fragile or lacking, social power has become a cherished, while scarce, commodity in international politics.

As we have seen, contemporary (global) governance embraces governmental institutions (be they states or IOs), but also involves informal, non-governmental mechanisms, all aspiring to frame debates and set the norms on a wide range of policy issues. States now compete with IOs, transgovernmental policy networks, as well as NGOs and private authorities in a new global governance game.[4] Clearly, the state is usually the *primes inter pares* among them, not least because its territorial embeddedness offers it unique authority as well as democratic legitimacy.[5]

But the state's enduring power base is no longer directly linked with its military capacity, since in a governance environment military force has been duly marginalized and delegitimized. Moreover, since the state can no longer take the loyalty of "its" citizens for granted, it has to work hard and smart to maintain what is left of the traditionally strong emotional bond between country and people. Place branding has become an effective mechanism for states (as well as cities and IOs) to charge citizens' emotional batteries, trying to obtain the attention, affection, and "brand loyalty" of communities living both inside and outside their borders by using practices developed in the commercial sector. Public diplomacy—both old and new—has similar ambitions.

In order to define the situation, states increasingly look at social power tools. Hard power still lurks in the background, though, reminding us of US President Teddy Roosevelt's famous dictum that smart policymakers "speak softly and carry a big stick." This relationship between hard and social power remains largely unresolved, since it is nigh impossible to clinically dissect their impact on the legitimacy and credibility of political actors and foreign policies. Scholars like Ian Manners maintain that the EU's normative power would be seriously undermined by the development of an ESDP worthy of its acronym. Others, like Robert Kagan, have famously argued that America's credibility is sustained by its massive military might, even—or perhaps: particularly—when it is not actually used. Examples can be found proving both scholars right: the EU's model of postnational policymaking has been attractive for Africa, for example, which tries to emulate the EU's experience with its African Union. At the same time, America's military preponderance has made it particularly popular in Central Europe, which still credits Ronald Reagan's power-politics with winning the Cold War. Or, as Thomas Friedman claims, "[t]he hidden hand of the market will never work without the hidden fist. McDonald's cannot flourish without McDonnell Douglas, the designer of the F-15. And the hidden fist that keeps the world safe for Silicon valley's technologies is called the U.S. Army, Air Force, Navy and Marine Corps."[6]

These two cases illustrate that social power is not simply the default option of the weak. Even hard-nosed Realpolitiker realize that the intangible qualities of social power are relevant, even to the use of military force. In all conflicts and wars, claims are made to transform brute force into legitimate rule. Whether it is God, communism, international law, or freedom, lofty goals have always been set to legitimate the use of force, confirming that hard power requires social power to ultimately achieve its goals. On the other hand, one should also recognize that normative power is not always "nice" power. Social power may certainly have a social ring to it, but it is conceptually neutral and says nothing about the moral qualities of the "situation" it endeavors to define, or the norms and values it attempts to upload to the next governance level.[7] For example, critics claim that Europe's global norm-setting is frequently a hidden form of protectionism. Take the EU's call upon all member states to ban inefficient light bulbs and to gradually introduce energy-saving CFLs (compact fluorescent light bulbs). Although a lofty plan from an environmental perspective, this decision also offers splendid new business opportunities for EU-based manufacturers such as Philips and Osram, and keeps the old-fashioned light bulbs out, which happen to be produced outside the EU, in the developing world.[8] The EU's efforts to upload its norms can therefore also be seen as a strategy to defend Europe's own social standards against worldwide competition.

Summarizing the ideas of Zaki Laïdi, we may therefore conclude that "norms" are not necessarily "nice", but that projecting (or uploading) norms is a major tool and source of social power.

8.2 MAKING IT WORK

I have argued that social power forms a central part of international politics, that it is a complex phenomenon, and forms a comprehensive feature of contemporary power—the three C's. This book has offered numerous examples, combining contemporary practices of social power with fragments of its genealogy. Although one could combine these examples and vignettes to a comprehensive and exhaustive taxonomy, this would be stretching it quite a bit. It took Michael Mann three hefty volumes to lift the veil on the sources of social power, which suggests that social power's place and role in international politics certainly still requires more scholarship, both historical and interdisciplinary (from IR, public administration, law, and economics, to cultural and media studies).[9] Still, the contours of several conclusions have become sharper, offering me the opportunity to draw them.

Central to all debates is the wielding problem: how can we connect the dots between power tools, instruments, and resources, and concrete policy outcomes? I have argued that social power has a Newtonian quality to it, since its effect may be visible, whereas the source of power normally is not. Since social power is most often set in institutions and relationships, it is difficult to actually wield it. Institutions and relationships are socially embedded, molded as they are by traditions, culture, media, as well as fads and fashions.

Whereas military power is visible and mediagenic, social power generally lacks visibility and public attention. By their very nature, institutions and relationships are visually unappealing, and often elusive. The simplicity and straightforward quality of military power stand in stark contrast to the complexity and ambiguity of social power. This makes the quality of social power less easy to understand and explain; it also makes it less easy to "sell" as a preferred tool of statecraft, both to the wider public and within bureaucratic organizations. Perhaps the current impasse in the wars in Afghanistan and Iraq offers a window of opportunity for social power to make its case. In Iraq (as well as Afghanistan), military power obviously has found its limits, whereas the struggle to win the hearts and minds of Muslim communities is an on-going effort. Obviously, winning the war of ideas requires social power, since it involves a struggle between the West and extremist Islamists to define the situation, and to upload conflicting sets of norms. Public diplomacy and place branding have emerged as social power tools to reach these foreign communities, instill legitimacy and credibility, and gain compliance. This is, of course, a tall order—but feasible, despite all odds.

So, which dots have been connected most clearly, giving us confidence that social power tools indeed form a central part of international politics? As in all social sciences, 100 percent proof is illusory. Still, some cases prove social power's value beyond any reasonable doubt. The case of culture, especially popular, or "low" culture, stands out. Since social power involves the capacity to shape and influence motives, attitudes, roles, and interests of actors in international politics (by non-coercive means), culture's qualities hardly come as a surprise. Popular culture, in particular, is uniquely capable of defining what is standard, normal, and legitimate.

These are, of course, rather unspectacular sociological observations. But applying them to the realm of international politics opens up new thinking space about the workings of power in general, and foreign policy in particular. Popular culture has been instrumentalized during the Cold War, when jazz and rock 'n' roll were used to spread the Western values of freedom and consumerism to the communist world and beyond. But arguably more influential has been the complete package of American (and more general Western) popular culture, which has offered the people of Soviet-dominated "captive nations" tempting vistas of freedom and affluence. Having myself frequently visited Central Europe in the 1980s, I recall the immense attraction these Western lifestyles had on ordinary Poles, Czechoslovaks, and East Germans, feeding the frustration and opposition which ultimately culminated in the 1989 revolutions.

The social power of popular culture permeates Western society, and is most notably visible through patterns of consumption and the impact of the media. Consumers' power of the purse is shaping notions of corporate social responsibility, whereas the rise of the Internet and me-media (blogs and wiki's) effectively limits the role and impact of traditional gatekeepers of information. The bearing of these modes of social power becomes most evident if we focus on the resistance and conflicts they provoke, especially with authoritarian governments keen on defending their bubble of identity against the perceived onslaught of a Western-dominated globalization. Obviously, countries like China realize all too well that the free flow of goods and images affects their identity, which in turn shapes the normative codex upon which both domestic and foreign policy are based. China has erected its own Great Firewall to manage the Internet, and is developing its public diplomacy network to counter the social power of its competitors. And so does the EU, which over the last decades has thrown up its own cultural Maginot line, in a rather desperate attempt to dam off American popular culture—to little avail, of course.

As we have seen, US administrations have persisted in their efforts to use, manage, and manipulate the social power instilled in America's pop culture. As a report of the US Advisory Commission on Public Diplomacy suggested, immediately after 9/11: "Brands, products, popular entertainment, higher education, corporations, and Web sites all may reinforce or undermine U.S. foreign policy objectives."[10] From cartoons to music, from movies to consumer brands, all modes of social power have been used by the US (and others) to upload their norms, and define the (global) situation—at times quite successfully.

The most impressive pool of social power comprises the images and narratives that inform the so-called "Hollywood aesthetic", which has turned itself into the globe's dominant visual language. The normative mode of communication that underlies this aesthetic offers the world a golden mean of images, which explains why it crosses boundaries easily. Hollywood has turned itself into the world's dream factory, producing its hopes and fears, based on shared desires and concerns. Olsen and Blumenberg's notion of the "Hollywood mythotypos" dissects Hollywood's social power, arguing that its movies are designed to overcome the "existential dread that our lives might be short, meaningless, and ultimately ephemeral", and appeal "to those emotions that block out the absolutism of reality: wonder, awe, purpose, and participation."[11] This offers popular culture (as well as the mass media) the social power to set standards and determine normalcy. Taken together, popular culture and media largely shape the general public's views of the world, and its notions of how the world is run, and by whom.

The relevance of these social power resources for international politics should be clear. For example, the fact that US popular culture is based on the dogma of the happy ending is reflected in (and in turn shaped by) America's can-do foreign policy ideology. The US entertainment and media industry supports this image, depicting America as a superhero who "reluctantly" steps in to rescue passive and usually incompetent communities and peoples. Ranging from Westerns to *Die Hard*-like movies, the notion that Americans should fight evil has become ingrained in the American psyche. This is the myth constructing the US as a redeemer nation. It is also an image which tickles the egos of US foreign policymakers, and informs their foreign policy decisions. But since these movies, stories, and images are consumed globally, this "natural" American role has also influenced the perceptions and expectations of the rest of the world.

Can Washington wield this pool of social power? Not really, but American policymakers are keenly aware of it, and realize the impact it has on their image and reputation as an actor in international politics. Unlike any other social power tool, America's popular culture shapes the imagination of a global community, and, more importantly, informs expectations of American foreign policy actions. Although trust in American leadership has fallen precipitously, the overall US brand remains strong, despite debacles such as the torture pictures of Abu Ghraib and Guantanamo Bay's prisoners, and the atrocities in Haditha, and other Iraqi villages. Imagine what would happen if other Great Powers like Russia or China were responsible for disasters of this magnitude—the consequences would be devastating, mainly because these states lack the massive pool of goodwill and visual hegemony the Hollywood aesthetic still offers. As long as America presents the world with its *Desperate Housewives* and *Mad Men*, it seems to get away with policy failures like Iraq.

Combined with the marginal success of America's public diplomacy efforts towards the Muslim world, the conclusion is warranted that social power is a key tool of statecraft, although inherently hard to employ effectively. As far as culture and media dominance is concerned, one can have social power without being really able to use it. In this sense, social power is structural.[12] America's popular culture offers it legitimacy and credibility, as well as visual and discursive hegemony over the global foreign policy agenda. This has given Washington the ability to dominate the agenda, and determine what issues warrant discussion; but it has not shaped ultimate policy decisions and outcomes. Al Jazeera and the surge of new media all add to the erosion of America's social power to frame the global international agenda. These new, and often powerful competitors, make it harder for political elites to control the nature, timing, and content of foreign policy debates. As a result, social power, at least in the realm of culture and media, may still involve the ability to influence and affect, but rarely to determine and control.

8.3 TILTING THE PLAYING FIELD

This makes social power uncomfortably fluffy for foreign policy analysts, but a great resource for experienced players of the global governance game. Setting rules is the core business in international politics. Both the US and EU are avid norm entrepreneurs, using every possible instrument in their toolbox to encourage others to join their normative spheres of influence. Strong states and IOs may still follow Realpolitik's rulebook of power-play and coercive diplomacy,[13] but the vast majority of rules, standards, and regulations that cover international society's *acquis communautaire* are set through non-hierarchical means of policymaking, involving such postmodern processes as best practices, benchmarking, and naming-and-shaming. In order to play this game well, policy actors have to acquire a particular sensitivity, mindset, and organizational structure to be successful. Here too, social capital assets like legitimacy and credibility, as well as trust, are indispensable.

It comes as no surprise that the EU feels comfortable in this new environment of governance and social power. The unique nature of EU policymaking, which comprises elements of intergovernmentalism, supranationalism, and comitology (i.e., the rule of committees and working groups), makes the European integration process a microcosm of global governance, be it on a regional basis.[14] Over the decades, the European Commission has spun a dense network of advisory, regulatory, and management committees which serve to set the agenda, prepare policy proposals, and implement agreed policies. Obviously, these committees are the preferred entry points for advocacy groups and NGOs, turning the EU's intrinsic hybridity and flexibility into a major *forte* to compete in today's global governance arena.

Interestingly, the soft underbelly of EU policymaking is duly compensated for by a rather tough institutional construction supporting Europe to project its norms and values to the global level. *The Economist* even suggested (in 2007) that "Brussels is becoming the world's regulatory capital."[15] EU Trade Commissioner Peter Mandelson clarified that it "is the rules of the single market which gives us the foundation to export our rules and standards around the world—an increasingly important part of my job as a trade commissioner. In short, no single market, no European project and no *Europe puissance*."[16]

Uploading one's norms is made easier by being a first mover, combined with a certain measure of economic and political power. As Mattli and Büthe suggest,

166 Conclusions

European firms "possess much better information about international standardization opportunities and proposals and, thanks to this information advantage and more effective interest representation, to be more involved—*earlier and more effectively*—than their American counterparts."[17] American firms usually learn about developments of new international standards too late, and therefore often have to pay high switching costs since international standards differ from their current practices. The EU's hybridity, combined with its institutional strictness, have made Brussels into the world champion of global governance, offering a good example of how social power is generated and used. It also suggests that social power facilititates other power resources, adding legitimacy and credibility to policy outcomes that might otherwise be deemed hegemonic. In particular, since the EU is considered a postnational actor, with a kaleidoscope of interests and norms, its policies acquire credence and authority, which are major elements determining its chances of success.

A similar route has been followed by emerging transgovernmental policy networks, which have become important conduits for social power. These transgovernmental arrangements (or global public policy networks—GPPNs) are loose alliances between government, IOs, firms, NGOs, professional organizations, and cultural and religious groups, which join together to achieve common goals. They embody the new fluid (or liquid) nature of today's governance environment, which privileges arrangements lacking institutional fixity, but rewards flexibility. This also explains the proliferation of Friends groupings, Troikas, Quartets, and Quints, which are merely the top of the iceberg of a major recalibration of the institutional foundation of global governance. The important novelty of these networks is that they are not driven by formal institutions and bureaucracies, and not managed in a modern, top-down, hierarchical style. Instead, GPPNs are "owned" by relevant slices of society, comprising as many stakeholders as is deemed necessary to be effective, efficient, and legitimate.

Transnational advocacy coalitions, in particular, whose power derives from managing information and mobilizing public support, have shown themselves remarkably adept at influencing both formal government channels and GPPNs. Norms established within the UN-sponsored Global Compact and Corporate Social Responsibility (CRS) agreements, for example, are encouraging firms to act as good, responsible corporate citizens. Firms selling directly to consumers realize that their credibility and likeability are essential elements of their brand. This implies that NGOs and the wider public of consumers may steer business actors to comply with a wide range of social and environmental goals. Together with the phenomenon of private authority—based on gentlemen agreements, codes of conduct, ethical guidelines, and partnerships—today's policymaking environment has become a crowded field of actors, all with diverging claims on legitimacy and credibility. The state has become only one of these competing actors, who are all trying to define the situation, and aiming to set rules and standards.

Social power can be used to tilt the playing field, by setting the structural conditions needed to achieve foreign policy goals and limit the costs to do so. The EU's institutional structure and its normative authority have proved to be effective social power tools. The US, however, has made use of the social power derived from its hegemonic pop culture, on top of all the other structural qualities inherent in its powerful Brand USA. In particular, public diplomacy and place branding are emerging as strategies used by new players—ranging from emerging Great Powers like China, to IOs such as NATO—in order to enhance and capitalize on their social capital. They are not always successful, to be sure, since many of these rather inexperienced actors are feeling their way forward, trying to learn the largely unwritten mores and mechanisms of global governance's rulebook.

One of the bigger challenges for *all* actors involved in public diplomacy and place branding has been the need to shed the mindset of power-politics, based on control and hierarchy. Instead, the new paradigm of social power has to be embraced, which does not use the megaphone, making claims, but aims to shape an idea or argument in the hope that they will eventually be taken up and reproduced by others, and hence get a life of their own. Social power is therefore less about authority, telling others what to do, as it is about showing others what we consider to be desirable, in the hope that it will be emulated.

Just as social power aims to tilt the playing field of international politics, this book has tried to tip the IR debate on the nature of power. As I indicated in Chapter 1, this book has not relied upon a single conception of power, but has instead looked beyond social power itself, trying to explain its role and place in international politics in relation to other, more traditional modes of power (such as military, symbolic, and soft power). In doing so, this book has offered numerous cases illustrating, if not confirming, the growing role of social power, especially in a global governance environment. Without appreciating the nature and workings of social power, contemporary international politics can no longer be understood.

Notes

1 Social power defined

1 Quoted in Michael Moran, "Losing the Cold Peace, *Op-Ed – Council on Foreign Relations* (July 20, 2008).
2 Eric Hobsbawm, *On Empire: America, War, and Global Supremacy* (New York: Pantheon, 2008); Fareed Zakaria, *The Post-American World* (New York: W.W. Norton, 2008); and Robert Kagan, *The Return of History and the End of Dreams* (New York: Knopf, 2008).
3 Kurt M. Campbell and Jonathon Price (eds.), *The Global Politics of Energy* (Washington DC: The Aspen Institute, 2008), and Jan H. Kalicki and David L. Goldwyn (eds.), *Energy and Security: Toward a New Foreign Policy Strategy* (Washington DC: Woodrow Wilson Center Press, 2005).
4 Thomas L. Friedman, *The World is Flat: A Brief History of the Twenty-First Century* (New York: Farrar, Straus, and Giroux, 2006).
5 Yale H. Ferguson, "Approaches to Defining 'Empire' and Characterizing United States Influence in the Contemporary World", *International Studies Perspectives*, vol. 9, no. 3 (August 2008), p. 279. See also Niall Ferguson, "A World Without Power", *Foreign Policy*, no. 143 (July/August 2004).
6 Chris Giles, "Time to Stop the Dominoes Falling", *Financial Times* (October 10, 2008), p. B1, and *Financial Times*, "Nationalise to Save the Free Market" (October 14, 2008).
7 Harold Lasswell, *Politics: Who Gets What, When, How* (Cleveland: Meridian Books, 1958), and Barry Hindess, *Discourses of Power: From Hobbes to Foucault* (Oxford: Blackwell, 1996).
8 James N. Rosenau, "Governance, Order, and Change in World Politics", in James N. Rosenau and Ernst-Otto Czempiel (eds.), *Governance Without Government: Order and Change in World Politics* (Cambridge: Cambridge University Press, 1992); Martin Hewson and Timothy J. Sinclair (eds.), *Approaches to Global Governance Theory* (Albany, NY: State University of New York Press, 1999); Michael Barnett and Raymond Duvall (eds.), *Power in Global Governance* (Cambridge: Cambridge University Press, 2005); and Doris Fuchs, *Business Power in Global Governance* (Boulder, CO: Lynne Rienner, 2007).
9 David Held, Antony McGrew, David Goldblatt, and Jonathan Perraton, *Global Transformations: Politics, Economics and Culture* (Oxford: Blackwell, 1999), p. 447.
10 Brigid C. Harrison and Thomas R. Dye, *Power and Society: An Introduction to the Social Sciences* (Florence KY: Wadsworth Publishing, 2007).
11 David A. Baldwin, *Paradoxes of Power* (Oxford: Blackwell, 1989), p. 1. See also Baldwin, *Economic Statecraft* (Princeton, NJ: Princeton University Press, 1985).
12 Anna Holzscheiter, "Discourse as Capability: Non-State Actors' Capital in Global Governance", *Millennium*, vol. 33, no. 3 (June 2005), pp. 724–25. See also

Cynthia Enloe, "Margins, Silences, and Bottom Rungs: How to Overcome the Underestimation of Power in the Study of International Relations", in Steve Smith, Ken Booth, and Marysia Zalewski (eds.), *International Relations Theory: Positivism and Beyond* (Cambridge: Cambridge University Press, 1996).
13 Joseph S. Nye, Jr., *Soft Power: The Means to Success in World Politics* (New York: Public Affairs, 2004); Ted Galen Carpenter, *Smart Power: Toward a Prudent Foreign Policy for America* (Washington DC: Cato Institute, 2008); and Walter Russel Mead, "America's Sticky Power", *Foreign Policy*, no. 141 (March/April 2004).
14 John J. Mearsheimer, *The Tragedy of Great Power Politics* (New York: W.W. Norton, 2001).
15 David A. Baldwin, "Power and International Relations", in Walter Carlsnaes, Thomas Risse, and Beth A. Simmons (eds.), *Handbook of International Relations* (London: Sage, 2002).
16 Friedrich Kratochwil, "Of False Promises and Good Bets: A Plea for a Pragmatic Approach to Theory Building (The Tartu Lecture)", *Journal of International Relations and Development*, vol. 10, no. 1 (March 2007).
17 For an overview of the sociological literature on power, see John Scott, *Power* (Cambridge: Polity Press, 2001). See also Michael Mann, *The Sources of Social Power: A History of Power from the Beginning to A.D. 1760* (Cambridge: Cambridge University Press, 1986), and Daniel Philpott, *Revolutions in Sovereignty: How Ideas Shaped Modern International Relations* (Princeton, NJ: Princeton University Press, 2001). See also Peter Morriss, *Power: A Philosophical Analysis* (Manchester: Manchester University Press, 2002).
18 Jennifer Sterling-Folker and Rosemary E. Shinko, "Discourses of Power: Traversing the Realist-Postmodern Divide", *Millennium*, vol. 33, no. 3 (June 2005), pp. 637–38.
19 Ferguson, "Approaches to Defining 'Empire'", p. 279.
20 David A. Baldwin, "Power Analysis and World Politics: New Trends versus Old Tendencies", *World Politics*, vol. 31, no. 1 (October 1978).
21 Alain Touraine, *Return of the Actor* (Minneapolis: University of Minnesota Press, 1988), p. 49.
22 Steven Lukes, "Power and the Battle for Hearts and Minds", *Millennium*, vol. 33, no. 3 (June 2005), p. 478.
23 Quoted in Daniel Philpott, "Ideas and the Evolution of Sovereignty", in Sohail H. Hashmi (ed.), *State Sovereignty: Change and Persistence in International Relations* (University Park: The Pennsylvania State University Press, 1997), p. 17.
24 Wolfgang Reinhard (ed.), *Power Elites and State Building* (Oxford: Oxford University Press, 1996), and Herbert C. Kelman, "Reflections on Social and Psychological Processes of Legitimization and Delegitimization", in John T. Jost and Brenda Major (eds.), *The Psychology of Legitimacy: Emerging Perspectives on Ideology, Justice, and Intergroup Relations* (Cambridge: Cambridge University Press, 2001).
25 Jill Esbenshade, *Monitoring Sweatshops: Workers, Consumers, and the Global Apparel Industry* (Philadelphia: Temple University Press, 2004), and Rebecca DeWinter, "The Anti-Sweatshop Movement: Constructing Corporate Moral Agency in the Global Apparel Industry", *Ethics & International Affairs*, vol. 15, no. 2 (December 2001).
26 John Lewis Gaddis, *The Cold War: A New History* (New York: Penguin, 2006).
27 Robert Service, *Stalin: A Biography* (Cambridge, MA: Belknap Press, 2006).
28 George Weigel, *Witness to Hope: The Biography of Pope John Paul II* (New York: Harper Perennial, 1999).
29 Hans-Henrik Holm and Georg Sørensen (eds.), *Whose World Order? Uneven Globalization and the End of the Cold War* (Boulder, CO: Westview Press, 1995).
30 Benjamin R. Barber, *Jihad vs. McWorld: How Globalism and Tribalism Are Reshaping the World* (New York: Ballantine Books, 1995).
31 Tina Rosenberg, *The Haunted Land: Facing Europe's Ghosts After Communism* (New York: Vintage Books, 1995), p. xviii.

32 Cynthia Weber, *Simulating Sovereignty: Intervention, the State and Symbolic Exchange* (Cambridge: Cambridge University Press, 1995).
33 Joseph S. Nye, Jr., "Soft Power and American Foreign Policy", *Political Science Quarterly*, vol. 119, no. 2 (Summer 2004), p. 256. See also Nye, *Soft Power*, and Kathryn Sikkink, "Restructuring World Politics: The Limits and Asymmetries of Soft Power", in Sanjeev Khagram, James V. Riker, and Kathryn Sikkink (eds.), *Restructuring World Politics: Transnational Social Movements* (Minneapolis: University of Minnesota Press, 2002).
34 Nye, *Soft Power*, p. 6.
35 Joseph S. Nye, Jr., *Bound to Lead: The Changing Nature of American Power* (New York: Basic Books, 1990), p. 32.
36 US Secretary of Defense Robert M. Gates, "Landon Lecture – Kansas State University", Manhattan, Kansas (November 26, 2007). See also Michael Cox and Adam Quinn, "Hard Times for Soft Power? America and the Atlantic Community", in David Held and Henrietta L. Moore (eds.), *Cultural Politics in a Global Age: Uncertainty, Solidarity and Innovation* (Oxford: Oneworld Publications, 2007).
37 Walter Russel Mead, *Power, Terror, Peace, and War: America's Grand Strategy in a World at Risk* (New York: Vintage Books, 2005), and Mead, "America's Sticky Power".
38 Mead, "America's Sticky Power", p. 50.
39 Robert O. Keohane and Joseph S. Nye, Jr., *Transnational Relations and World Politics* (Cambridge, MA: Harvard University Press, 1972); and John D.B. Miller, *Norman Angell and the Futility of War: Peace and the Public Mind* (London: Palgrave Macmillan, 1986).
40 Proponents of liberal institutionalism include Robert O. Keohane, Oran Young, Kenneth Oye, Helen Milner, and Robert Axelrod. For a Realist critique of liberal institutionalism, see John J. Mearsheimer, "The False Promise of International Institutions", *International Security*, vol. 19, no. 3 (Winter 1994).
41 Stephen D. Krasner, "Structural Causes and Regime Consequences: Regimes as Intervening Variables", *International Organization*, vol. 36, no. 2 (Spring 1982).
42 E.H. Carr, *The Twenty Years' Crisis* (New York: HarperCollins, 2001/1939), pp. 79–80.
43 Mearsheimer, *The Tragedy of Great Power Politics*, pp. 55; 12.
44 These schools are epitomized by the work of respectively Hedley Bull and Timothy Dunne; Robert Keohane and Thomas Risse; Stephen Krasner; and Audie Klotz and Martha Finnemore. See Cynthia Weber (ed.), *International Relations Theory: A Critical Introduction* (New York: Routledge, 2001), and Andrew Linklater, Matthew Paterson, Christian Reus-Smit, and Jacqui True (eds.), *Theories of International Relations* (New York: Palgrave, 2001).
45 Doris Fuchs, "Commanding Heights? The Strength and Fragility of Business Power in Global Politics", *Millennium*, vol. 33, no. 3 (June 2005), p. 771.
46 Richard Ned Lebow, *The Tragic Vision of Politics: Ethics, Interests and Orders* (Cambridge: Cambridge University Press, 2003), and Ronnie D. Lipschutz, "Power, Politics and Global Civil Society", *Millennium*, vol. 33, no. 3 (June 2005).
47 Thomas C. Schelling, *Arms and Influence* (New Haven: Yale University Press, 1966), p. 3.
48 Maria Sperandei, "Bridging Deterrence and Compellence: An Alternative Approach to the Study of Coercive Diplomacy", *International Studies Review*, vol. 8, no. 2 (June 2006), p. 253.
49 Mead, "America's Sticky Power", p. 53.
50 Mead, "America's Sticky Power", p. 48.
51 Philpott makes frequent use of the notion of social power (without, however, defining the concept itself), arguing that it explains how "identities mould political interests." Philpott, *Revolutions in Sovereignty*, p. 49.
52 Alexander Wendt, *Social Theory of International Politics* (Cambridge: Cambridge University Press, 1999), p. 161.
53 Holzscheiter, "Discourse as Capability", p. 735.

54 Martha Finnemore and Kathryn Sikkink, "International Norm Dynamics and Political Change", *International Organization*, vol. 52, no. 4 (Autumn 1998), p. 897.
55 Finnemore and Sikkink, "International Norm Dynamics and Political Change", p. 893.
56 Christian Spielvogel, "'You Know Where I Stand': Moral Framing of the War on Terrorism and the Iraq War in the 2004 Presidential Campaign", *Rhetoric & Public Affairs*, vol. 8, no. 4 (Winter 2005), p. 551. See also Karen Callaghan and Frauke Schnell (eds.), *Framing American Politics* (Pittsburgh, PA: University of Pittsburgh Press, 2005); George Lakoff, *Don't Think of an Elephant: Know Your Values and Frame the Debate* (White River Jct.: Chelsea Green Publishers, 2004); Mark Allen Peterson, "American Warriors Speaking American: The Metapragmatics of Performance in the Nation State", in Mirjana N. Dedaic and Daniel N. Nelson (eds.), *At War With Words* (Berlin/New York: Mouton de Gruyter, 2003); Robert D. Benford and David A. Snow, "Framing Processes and Social Movements: An Overview and Assessment, *Annual Review of Sociology*, vol. 26 (2000); and Rodger A. Payne, "Persuasion, Frames, and Norm Construction", *European Journal of International Relations*, vol. 7, no. 1 (March 2001).
57 Finnemore and Sikkink, "International Norm Dynamics and Political Change", p. 908.
58 Theo Farrell, "Transnational Norms and Military Development: Constructing Ireland's Professional Army", *European Journal of International Relations*, vol. 7, no. 1 (March 2001).
59 Mayer N. Zald, "Culture, Ideology, and Strategic Framing", in Doug McAdam, John D. McCarthy, and Mayer N. Zald (eds.), *Comparative Perspectives on Social Movements: Political Opportunities, Mobilizing Structures, and Cultural Framings* (Cambridge: Cambridge University Press, 1996), p. 268.
60 Pepper D. Culpepper, "The Politics of Common Knowledge: Ideas and Institutional Change in Wage Bargaining", *International Organization*, vol. 62, no. 1 (Winter 2008), p. 5.
61 Culpepper, "The Politics of Common Knowledge", p. 9.
62 Margaret E. Keck and Kathryn Sikkink, *Activists Beyond Borders: Advocacy Networks in International Politics* (Ithaca, NY: Cornell University Press, 1998), p. 35.
63 Ann Florini, "The Evolution of International Norms", *International Studies Quarterly*, vol. 40, no. 3 (September 1996); Audie Klotz, *Norms in International Relations: The Struggle Against Apartheid* (Ithaca, NY: Cornell University Press, 1995); and Edna Ullmann-Margalit, *The Emergence of Norms* (Oxford: Clarendon Press, 1977).
64 Robert M. Entman, *Projections of Power: Framing News, Public Opinion, and U.S. Foreign Policy* (Chicago: University of Chicago Press, 2004).
65 Donald A. Schön and Martin Rein, *Frame Reflection: Toward the Resolution of Intractable Policy Controversies* (New York: Basic Books, 1994), p. 29.
66 US President George W. Bush, *National Strategy for Combating Terrorism* (2003), pp. 23–24.
67 Brian Steensland, "Why Do Policy Frames Change? Actor-Idea Coevolution in Debates Over Welfare Reform", *Social Forces*, vol. 86, no. 3 (March 2008), p. 1028.
68 Myra Marx Ferree, William A. Gamson, Jürgen Gerhards, and Dieter Ruchs, *Shaping Abortion Discourse: Democracy and the Public Sphere in Germany and the United States* (Cambridge: Cambridge University Press, 2002).
69 Katharina Holzinger and Christoph Knill, "Causes and Conditions of Cross-National Policy Convergence", *Journal of European Public Policy*, vol. 12, no. 5 (October 2005), p. 779.
70 Holzinger and Knill. "Causes and Conditions of Cross-National Policy Convergence", p. 786.
71 Erving Goffman, *Frame Analysis: An Essay on the Organization of Experience* (New York: Harper & Row, 1974).
72 Amitav Acharya, "How Ideas Spread: Whose Norms Matter? Norm Localization and Institutional Change in Asian Regionalism", *International Organization*, vol. 58, no. 2 (Spring 2004), p. 241.

73 Jeffrey W. Legro, "Which Norms Matter? Revisiting the 'Failure' of Internationalism", *International Organization*, vol. 51, no. 1 (Winter 1997), and Jeffrey T. Checkel, "Why Comply? Social Learning and European Identity Change", *International Organization*, vol. 55, no. 2 (Summer 2001).
74 Acharya, "How Ideas Spread", pp. 247–48.
75 Ian Hurd, *After Anarchy: Legitimacy and Power in the United Nations Security Council* (Princeton, NJ: Princeton University Press, 2007), p. 30.
76 Morris Zelditch, Jr., "Theories of Legitimacy", in John T. Jost and Brenda Major (eds.), *The Psychology of Legitimacy: Emerging Perspectives on Ideology, Justice, and Intergroup Relations* (Cambridge: Cambridge University Press, 2001), p. 51.
77 See in the rich literature on legitimacy in international politics, especially Andrew Hurrell, *On Global Order: Power, Values, and the Constitution of International Society* (Oxford: Oxford University Press, 2007); Friedrich Kratochwil, "On Legitimacy", *International Relations*, vol. 20, no. 3 (September 2006); Shane P. Mulligan, "The Uses of Legitimacy in International Relations", *Millennium*, vol. 34, no. 2 (February 2006); Corneliu Bjola, "Legitimating the Use of Force in International Politics: A Communicative Action Perspective", *European Journal of International Relations*, vol. 11, no. 2 (June 2005); Andrew Hurrell, "Legitimacy and the Use of Force: Can the Circle Be Squared?", *Review of International Studies*, vol. 31, Special Issue (December 2005); Ian Clark, *Legitimacy in International Society* (Oxford: Oxford University Press, 2005); Shane P. Mulligan, "Questioning (the Question of) Legitimacy in IR: A Reply to Jens Steffek", *European Journal of International Relations*, vol. 10, no. 3 (September 2004); Jens Steffek, "The Legitimacy of International Governance: A Discourse Approach", *European Journal of International Relations*, vol. 9, no. 2 (June 2003); Allen Buchanan, "Political Legitimacy and Democracy", *Ethics*, vol. 112, no. 4 (July 2002); Mlada Bukovansky, *Legitimacy and Power Politics: The American and French Revolutions in International Political Culture* (Princeton, NJ: Princeton University Press, 2002); Kenneth W. Abbott, Robert O. Keohane, Andrew Moravcsik, Anne-Marie Slaughter, and Duncan Snidal. "The Concept of Legalization", *International Organization*, vol. 54, no. 3 (Summer 2000); Rosemary H.T. O'Kane and David Beetham, "Against Legitimacy – Comment/Reply", *Political Studies*, vol. 41, no. 3 (September 1993); David Beetham, *The Legitimation of Power* (Basingstoke: Palgrave, 1991); and Thomas M. Franck, *The Power of Legitimacy Among Nations* (New York: Oxford University Press, 1990).
78 Daniel C. Esty, "Good Governance at the Supranational Scale: Globalizing Administrative Law", *The Yale Law Journal*, vol. 115, no. 7 (May 2006), p. 1504. See also Nicholas Rengger, "The Ethics of Trust in World Politics", *International Affairs*, vol. 73, no. 3 (July 1997).
79 Thomas M. Franck, "The Power of Legitimacy and the Legitimacy of Power: International Law in an Age of Power Disequilibrium", *The American Journal of International Law*, vol. 100, no. 1 (June 2006), p. 91.
80 Andrew Linklater, *The Transformation of Political Community* (Cambridge: Polity Press, 1998).
81 Francis Fukuyama, "Social Capital and the Global Economy", *Foreign Affairs*, vol. 74, no. 5 (September/October 1995); Carles Boix and Daniel N. Posner, "Social Capital: Explaining Its Origins and Effects on Goverment Performance", *British Journal of Political Science*, vol. 28, no. 4 (October 1998); Robert W. Jackman and Ross A. Miller, "Social Capital and Politics", *Annual Review of Political Science*, vol. 1 (June 1998); Alejandro Portes, "Social Capital: Its Origins and Application in Modern Sociology", *American Review of Sociology*, vol. 24 (August 1998); John R. Searle, *The Construction of Social Reality* (New York: The Free Press, 1995); and James S. Coleman, "Social Capital in the Creation of Human Capital", *American Journal of Sociology*, vol. 94, no. 1 (January 1988).
82 Ferdinand Toennies, *Community and Association* (London: Routledge, 1974).

83 Francis Fukuyama, *Trust: The Social Virtues and the Creation of Prosperity* (New York: The Free Press, 1996); and Fukuyama, *The Great Disruption: Human Nature and the Reconstitution of Social Order* (New York: The Free Press, 1999).
84 Esty, "Good Governance", p. 1505.
85 Richard Ned Lebow, "Reason, Emotion and Cooperation", *International Politics*, vol. 42, no. 3 (September 2005); Jeffrey T. Checkel, "Social Constructivisms in Global and European Politics: A Review Essay", *Review of International Studies*, vol. 30, no. 2 (April 2004); John T. Jost and Brenda Major (eds.), *The Psychology of Legitimacy: Emerging Perspectives on Ideology, Justice, and Intergroup Relations* (Cambridge: Cambridge University Press, 2001); and Emanuel Adler and Michael Barnett (eds.), *Security Communities* (Cambridge: Cambridge University Press, 1998).
86 Robert A. Dahl, *Democracy and Its Critics* (New Haven: Yale University Press, 1989).
87 Ian Hurd, "Legitimacy and Authority in International Politics", *International Organization*, vol. 53, no. 2 (Spring 1999).
88 Esty, "Good Governance", p. 1517.
89 Thomas Diez and Jill Steans, "A Useful Dialogue? Habermas and International Relations", *Review of International Studies*, vol. 31, no. 1 (January 2005); Jennifer Milliken, "The Study of Discourse in International Relations", *European Journal of International Relations*, vol. 5, no. 2 (June 1999); and James J. Chriss, "Habermas, Goffman, and Communicative Action: Implications for Professional Practice", *American Sociological Review*, vol. 60, no. 4 (August 1995).
90 Angela Merkel, "Germany's Foreign and Security Policy in the Face of Global Challenges – Speech at the 41st Munich Conference on Security Policy", Munich (4 February 2006).
91 Hewson and Sinclair (eds.), *Approaches to Global Governance Theory*.
92 Lisa Martin, *Global Governance* (Farnham: Ashgate, 2008).
93 Rosenau, "Governance, Order, and Change in World Politics", p. 3.
94 See on the importance of "reasonable" principles and standards of behavior and governance, John Rawls, *Political Liberalism* (New York: Columbia University Press, 1993).
95 Anne-Marie Slaughter, "Everyday Global Governance", *Daedalus*, vol. 132, no. 1 (Winter 2003), p. 83.
96 Rosenau, "Governance, Order, and Change in World Politics", p. 4.
97 Jens Steffek, *Embedded Liberalism and Its Critics: Justifying Global Governance in the American Century* (New York: Palgrave Macmillan, 2006); Allen Buchanan and Robert O. Keohane, "The Legitimacy of Global Governance Institutions", *Ethics & International Affairs*, vol. 20, no. 4 (Winter 2006); Ole Jacob Sending and Iver B. Neumann, "Governance to Governmentality: Analyzing NGOs, States, and Power", *International Studies Quarterly*, vol. 50, no. 3 (September 2006); Miles Kahler and David A Lake (eds.), *Governance in a Global Economy: Political Authority in Transition* (Princeton, NJ: Princeton University Press, 2003); Pascal Lamy and Zaki Laïdi, "A European Approach to Global Governance", *Progressive Politics*, vol. 1, no. 1 (September 2002); and Kal Raustiala, "Governance in World Affairs", *The American Journal of International Law*, vol. 94, no. 4 (October 2000).
98 Michael Barnett, "Culture, Strategy, and Foreign Policy Change: Israel's Road to Oslo", *European Journal of International Relations*, vol. 5, no. 1 (March 1999), p. 7.
99 James Traub, "The New Hard-Soft Power", *New York Times Magazine* (January 30, 2005), and Philip Manning, "Credibility, Agency, and the Interaction Order", *Symbolic Interaction*, vol. 23, no. 3 (August 2000).
100 Lukes, "Power and the Battle for Hearts and Minds", p. 480. Contrasting normative power and persuasion to coercion, is too simple and highly problematic. Legitimacy generally confers power, but the reverse is oftentimes also true: power can help to establish legitimacy. As Philpott suggests: "If early modern states had never developed means of coercion—bureaucracies, the power to tax and raise armies—the legitimate authority of Hobbes's sovereign would never have been possible." Moreover, as we will

see in our analysis of geopolitical power and hegemony (Chapter 2), social power is not necessarily benign. See Philpott, "Ideas and the Evolution of Sovereignty", p. 17.
101 Conor Foley, *The Thin Blue Line: How Humanitarianism Went to War* (London: Verso, 2008).
102 Mary Elise Sarotte, *Dealing With the Devil: East Germany, Détente, and Ostpolitik, 1969–1973* (Chapel Hill: The University of North Carolina Press, 2000).
103 "Ronald Reagan, Surprising Victor of the Cold War", *The Economist* (June 10, 2004).
104 Renée De Nevers, "Imposing International Norms: Great Powers and Norm Enforcement", *International Studies Review*, vol. 9, no. 1 (Spring 2007), p. 54.
105 De Nevers, "Imposing International Norms", p. 76.
106 Janice Bially Mattern, "Why 'Soft Power' Isn't So Soft: Representational Force and the Sociolinguistic Construction of Attraction in World Politics", *Millennium*, vol. 33, no. 3 (June 2005), pp. 586–87.
107 Linda S. Bishai, "Liberal Empire", *Journal of International Relations and Development*, vol. 7, no. 1 (April 2004), p. 54.
108 Neta C. Crawford, "Decolonization as an International Norm: The Evolution of Practices, Arguments, and Beliefs", in Laura W. Reed and Carl Kaysen (eds.), *Emerging Norms of Justified Intervention* (Cambridge, MA: American Academy of Arts and Sciences, 1993), p. 52.
109 Mattern, "Why 'Soft Power' Isn't So Soft", p. 602.
110 Thomas Risse, " 'Let's Argue!', Communicative Action in World Politics", *International Organization*, vol. 54, no. 1 (Winter 2000).
111 Thomas Risse and Kathryn Sikkink, "The Socialization of International Human Rights Norms into Domestic Practices", in Thomas Risse, Stephen C. Ropp, and Kathryn Sikkink (eds.), *The Power of Human Rights: International Norms and Domestic Change* (Cambridge: Cambridge University Press, 1999), pp. 37–38.
112 Barry M. Blechman, "Book Review of Nye's *Soft Power*", *Political Science Quarterly*, vol. 119, no. 4 (Winter 2004/5), p. 608.
113 Blechman, "Book Review", p. 681.
114 Jeffrey M. Chwieroth, "Testing and Measuring the Role of Ideas: The Case of Neoliberalism in the International Monetary Fund", *International Studies Quarterly*, vol. 51, no. 1 (March 2007), p. 5. See also Pierre C. Pahlavi, "Evaluating Public Diplomacy Programmes", *The Hague Journal of Diplomacy*, vol. 2, no. 3 (October 2007).
115 Doris Fuchs, "Commanding Heights?", p. 780.
116 Craig Parsons, "Showing Ideas as Causes: The Origins of the European Union", *International Organization*, vol. 56, no. 1 (Winter 2002), p. 48.
117 Jeffrey T. Checkel, "The Constructivist Turn in International Relations Theory", *World Politics*, vol. 50, no. 2 (January 1998), p. 339. Emphasis added.
118 Anne E. Sartori, "The Might of the Pen: A Reputational Theory of Communication in International Disputes", *International Organization*, vol. 56, no. 1 (Winter 2002).
119 Parsons, "Showing Ideas as Causes", p. 76.
120 Parsons, "Showing Ideas as Causes", p. 79.
121 Robert Adcock and David Collier, "Measurement Validity: A Shared Standard for Qualitative and Quantitative Research", *American Political Science Review*, vol. 95, no. 3 (September 2001), and Henry E. Brady and David Collier (eds.), *Rethinking Social Inquiry: Diverse Tools, Shared Standards* (Lanham, MD: Rowman & Littlefield, 2004).
122 Michael Barnett and Raymond Duvall, "Power in International Politics", *International Organization*, vol. 59, no. 1 (Winter 2005), p. 44. See also Barnet and Duvall (eds.), *Power in Global Governance*.
123 Barnett and Duvall, "Power in International Politics", p. 44. See also Stefano Guzzini, "The Use and Misuse of Power Analysis in International Theory", in Ronen Palan (ed.), *Global Political Economy: Contemporary Analysis* (London: Routledge, 2000).

124 Barnett and Duvall, "Power in International Politics", p. 46.
125 Barnett and Duvall, "Power in International Politics", p. 67.

2 Geopolitics and hegemony

1 Honor Mahony, "Barroso Says EU is an 'Empire' ", *EUObserver.com* (July 11, 2007).
2 Bruno Waterfield, "Barroso Hails the European 'Empire' ", *Daily Telegraph* (July 12, 2007). Emphasis added.
3 Quoted in Samuel P. Huntington, "The Lonely Superpower" *Foreign Affairs*, vol. 78, no. 2 (March/April 1999), p. 38. See also Alexander K. Motyl, "Empire Falls: Washington May Be Imperious But It Is Not Imperial", *Foreign Affairs*, vol. 85, no. 4 (July/August 2006), and Niall Ferguson, "An Empire in Denial", *Harvard International Review*, vol. 25, no. 3 (Fall 2003).
4 Alan Ryan, "What Happened to the American Empire?" *The New York Review of Books*, vol. 55, no. 16 (October 23, 2008), p. 59.
5 Andrew J. Bacevich, *American Empire: The Realities and Consequences of U.S. Diplomacy* (Cambridge, MA: Harvard University Press, 2004); Niall Ferguson, *Colossus: The Price of America's Empire* (New York: Penguin, 2004); Christian Reus-Smith, *American Power and World Order* (London: Polity, 2004); Thanh Duong, *Hegemonic Globalisation: U.S. Centrality and Global Strategy in the Emerging World Order* (New York: Ashgate, 2002); William C. Wohlforth, "The Stability of a Unipolar World", *International Security*, vol. 24, no. 1 (Summer 1999); Fareed Zakaria, *From Wealth to Power: The Unusual Origins of America's World Role* (Princeton, NJ: Princeton University Press, 1998); and Richard N. Haass, *The Reluctant Sheriff: The United States After the Cold War* (New York: Council on Foreign Relations Press, 1997).
6 Parag Khanna, *The Second World: Empires and Influence in the New Global Order* (New York: Random House, 2008); Amy Chua, *Day of Empire: How Hyperpowers Rise to Global Dominance—And Why They Fall* (New York: Doubleday, 2008); Deepak Lal, *In Praise of Empires: Globalization and Order* (New York: Palgrave Macmillan, 2004); Francis Fukuyama, "US Must Balance Hard Power with Soft Power", *New Perspectives Quarterly*, vol. 21, no. 3 (Summer 2004); and Charles A. Kupchan, *The Vulnerability of Empire* (Ithaca, NY: Cornell University Press, 1994).
7 David A. Lake, "The New American Empire?", *International Studies Perspectives*, vol. 9, no. 3 (August 2008), p. 284.
8 Thomas F. Madden, *Empires of Trust: How Rome Built—And America Is Building—A New* World (New York: Dutton, 2008).
9 Theo Farrell, "Strategic Culture and American Empire", *SAIS Review*, vol. 25, no. 2 (Summer 2005), p. 3.
10 Farrell, "Strategic Culture and American Empire", p. 11.
11 Richard Ned Lebow and Robert Kelly, "Thucydides and Hegemony: Athens and the United States", *Review of International Studies*, vol. 27, no. 4 (October 2001), p. 595.
12 Philpott, *Revolutions in Sovereignty*. See esp. Chapter 8 ("Ideas and the End of Empire").
13 Samuel P. Huntington, *The Clash of Civilizations and the Remaking of World Order* (New York: Simon & Schuster, 1996).
14 Richard Ned Lebow, "Power, Persuasion and Justice", *Millennium*, vol. 33, no. 3 (June 2005), and Lebow, *A Cultural Theory of International Relations* (Cambridge: Cambridge University Press, 2008).
15 Jonathan Monten, "Thucydides and Modern Realism", *International Studies Quarterly*, vol. 50, no. 1 (March 2006).
16 Lebow, "Power, Persuasion and Justice", p. 555.
17 Lebow, "Power, Persuasion and Justice", pp. 572–73.
18 Lebow and Kelly, "Thucydides and Hegemony".
19 Lebow, "Power, Persuasion and Justice", p. 579. Using a different metaphor, Candace Archer suggests that hegemons are (or should be) like the casinos in Las Vegas: they

"make the rules, but they do not win every bet. If they did, nobody would gamble (...) Being powerful enough to make the rules does not mean that you should make them in such a way that you win every time (...) But make the rules so that however many other winners there are, you come out the big winner, and you are hegemonic." See Candace Archer, "Hegemony and Las Vegas", *International Studies Perpsectives*, vol. 5, no. 2 (May 2004), inside backcover. For America's enlighted hegemony after World War II, see Geir Lundestad, *The United States and Western Europe Since 1945: From "Empire" by Invitation to Transatlantic Drift* (Oxford: Oxford University Press, 2003).

20 G. John Ikenberry and Charles A. Kupchan, "Socialization and Hegemonic Power", *International Organization*, vol. 44, no. 3 (Summer 1990).

21 Robert W. Cox, "Social Forces, States and World Orders: Beyond International Relations Theory", *Millennium*, vol. 10, no. 2 (June 1981), and Andreas Bieler and Adam David Morton, "A Critical Theory Route to Hegemony, World Order and Historical Change", *Capital and Class*, vol. 85 (Spring 2004).

22 Cox, "Social Forces, States and World Orders", p. 139. See also William I. Robinson, "Gramsci and Globalisation: From Nation-State to Transnational Hegemony", *Critical Review of Social and Political Philosophy*, vol. 8, no. 4 (December 2005); Jacques Dufresne, "Soft Opposition to Soft Domination", *Technology in Society*, vol. 20, no. 3 (August 1998); and Chantal Mouffe, "Hegemony and Ideology in Gramsci", in Chantal Mouffe (ed.), *Gramsci and Marxist Theory* (London: Routledge, 1979).

23 Robert W. Cox, *Production, Power and World Order: Social Forces in the Making of History* (New York: Columbia University Press, 1987), p. 4.

24 Gramsci identified three mechanisms: universalization, naturalization, and rationalization. *Universalization* implies the dissemination of norms and practices; *naturalization* implies the process where hegemonic culture becomes "natural", based on the assumption that there is no point in questioning or fighting against "nature"; and *rationalization* implies a process where intellectuals and opinion-shapers (ranging from politicians, scientists to journalists) rationalize the dominant norm at all levels of societal activity, from politics, academia, education to entertainment. In all three mechanisms, social relations are the main vehicles of norm dissemination, hence confirming the centrality of social power in creating and sustaining hegemony. See Mouffe, "Hegemony and Ideology in Gramsci".

25 Ikenberry and Kupchan, "Socialization and Hegemonic Power", p. 283. Ann Florini argues that "[i]nternational norms may also begin to spread in the absence of a norm entrepreneur if some states simply emulate the behaviour of some prestigious or otherwise well-known actor, even if the emulated actor is not attempting to communicate its behaviour." Florini, "The Evolution of International Norms", p. 375. See also Benjamin O. Fordham and Victor Asal, "Billiard Balls or Snowflakes? Major Power Prestige and the International Diffusion of Institutions and Practices", *International Studies Quarterly*, vol. 51, no. 1 (March 2007).

26 Dennis K. Mumby, "The Problem of Hegemony: Rereading Gramsci for Organizational Communication Studies", *Western Journal of Communication*, vol. 61, no. 4 (Fall 1997), p. 344.

27 Tanja A. Börzel, "Pace-Setting, Foot-Dragging, and Fence-Sitting: Member State Responses to Europeanization", *Journal of Common Market Studies*, vol. 40, no. 2 (June 2002).

28 Finnemore and Sikkink, "International Norm Dynamics and Political Change".

29 Ellen Lutz and Kathryn Sikkink, "The Justice Cascade: The Evolution and Impact of Foreign Human Rights Trials in Latin America", *Chicago Journal of International Law*, vol. 2, no. 1 (Spring 2001), p. 5.

30 Annika Björkdahl, "Norm Advocacy: A Small State Strategy to Influence the EU", *Journal of European Public Policy*, vol. 15, no. 1 (January 2008).

31 Checkel, "Why Comply?".

32 Björkdahl, "Norm Advocacy", pp. 137–38.

33 Barry Buzan and Gerald Segal, "The Rise of 'Lite' Powers: A Strategy for the Postmodern State", *World Policy Journal*, vol. 13, no. 3 (Fall 1996).
34 Buzan and Segal, "The Rise of 'Lite' Powers", p. 2. See also Richard Rosecrance, *The Rise of the Virtual State: Wealth and Power in the Coming Century* (New York: Basic Books, 1999), and Richard Rosecrance, *The Rise of the Trading State* (New York: HarperCollins, 1985).
35 See also Zygmunt Bauman, *Liquid Modernity* (Cambridge: Polity Press, 2000); Bauman, *Liquid Times: Living in an Age of Uncertainty* (Cambridge: Polity Press, 2007); and Rajan Menon, *The End of Alliances* (Oxford: Oxford University Press, 2007).
36 Buzan and Segal, "The Rise of 'Lite' Powers", p. 3.
37 Robert Kagan, "Power and Weakness", *Policy Review*, no. 113 (June/July 2002).
38 Robert Cooper, *The Breaking of Nations: Order and Chaos in the Twenty-First Century* (London: Atlantic Books, 2003), p. 159. See also Cooper, "The New Liberal Imperialism", *Observer* (April 7, 2002), and Cooper, *The Post-Modern State and the World Order* (London: Demos, 1996).
39 Henrik Larsen, "The EU: A Global Military Actor?", *Cooperation and Conflict*, vol. 37, no. 3 (September 2002). See also Alyson J.K. Bailes, "The EU and a 'Better World': What Role for the European Security and Defence Policy?", *International Affairs*, vol. 84, no. 1 (January 2008), and Jolyon Howorth, "European Defence and the Changing Politics of the European Union: Hanging Together or Hanging Separately?", *Journal of Common Market Studies*, vol. 39, no. 4 (November 2001).
40 Dimitri K. Simes, "America's Imperial Dilemma", *Foreign Affairs*, vol. 82, no. 6 (November/December 2003).
41 Andrew J. Bacevich, "New Rome, New Jerusalem", *The Wilson Quarterly*, vol. 26, no. 3 (Summer 2002), pp. 51, 54.
42 Charles Krauthammer, "America Rules, Thank God", *Time* (August 4, 1997).
43 Charles Krauthammer, "The New Unilateralism", *Washington Post* (June 8, 2001).
44 US President George W. Bush, "Remarks at the 20th Anniversary of the National Endowment for Democracy, United States Chamber of Commerce", Washington DC (November 6, 2003).
45 "Cheney Exhorts Europe to Promote Diplomacy", *Los Angeles Times* (January 25, 2004).
46 George Lakoff has argued that President Bush quickly framed the attack as a "strict father" should: protecting his family against outside evil. President Bush used the good-vs.-evil frame, promising "I will not waver!" The alternative frame of a "nurturant parent", stressing empathy and mutual responsibility, just did not fit the neoconservative and Realist mindsets dominating the White House. See George Lakoff, *Moral Politics: How Liberals and Conservatives Think* (Chicago: University of Chicago Press, 2002), and Benjamin Wolozin, "The Art of Persuasion in Politics (and Science)", *The Skeptical Inquirer*, vol. 31, no. 1 (January/February 2007).
47 Daniel N. Nelson, "Conclusion: Word Peace", Dedaic and Nelson (eds.), *At War With Words*.
48 G. John Ikenberry, *After Victory: Institutions, Strategic Restraint, and the Rebuilding of Order After Major Wars* (Princeton NJ: Princeton University Press, 2000).
49 Jim Rutenberg, "In Farewell, Rumsfeld Warns Weakness is 'Provocative'", *New York Times* (December 16, 2006).
50 Quoted in Carla Anne Roberts, "The U.N.: Searching for Relevance", *The Wall Street Journal* (October 21, 2003). In a similar vein, Lion Brooks, acting director of the US National Nuclear Security Administration (NNSA), argued in 2003 that the US is "seeking to free [itself] from intellectual prohibitions against exploring a full range of technical options (…) I have a bias in favor of things that might be usable." Quoted in Senators Carl Levin and Jack Reed, "Toward a More Responsible Nuclear Nonproliferation Strategy", *Arms Control Today*, vol. 34, no. 2 (January/February 2004).

51 Quoted in Robert W. Tucker and David C. Hendrickson, "The Sources of American Legitimacy", *Foreign Affairs*, vol. 83, no. 6 (November/December 2004), p. 18.
52 Quoted in James K. Glassman, "Winning the War of Ideas", *The New York Sun* (July 23, 2008). Even the US *National Strategy for Combating Terrorism* (September 2006) acknowledges that "[i]n the long run, winning the War on Terror means winning the battle of ideas." *National Strategy for Combating Terrorism* (Washington DC, September 2006), p. 7.
53 Alexandra Marks, "Rethinking the Post-9/11 Strategy", *The Christian Science Monitor* (August 1, 2008). See Seth G. Jones and Martin C. Libicki, *How Terrorist Groups End: Lessons for Countering Al Qa'ida* (Santa Monica, CA: RAND, 2008).
54 Jean-Marie Colombani, "Nous Sommes Tous Américains", *Le Monde* (September 12, 2001).
55 Irwin Stelzer, "Bush Turns Away from the Weaklings of Europe", *Times* (February 19, 2002).
56 Pew Global Attitudes Project, *A Year After Iraq: A Nine-Country Survey* (Washington DC: 2004).
57 GMF Transatlantic Trends 2003 and the Pew Global Attitudes Project. Internet: www.transatlantictrends.org and www.pewtrusts.org
58 Daniel Dombrey, "Transatlantic Climate Shift", *Financial Times* (June 4, 2007).
59 Sidney Weintraub, *U.S.-Latin American Attitudes: Mistrust and Indifference* (Washington DC: CSIS Issues in International Political Economy 41, 2003).
60 Acharya, "How Ideas Spread." Ikenberry and Kupchan suggest that "[e]lites in secondary states buy into and internalize norms that are articulated by the hegemon and therefore pursue policies that are consistent with the hegemon's notion of world order." Ikenberry and Kupchan, "Socialization and Hegemonic Power", p. 283.
61 Lebow, "Power, Persuasion and Justice", p. 557.
62 Isaiah Berlin, "The Bent Twig: A Note on Nationalism", *Foreign Affairs*, vol. 51, no. 1 (October 1972), pp. 17–18. See also Stephen M. Walt, *Taming American Power: The Global Response to U.S. Primacy* (New York: W.W. Norton, 2006); Shibley Telhami, "History and Humiliation", *Washington Post* (March 28, 2003); and Ulrich Beck, *Macht und Gegenmacht im Globalen Zeitalter* (Frankfurt a/M: Suhrkamp, 2002).
63 Simes, "America's Imperial Dilemma", p. 93.
64 Quoted in Jonathan Freedland, "Patten Lays into Bush's America", *Guardian* (February 9, 2002). Similar ideas and points of criticism could be heard from French Minister of Foreign Affairs Hubert Védrine and his German counterpart Joschka Fischer. See Suzanne Daley, "France Upbraids U.S. as 'Simplistic'", *International Herald Tribune* (February 7, 2002), and Stephan Haselberger and Nikolaus Blome, "Wir sind keine Satelliten", *Die Welt* (February 12, 2002).
65 Francis Fukuyama, "The Damage to Brand USA Needs Urgent Repair", *Times* (October 14, 2008), p. 18.
66 Chicago Council on Global Affairs, *Global Views 2008* (Chicago, 2008). Internet: www.thechicagocouncil.org
67 Josef Joffe, "Who's Afraid of Mr. Big?", *The National Interest*, no. 64 (Summer 2001), p. 52.
68 Joseph Nye, Jr., "Barack Obama and Soft Power", *Huffington Post* (June 12, 2008). See also Nye, "Beware an October Surprise From Bin Laden", *Financial Times* (October 16, 2008).
69 See for a good debate on "Ethical Power Europe", the Special Issue of *International Affairs*, vol. 84, no. 1 (January 2008). See also Hartmut Behr, "The European Union in the Legacies of Imperial Rule? EU Accession Politics Viewed from a Historical Comparative Perspective", *European Journal of International Affairs*, vol. 13, no. 2 (June 2007); Michelle Pace, "The Construction of EU Normative Power", *Journal of Common Market Studies*, vol. 45, no. 5 (December 2007); Adrian Hyde-Price, "'Normative' Power Europe: A Realist Critique", *Journal of European Public Policy*,

vol. 13, no. 2 (March 2006); Thomas Diez, "Constructing the Self and Changing Others: Reconsidering 'Normative Power Europe'", *Millennium*, vol. 33, no. 3 (June 2005); Richard Youngs, "Normative Dynamics and Strategic Interests in the EU's External Identity", *Journal of Common Market Studies*, vol. 42, no. 2 (June 2004); Tommaso Padoa-Schioppa, *Europe, a Civilian Power: Lessons from EU Experience* (London: The Federal Trust, 2004); Thomas Diez, "Europe as a Discursive Battleground: Discourse Analysis and European Integration Studies", *Cooperation and Conflict*, vol. 36, no. 1 (March 2001); Thomas Christiansen, Knud-Erik Jørgensen, and Antje Wiener (eds.), *The Social Construction of Europe* (London: Sage, 2001); Hedley Bull, "Civilian Power Europe: A Contradiction in Terms?", *Journal of Common Market Studies*, vol. 21, nos. 1–2 (September/December 1982).
70 Michel Foucault, "Governmentality", in Graham Burchell, Colin Cordon, and Peter Miller (eds.), *The Foucault Effect: Studies in Governmentality* (Chicago: University of Chicago Press, 1991).
71 Ian Manners, "Normative Power Europe: A Contradiction in Terms?", *Journal of Common Market Studies*, vol. 40, no. 2 (June 2002), p. 252.
72 Jeremy Rifkin, *The European Dream: How Europe's Vision of the Future is Quietly Eclipsing the American Dream* (Oxford: Blackwell, 2004), p. 3.
73 Colin S. Gray, "Strategy in the Nuclear Age: The United States, 1945–91", in Williamson Murray, MacGregor Knox, and Alvin Bernstein (eds.), *The Making of Strategy: Rulers, States, and War* (Cambridge: Cambridge University Press, 1994), pp. 593, 597.
74 François Duchêne, *Jean Monnet: The First Statesman of Interdependence* (London: W.W. Norton, 1994), pp. 368, 388.
75 Romano Prodi, *Europe as I See It* (Cambridge: Polity Press, 2000), p. 40. Indeed, key EU documents generally refer to Europe's values and mission in lofty terms, confirming the Monnet line on the Union's morally superior social power. For example, Article 6 of the Treaty on European Union claims that "[t]he Union is founded on the principles of liberty, democracy, respect for human rights and fundamental freedoms, and the rule of law, principles which are common to the Member States." The Constitutional Treaty (which was voted down by the French and Dutch electorates in 2005) has been replaced by the Lisbon Treaty, and now incorporates an even broader list of principles the EU stands for: equality, social solidarity, sustainable development, and good governance. See also Chapter 7.
76 Romano Prodi, "2000–2005: Shaping the New Europe – Speech at the European Parliament", Strasbourg (February 15, 2000).
77 European Commission, *Shaping the New Europe: Strategic Objectives 2000–2005*, Brussels (COM(2000) 154 final, 2000).
78 "Sarkozy to Go to North Africa to Sell Proposal for Mediterranean Union", *International Herald Tribune* (July 9, 2007).
79 Ben Rosamond, "Conceptualizing the EU Model of Governance in World Politics", *European Foreign Policy Review*, vol. 10, no. 4 (Winter 2005), p. 478.
80 Manners, "Normative Power Europe: A Contradiction in Terms?", p. 253.
81 Manners, "Normative Power Europe: A Contradiction in Terms?", p. 238.
82 Ludger Kühnhardt, *The Global Proliferation of Regional Integration: European Experience and Worldwide Trends* (Bonn: ZEI Discussion Paper, 2004), p. 3.
83 Mitchell P. Smith, "Soft Power Rising: Romantic Europe in the Service of Practical Europe", *World Literature Today*, vol. 80, no. 1 (January/February 2006), p. 22. See also Peter van Ham, *European Integration and the Postmodern Condition: Governance, Democracy, Identity* (London: Routledge, 2001), and Van Ham, *Identity Beyond the State: The Case of the European Union* (Copenhagen: COPRI Working Paper 15, 2000).
84 Non-EU European countries like Norway and Switzerland are the notable exceptions confirming this rule.
85 But since the EU is experiencing "enlargement fatigue", and like all empires is afraid to fall prey to imperial overstretch, the natural limits of this strategy seem to be reached.

The EU's European Security Strategy of 2003 still suggests that the Union's aim is to be surrounded by a "ring of friends", stretching from Eastern Europe to the Mediterranean, which is held together by shared values, open markets, and (to a lesser extent) open borders, enhanced cooperation in the areas of research, energy, and law enforcement. The EU offers neighbouring countries "everything but institutions", which is another way of extending the European "empire" without overburdening an already strained institutional framework. See Felix Berenskoetter, "Mapping the Mind Gap: A Comparison of US and European Security Strategies", *Security Dialogue*, vol. 36, no. 1 (March 2005); Christopher Hill, "The Geopolitical Implications of Enlargement", in Jan Zielonka (ed.), *Europe Unbound: Enlarging and Reshaping the Boundaries of the European Union* (London: Routledge, 2002); and Frank Schimmelpfennig, "The Community Trap: Liberal Norms, Rhetorical Action, and the Eastern Enlargement of the European Union", *International Organization*, vol. 55, no. 1 (Winter 2001).

86 The notion of the EU (or "Europe", in short), as a "normative authority" has been developed further by Ian Manners, who introduced the notion of "Normative Power Europe" (NPE). Manners claims that the EU embodies "European norms" as peace, liberty, democracy, the rule of law, and respect for human rights, which find expression in "minor norms" like social solidarity, anti-discrimination, sustainable development, and good governance. See Ian Manners, "Normative Power Europe Reconsidered – Paper presented at the CIDEL Workshop", Oslo (October 22–23, 2004). See also Helene Sjursen, "What Kind of Power?", *Journal of European Public Policy*, vol. 13, no. 2 (March 2006).

87 European Commission, *The Trade and Development Aspects of EPA Negotiations: Commission Staff Working Report*, Brussels (SEC(2005) 1459, November 9, 2005), p. 32.

88 James Dobbins, *Europe's Role in Nation-Building: From the Balkans to the Congo* (Santa Monica CA: RAND, 2008).

89 Manners, "Normative Power Europe Reconsidered", pp. 12–13.

90 Finnemore and Sikkink, "International Norm Dynamics and Political Change", p. 272.

91 Zaki Laïdi, "Are European Preferences Shared by Others? – Keynote speech at SciencesPo", Paris (June 23–24, 2006), p. 3.

92 Laïdi, "Are European Preferences Shared by Others?", pp. 4–6.

93 Zaki Laïdi, "The Normative Empire: The Unintended Consequences of European Power", *Les Essays de Telos* (Paris: Telos, 2008).

94 Carsten Daugbjerk and Alan Swinbank. "The Politics of CAP Reform: Trade Negotiations, Institutional Settings and Blame Avoidance", *Journal of Common Market Studies*, vol. 45, no. 1 (March 2007).

95 Kishore Mahbubani, *The New Asian Hemisphere: The Irresistible Shift of Global Power to the East* (New York: PublicAffairs, 2008).

96 Mahbubani, *The New Asian Hemisphere*, pp. 5, 8.

97 Orville Schell, "China's Quest for Moral Authority", *The Nation*, vol. 287, no. 12 (October 20, 2008).

98 R. Bin Wong, "Asian Values: In Search of Possibilities", *Korea Journal*, vol. 42, no. 2 (Summer 2002). See also Martin Roll, *Asian Brand Strategy: How Asia Builds Strong Brands* (New York: Palgrave Macmillan, 2006).

99 Jing Tsu, *Failure, Nationalism, and Literature: The Making of Modern Chinese Identity* (Stanford: Stanford University Press, 2005).

100 Yong Deng and Fei-ling Wang (eds.), *China Rising: Power and Motivation in Chinese Foreign Policy* (Lanham, MD: Rowman & Littlefield, 2005).

101 Cho and Jeong, "China's Soft Power", pp. 456–58.

102 Cho and Jeong, "China's Soft Power", p. 461.

103 For an overview, see Randall Peerenboom, *China Modernizes: Threat to the West or Model for the Rest?* (Oxford: Oxford University Press, 2008). See also Ashton B. Carter and William J. Perry, "China on the March", *The National Interest*, no. 88 (March/April 2007); John Wilson Lewis and Xue Litai, *Imagined Enemies: China*

Prepares for Uncertain War (Stanford: Stanford University Press, 2006); and Lydia H. Liu, *The Clash of Empires: The Invention of China in Modern World Making* (Cambridge, MA: Harvard University Press, 2006).
104 Avery Goldstein, *Rising to the Challenge: China's Grand Strategy and International Security* (Stanford: Stanford University Press, 2005), and Wu Guoguang, "The Peaceful Emergence of a Great Power?", *Social Research*, vol. 73, no. 1 (Spring 2006).
105 Joshua Kurlantzick, *China's Charm: Implications of Chinese Soft Power* (Washington DC: Carnegie Endowment Policy Brief 47, 2006), p. 1. See also Ingrid d'Hooghe, *The Rise of China's Public Diplomacy* (The Hague: Clingendael Diplomacy Paper 12, 2007).
106 Joshua Kurlantzick, *Charm Offensive: How China's Soft Power Is Transforming the World* (New Haven: Yale University Press, 2008); David Shambaugh, "China's Propaganda System: Institutions, Processes and Efficacy", *The China Journal*, no. 57 (January 2007); and Pamela Kyle Crossley, Helen F. Siu, and Donald S. Sutton (eds.), *Empire at the Margins: Culture, Ethnicity, and Frontier in Early Modern China* (Berkeley: University of California Press, 2006).
107 Bates Gill and Yanzhong Huang, "Sources and Limits of Chinese 'Soft Power'", *Survival*, vol. 48, no. 2 (Summer 2006), p. 19.
108 Cho and Jeong, "China's Soft Power", pp. 470–71.
109 Mara Hvistendahl, "China Moves Up To Fifth as Importer of Students", *The Chronicle of Higher Education*, vol. 55, no. 4 (September 19, 2008).
110 Joshua Cooper Ramo, *The Beijing Consensus* (London: The Foreign Policy Centre, 2004). The concept of the "Beijing Consensus" has been looked upon with mixed feeling by Chinese officials, mainly since it may be considered as a call to begin an anti-capitalist, even anti-globalization movement led by Beijing itself, which would hardly serve China's economic and political goals. Chinese officials therefore stress the more neutral "Chinese development model", which still offers an alternative to America's continued belief in the blessings of the market economy, without excluding China's own special economic zones and export-led growth.
111 Yong Deng, "The Asianization of East Asian Security and the United States' Role", *East Asia*, vol. 16, nos. 3/4 (Autumn 1998), p. 100.
112 Gill and Huang, "Sources and Limits of Chinese 'Soft Power'", p. 24.
113 Gill and Huang, "Sources and Limits of Chinese 'Soft Power'", p. 24.
114 Gill and Huang, "Sources and Limits of Chinese 'Soft Power'", p. 25.
115 Joshua Eisenman and Joshua Kurlantzick, "China's Africa Strategy", *Current History*, vol. 105, no. 691 (May 2006), pp. 219–20.
116 Chris Alden, *China in Africa: Competitor or Hegemon?* (London: Zed Books, 2007), and Joshua Eisenman, Eric Heginbotham, and Derek Mitchell (eds.), *China and the Developing World: Beijing's Strategy for the Twenty-First Century* (Armonk NY: M.E. Sharpe, 2007).
117 Kurlantzick, *China's Charm*, p. 2.
118 Mark Leonard, "The Road Obscured: New Left or 'Neo-Comm'?", *Financial Times* (July 8, 2005).
119 Philip Stevens, "Hollywood's Geopolitics Lesson for China", *Financial Times* (February 14, 2008).
120 Joseph Kahn, "China Disputes Defense Assessment", *New York Times* (May 28, 2007), p. A6.
121 Dingli Shen, "Why China Sees the EU as a Counterweight to America", *Europe's World*, no. 10 (Autumn 2008).
122 Yong Deng, "Hegemon on the Offensive: Chinese Perspectives on U.S. Global Strategy", *Political Science Quarterly*, vol. 116, no. 3 (Fall 2001).
123 Nye, "Soft Power and American Foreign Policy", p. 258.
124 Lee Feinstein and Anne-Marie Slaughter, "A Duty to Prevent", *Foreign Affairs*, vol. 83, no. 1 (January/February 2004); Charles D. Ferguson and Peter van Ham, "Beyond the

NRA Doctrine", *The National Interest*, no. 87 (January/February 2007); and Gareth Evans, "The Responsibility to Protect: When It's Right to Fight", *Progressive Politics*, vol. 2, no. 2 (July 2003).
125 US President Barack Obama, *Remarks by the President on a New Beginning* (Cairo, June 4, 2009). Internet: www.whitehouse.gov
126 James K. Glassman, "Lecture at the Council on Foreign Relations" (Washington DC, June 30, 2008). See also Azar Gat, "The Return of Authoritarian Great Powers", *Foreign Affairs*, vol. 86, no. 4 (July/August 2007).
127 James K. Glassman, "Foreign Press Center Briefing" (Washington DC, July 15, 2008).

3 Culture and constructivism

1 Generally, this phrase is linked to Nazi propaganda-chief Joseph Goebbels, which is not correct. The expression originates from Hanns Johst's play *Schlageter*, in which a character says: "Wenn ich Kultur höre, entsichere ich meinen Browning" ("Whenever I hear of culture, I release the safety-catch of my Browning.")
2 Peter J. Katzenstein, "Introduction: Alternative Perspectives on National Security", in Peter J. Katzenstein (ed.), *The Culture of National Security: Norms and Identity in World Politics* (New York: Columbia University Press, 1996), p. 17.
3 Yosef Lapid and Friedrich Kratochwil (eds.), *The Return of Culture and Identity in IR Theory* (Boulder, CO: Lynne Rienner, 1996), and Katzenstein (ed.), *The Culture of National Security*. See also Nicholas G. Onuf, *The World of Our Making: Rules and Rule in Social Theory and International Relations* (Columbia, SC: University of South Carolina Press, 1989). Even students of security studies are showing remarkable interest in the role of norms, values, and culture, having agreed among themselves that the concept of security should be contested and made "insecure." See Steve Smith, "The Increasing Insecurity of Security Studies: Conceptualizing Security in the Last Twenty Years", *Contemporary Security Studies*, vol. 20, no. 3 (December 1999).
4 Stefano Guzzini and Anna Leander (eds.), *Constructivism and International Relations: Alexander Wendt and His Critics* (London: Routledge, 2006).
5 Clifford Geertz, *The Interpretation of Cultures* (New York: Basic Books, 1973).
6 Maja Zehfuss, *Constructivism in International Relations: The Politics of Reality* (Cambridge: Cambridge University Press, 2002).
7 Lapid and Kratochwil (eds.), *The Return of Culture and Identity in IR Theory*; Alexander Wendt, "Anarchy is What States Make of It: The Social Construction of Power Politics", *International Organization*, vol. 46, no. 2 (Spring 1992); and Emanuel Adler, "Seizing the Middle Ground: Constructivism in World Politics", *European Journal of International Relations*, vol. 3, no. 3 (September 1997).
8 Ted Hopf, "The Promise of Constructivism in International Relations Theory", *International Security*, vol. 23, no. 1 (Summer 1998), p. 173.
9 Hopf, "The Promise of Constructivism", p. 175.
10 Hopf, "The Promise of Constructivism", p. 178.
11 Ronald L. Jepperson, Alexander Wendt, and Peter J. Katzenstein, "Norms, Identity, and Culture in National Security", in Katzenstein (ed.), *The Culture of National Security*.
12 Jepperson, Wendt, and Katzenstein, "Norms, Identity, and Culture in National Security", p. 54.
13 Michael S. Billig, "Institutions and Culture: Neo-Weberian Economic Anthropology", *Journal of Economic Issues*, vol. 34, no. 4 (December 2000), p. 777.
14 Quoted in Billig, "Institutions and Culture", p. 779.
15 Stefano Guzzini, "The Concept of Power: A Constructivist Analysis", *Millennium*, vol. 33, no. 3 (June 2005).
16 See, for example, Tom Stoppard and Derek Walcott, *Cultural Power: A Conversation* (New York: The City University of New York, November 10, 2008). Internet: www.greatissuesforum.org

17 David Swartz, *Culture and Power: The Sociology of Pierre Bourdieu* (Chicago: University of Chicago Press, 1998). See also John F. Stolte and Shanon Fender, "Framing Social Values: An Experimental Study of Culture and Cognition", *Social Psychology Quarterly*, vol. 70, no. 1 (March 2007); Edward W. Said, *Power, Politics, and Culture* (New York: Vintage Books, 2002); and James Davison Hunter, *Culture Wars: The Struggle to Define America* (New York: Basic Books, 1991).
18 Graham Murdock, "Notes From the Number One Country: Herbert Schiller on Culture, Commerce and American Power", *International Journal of Cultural Policy*, vol. 12, no. 2 (July 2006).
19 Lukes, *Power*, p. 23.
20 Douglas Litowitz, "Gramsci, Hegemony, and the Law", *Brigham Young University Law Review*, vol. 2000, no. 2 (2000), p. 525.
21 Pierre Bourdieu, *Language and Symbolic Power* (Cambridge: Polity Press, 1991), and Mara Loveman, "The Modern State and the Primitive Accumulation of Symbolic Power", *The American Journal of Sociology*, vol. 110, no. 6 (May 2005).
22 David L. Altheide, "Consuming Terrorism", *Symbolic Interaction*, vol. 27, no. 3 (Summer 2004), p. 292. See also David L. Altheide, *Creating Fear: News and the Construction of Crisis* (New York: Aldine de Gruyter, 2002).
23 Oran R. Young, *International Governance: Protecting the Environment in a Stateless Society* (Ithaca, NY: Cornell University Press, 1994), pp. 3–4.
24 John G. Ruggie, "International Regimes, Transactions, and Change: Embedded Liberalism in the Postwar Economic Order", in Stephen D. Krasner (ed.), *International Regimes* (Ithaca, NY: Cornell University Press, 1983), p. 201. See also Ruggie, "Reconstituting the Global Public Domain: Issues, Actors, and Practices", *European Journal of International Relations*, vol. 10, no. 4 (2004).
25 Michael Hardt and Antonio Negri, *Empire* (Cambridge, MA: Harvard University Press, 2000), p. xiii.
26 Hardt and Negri, *Empire*, p. 24.
27 Monroe E. Price, *Media and Sovereignty: The Global Information Revolution and Its Challenge to State Power* (Cambridge, MA: The MIT Press, 2002), p. 19.
28 Friedrich Kratochwil, "Is the Ship of Culture at Sea or Returning?", in Friedrich Kratochwil and Yosef Lapid (ed.), *Nationalism, Citizenship and Identity* (Boulder, CO: Lynne Rienner, 1996), p. 206. See also David Held and Henrietta L. Moore (eds.), *Cultural Politics in a Global Age: Uncertainty, Solidarity and Innovation* (Oxford: Oneworld Publications, 2007).
29 Walter LaFeber, *Michael Jordan and the New Global Capitalism* (New York: W.W. Norton, 1999), pp. 17–18.
30 Huntington, *The Clash of Civilizations*, p. 20.
31 See the cover of Huntington's *Clash of Civilizations* of the 2002-imprint by The Free Press.
32 Nicholas Evan Sarantakes, "Cold War Pop Culture and the Image of U.S. Foreign Policy: The Perspective of the Original Star Trek Series", *Journal of Cold War Studies*, vol. 7, no. 4 (Fall 2005), and Stephen J. Whitfield, *The Culture of the Cold War* (Baltimore: The Johns Hopkins University Press, 1991).
33 Penny M. von Eschen, *Satchmo Blows Up the World: Jazz Ambassadors Play the Cold War* (Cambridge, MA: Harvard University Press, 2004).
34 Toby Miller, Nitin Govil, John McMurrian, and Richard Maxwell, *Global Hollywood* (Berkeley: University of California Press, 2002).
35 Joost Smiers, *Arts Under Pressure: Promoting Cultural Diversity in the Age of Globalisation* (London: Zed Books, 2003), p. 35.
36 Reinhold Wagnleiter, *Coca-Colonization and the Cold War: The Cultural Mission of the United States in Austria After the Second World War* (Chapel Hill: University of North Carolina Press, 1994).

37 Michael Nelson, *Wars of the Black Heavens: The Battles of Western Broadcasting in the Cold War* (Syracuse, NY: Syracuse University Press, 1997).
38 Kenneth A. Osgood, "Hearts and Minds: The Unconventional Cold War", *Journal of Cold War Studies*, vol. 4, no. 2 (Spring 2002); Daniel C. Thomas, "Human Rights Ideas, The Demise of Communism and the End of the Cold War", *Journal of Cold War Studies*, vol. 7, no. 2 (Spring 2005); and Nancy E. Bernhard, *US Television News and Cold War Propaganda, 1947–1960* (Cambridge: Cambridge University Press, 1999). See also Cynthia P. Schneider, "Culture Communicates: US Diplomacy that Works", in Jan Melissen (ed.), *The New Public Diplomacy: Soft Power in International Relations* (New York: Palgrave Macmillan, 2005).
39 Benjamin R. Barber, "Imperial Emporium", *Raritan*, vol. 26, no. 3 (Winter 2007), p. 50.
40 James K. Glassman, "Lecture at the Council on Foreign Relations", Washington DC (June 30, 2008).
41 Nick Gillespie and Matt Welch, "How 'Dallas' Won the Cold War", *Washington Post* (April 27, 2008), p. B02.
42 Buzan and Segal, "The Rise of 'Lite' Powers", p. 10.
43 If only because *Baywatch* was aired for the first time in 1989 by the American TV network NBC.
44 M. Mehdi Semati and Patty J. Sotirin, "Hollywood's Transnational Appeal: Hegemony and Democratic Potential?", *Journal of Popular Film & Television*, vol. 29, no. 4 (Winter 1999).
45 Kagan, "Power and Weakness", p. 7.
46 Jennifer Sterling-Folker, "The Emperor Wore Cowboy Boots", *International Studies Perspectives*, vol. 9, no. 3 (August 2008), p. 326. Sterling-Folker further asks attention to be focused on the benevolent framing of US "hegemony" as the legitimate role of a Great Power, or even a superpower: "The very term 'great' suggests something wonderful and grand; the term 'super' implies something marvelous and fantastic. In fact Americans love 'power' which is why they give it such qualifiers. And if they mistakenly think the use of military power will automatically 'shock and awe' others, it is because power shocks and awes them." (p. 327). See also Andrew J. Bacevich, *The New American Militarism: How Americans are Seduced by War* (New York: Oxford University Press, 2006), and Max Boot, *The Savage Wars of Peace: Small Wars and the Rise of American Power* (New York: Basic Books, 2003).
47 Eugene Secunda and Terence P. Moran, *Selling War to America: From the Spanish American War to the Global War on Terror* (Westport, CT: Praeger, 2007), pp. 3–4.
48 *Der Spiegel* (February 18, 2002). See Lillian Daniel, "Doubting Tom", *The Christian Century*, vol. 120, no. 17 (August 23, 2003), p. 38.
49 Michael J. Zwiebel, "Why We Need To Reestablish the USIA", *Military Review*, vol. 86, no. 6 (November/December 2006).
50 Jim Rutenberg, "Hollywood Seeks Role in the War", *New York Times* (October 20, 2001), p. B9.
51 Edward Buscombe, quoted in Semati and Sotirin, "Hollywood's Transnational Appeal", p. 178.
52 Scott R. Olson, "The Globalization of Hollywood", *International Journal on World Peace*, vol. 17, no. 4 (December 2000), p. 10. See also Hans Blumenberg, *Work on Myth* (Cambridge, MA: The MIT Press, 1985).
53 "Pop Anti-Americanism", *Foreign Policy*, no. 134 (January/February 2003), p. 16. See also Margaret H. DeFleur and Melvin L. DeFleur, *The Next Generation's Image of Americans: Attitudes and Beliefs Held by Teen-Agers in Twelve Countries* (Boston: Boston University College of Communication, 2002).
54 Conn Carroll, "Once Upon a Time, Hollywood Helped U.S. Image Abroad", *Heritage Foundation Blog* (July 7, 2008). See also Jonathan Gray, "Imagining America: The Simpsons Go Global", *Popular Communication*, vol. 5, no. 2 (March 2007).

55 Jack G. Shaheen, *Guilty—Hollywood's Verdict on Arabs After 9/11* (Northampton, MA: Interlink Publishing, 2008), and Tom Perry, "Critics Accuse Hollywood of Vilifying Arabs", *Reuters.com* (May 1, 2008).
56 Mel van Elteren, "U.S. Cultural Imperialism Today: Only a Chimera?", *SAIS Review*, vol. 23, no. 2 (Summer 2003), p. 171. See also Janet Wasko, "Can Hollywood Still Rule the Word?", in David Held and Henrietta L. Moore (eds.), *Cultural Politics in a Global Age: Uncertainty, Solidarity and Innovation* (Oxford: Oneworld Publications, 2007).
57 Peter J. Katzenstein and Robert O. Keohane, "Anti-Americanisms", *Policy Review*, no. 139 (October/November, 2006), p. 35. Hollywood's transnationalism is also deeply rooted in its history of accommodating émigrés and its willingness to use other countries and cultures as the setting of its exotic films.
58 Katzenstein and Keohane, "Anti-Americanisms", p. 35.
59 Olson, "The Globalization of Hollywood".
60 Barber, *Jihad vs. McWorld*, p. 17.
61 Barry Schwartz, *The Costs of Living: How Market Freedom Erodes the Best Things in Life* (New York: W.W. Norton, 1994).
62 Benjamin R. Barber, *Consume: How Markets Corrupt Children, Infantilize Adults and Swallow Citizens Whole* (New York: W.W. Norton, 2007); Lizabeth Cohen, *A Consumers' Republic: The Politics of Mass Consumption in Postwar America* (New York: Knopf, 2003); and Victoria de Grazia, *Irresistible Empire: America's Advance Through Twentieth-Century Europe* (Cambridge, MA: Harvard University Press, 2006).
63 This applies to consumers across the globe. For example, as Güliz Ger and Russell W. Belk conclude in their study on global consumerscapes, "[w]hen the Congolese consume, the satisfaction gained is not in the small contribution to lifestyle experience that these objects convey in the West, but in the constitution of an entirely different and more prestigious self." See Güliz Ger and Russell W. Belk, "I'd Like to Buy the World a Coke: Consumptionscapes of the 'Less Affluent World'", *Journal of Consumer Policy*, vol. 19, no. 3 (September 1996), p. 273.
64 Hardt and Negri, *Empire*, p. xiii.
65 Duncan Campbell, "Bush Tars Drug Takers with Aiding Terrorists", *Guardian* (August 8, 2002).
66 Altheide, "Consuming Terrorism", p. 291.
67 Altheide, "Consuming Terrorism", p. 299.
68 Altheide, "Consuming Terrorism", p. 298.
69 David Campbell, "The Biopolitics of Security: Oil, Empire, and the Sports Utility Vehicle", *American Quarterly*, vol. 57, no. 3 (September 2005).
70 Patricia Leigh Brown, "Among California's S.U.V. Owners, Only a Bit of Guilt in a New 'Anti' Effort", *New York Times* (February 8, 2003).
71 Leigh Brown, "Among California's S.U.V. Owners".
72 Campbell, "The Biopolitics of Security", p. 964.
73 This also applied to Danish commercial brands (like Lego, in 2006), who were boycotted by angry Muslim consumers after the controversy over the well-known "Muhammed cartoons" (see Chapter 7).
74 Walter LaFeber, "The Post-September 11 Debate Over Empire, Globalization, and Fragmentation", *Political Science Quarterly*, vol. 117, no. 1 (Spring 2002), pp. 10–11.
75 Jonathan Bignell, *Big Brother: Reality TV in the Twenty-First Century* (New York: Palgrave Macmillan, 2006), and Susan Murray (ed.), *Reality TV: Remaking Television Culture* (New York: New York University Press, 2004).
76 Philip R. Schlesinger, "Europe's Contradictory Communicative Space", *Daedalus*, vol. 123, no. 2 (Spring 1994), p. 33.
77 Quoted in "Sarkozy Defends 'Offensive' Francophony Concept", *EurActiv.com* (March 21, 2008).
78 Barber, *Jihad vs. McWorld*, p. 89.

186　*Notes*

79　Kevin V. Mulcahy, "Cultural Imperialism and Cultural Sovereignty: U.S.-Canadian Cultural Relations", *Journal of Arts Management, Law, and Society*, vol. 31. no. 4 (Winter 2002).
80　Smiers, *Arts Under Pressure*, pp. 30–31.
81　A new EU project, called *Media Mundus*, earmarks Euro 60 million from 2011 onwards to promote cooperation with third countries (and Canada, Australia, Japan, India, and China in particular), aimed at improving access of EU films and series into their markets (and, officially at least, *vice versa*). Still, most cinemas screen Hollywood productions (around 60 percent of the total in 2007), and the extra-EU market share of EU movies is only between 2 and 5 percent. See "EU To Challenge Hollywood Rule", *EurActiv.com* (June 11, 2008), and Tim Arango, "U.S. Media Thrive Worldwide, But Not U.S. Image", *International Herald Tribune* (December 1, 2008).
82　David Puttnam, *Movies and Money: The Undeclared War Between Europe and America* (New York: David McKay Company, 1998).
83　Mel van Elteren, "GATT and Beyond: World Trade, the Arts and American Popular Culture in Western Europe", *Journal of American Culture*, vol. 19, no. 3 (Fall 1996).
84　SACD stands for *Societé des Auteurs et Compositeurs Dramatiques*.
85　SACD, *L'AMI: l'Ennemi* (Paris: pamphlet, 1998). Internet: www.sacd.fr
86　Quoted in Van Ham, *European Integration and the Postmodern Condition*, p. 83.
87　Interview with De Charette in *Le Monde* (March 18, 1997), quoted in Van Ham, *European Integration and the Postmodern Condition*, p. 83. Emphasis added.
88　Keith Acheson and Christopher Maule, "Convention on Cultural Diversity", *Journal of Cultural Economics*, vol. 28, no. 4 (November 2004).
89　Bill Grantham, "America the Menace: France's Feud with Hollywood", *World Policy Journal*, vol. 15, no. 2 (Summer 1998). See also LaFeber, *Michael Jordan and the New Global Capitalism*, p. 82.
90　A July 2008 European Commission Report observed that European movies and series now dominate programme schedules on most EU television channels, with broadcasters preferring European works over Hollywood. On average, 64 percent of EU programming time is now devoted to European films and fictions (in 2005 and 2006). See European Commission, *Eighth Communication on the Application of Articles 4 and 5 of Directive 89/552/EEC "Television Without Frontiers"*, Brussels (July 22, 2008). See also Arango, "U.S. Media Thrive Worldwide, But Not U.S. Image".
91　Wendie Curry, *The Global Information Society: A New Paradigm for the 21st Century* (Chichester: John Wiley & Sons, 2000), and Frank Webster, *Theories of the Information Society* (New York: Routledge, 2006).
92　Toennies, *Community and Association*.
93　The Arab and Islamic world, in particular, has effectively filtered Hollywood's images to keep out politically undesirable messages. For example, Steven Spielberg's epic *Schindler's List* was effectively barred from most movie theatres in the Arab and Islamic world, on the basis of its alleged Zionist character. See Bernard Weinraub, "Islamic Nations Move to Keep Out 'Schindler's List'", *New York Times* (April 7, 1994), p. C15.
94　Cris Shore, "'In Uno Plures' (?) EU Cultural Policy and the Governance of Europe", *Cultural Analysis*, vol. 5 (2006), p. 15.
95　European Commission, *First Report on the Consideration of Cultural Aspects in European Community Action* (Luxembourg: Office for Official Publications of the European Communities, April 17, 1996), p. 92.
96　European Commission, *Unifying Europe Through Culture*, Brussels (November 17, 2006).
97　European Council, *Council Resolution of 21 January 2002 on the Role of Culture in the Development of the European Union*, Brussels (2002/C 32/02, January 21, 2002).

98 European Commission, *Communication from the Commission to the European Parliament, the Council, the European Economic and Social Committee and the Committee of the Regions on a European Agenda for Culture in a Globalizing World*, Brussels (COM(2007) 242 final, May 25, 2007).
 99 *Communication from the Commission to the European Parliament, the Council, the European and Social Committee and the Committee of the Regions on a European Agenda for Culture in a Globalizing World* (Brussels, May 5, 2007).
100 José Manuel Barroso, "How Can European Culture Promote European Integration? – Speech for the European Cultural Parliament", Lisbon (December 3, 2005).
101 Most Europeans do not look forward to an imperial Europe, although the academic debate about "Europe as Empire" has been engaging and intellectually inspiring. The notions of multi-level governance and neo-medievalism, in particular, have enriched the debate about the EU as a new, post-sovereign and post-territorial entity which bears some resemblance to past empires. See Jan Zielonka, *Europe as Empire: The Nature of the Enlarged European Union* (Oxford: Oxford University Press, 2006), and Liesbet Hooghe and Gary Marks, *Multi-Level Governance and European Integration* (Lanham, MD: Rowman & Littlefield, 2001).
102 Ernest Gelner, *Nations and Nationalism* (Oxford: Blackwell, 1983), p. 86.
103 Staffan Zetterholm (ed.), *National Cultures and European Integration* (Oxford: Berg, 1994).
104 "Europe: Euro Visions", *The Economist* (May 14, 2005), p. 46.
105 Ukraine and Serbia have not applied for EU membership yet, but certainly have a "European vocation".
106 European Commission, *European Agenda for Culture in a Globalizing World*, p. 6.
107 European Commission, *European Agenda for Culture in a Globalizing World*, p. 7. See also Javier Solana Madariaga, "The New Paradigm of Cooperation in Europe", *Hampton Roads International Security Quarterly*, vol. 8, no. 2 (April 2008).
108 Andrew F. Cooper, "Beyond Hollywood and the Boardroom: Celebrity Diplomacy", *Georgetown Journal of International Affairs*, vol. 8, no. 2 (Summer/Fall 2007), and Cooper, *Celebrity Diplomacy* (Boulder, CO: Paradigm Publishers, 2007).
109 Teresa Küchler, "Europe Has Forgotten Its Emigration Past, Says EU Cultural Ambassador", *EUObserver.com* (February 2, 2008).
110 European Commission, *European Agenda for Culture in a Globalizing World*, p. 9.
111 *The Economy of Culture in Europe*, conducted by KEA European Affairs for the European Commission (2006).
112 Benjamin R. Barber, "Shrunken Sovereign: Consumerism, Globalization, and American Emptiness", *World Affairs*, vol. 170, no. 4 (Spring 2008), p. 79.
113 John Tomlinson, *Cultural Imperialism: A Critical Introduction* (London: Pinter, 1991).
114 Neal M. Rosendorf, "Social and Cultural Globalization: Concepts, History, and America's Role", in Joseph S. Nye, Jr. and John D. Donahue (eds.), *Governance in a Globalizing World* (Washington DC: Brookings Institution Press, 2000).
115 Van Elteren, "U.S. Cultural Imperialism Today", p. 183.
116 Van Elteren, "U.S. Cultural Imperialism Today", p. 177.
117 Van Elteren, "U.S. Cultural Imperialism Today", p. 179.
118 R. Daniel Kelemen and Eric C. Sibbitt, "The Globalization of American Law", *International Organization*, vol. 58, no. 1 (Winter 2004).

4 Institutions and law

 1 Bas Arts and Jan van Tatenhove, "Policy and Power: A Conceptual Framework Between the 'Old' and 'New' Policy Idioms", *Policy Sciences*, vol. 37, no. 3 (December 2004), p. 343.
 2 Mann, *The Sources of Social Power*, p. 7.

Notes

3 Kathleen R. McNamara, *Constructing Authority in the European Union* (Washington DC: Georgetown University Mortara Center for International Studies Working Paper, 2007), p. 1.
4 Young, *International Governance*. In contrast, organizations "are material entities possessing offices, personnel, budgets, equipment, and, more often than not, legal personality" (pp. 3–4).
5 John G. Ruggie, "Multilateralism: The Anatomy of an Institution", *International Organization*, vol. 46, no. 3 (Summer 1992).
6 Nico Krisch, "International Law in Times of Hegemony: Unequal Power and the Shaping of the International Legal Order", *European Journal of International Law*, vol. 16, no. 3 (June 2005), p. 370. See also Christian Reus-Smith (ed.), *The Politics of International Law* (Cambridge: Cambridge University Press, 2004).
7 Douglas Howland and Luise White (eds.), *The State of Sovereignty: Territories, Laws, Populations* (Bloomington, IN: Indiana University Press, 2008), and Robert O. Keohane, "International Relations and International Law: Two Optics", *Harvard International Law Journal*, vol. 38, no. 2 (Spring 1997).
8 Javier Solana, "Mars and Venus Reconciled: A New Era for Transatlantic Relations", Albert H. Gordon Lecture at the Kennedy School of Government, Harvard University (April 3, 2003).
9 Lisa Martin, "Interests, Power, and Multilateralism", *International Organization*, vol. 46, no. 4 (Autumn 1992), pp. 783–89. See also Anthony Pagden, *Lords of All the Worlds: Ideologies of Empire in Spain, Britain and France c. 1500–c. 1800* (New Haven: Yale University Press, 1998).
10 Paul D. Wolfowitz, "Speech at the 38th Munich Conference on Security Policy", Munich (February 2, 2002).
11 "The New Multilateralism", *The Wall Street Journal* (January 8, 2004).
12 Michael Barnett and Martha Finnemore, *Rules for the World: International Organizations in Global Politics* (Ithaca, NY: Cornell University Press, 2004).
13 Bauman, *Liquid Modernity*, and Bauman, *Liquid Times*. See also Christopher Coker, "NATO's Unbearable Lightness of Being", *RUSI Journal*, vol. 149, no. 3 (June 2004).
14 Teresa Whitfield, *A Crowded Field: Groups of Friends, the UN, and the Resolution of Conflict* (New York: New York University CIC Occasional Paper, 2005).
15 See also Virginia Haufler, "International Diplomacy and the Privatization of Conflict Prevention", *International Studies Perspectives*, vol. 5, no. 2 (May 2004).
16 Internet: www.g8.utoronto.ca/ and www.g20.org
17 Richard Sennett, *The Corrosion of Character: The Personal Consequences of Work in the New Capitalism* (New York: W.W. Norton, 1998), p. 47.
18 Ruggie, "International Regimes", p. 198.
19 Ruggie, "International Regimes", p. 201.
20 Kal Raustiala, "The Architecture of International Cooperation: Transgovernmental Networks and the Future of International Law", *Virginia Journal of International Law*, vol. 43, no. 1 (Fall 2002). See also Kal Raustiala, "Form and Substance in International Agreements", *The American Journal of International Law*, vol. 99, no. 3 (July 2005).
21 Börzel, "Pace-Setting, Foot-Dragging, and Fence-Sitting".
22 Mark Pollack, *The Engines of European Integration: Delegation, Agency and Agenda-Setting in the EU* (Oxford: Oxford University Press, 2003); Dermott Hudson and Imelda Mahler, "The Open Method as a New Mode of Governance: The Case of Soft Economic Policy Co-ordination", *Journal of Common Market Studies*, vol. 39, no. 4 (November 2001); and Sonja Mazey and Jeremy Richardson, "Policy Framing: Interest Groups and the Lead Up To the 1996 Inter-Governmental Conference", *West European Politics*, vol. 20. no. 3 (June 1997).
23 Edoardo Chiti, "Regulation Through Agencies in the EU: A New Paradigm of European Governance", *Common Market Law Review*, vol. 44, no. 2 (April 2007).

24 Fabio Franchino, *The Powers of the Union: Delegation in the EU* (Cambridge: Cambridge University Press, 2007).
25 See for a recent example, Celeste Montoya, "The European Union, Capacity Building, and Transnational Networks: Combating Violence Against Women Through the Daphne Program", *International Organization*, vol. 62, no. 2 (April 2008).
26 Hanspeter Neuhold, "The Legal Dimension of Transatlantic Relations: Basic Positions and Some Key Issues", in Neuhold (ed.), *Transatlantic Legal Issues – European Views* (Vienna: Favorita Papers, 2005), p. 14.
27 Neuhold, "The Legal Dimension of Transatlantic Relations", p. 14.
28 "Brussels Rules OK", *The Economist* (September 22, 2007), p. 42.
29 "Brussels Rules OK", *The Economist* (September 22, 2007), p. 42. See also Laïdi, "The Normative Empire".
30 Walter Mattli and Tim Büthe, "Setting International Standards: Technological Rationality or Primacy of Power?", *World Politics*, vol. 56, no. 1 (October 2003).
31 Mattli and Büthe, "Setting International Standards", p. 26.
32 Mattli and Büthe, "Setting International Standards", p. 27.
33 Mattli and Büthe, "Setting International Standards", p. 27. Emphasis added.
34 Quoted in Mattli and Büthe, "Setting International Standards", p. 29.
35 Peter Mandelson, "Biotech and the EU – Speech at the European Biotechnology Info Day, Bavarian Representation", Brussels (June 14, 2007). See also Sarah Lieberman and Tim Gray, "GMOs and the Developing World: A Precautionary Interpretation of Biotechnology", *British Journal of Politics & International Relations*, vol. 10, no. 3 (August 2008).
36 Peter Mandelson, "Openness, Trade and the European Union – Speech at the Chambre de Commerce et de l'Industrie de Paris", Paris (June 30, 2007).
37 *A Single Market for Citizens*, COM(2007) 60 final (Brussels, February 21, 2007), p. 7.
38 Mark Schapiro, *Exposed: The Toxic Chemistry of Everyday Products and What's at Stake for American Power* (White River Jct., VT: Chelsea Green Publishing, 2007).
39 Khalid Nadvi, "Global Standards, Global Governance and the Organization of Global Value Chains", *Journal of Economic Geography*, vol. 8, no. 3 (May 2008).
40 John Braithwaite and Peter Drahos, *Global Business Regulation* (Cambridge: Cambridge University Press, 2000).
41 Braithwaite and Drahos, *Global Business Regulation*, p. 10.
42 Braithwaite and Drahos, *Global Business Regulation*, p. 10.
43 Braithwaite and Drahos, *Global Business Regulation*, p. 31.
44 Braithwaite and Drahos, *Global Business Regulation*, p. 17.
45 Braithwaite and Drahos, *Global Business Regulation*, p. 25.
46 Andrew P. Cortell and James W. Davis, "When Norms Clash: International Norms, Domestic Practices, and Japan's Internalisation of the GATT/WTO", *Review of International Studies*, vol. 31, no. 1 (January 2005); Judith E. Innes and David E. Booher, "Collaborative Policymaking: Governance Through Dialogue", in Maarten A. Hajer and Hendrik Wagenaar (eds.), *Deliberative Policy Analysis: Understanding Governance in the Network Society* (Cambridge: Cambridge University Press, 2003); Ian Johnstone, "Security Council Deliberations: The Power of the Better Argument", *European Journal of International Law*, vol. 14, no. 3 (June 2003); Neta C. Crawford, *Argument and Change in World Politics* (Cambridge: Cambridge University Press, 2002); and Maarten A. Hajer, *The Politics of Environmental Discourse: Ecological Modernization and the Policy Process* (Oxford: Oxford University Press, 1995).
47 Risse, "'Let's Argue!'".
48 Henry Farrell, "Constructing the International Foundations of E-Commerce—The EU-U.S. Safe Harbor Arrangement", *International Organization*, vol. 57, no. 2 (Spring 2003).
49 Curzio Giannini, "Promoting Financial Stability in Emerging-Market Countries: The Soft Law Approach and Beyond", *Comparative Economic Studies*, vol. 44, nos. 2/3

(Summer 2002), p. 126. See also Mariely Lopez-Santana, "The Domestic Implications of European Soft Law: Framing and Transmitting Change in Employment Policy", *Journal of European Public Policy*, vol. 13, no. 4 (June 2006).
50 Hartmut Hillgenberg, "A Fresh Look at Soft Law", *European Journal of International Law*, vol. 10, no. 3 (June 1999), p. 501.
51 Shareen Hertel, *Unexpected Power: Conflict and Change Among Transnational Activists* (Ithaca, NY: Cornell University Press, 2006); William E. DeMars, *NGOs and Transnational Networks: Wild Cards in World Politics* (London: Pluto Press, 2005); Thorsten Benner, Wolfgang H. Reinicke, and Jan Martin Witte, "Multisectoral Networks in Global Governance: Towards a Pluralistic System of Accountability", *Government and Opposition*, vol. 39, no. 2 (Spring 2004); Jonathan P. Doh and Hildy Teegen (eds.), *Globalization and NGOs: Transforming Business, Government and Society* (Westport CT: Praeger, 2003); Howard Rheingold, *Smart Mobs: The Next Social Revolution* (New York: Basic Books, 2003); Sanjeev Khagram, James V. Riker, and Kathryn Sikkink (eds.), *Restructuring World Politics: Transnational Social Movements* (Minneapolis: University of Minnesota Press, 2002); and Ariel Colonomos, "Non-State Actors as Moral Entrepreneurs: A Transnational Perspective on Ethics Networks", in Daphne Josselin and William Wallace (eds.), *Non-State Actors in World Politics* (London: Palgrave, 2001).
52 Slaughter, "Everyday Global Governance", p. 84.
53 Slaughter, "Everyday Global Governance", p. 87.
54 Slaughter, "Everyday Global Governance", p. 84. See also Anne-Marie Slaughter, *A New World Order* (Princeton, NJ: Princeton University Press, 2004).
55 Slaughter, "Everyday Global Governance", p. 88.
56 Jutta Joachim, "Framing Issues and Seizing Opportunities: The UN, NGOs and Women's Rights", *International Studies Quarterly*, vol. 47, no. 2 (June 2003), and Thomas Risse, Stephen C. Ropp, and Kathryn Sikkink (eds.), *The Power of Human Rights: International Norms and Domestic Change* (Cambridge: Cambridge University Press, 1999).
57 Anne-Marie Slaughter, "Courting the World", *Foreign Policy*, no. 141 (March/April 2004), p. 79.
58 Slaughter, "Everyday Global Governance", p. 89.
59 Anne-Marie Slaughter, "Leading Through Law", *The Wilson Quarterly*, vol. 27, no. 4 (Autumn 2003), p. 42.
60 Wolfgang H. Reinicke, "The Other World Wide Web: Global Public Policy Networks", *Foreign Policy*, no. 117 (Winter 1999), p. 44. Reinicke has been on the forefront of thinking on these emerging trisectoral alliances as the director of the UN's Vision Project on Global Public Policy Networks. See also Benedicte Bull and Desmond McNeill, *Development Issues in Global Governance: Public-Private Partnerships and Market Multilateralism* (London: Routledge, 2007); Jutta Joachim, *Agenda Setting, the UN and NGOs: Gender Violence and Reproductive Rights* (Washington DC: Georgetown University Press, 2007); Errol Meidinger, "The Administrative Law of Global Private-Public Regulation: The Case of Forestry", *European Journal of International Law*, vol. 17, no. 1 (February 2006); Morten Ougaard, *Political Globalization: State, Power and Social Forces* (New York: Palgrave Macmillan, 2004); and Laura Cram, "Governance 'To Go': Domestic Actors, Institutions and the Boundaries of the Possible", *Journal of Common Market Studies*, vol. 39, no. 4 (November 2001).
61 Klaus Dingwerth, "The Democratic Legitimacy of Public-Private Rule Making: What Can We Learn from the World Commission on Dams?", *Global Governance*, vol. 11, no. 1 (January/March 2005).
62 Tagi Sagafi-nejad, *The UN and Transnational Corporations: From Code of Conduct to Global Compact* (Bloomington, IN: Indiana University Press, 2008). See also www.globalcompactfoundation.org
63 Georg Kell, Anne-Marie Slaughter, and Thomas Hale, "Silent Reform Through the Global Compact", *UN Chronicle*, vol. 44, no. 1 (March 2007).

64 Dilek Cetindamar and Kristoffer Husoy, "Corporate Social Responsibility Practices and Environmentally Responsible Behavior: The Case of the United Nations Global Compact", *Journal of Business Ethics*, vol. 76, no. 2 (December 2007), and Lyn Bennie, Patrick Bernhagen, and Neil J. Mitchell, "The Logic of Transnational Action: The Good Corporation and the Global Compact", *Political Studies*, vol. 55, no. 4 (December 2007).
65 Kelly Kollman, "The Regulatory Power of Business Norms: A Call for a New Research Agenda", *International Studies Review*, vol. 10, no. 3 (September 2008); Ans Kolk, "Corporate Social Responsibility in the Coffee Sector: The Dynamics of MNC Responses and Code Development", *European Management Journal*, vol. 23, no. 2 (April 2005); David Levy and Daniel Egan, "Corporate Political Action in the Global Polity", in Richard Higgott, Geoffrey Underhill, and Andreas Bieler (eds.), *Non-State Actors and Authority in the Global System* (London: Routledge, 2000); Andrew King and Michael Lenox, "Industry Self-Regulation Without Sanctions", *Academy of Management Journal*, vol. 43, no. 4 (August 2000); and Frans Stokman, Rolf Ziegler, and John Scott, *Networks of Corporate Power* (Cambridge: Cambridge University Press, 1985).
66 David Antony Detomasi, "The Multinational Corporation and Global Governance: Modelling Global Public Policy Networks", *Journal of Business Ethics*, vol. 71, no. 3 (March 2007).
67 Daniel W. Drezner, *All Politics Is Global: Explaining International Regulatory Regimes* (Princeton, NJ: Princeton University Press, 2007).
68 Richard Price, "Reversing the Gun Sights: Transnational Civil Society Targets Land Mines", *International Organization*, vol. 52, no. 3 (Summer 1998).
69 Daniel C. Esty, "What Stakeholders Demand", *Harvard Business Review*, vol. 85, no. 10 (October 2007).
70 Esbenshade, *Monitoring Sweatshops*; DeWinter, "The Anti-Sweatshop Movement"; and Shareen Hertel, "New Moves in Transnational Advocacy: Getting Labor and Economic Rights on the Agenda in Unexpected Ways", *Global Governance*, vol. 12, no. 3 (July/September 2006).
71 Sheldon S. Wolin, "Fugitive Democracy", in Seyla Benhabib (ed.), *Democracy and Difference* (Princeton, NJ: Princeton University Press, 1996). See also Sheldon S. Wolin, *Democracy Incorporated: Managed Democracy and the Specter of Inverted Totalitarianism* (Princeton, NJ: Princeton University Press, 2008).
72 Kim D. Reimann, "A View From the Top: International Politics, Norms and the Worldwide Growth of NGOs", *International Studies Quarterly*, vol. 50, no. 1 (March 2006), p. 45.
73 Reimann, "A View From the Top", p. 59.
74 Quoted in Shepard Forman and Derk Segaar, "New Coalitions for Global Governance: The Changing Dynamics of Multilateralism", *Global Governance*, vol. 12, no. 2 (April/June 2006), p. 216.
75 Ronnie D. Lipschutz and James K. Rowe (eds.), *Globalization, Governmentality, and Global Politics: Regulation for the Rest of Us?* (London: Routledge, 2005); Jan Aart Scholte, "Civil Society and Democratically Accountable Global Governance", *Government and Opposition*, vol. 39, no. 2 (Spring 2004); Mathias Koenig-Archibugi, "Transnational Corporations and Public Accountability", *Government and Opposition*, vol. 39, no. 2 (Spring 2004); and Mathias Zürn, "Global Governance and Legitimacy Problems", *Government and Opposition*, vol. 39, no. 2 (Spring 2004).
76 Elliott A. Krause, *Death of the Guilds: Professions, States, and the Advance of Capitalism, 1930s to the Present* (New Haven: Yale University Press, 1996).
77 Rodney Bruce Hall and Thomas J. Biersteker, "The Emergence of Private Authority in the International System", in Hall and Biersteker (eds.), *The Emergence of Private Authority in Global Governance* (Cambridge: Cambridge University Press, 2003).

78 Jean-Christophe Graz and Andreas Nölke (eds.), *Transnational Private Governance and Its Limits* (London: Routledge, 2008); Hans Krause Hansen and Dorte Salskov-Iversen (eds.), *Critical Perspectives on Private Authority in Global Politics* (New York: Palgrave Macmillan, 2008); Philipp H. Pattberg, *Private Institutions and Global Governance: The New Politics of Environmental Sustainability* (Northhampton, MA: Edward Elgar, 2007); Stefan Schirm (ed.), *New Rules for Global Markets: Public and Private Governance in the World Economy* (New York: Palgrave Macmillan, 2004); Ben Cashore, Graeme Auld, and Deanne Newsom, *Governing Through Markets: Forest Certification and the Emergence of Non-State Authority* (New Haven: Yale University Press, 2004); Shareen Hertel, "The Private Side of Global Governance", *Journal of International Affairs*, vol. 57, no. 1 (Fall 2003); Virginia Haufler, *A Public Role for the Private Sector* (Washington DC: Carnegie Endowment for International Peace, 2001); Daniel Drache (ed.), *The Market or the Public Domain?* (London: Routledge, 2001); Claire Cutler, Virginia Haufler, and Tony Porter (eds.), *Private Authority and International Affairs* (Albany: SUNY Press, 1999); and Gunther Teubner (ed.), *Global Law Without a State* (Aldershot: Dartmouth, 1997).
79 Tony Porter and Karsten Ronit, "Self-Regulation as Policy Process: The Multiple and Criss-Crossing Stages of Private Rule-Making", *Policy Sciences*, vol. 39, no. 1 (March 2006), p. 42.
80 Leonard J. Schoppa, "The Social Context in Coercive International Bargaining", *International Organization*, vol. 53, no. 2 (Spring 1999).
81 Quoted in Hall and Biersteker (eds.), *The Emergence of Private Authority in Global Governance*, p. 205.
82 Drezner, *All Politics Is Global*, p. 5.
83 Hall and Biersteker, "The Emergence of Private Authority", p. 6.
84 Lisa Blomgren Bingham, Tina Nabatchi, and Rosemanry O'Leary, "The New Governance: Practices and Processes for Stakeholder and Citizen Participation in the Work of Government", *Public Administration Review*, vol. 65, no. 5 (September/October 2005), p. 547. See also Andrew Linklater, "Dialogic Politics and the Civilising Process", *Review of International Studies*, vol. 31, no. 1 (January 2005), and Thomas Risse, "Global Governance and Communicative Action", *Government and Opposition*, vol. 39, no. 2 (Spring 2004).
85 Rodney Bruce Hall, "Private Authority: Non-State Actors and Global Governance", *Harvard International Review*, vol. 27, no. 2 (Summer 2005).
86 The notions "institutional market authority" and "normative market authority" are derived from Hall and Biersteker (eds.), *The Emergence of Private Authority in Global Governance*.
87 Stanley Holmes, "Nike Goes for the Green", *Business Week* (September 25, 2006).
88 Internet: www.icann.org
89 Cees N.J. de Vey Mestdagh and Rudolf W. Rijgersberg, "Rethinking Accountability in Cyberspace: A New Perspective on ICANN", *International Review of Law, Computers & Technology*, vol. 21, no. 1 (March 2007).
90 Fuchs, "Commanding Heights?", p. 773.
91 Paul J. Davies, Joanna Chung, and Gillian Tett, "Reputations To Restore", *Financial Times* (July 22, 2008). See also Susan Strange, "Finance, Information and Power", *Review of International Studies*, vol. 16, no. 3 (July 1990).
92 Baldwin, "Power Analysis and World Politics".
93 Ans Kolk and Rob van Tulder, "Setting New Global Rules? TNCs and Codes of Conduct", *Transnational Corporations*, vol. 14, no. 3 (December 2005).
94 Magali Delmas and Ivan Montiel, "The Diffusion of Voluntary International Management Standards: Responsible Care, ISO 9000, and ISO 14001 in the Chemical Industry", *Policy Studies Journal*, vol. 36, no. 1 (February 2008).

95 Klaus Dingwerth, *The New Transnationalism: Transnational Governance and Democratic Legitimacy* (New York: Palgrave Macmillan, 2007), and Robert O. Keohane and Joseph S. Nye, Jr., "Redefining Accountability for Global Governance", in Miles Kahler and David A Lake (eds.), *Governance in a Global Economy: Political Authority in Transition* (Princeton, NJ: Princeton University Press, 2003).
96 Fritz W. Scharpf, *Regieren in Europa: Effectiv und Demokratisch?* (Frankfurt a/M: Campus Verlag, 1999).
97 Marco Schäferhoff, Sabine Campe, and Christopher Kaan, *Transnational Public-Private Partnerships in International Relations: Making Sense of Concepts, Research Frameworks and Results* (Berlin: SFB-Governance Working Papers 6, 2007), p. 25.
98 Risse, " 'Let's Argue!' ", p. 15.
99 Kathryn Sikkink, "Transnational Politics, International Relations Theory, and Human Rights", *PS, Political Science & Politics*, vol. 31, no. 3 (September 1998), p. 518.
100 Sikkink, "Transnational Politics", p. 519.
101 Sikkink, "Transnational Politics", p. 520.
102 Abram Chayes and Antonia Handler Chayes, *The New Sovereignty: Compliance with International Regulatory Agreements* (Cambridge, MA: Harvard University Press, 1995).
103 Harold Hongju Koh, "Why Do Nations Obey International Law?", *The Yale Law Journal*, vol. 106, no. 8 (June 1997), p. 2602. Italics in the original.
104 Hongju Koh, "Why Do Nations Obey International Law?", p. 2613.
105 Hongju Koh, "Why Do Nations Obey International Law?", p. 2617.
106 Quoted in Hongju Koh, "Why Do Nations Obey International Law?", p. 2599.
107 Nan Lin, "Building a Network Theory of Social Capital", *Connections*, vol. 22, no. 1 (1999), p. 35.
108 Loveman, "The Modern State". See also Bourdieu, *Language and Symbolic Power*. For an assessment of the impact of global administrative law on IOs, see Nico Krisch and Benedict Kingbury, "Introduction: Global Governance and Global Administrative Law in the International Legal Order", *European Journal of International Law*, vol. 17, no. 1 (February 2006); Krisch, "The Pluralism of Global Administrative Law", *European Journal of International Law*, vol. 17, no. 1 (February 2006); and Carol Harlow, "Global Administrative Law: The Quest for Principles and Values", *European Journal of International Law*, vol. 17, no. 1 (February 2006).
109 Michael C. Williams, *Culture and Security: Symbolic Power and the Politics of International Security* (London: Routledge, 2007).
110 Quoted in Williams, *Culture and Security*, p. 33.
111 Loveman, "The Modern State", p. 1655.
112 Loveman, "The Modern State", p. 1655.
113 Loveman, "The Modern State", p. 1655.
114 Quoted in William F. Hanks, "Pierre Bourdieu and the Practices of Language", *Annual Review of Anthropology*, vol. 34, no. 1 (October 2005), p. 77.
115 Quoted in Ian Hurd, "Legitimacy, Power, and the Symbolic Life of the UN Security Council", *Global Governance*, vol. 8, no. 1 (January/March 2002), p. 37.
116 A. Claire Cutler, *Private Power and Global Authority: Transnational Merchant Law in the Global Political Economy* (Cambridge: Cambridge University Press, 2003).
117 James N. Rosenau, *People Count! The Networked Individual in World Politics* (Boulder, CO: Paradigm Publishers, 2007).
118 Karen Tindall and Paul 't Hart, "Leadership by the Famous: Celebrity as Political Capital", in John Kane, Haig Patapan, and Paul 't Hart (eds.), *Dispersed Leadership in Democracies* (Oxford: Oxford University Press, 2009); Andrew F. Cooper, "Beyond One Image Fits All: Bono and the Complexity of Celebrity Diplomacy", *Global Governance*, vol. 14, no. 3 (July/September 2008); Heribert Dieter and Rajiv Kumar, "The Downside of Celebrity Diplomacy: The Neglected Complexity of Development", *Global Governance*, vol. 14, no. 3 (July/September 2008); Andrew F. Cooper,

"Beyond Hollywood and the Boardroom: Celebrity Diplomacy", *Georgetown Journal of International Affairs*, vol. 8, no. 2 (Summer/Fall 2007); Cooper, *Celebrity Diplomacy* (Boulder, CO: Paradigm Publishers, 2007); Mark D. Alleyne, "The United Nations' Celebrity Diplomacy", *SAIS Journal*, vol. 25, no. 1 (Winter-Spring 2005); and P. David Marshall, *Celebrity and Power: Fame in Contemporary Culture* (Minneapolis: University of Minnesota Press, 1997).
119 See Internet: www.one.org
120 Neal Gabler, *Life: The Movie. How Entertainment Conquered Reality* (New York: Vintage Books, 2000).
121 James Traub, "The Celebrity Solution", *New York Times* (March 9, 2008).
122 Traub, "The Celebrity Solution".
123 Barber, "Shrunken Sovereign", p. 78.
124 Traub, "The Celebrity Solution".
125 Schäferhoff, Campe, and Kaan, *Transnational Public-Private Partnerships in International Relations*, p. 17, and Hurd, "Legitimacy and Authority in International Politics".
126 Checkel, "Why Comply?".
127 Maarten A. Hajer and Hendrik Wagenaar (eds.), *Deliberative Policy Analysis: Understanding Governance in the Network Society* (Cambridge: Cambridge University Press, 2003). See also Göktuğ Morçöl, *A New Mind for Policy Analysis: Toward a Post-Newtonian and Postpositivist Epistemology and Methodology* (Westport, CT: Praeger Publishers, 2002).

5 Media and globalization

1 Price, *Media and Sovereignty*, p. 3.
2 Göran Bolin, "Visions of Europe—Cultural Technologies of Nation-States", *International Journal of Cultural Studies*, vol. 9, no. 2 (2006).
3 Neil Postman, *Amusing Ourselves To Death: Public Discourse in the Age of Show Business* (London: Penguin, 1985).
4 Robert M. Entman, "Framing: Towards Clarification of a Fractured Paradigm", *Journal of Communication*, vol. 43, no. 4 (Autumn 1993), p. 53. See also Entman, "Framing Bias: Media in the Distribution of Power", *Journal of Communication*, vol. 57, no. 1 (March 2007), and Entman, "How the Media Affect What People Think: An Information Processing Approach", *The Journal of Politics*, vol. 51, no. 2 (May 1989).
5 Benedict Anderson, *Imagined Communities* (London: Verso, 1991), p. 25.
6 Dedaic and Nelson (eds.), *At War With Words*, and Richard Biernacki, "Language and the Shift from Signs to Practices in Cultural Inquiry", *History and Theory*, vol. 39, no. 3 (October 2000).
7 Susan J. Douglas, "The Turn Within: The Irony of Technology in a Globalized World", *American Quarterly*, vol. 58, no. 3 (September 2006), p. 637.
8 Cornel Sandvoss, "On the Couch With Europe: The Eurovision Song Contest, the European Broadcast Union and Belonging on the Old Continent", *Popular Communication*, vol. 6, no. 3 (July 2008).
9 Ithiel de Sola Pool, *Technologies of Freedom: On Free Speech in an Electronic Age* (Cambridge, MA: Belknap Press, 1983).
10 Edwin L. Armistead, *Information Operations: Warfare and the Hard Reality of Soft Power* (Washington DC: Potomac Books, 2004).
11 Dennis Behreandt, "Satellite Wars", *The New American*, vol. 23, no. 7 (April 2007).
12 Quoted in Tony Blankley and Oliver Horn, "Strategizing Strategic Communication", *The Heritage Foundation WebMemo*, no. 1939 (May 29, 2008), p. 2.
13 Jerry W. Knudson, "Rebellion In Chiapas: Insurrection by Internet and Public Relations", *Media, Culture & Society*, vol. 20, no. 3 (July 1998).

14 Jerry Everard, *Virtual States: The Internet and the Boundaries of the Nation-State* (London: Routledge, 2000); H. Frederick, *Global Communication and International Relations* (Belmont, CA: Wadsworth Publishing, 1993); Benjamin Woolley, *Virtual Worlds: A Journey in Hype and Hyperreality* (Harmondsworth: Penguin, 1993); and Howard Rheingold, *Virtual Reality: The Revolutionary Technology of Computer-Generated Artificial Worlds – And How It Promises To Transform Society* (New York: Simon & Schuster, 1992).
15 Wayne Wanta, Guy Golan, and Cheolhan Lee, "Agenda Setting and International News: Media Influence on Public Perceptions of Foreign Policy", *Journalism and Mass Communication Quarterly*, vol. 81, no. 2 (Summer 2004).
16 Gary C. Woodward, *Center Stage: Media and the Performance of American Politics* (Lanham, MD: Rowman & Littlefield, 2007), and Eytan Gilboa, "Global Communication and Foreign Policy", *Journal of Communication*, vol. 52, no. 4 (December 2002).
17 Dan Steinbock, "Mobile Service Revolution: CNN Effect Goes Mobile", *Georgetown Journal of International Affairs*, vol. 6, no. 2 (Summer 2005), pp. 133–34.
18 Monroe E. Price, *Television: The Public Sphere and National Identity* (Oxford: Clarendon Press, 1995).
19 Andrew Sullivan, "Andrew Sullivan on America: An Honest Blogger Will Never Make a Quick Buck", *The Sunday Times* (October 13, 2002), p. A4.
20 Mahbubani, *The New Asian Hemisphere*, pp. 8–9.
21 Martin Walker, "Globalization 3.0", *The Wilson Quarterly*, vol. 31, no. 4 (Autumn 2007), p. 19.
22 Bruce Bimber, *Information and American Diplomacy: Technology in the Evolution of Political Power* (Cambridge: Cambridge University Press, 2003), p. 13.
23 Mark Tremayne (eds.), *Blogging, Citizenship, and the Future of the Media* (London: Routledge, 2007).
24 Joseph S. Nye, Jr., and William Owens, "America's Information Edge", *Foreign Affairs*, vol. 75, no. 2 (March/April 1996), p. 27.
25 Philip Seib, *The Al Jazeera Effect: How the New Global Media are Reshaping World Politics* (Washington DC: Potomac Books, 2008); Hugh Miles, *Al-Jazeera: The Inside Story of the Arab News Channel That is Challenging the West* (New York: Grove Press, 2006); and Khalil Rinnawi, *Instant Nationalism: McArabism, Al-Jazeera, and Transnational Media in the Arab World* (Lanham, MD: University Press of America, 2006).
26 Thomas L. Friedman, "Glasnost in the Gulf", *New York Times* (February 27, 2001), p. 23.
27 Philip Seib, "Hegemonic No More: Western Media, the Rise of Al-Jazeera, and the Influence of Diverse Voices", *International Studies Review*, vol. 7, no. 4 (December 2005), p. 613.
28 Marshall McLuhan, *Understanding Media: The Extensions of Man* (New York: Signet, 1964), pp. 19–20.
29 Douglas, "The Turn Within", p. 621. See also Norbert Elias, *The Society of Individuals* (Oxford: Blackwell, 1991).
30 James Lull, *Media, Communication, Culture: A Global Approach* (New York: Columbia University Press, 2000).
31 Mark Tremayne (eds.), *Blogging, Citizenship, and the Future of the Media* (London: Routledge, 2007), and Stephen D. Cooper, *Watching the Watchdog: Bloggers as the Fifth Estate* (Spokan, WA: Marquette Books, 2006).
32 Lev Grossman, "Blogs Have Their Day", *Time* (December 27, 2004), p. 110.
33 David Weigel, "An Army of Bloggers", *Reason*, vol. 38, no. 3 (July 2006), p. 51.
34 Ray Maratea, "The E-Rise and Fall of Social Problems: The Blogosphere as a Public Arena", *Social Problems*, vol. 55, no. 1 (February 2008), p. 143.
35 Bara Vaida, "Blogging On", *National Journal*, vol. 39, no. 40 (October 6, 2007), p. 27.

36 Matthew Currier Burden, *The Blog of War: Frontline Dispatches from Soldiers in Iraq and Afghanistan* (New York: Simon & Schuster, 2006).
37 Nicholson Baker, "The Charms of Wikipedia", *The New York Review of Books*, vol. 55, no. 4 (March 20, 2008).
38 John Cassidy, "Me Media", *The New Yorker* (May 15, 2006).
39 Lucas Hilderbrand, "YouTube: Where Cultural Memory and Copyright Converge", *Film Quarterly*, vol. 61, no. 1 (Fall 2007), p. 48.
40 Vaida, "Blogging On", p. 29.
41 World Information Access, *Blogger Arrests* (Seattle: University of Washington, 2008).
42 Friedman, *The World is Flat*, pp. 205–6.
43 Price, *Media and Sovereignty*, p. 29.
44 Taylor C. Boas, "Weaving the Authoritarian Web", *Current History*, vol. 103, no. 677 (December 2004).
45 James Mulvenon, "Golden Shields and Panopticons: Beijing's Internet Control Policies", *Georgetown Journal of International Affairs*, vol. 9, no. 2 (Summer 2008), and Naomi Klein, "China's All-Seeing Eye", *Rolling Stone*, no. 1053 (May 29, 2008).
46 Howard W. French, "Will the Great Firewall Stand?", *New York Times Upfront*, vol. 140, no. 11 (March 10, 2008), p. 12.
47 Peter Ford, "China Blocks YouTube, Reporters Over Tibet News", *The Christian Science Monitor* (March 18, 2008), p. 6.
48 Shanthi Kalathil and Taylor C. Boas, *Open Networks, Closed Regimes: The Impact of the Internet on Authoritarian Rule* (Washington DC: Carnegie Endowment for International Peace, 2003), p. 3. See also Michael Chase and James Mulvenon, *You've Got Dissent: Chinese Dissident Use of the Internet and Beijing's Counter-Strategies* (Santa Monica, CA: RAND, 2002), and Jack Goldsmith and Tim Wu, *Who Controls the Internet? Illusions of a Borderless World* (New York: Oxford University Press, 2006).
49 William Thatcher Dowell, "The Internet, Censorship, and China", *Georgetown Journal of International Affairs*, vol. 7, no. 2 (Summer 2006), p. 113.
50 BDA Connect, "China Surpasses the US to Become the World's Largest Internet Population" (March 13, 2008).
51 Xiao Qiang, "The Rising Tide of Internet Opinion in China", *Nieman Reports*, vol. 58, no. 2 (Summer 2004), p. 103.
52 Shaoguang Wang, "Changing Models of China's Policy Agenda Setting", *Modern China*, vol. 34, no. 1 (January 2008).
53 Qiang, "The Rising Tide of Internet Opinion in China", p. 104.
54 Edmund Ghareeb, "New Media and the Information Revolution in the Arab World: An Assessment", *The Middle East Journal*, vol. 54, no. 3 (Summer 2000), pp. 398–99.
55 Ghareeb, "New Media and the Information Revolution in the Arab World", p. 416.
56 Jon B. Alterman, "The Middle East's Information Revolution", *Current History*, vol. 99, no. 633 (January 2000), p. 24.
57 Jonathan Rauch, "In Arabic, 'Internet' Means 'Freedom' ", *National Journal*, vol. 38, no. 9 (March 4, 2006), p. 17.
58 "Watch Out, Arabs and the Internet", *The Economist* (July 10, 2004), p. 53.
59 Rauch, "In Arabic, 'Internet' Means 'Freedom' ", p. 17.
60 David Ignatius, "From 'Connectedness' to Conflict", *Washington Post* (February 22, 2006), p. A15.
61 Thomas L. Friedman, "Global Village Idiocy", *New York Times* (May 12, 2002), p. 15.
62 Roger Cohen, "Democracy as a Brand: Wooing Hearts, European or Muslim", *New York Times* (October 16, 2004), p. B7.
63 Laïdi, "Are European Preferences Shared by Others?", and Laïdi, "The Normative Empire".
64 Alvin Toffler and Heidi Toffler, *War and Anti-War* (Boston: Little, Brown, 1993), p. 147.
65 David Barstow, "Behind TV Analysts, Pentagon's Hidden Hand", *International Herald Tribune* (April 20, 2008).

66 Eytan Gilboa, "Global Television News and Foreign Policy: Debating the CNN Effect", *International Studies Perspectives*, vol. 6, no. 3 (August 2005), and Gilboa (ed.), *Media and Conflict: Framing Issues, Making Policy, Shaping Opinions* (Ardsley, NY: Transnational Publishers, 2002).
67 Myriam Dunn Cavelty, *Cyber-Security and Threat Politics: US Efforts to Secure the Information Age* (London: Routledge, 2008); Joelien Pretorius, "The Security Imaginary: Explaining Military Isomorphism", *Security Dialogue*, vol. 39, no. 1 (March 2008); Chris Hables Gray, *Peace, War, and Computers* (London: Routledge, 2005); and Henry C. Ryan and Edward C. Peartree (eds.), *Information Revolution and International Security* (Washington DC: Center for Strategic and International Studies, 1998).
68 Margaret H. Belknap, "The CNN Effect: Strategic Enabler or Operational Risk?", *Parameters*, vol. 32. no. 3 (Autumn 2002), pp. 105–7.
69 Daya Kishan Thussu and Des Freedman (eds.), *War and the Media: Reporting Conflict 24/7* (Thousand Oaks, CA: Sage, 2003).
70 Marvin Kalb, *The Israeli-Hezbollah War of 2006: The Media as a Weapon in Asymmetrical Conflict* (Cambridge, MA: Harvard University Shorenstein Center Working Paper, 2007), pp. 33–34. See also Winn Schwartau, *Information Warfare: Chaos on the Electronic Superhighway* (New York: Thunder's Mouth Press, 1994).
71 Gal Mor, "The First Photoshop War", *Ynetnews.com* (August 17, 2006).
72 Lorne Manly, "In Wars, Quest for Media Balance is Also a Battlefield", *New York Times* (August 14, 2006).
73 Kalb, *The Israeli-Hezbollah War of 2006*, p. 6.
74 M. Rex Miller, "The Digital Dynamic: How Communications Media Shape Our World", *The Futurist*, vol. 39, no. 3 (May/June 2005), p. 32.
75 Steven Livingston, "Diplomacy in the New Information Environment", *Georgetown Journal of International Affairs*, vol. 4, no. 2 (Summer 2003), p. 114.
76 Lila Rajiva, *The Language of Empire: Abu Ghraib and the American Media* (New York: Monthly Review Press, 2005).
77 Nancy Pauly, "Abu Ghraib (Un)becoming Photographs: How Can Art Educators Address Current Images From Visual Culture Perspectives?", *The Journal of Social Theory in Art Education*, vol. 25 (2005), pp. 159, 164.
78 Ian Buruma, "Ghosts", *The New York Review of Books*, vol. 55, no. 11 (June 26, 2008).
79 Douglas, "The Turn Within", p. 629.
80 Herbert Gans, *Deciding What's News* (New York: Vintage Books, 1979).
81 W. Lance Bennett, Regina G. Lawrence, and Steven Livingston, *When the Press Fails: Political Power and the News Media from Iraq to Katrina* (Chicago: University of Chicago Press, 2008), and Neil Henry, *American Carnival: Journalism Under Siege in an Age of New Media* (Berkeley: University of California Press, 2007).
82 Colin Powell, *My American Journey* (New York: Random House, 1995), p. 529.
83 Thussu and Freedman (eds.), *War and the Media*.
84 Claude Brodesser, "Feds Seek H'wood Help", *Variety* (October 7, 2001).
85 The US Pentagon is developing its newly formed Defense Media Activity (DMA), whose US$68 million, 186.000-square-foot headquarters should be finished by 2011 on the grounds of Fort Meade (Maryland). DMA's mission is to provide "the American public [with] high quality visual information, including Combat Camera imagery depicting U.S. military activities and operation." See Walter Pincus, "New Pentagon Media Agency Seeks to Fill Top Job", *Washington Post* (August 25, 2008), p. A15.
86 David L. Robb, *Operation Hollywood: How the Pentagon Shapes and Censors the Movies* (Amherst, NY: Prometheus Books, 2004).
87 James Der Derian, *Virtuous War: Mapping the Military-Industrial-Medial-Entertainment Network* (Boulder, CO: Westview, 2001).
88 James Castonguay, "Conglomeration, New Media, and the Cultural Production of the 'War on Terror' ", *Cinema Journal*, vol. 43, no. 4 (Summer 2004), p. 103.

89 Dennis Broe, "Fox and Its Friends: Global Commodification and the New Cold War", *Cinema Journal*, vol. 43, no. 4 (Summer 2004).
90 Matthew A. Baum, "Sex, Lies, and War: How Soft News Brings Foreign Policy to the Inattentive Public", *American Political Science Review*, vol. 96, no. 1 (March 2002), p. 91. See also Matthew A. Baum, *Soft News Goes to War: Public Opinion and American Foreign Policy in the New Media Age* (Princeton, NJ: Princeton University Press, 2003).
91 Baum, *Soft News Goes to War*.
92 Baum, "Sex, Lies, and War", pp. 94, 96.
93 François Debrix, *Tabloid Terror: War, Culture, and Geopolitics* (London: Routledge, 2008), p. 6. See also Ishita Sinha Roy, "Worlds Apart: Nation-Branding on the National Geographic Channel", *Media, Culture & Society*, vol. 29, no. 4 (July 2007).
94 Baum, *Soft News Goes to War*, p. 7.
95 Edward S. Herman and Noam Chomsky, *Manufacturing Consent: The Political Economy of the Mass Media* (New York: Pantheon Books, 1988).
96 Lisa Nakamura, *Cybertypes: Race, Ethnicity, and Identity on the Internet* (London: Routledge, 2002).
97 Miller, "The Digital Dynamic", p. 33.
98 David J. Rothkopf, "Cyberpolitik: The Changing Nature of Power in the Information Age", *Journal of International Affairs*, vol. 51, no. 2 (Spring 1998), p. 326. See also Stanley Aronowitz, Barbara Martinsons, and Michael Menser (eds.), *Technoscience and Cyberculture* (London: Routledge, 1996), and Douglas Rushkoff, *Cyberia: Life in the Trenches of Hyperspace* (London: HarperCollins, 1994).
99 Jessica T. Mathews, "Power Shift", *Foreign Affairs*, vol. 76, no.1 (January/February 1997), p. 57.
100 Nye and Owens, "America's Information Edge." For example, during the August 2008 Caucassus conflict, websites of the Georgian government were jammed, blocking the access of the international community to information originating from the Georgian authorities. Georgia's Internet exposed its reliance on Russian infrastructure, indicating that any modern conflict will now inevitably have a cyberwar component to it, simply because hacking foreign websites is too inexpensive to be passed up. See Ben Arnoldy, "Cyberspace: New Frontier in Conflicts", *The Christian Science Monitor* (August 13, 2008).
101 Nye and Owens, "America's Information Edge", p. 20.
102 Nye and Owens, "America's Information Edge", p. 20.

6 Public diplomacy

1 Ladislav Bittman, *The KGB and Soviet Disinformation: An Insider's View* (Washington DC: Potomac Books, 1985).
2 Israel's public diplomacy is usually called *Hasbara*, Hebrew for "explanation." See Internet: www.hasbara.com
3 Karl Theodor Paschke, *Report on the Special Inspection of 14 German Embassies in the Countries of the European Union* (Berlin: Auswärtiges Amt, 2002).
4 Jolyon Welsh and Daniel Fearn (eds.), *Engagement: Public Diplomacy in a Globalised World* (London: Foreign and Commonwealth Office, 2008).
5 David Blair, "UK Using Public Opinion to change US Climate Policy", *Daily Telegraph* (July 20, 2008).
6 Quoted in Ferguson, "Approaches to Defining 'Empire'", p. 279. See Hans J. Morgenthau, *Politics Among Nations: The Struggle for Power and Peace* (New York: Knopf, 1978/1948).
7 Michael A. Cohen and Maria Figueroa Küpçü, "Privatizing Foreign Policy", *World Policy Journal*, vol. 22, no. 3 (Fall 2005); Cooper, "Beyond Hollywood and the Boardroom"; and Alleyne, "The United Nations' Celebrity Diplomacy".

8 Nancy Snow and Philip N. Taylor (eds.), *Routledge Handbook of Public Diplomacy* (New York: Routledge, 2008), and J. Michael Waller, *The Public Diplomacy Reader* (Washington DC: Institute of World Politics Press, 2007).
9 Nicholas J. Cull, "Public Diplomacy: Lessons from the Past" (April 2007), unpublished report.
10 Both quoted in Jan Melissen, "The New Public Diplomacy: Between Theory and Practice", in Jan Melissen (ed.), *The New Public Diplomacy: Soft Power in International Relations* (New York: Palgrave, 2005), pp. 11–12. See also Hans N. Tuch, *Communicating With the World: U.S. Public Diplomacy Overseas* (New York: St. Martin's Press, 1990).
11 Bruce Gregory, "Public Diplomacy and National Security: Lessons from the U.S. Experience", *Smallwarsjournal.com* (2008). Emphasis added.
12 Eytan Gilboa, "Searching for a Theory of Public Diplomacy", *The Annals of the American Academy of Political and Social Science*, vol. 616 (March 2008), and Gilboa, "Mass Communication and Diplomacy: A Theoretical Framework", *Communication Theory*, vol. 10, no. 3 (August 2000).
13 Cull, "Public Diplomacy: Lessons from the Past", p. 15.
14 Nicholas J. Cull, David Culbert, and David Welch (eds.), *Propaganda and Mass Pursuasion: A Historical Encyclopedia, 1500 to the Present* (Santa Barbara, CA: ABC-Clio, 2003).
15 Naima Prevots, *Dance for Export: Cultural Diplomacy in the Cold War* (Middletown, CT: Wesleyan University Press, 1998), and Carol Bellamy and Adam Weinberg, "Educational and Cultural Exchanges to Restore America's Image", *The Washington Quarterly*, vol. 31, no. 3 (Summer 2008).
16 Cynthia P. Schneider, "Culture Communicates: US Diplomacy That Works", in Melissen (ed.) *The New Public Diplomacy*.
17 Richard T. Arndt, *The First Resort of Kings: American Cultural Diplomacy in the Twentieth Century* (Washington DC: Potomac Books, 2005).
18 Cho and Jeong, "China's Soft Power".
19 Michael True, *People Power: Fifty Peacemakers and Their Communities* (Jaipur: Rawat, 2007).
20 See, for example, the special issue on human security of *Security Dialogue*, vol. 35, no. 3 (September 2004).
21 Mark Leonard and Vidhya Alakeson, *Going Public: Diplomacy for the Information Society* (London: The Foreign Policy Center, 2000), p. 3.
22 Kathy Fitzpatrick, "Advancing the New Public Diplomacy: A Public Relations Perspective", *The Hague Journal of Diplomacy*, vol. 2, no. 3 (October 2007).
23 Nicholas J. Cull, *Public Diplomacy Before Gullion: The Evolution of a Phrase* (Los Angeles: USC Center on Public Diplomacy, April 2006).
24 Kristin M. Lord, "Public Diplomacy and the New Transatlantic Agenda", *Brookings US-Europe Analysis* (August 15, 2008).
25 Cull, "Public Diplomacy: Lessons from the Past".
26 See also Melissa A. Rudderham, *Middle Power Pull: Can Middle Powers Use Public Diplomacy to Ameliorate the Image of the West?* (Toronto: York University YCISS Working Paper 46, 2008).
27 David Styan, "Tony Blair and Africa: Old Images, New Realities", *OpenDemocracy.net* (May 25, 2005).
28 Leonard and Alakeson, *Going Public*, p. 13.
29 Leonard and Alakeson, *Going Public*, p. 13.
30 Iver B. Neumann, "Returning Practice to the Linguistic Turn: The Case of Diplomacy", *Millennium*, vol. 31, no. 3 (July 2002).
31 Charlotte L. Beers, "Prepared Testimony Before the Committee on Foreign Relations of the United States Senate on American Public Diplomacy and Islam", Washington DC (February 27, 2003).

Notes

32. David E. Kaplan, "Hearts, Minds, and Dollars: In an Unseen Front in the War on Terrorism, America is Spending Millions... To Change the Very Face of Islam", *US News and World Report* (April 17, 2005), and Rosaleen Smyth, "Mapping US Public Diplomacy in the 21st Century", *Australian Journal of International Affairs*, vol. 55, no. 3 (November 2001).
33. Richard Holbrooke, "Get the Message Out", *Washington Post* (October 28, 2001), p. B07. See also Nicholas D. Kristof, "Make Diplomacy, Not War", *New York Times* (August 10, 2008); Joshua Muravchik, "America Loses Its Voice", *The Weekly Standard* (June 9, 2003); and David E. Morey and Ted Dalen Carpenter, "Should the United States Invest Heavily in New Efforts to Advance Public Diplomacy?", *Insight on the News* (September 30, 2002).
34. Salman Rushdie, "Anti-Americanism Has Taken the World by Storm", *Guardian* (February 6, 2002). Lamis Andoni argues that "U.S. policy has been an utter failure in the Arab and Muslim world", in Andoni, "Deeds Speak Louder Than Words", *The Washington Quarterly*, vol. 25, no. 2 (Spring 2002), p. 87. See also Barry Rubin and Judith Colp Rubin, *Anti-American Terrorism and the Middle East: A Documentary Reader* (Oxford: Oxford University Press, 2002).
35. Joffe, "Who's Afraid of Mr. Big?".
36. "Brand U.S.A.", *Foreign Policy*, no. 127 (November/December 2001), p. 19.
37. Mrs Beers left this position in March 2003, officially for health reasons.
38. Rutenberg, "Hollywood Seeks Role in the War", and Nina Teicholz, "Privatizing Propaganda", *Washington Monthly*, vol. 34, no. 12 (October 2002), pp. 16–18. See also Catherine Scott, "Americans Aren't Consumers Who Have to be Sold on War', *Atlanta Journal-Constitution* (January 22, 2003).
39. Philip M. Taylor, *Munitions of the Mind: A History of Propaganda from the Ancient World to the Present Day* (Manchester: Manchester University Press, 1995).
40. Arthur A. Bardos, " 'Public Diplomacy': An Old Art, A New Profession", *The Virginia Quarterly Review*, vol. 77, no. 3 (Summer 2001). See also Yale Richmond, *Practicing Public Diplomacy: A Cold War Odyssey* (New York: Berghahn Books, 2008), and Alvin Snyder, *Warriors of Disinformation: American Propaganda, Soviet Lies, and the Winning of the Cold War* (New York: Arcade Publishing, 1995).
41. Nancy Snow, *Propaganda Inc.: Selling America's Culture to the World* (New York: Seven Stories Press, 2002), and Nancy Snow, *Information War: American Propaganda, Free Speech, and Opinion Control After 9/11* (New York: Seven Stories Press, 2003). See also Gifford D. Malone, *Political Advocacy and Cultural Communication: Organizing the Nation's Public Diplomacy* (Lanham, MD: University Press of America, 1988).
42. *Finding America's Voice: A Strategy for Reinvigorating U.S. Public Diplomacy*, Report of an Independent Task Force Sponsored by the Council on Foreign Relations (Washington DC: Council on Foreign Relations, 2003), p. v.
43. Nye, *Soft Power*, pp. 99–100.
44. An Independent Task Force on Public Diplomacy was set up by the Council on Foreign Relations; the US Advisory Commission on Public Diplomacy is a long-standing bipartisan panel created by Congress and appointed by the President; Hearings were conducted by the Committee on International Relations in the House of Representatives in November 2001.
45. Sheldon Rampton and John Stauber, *Weapons of Mass Deception: The Uses of Propaganda in Bush's War on Iraq* (London: Constable & Robinson, 2003).
46. Joseph S. Nye, Jr., "The Decline of America's Soft Power", *Foreign Affairs*, vol. 83, no. 3 (May/June 2004), p. 16. See also Nye, "Squandering the U.S. 'Soft Power' Edge", *International Educator*, vol. 16, no. 1 (January/February 2007); Nye, "When Hard Power Undermines Soft Power", *New Perspectives Quarterly*, vol. 21, no. 3 (Summer 2004); and Nye, "Propaganda Isn't the Way: Soft Power", *International Herald Tribune* (January 10, 2003).

47 US President George W. Bush, "Freedom in Iraq and the Middle East – Remarks at the 20th Anniversary of the National Endowment for Democracy, United States Chamber of Commerce", Washington DC (November 6, 2003).
48 Walter Laqueur, "Save Public Diplomacy: Broadcasting America's Message Matters", *Foreign Affairs*, vol. 73, no. 5 (September/October, 1994), and Aryeh Neier, "Warring Against Modernity", *Washington Post* (October 9, 2001).
49 Quoted in John Hughes, "The Key To a Better U.S. Image", *The Christian Science Monitor* (June 26, 2008).
50 Mark Leonard and Conrad Smewing, *Public Diplomacy and the Middle East* (London: The Foreign Policy Centre, 2003).
51 Mattern, "Why 'Soft Power' Isn't So Soft", p. 602.
52 See also Craig Harden, "Arguing Public Diplomacy: The Role of Argument Formation in US Foreign Policy Rhetoric", *The Hague Journal of Diplomacy*, vol. 2, no. 3 (October 2007).
53 Francis Fukuyama argued a few weeks after 9/11, "We remain at the end of history because there is only one system that will continue to dominate world politics—that of the liberal democratic West." See Fukuyama, "We Remain at the End of History", *The Independent* (October 11, 2001).
54 *The National Security Strategy of the United States of America* (Washington DC, September 2002).
55 Henry J. Hyde, *The Message is America: Rethinking U.S. Public Diplomacy*, Hearing before the Committee on International Relations, House of Representatives, Washington DC (November 14, 2002), p. 2.
56 Hyde, *The Message is America*, p. 1.
57 U.S. Advisory Commission on Public Diplomacy, *Building America's Public Diplomacy Through a Reformed Structure and Additional Resources* (Washington DC: U.S. Department of State, 2002).
58 Philip Kotler, Somkid Jatusripitak, and Suvit Mausincee, *The Marketing of Nations: A Strategic Approach to Building National Wealth* (New York: The Free Press, 1997).
59 Samuel Blumenfeld, "Hollywood et le Pentagone, frères d'armes contre Al-Qaida", *Le Monde* (September 11, 2002).
60 Grey E. Burkhart and Susan Older, *The Information Revolution in the Middle East and North Africa* (Santa Monica, CA: RAND, 2003).
61 R.S. Zaharna, "American Public Diplomacy in the Arab and Muslim Worlds: A Strategic Communication Analysis", *Foreign Policy in Focus* (November 2001), p. 4. See also Zaharna, "The Soft Power Differential: Network Communication and Mass Communication in Public Diplomacy", *The Hague Journal of Diplomacy*, vol. 2, no. 3 (October 2007), and Zaharna, "Intercultural Communication and International Public Relations: Exploring Parallels", *Communication Quarterly*, vol. 48, no. 1 (Winter 2000).
62 See for in-depth analyses of HBO hit-series *The Sopranos*, Richard Greene and Peter Vernezze (eds.), *The Sopranos and Philosophy: I Kill Therefore I Am* (Chicago and La Salle, IL: Open Court, 2004), and David Lavery (ed.), *Reading The Sopranos* (London: I.B. Tauris, 2006). See also Johanna Blakley, "Entertainment, Politics & Cultural Diplomacy", *Public Diplomacy Blog* (October 23, 2008). Internet: www.uscpublicdiplomacy.com
63 Baldwin, "Power Analysis and World Politics".
64 Lou Morano, "Propaganda: Remember the Kuwaiti Babies?" *United Press International* (February 26, 2002).
65 The Iraq Public Diplomacy Group included representatives from the CIA, the National Security Council, the Pentagon, the State Department, and the US Agency for International Development. It was formed under President Clinton to counter Saddam Hussein's public relations campaign against the UN sanctions regime.
66 In October 2001, The Rendon Group (or TRG, a strategic communications firm) obtained a multi-million dollar contract from the Pentagon and has subsequently

managed America's image across the world using a wide range of tools, from focus groups to websites, and beyond. The firm's CEO, John Rendon, describes himself as "an information warrior and a perception manager." See Franklin Foer, "Flacks Americana: John Rendon's Shallow PR War on Terrorism", *The New Republic* (May 20, 2002).
67 Charles Pappas, "Should American Values Be Marketed to Muslim Nations?", *AdAge.com* (December 17, 2001).
68 Zaharna, "American Public Diplomacy in the Arab and Muslim Worlds", p. 3.
69 Private firms are also involved in activities so far removed from accepted diplomatic practice (due to their controversial nature or the risks involved) that official government agencies are all too happy to outsource them. TRG, for example, has produced a wide range of propaganda programs aired in Iraq. One of them involved spoof Saddam Hussein speeches and other satirical newscasts aimed at undermining support for the Iraqi regime. See Ian Urbina, "This War Brought to You by Rendon Group", *Asia Times* (November 13, 2002). In August 2002, the State Department asked another consultancy agency to begin mobilizing Iraqis in North America, Europe, and the Arab world, preparing them to perform on talk shows, writing newspaper opinion pieces, and giving lectures on the necessity of regime change in Iraq. Although these activities may well be crucial to reach American foreign policy goals, their sensitive nature makes them anathema to diplomats and other governmental officials. Only the imagination places limits on what kind of programs may be developed behind the screens. But if the past offers any guide, we should assume that this ranges from spin-doctoring, information warfare to outright devious lies (and worse). See Rampton and Stauber, *Weapons of Mass Deception*, and Michael Cohen, "What We Say, Goes! How Bush Sr. Sold the Bombing of Iraq", *Counterpunch* (December 28, 2002). Internet: www.counterpunch.org
70 Mark Leonard, "Diplomacy by Other Means", *Foreign Policy*, no. 132 (September/October 2002), and Leonard, "Velvet Fist in the Iron Glove", *Observer* (June 16, 2002).
71 Lynette Clemetson and Nazila Fathi, "U.S.'s Powerful Weapon in Iran: TV", *New York Times* (December 7, 2002), p. 7.
72 Simon Dumenco, "Stopping Spin Laden", *New York Magazine* (November 12, 2001).
73 Greg Bruno, "The Soft Power Surge", *Daily Analysis – Council on Foreign Relations* (July 21, 2008).
74 Snow, *Information War*.
75 Joel Bleifuss, "Selling the War", *InThese Times* (November 25, 2002). Internet: http://inthesetimes.com
76 Jane Kirtley, "News or Propaganda?", *American Journalism Review*, vol. 23, no. 10 (December 2001), p. 66, and Joe Murphy, "Blair Tells BBC to Censor Bin Laden", *Daily Telegraph* (October 14, 2001).
77 Gregory, "Public Diplomacy and National Security".
78 See also Steven R. Corman, Angela Trethewey, and Bud Goodall, *A 21st Century Model for Communication in the Global War of Ideas: From Simplistic Influence to Pragmatic Complexity* (Tempe, AZ: Arizona State Consortium for Strategic Communication Report, 2007).
79 Gregory, "Public Diplomacy and National Security". America's response to the 2004 Asian tsunami offers an excellent example, since US military ships and aircraft brought food and medical assistance instead of arms to the world's most populous Muslim country. See the editorial, "Food Diplomacy Works", *Los Angeles Times* (June 9, 2008). Interestingly, the Pentagon now uses humanitarian assistance as a public diplomacy tool, making the US military more palatable to local populations. In 2007, 22 percent of US government foreign assistance funding was allocated to the Pentagon, up from 5.6 percent five years earlier. See Peter A. Buxbaum, "Winning the World's Hearts and Minds", *ISN Security Watch* (July 28, 2008), and William Easterly, "Foreign

Aid Goes Military!", *The New York Review of Books*, vol. 55, no. 19 (December 4, 2008).
80 James K. Glassman, "Lecture at the Council on Foreign Relations", Washington DC (June 30, 2008).
81 James K. Glassman, "Foreign Press Center Briefing", Washington DC (July 15, 2008).
82 Glassman, "Winning the War of Ideas".
83 Glassman, "Winning the War of Ideas".
84 Glassman, "Winning the War of Ideas".
85 Glassman, "Lecture at the Council on Foreign Relations".
86 Glassman framed it as follows: "Think of it this way: we're Coke; they're Pepsi. Our job is not to get people to drink Coke in this instance, but to get people not to drink Pepsi. They can drink anything else they want. They can drink milk, ginger ale, tomato juice. We think that ultimately they will come around to Coke; that is to say, come around to principles of freedom and democracy. But in the meantime, we want them to stay away from Pepsi—that is to say, violent extremism. And my apologies to Pepsi for this metaphor." See Glassman, "Lecture at the Council on Foreign Relations".
87 Ingrid d'Hooghe, "Public Diplomacy in the People's Republic of China", in Melissen (ed.), *The New Public Diplomacy*.
88 Quoted in d'Hooghe, "Public Diplomacy in the People's Republic of China", p. 98.
89 d'Hooghe, "Public Diplomacy in the People's Republic of China", p. 102.
90 d'Hooghe, "Public Diplomacy in the People's Republic of China", p. 103.
91 Philip Fiske de Gouveia and Hester Plumridge, *European Infopolitik: Developing EU Public Diplomacy Strategy* (London : The Foreign Policy Centre, 2005).
92 Speech by Vice-President of the European Commission Margot Wallström, "Public Diplomacy and Its Role in the EU's External Relations", Mortara Center for International Studies, Georgetown University (Washington DC, October 2, 2008).
93 European Commission, *Action Plan to Improve Communicating Europe by the Commission*, Brussels (SEC(2005) 985 final, July 2005), pp. 2–3.
94 European Commission, *Communicating About Europe via the Internet: Engaging the Citizens* (Brussels, December 21, 2007).
95 European Commission, *Information and Communication Strategy 2005–2009* (Brussels, 2005).
96 De Gouveia and Plumridge, *European Infopolitik*.
97 Stefanie Babst, *Reinventing NATO's Public Diplomacy* (Rome: NATO Defence College Research Paper, 2008).
98 Speech by NATO Secretary General Jaap de Hoop Scheffer at the Seminar on "Public Diplomacy in NATO-led Operations", Copenhagen (October 8, 2007).
99 De Hoop Scheffer, "Speech at the Seminar on Public Diplomacy in NATO-led Operations".
100 Melissen, "The New Public Diplomacy: Between Theory and Practice", p. 8.
101 The following section draws on the ideas of the most influential thinkers on the "new public diplomacy", to be found in Leonard and Alakeson, *Going Public*; Melissen (ed.), *The New Public Diplomacy*; and Cull, "Public Diplomacy: Lessons from the Past".
102 Yossi Alpher, "Bitterlemons.org and the Lebanon War", *Foreign Service Journal*, vol. 83, no. 12 (December 2006).
103 A conscise history can be found in Nicola Short, "A Review of the Ottawa Process to Ban Landmines", *ISIS Briefing Paper*, no. 15 (November 1997).
104 Evan H. Potter, *Cyber-Diplomacy: Managing Foreign Policy in the Twenty-First Century* (Montreal: McGill-Queen's University Press, 2003).
105 "Philantropists Take a Closer Look at Second Life", *The Chronicle of Higher Education* (June 22, 2007).
106 Wolfgang H. Reinecke, *Global Public Policy: Governing Without Government?* (Washington DC: Brookings Institution Press, 1998).

107 Lee Edwards, *Mediapolitik: How the Mass Media Have Transformed World Politics* (Washington DC: Catholic University of America Press, 2001); Rothkopf, "Cyberpolitik"; and John Arquilla and David Ronfeld, *The Emergence of Noopolitik* (Santa Monica, CA: RAND, 1999). See also Parag Khanna, "America in the Age of Geodiplomacy", *Georgetown Journal of International Affairs*, vol. 4, no. 1 (Winter/Spring 2003), and Jarol B. Manheim, *Strategic Public Diplomacy and American Foreign Policy: The Evolution of Influence* (Oxford: Oxford University Press, 1994).

7 Place branding

1 Peter van Ham, "The Rise of the Brand State: The Postmodern Politics of Image and Reputation", *Foreign Affairs*, vol. 80, no. 5 (September/October 2001), and Van Ham, "Branding European Territory: Inside the Wonderful Worlds of PR and IR Theory", *Millennium*, vol. 31, no. 2 (March 2002).
2 Douglas B. Holt, *How Brands Become Icons: The Principles of Cultural Branding* (Boston: Harvard Business School Publishing, 2004); Graham Hankinson, "Relational Network Branding: Towards a Conceptual Model of Place Brands", *Journal of Vacation Marketing*, vol. 10, no. 2 (April 2004); Lynne R. Kahle and Chung-Hyun Kim (ed.), *Creating Images and the Psychology of Marketing Communication* (Mahwah, NJ: Lawrence Erlbaum Associates, 2006); C. Lury, *Brands: The Logos of the Global Economy* (New York: Routledge, 2004); and Paul Stobart, *Brand Power* (New York: New York University Press, 1994).
3 Gyorgy Szondi, *Public Diplomacy and Nation Branding: Conceptual Similarities and Differences* (The Hague: Clingendael Discussion Paper in Diplomacy, 2008).
4 Kotler, Jatusripitak, Mausincee, *The Marketing of Nations*, and Michael Kunczik, *Images of Nations and International Public Relations* (Mahwah, NJ: Lawrence Erlbaum Associates, 1997).
5 See Keith Dinnie, *Nation Branding: Concepts, Issues, Practice* (Oxford: Butterworth-Heinemann, 2008); Simon Anholt, *Competitive Identity: The New Brand Management for Nations, Cities and Regions* (New York: Palgrave Macmillan, 2007); J. De Vincente, *State Branding in the 21st Century* (Medford, Mass.: Tufts University, Fletcher School of Diplomacy MA Thesis, 2004); Simon Anholt, *Brand New Justice: The Upside of Global Branding* (Oxford: Butterworth-Heinemann, 2003); Eugene D. Jaffe and Israel D. Nebenzahl, *National Image and Competitive Advantage: The Theory and Practice of Place Branding* (Copenhagen: Copenhagen Business School Press, 2001); John O'Shaughnessy and Nicholas Jackson O'Shaughnessy, "Treating the Nation as a Brand: Some Neglected Issues", *Journal of Macromarketing*, vol. 20, no. 1 (June 2000); David A. Aaker and Alexander L. Biel, *Brand Equity and Advertising: Advertising's Role in Building Strong Brands* (Hillsdale, NJ: Lawrence Erlbaum Associates, 1993); and Michael E. Porter, *The Competitive Advantage of Nations* (New York: The Free Press, 1990).
6 Robert O. Keohane and Joseph S. Nye, Jr., "Power and Interdependence in the Information Age", *Foreign Affairs*, vol. 77, no. 5 (September/October 1998), p. 7.
7 Marsha Lindsay, "The Brand Called Wisconsin™: Can We Make It Relevant and Different for Competitive Advantage?" *Economic Summit White Paper* (October 2000).
8 Dennis Chong and James N. Druckman, "Framing Public Opinion in Competitive Democracies", *The American Political Science Review*, vol. 101. no. 4 (November 2007).
9 Consuelo Cruz, "Identity and Persuasion: How Nations Remember Their Pasts and Make Their Futures", *World Politics*, vol. 52, no. 3 (April 2000).
10 Anderson, *Imagined Communities*.
11 Michael Ha, "Samsung Shapes Korea's Image", *Korea Times* (June 23, 2008). Internet: www.coreaimage.org

12 Michele G. Alexander, Shana Levin, and P.J. Henry, "Image Theory, Social Identity, and Social Dominance: Structural Characteristics and Individual Motives Underlying International Images", *Political Psychology*, vol. 26, no. 1 (February 2005); Michele G. Alexander, Marilynn B. Brewer, and Richard K. Herrmann, "Images and Affect: A Functional Analysis of Out-Group Stereotypes", *Journal of Personality and Social Psychology*, vol. 77, no. 1 (July 1999); Richard K. Herrmann, "Image Theory and Strategic Interaction in International Relations", in David O. Sears, Leonie Huddy, and Robert Jervis (eds.), *Oxford Handbook of Political Psychology* (New York: Oxford University Press, 2003); Robert Jervis, *Perception and Misperception in International Politics* (Princeton, NJ: Princeton University Press, 1976); Jervis, *The Logic of Images in International Relations* (Princeton, NJ: Princeton University Press, 1970); Kenneth E. Boulding, "National Images and International Stereotypes", *Journal of Conflict Resolution*, vol. 3, no. 2 (June 1959); and Boulding, *The Image* (Ann Arbor, MI: University of Michigan Press, 1956).
13 Sicco van Gelder, "A View on the Future of Branding", unpublished paper (April 2002).
14 Kenichi Ohmea, *The End of the Nation State: The Rise of Regional Economies* (New York: The Free Press, 1996); Jean-Marie Guéhenno, *The End of the Nation-State* (Minneapolis: University of Minnesota Press, 2003); and Don Tapscott and Anthony D. Williams, *Wikinomics: How Mass Collaboration Changes Everything* (New York: Portfolio/Penguin, 2006).
15 John Williamson, "Putting the Fizz Back into the Tory Party" (October 7, 2001). Internet: www.wallyolins.com
16 Peter van Ham and Jon Coaffee, "Guest Editorial – Security Branding: The Role of Security in Marketing the City, Region or State", *Place Branding and Public Diplomacy*, vol. 4, no. 3 (August 2008), and Van Ham, "Place Branding Within a Security Paradigm – Concepts and Cases", *Place Branding and Public Diplomacy*, vol. 4, no. 3 (August 2008).
17 Although the Bin Laden-name has already been granted a trademark (given to Yeslam Bin Laden, one of the terrorist's siblings), and may be used to brand casual clothing around the world, politically this brand of "evil" is unlikely to be profitable. See Julia Day, "Swiss Move to Ban Bin Laden Fashion Line", *Guardian* (January 18, 2002), and Erik van Lit, "Osama Bin Laden Als Popidool", *ZemZem*, vol. 4, no. 2 (2008).
18 Ryszard Kapuscinski, *The Other* (London: Verso, 2008).
19 Some states are new (like Slovenia and Kosovo), or perhaps want to be new (like Scotland). To reflect these changes, these nations (and would-be states) have rebranded themselves, using (and abusing) all the paraphernalia of statehood by all the media available, and pursuing these efforts relentlessly. See Sue Curry Jansen, "Designer Nations: Neo-Liberal Nation Branding—Brand Estonia", *Social Identities*, vol. 14, no. 1 (January 2008).
20 Wally Olins, *Trading Identities: Why Countries and Companies are Taking on Each Others' Roles* (London: The Foreign Policy Centre, 1999).
21 Theodore Dalrymple, *In Praise of Prejudice: The Necessity of Preconceived Ideas* (New York: Encounter Books, 2006).
22 Kunczik, *Images of Nations and International Public Relations*.
23 Iver B. Neumann, *Russia and the Idea of Europe: A Study in Identity and International Relations* (New York: Routledge, 1996).
24 For an account on the role of images during the Cold War, see Richard Little and Steve Smith (eds.), *Belief Systems and International Relations* (Oxford: Blackwell, 1988).
25 Larry Wolff, *Inventing Eastern Europe: The Map of Civilization on the Mind of the Enlightenment* (Stanford: Stanford University Press, 1994).
26 Quoted in Van Ham, "The Rise of the Brand State", p. 5.
27 Zala Volcic, "Former Yugoslavia on the World Wide Web: Commercialization and Branding of Nation-States", *The International Communication Gazette*, vol. 70, no. 5 (October 2008). See also David Owen, *Balkan Odyssey* (London: Victor Gollancz, 1995).

28 Wally Olins, "Branding the Nation – The Historical Context", *The Journal of Brand Management*, vol. 9, nos. 4–5 (April 2002).
29 Olins, "Branding the Nation – The Historical Context", p. 242.
30 Olins, "Branding the Nation – The Historical Context", p. 244.
31 "The Case For Brands", *The Economist* (September 6, 2001).
32 Vance Packard, *The Hidden Persuaders* (New York: Mackay & Co, 1957).
33 Simon Anholt, "Foreword" (to the special issue on nation branding of) *The Journal of Brand Management*, vol. 9, no. 4–5 (April 2002).
34 Stephen Castle, "NATO Hires a Coke Executive to Retool Its Brand", *New York Times* (July 16, 2008).
35 Castle, "NATO Hires a Coke Executive".
36 Natalia Chaban, Ole Elgström, and Martin Holland. "The European Union as Others See It", *European Foreign Affairs Review*, vol. 11, no 2 (Summer 2006).
37 Gerald Segal, "'Asianism' and Asian Security", *The National Interest*, no. 42 (Winter 1995), and Mahbubani, *The New Asian Hemisphere*.
38 Tonia Novitz, "Legal Power and Normative Sources in the Field of Social Policy: Normative Power Europe at Work?", in Jan Orbie (ed.), *Europe's Global Role: External Policies of the European Union* (Aldershot: Ashgate, 2008), and Edith Vanden Brande, "Green Civilain Power Europe", in Orbie (ed.), *Europe's Global Role*.
39 John Hale, "The Renaissance Idea of Europe", in Soledad Garcia (ed.), *European Identity and the Search for Legitimacy* (London: Pinter, 1993), p. 48.
40 Michael Billig, *Banal Nationalism* (London: Sage, 1995).
41 Peter van Ham, "Branding European Power", *Journal of Place Branding*, vol. 1, no.2 (March 2005).
42 Timothy Garton Ash, "Europe Needs a Bold New Story—And to Invent New Ways to Tell It", *Guardian* (March 22, 2007).
43 European Commission, *Shaping the New Europe*, Brussels, 9.2.2000 COM (2000) 154 final.
44 Rosamond, "Conceptualizing the EU Model of Governance in World Politics", p. 478.
45 Martin Ortega (ed.), *Global Views on the European Union* (Paris: European Union Institute for Security Studies, 2004).
46 Christoph O. Meyer, *The Quest for a European Strategic Culture: Changing Norms on Security and Defence in the European Union* (London: Palgrave Macmillan, 2007).
47 Paul Cornish and Geoffrey Edwards, "The Strategic Culture of the European Union: A Progress Report", *International Affairs*, vol. 81, no. 4 (July 2005), and François Duchêne, "Europe's Role in World Politics", in Richard Mayne (ed.), *Europe Tomorrow: Sixteen Europeans Look Ahead* (London: Fontana, 1972).
48 Julian Lindley-French, *A Chronology of European Security and Defence, 1945–2006* (Oxford: Oxford University Press, 2007), and Dobbins, *Europe's Role in Nation-Building*.
49 Peter van Ham, "Europe, War, and Territory", in Michael Burgess and Hans Vollaard (eds.), *State Territoriality and European Integration* (London: Routledge, 2006).
50 On the relationship between war an national roles and identity, see Ole Elgström, "Do Images Matter? The Making of Swedish Neutrality: 1834 and 1856", *Cooperation and Conflict*, vol. 35, no. 3 (September 2000); Knut Kirste and Hanns W. Maull, "Zivilmacht und Rollentheorie", *Zeitschrift für Internationale Beziehungen*, vol. 3, no. 2 (1996); Erik Ringmar, *Identity, Interest and Action: A Cultural Explanation of Sweden's Intervention in the Thirty Years' War* (Cambridge: Cambridge University Press, 1996); Karen A. Rasle and William R. Thompson, *War and State Making: The Shaping of the Global Powers* (Boston: Unwin Hyman, 1989); and Charles Tilly, "War Making and State Making as Organized Crime," in Peter B. Evans, Dietrich Rueschmeyer, and Theda Skocpol (eds.), *Bringing the State Back In* (Cambridge: Cambridge University Press, 1985).

51 Simon Anholt told the author (in July 2007) that the meeting did not take place, but that the rumour of the European Commission even *thinking* about hiring a branding expert was obviously sufficient to cause a stir.
52 Peter Sain, "In Search of a European Brand", *EuropaWorld* (May 4, 2006).
53 Andrew Bounds, "Brand Experts Study EU Identity Crisis", *Financial Times* (May 1, 2006).
54 Helena Spongenberg, "EU Considers Going Virtual", *EUObserver.com* (March 2, 2007). For the Second Life website, see www.secondlife.com
55 Tobias Buck, "Brussels Plan for 'Made in EU' Label Could End Marks of National Origin", *Financial Times* (January 12, 2003).
56 Simon Anholt and Jeremy Hildreth, *Brand America: The Mother of All Brands* (London: Cyan Books, 2004).
57 Anholt and Hildreth, *Brand America*, p. 6.
58 Anholt and Hildreth, *Brand America*, p. 20.
59 Suzanne Nossel, "Smart Power", *Foreign Affairs*, vol. 83, no. 2 (March/April 2004).
60 Clark S. Judge, "Hegemony of the Heart", *Policy Review*, no. 110 (January 2002), pp. 12–13.
61 Glassman, "Foreign Press Center Briefing" (Washington DC, July 15, 2008).
62 Holbrooke, "Get the Message Out".
63 Szondi, *Public Diplomacy and Nation Branding*.
64 Margaret Carlson, "Can Charlotte Beers Sell Uncle Sam", *Time* (November 14, 2001).
65 Joshua Muravchik, "Hearts, Minds, and the War Against Terror", *Commentary*, vol. 113, no. 5 (May 2002), p. 25. See also Beers, "Prepared Testimony Before the Committee on Foreign Relations".
66 Jon Western, "The War Over Iraq: Selling War To the American Public", *Security Studies*, vol. 14, no. 1 (January/March 2005).
67 Elen Lewis, "Branding War and Peace", *Brand Strategy*, no. 167 (January 2, 2003).
68 Bret Stephens. "A President, Not a Symbol", *The Wall Street Journal* (March 11, 2008), p. A20.
69 Reza Aslan, "He Could Care Less About Obama's Story", *Washington Post* (December 30, 2007), p. B03.
70 Saskia Sassen, *The Global City: New York, London, Tokyo* (Princeton, NJ: Princeton University Press, 1991); Saskia Sassen, *Global Networks, Linked Cities* (London: Routledge, 2002); Stephanie Hemelrijk Donald, Eleonore Kofman, and Catherine Kevin (eds.), *Branding Cities: Cosmopolitanism, Parochialism, and Social Change* (London: Routledge, 2008); and Richard Florida, *Who's Your City? How the Creative Economy is Making Where You Live the Most Important Decision in Your Life* (New York: Basic Books, 2008).
71 John Brown, "Why Uncle Ben Hasn't Sold Uncle Sam", *Counterpunch* (April 8, 2003), and Lilie Chouliaraki, *The Soft Power of War* (Amsterdam: John Benjamins Publishing, 2003).
72 Naomi Klein, *No Logo: Taking Aim at the Brand Bullies* (New York: Picador, 1999), Chapters 12–14, and Kalle Lasn, *Culture Jam: The Uncooling of America™* (New York: HarperCollins, 2000).
73 Josh Grossberg, "Kazakhstan on Borat: Not Nice", *E! News* (November 14, 2005).
74 Abram Sauer, "Borat vs. Kazakhstan – Identity Crisis?", *Brandchannel.com* (October 30, 2006). It should be noted that the controversy Borat–Kazakhstan was a bit older than the actual movie since Cohen had already used the character in earlier TV shows such as *Ali G Indahouse*.
75 Kenneth Neil Cukier, "No Joke", *Foreignaffairs.org* (December 28, 2005).
76 Quoted in "Bush to Hold Talks on Ali G Creator After Diplomatic Row", *Daily Mail* (September 12, 2006). It may be useful to note here that Mr Cohen is Jewish.

Notes

77 Daniel Radosh, "The Borat Doctrine", *The New Yorker* (September 20, 2004), and "Kazakh Anger has Yet to Subside Over Borat", *International Herald Tribune* (October 21, 2006).
78 Edward Schatz, "Transnational Image Making and Soft Authoritarian Kazakhstan", *Slavic Review*, vol. 67, no. 1 (Spring 2008).
79 Jami Fullerton, Alice Kendrick, and Courtney Wallis, "Brand Borat? Americans' Reactions to a Kazakhstani Place Branding Campaign", *Place Branding and Public Diplomacy*, vol. 4, no. 2 (May 2008). See also Dickie Wallace, "Hyperrealizing 'Borat' With the Map of the European 'Other' ", *Slavic Review*, vol. 67, no. 1 (Spring 2008).
80 Robert A. Saunders, "Buying into Brand Borat: Kazakhstan's Cautious Embrace of its Unwanted 'Son' ", *Slavic Review*, vol. 67, no. 1 (Spring 2008).
81 "Muslim Cartoon Row Timeline", *BBC News* (February 19, 2006).
82 "70,000 Gather for Violent Pakistan Cartoons Protest", *TimesOnline* (February 15, 2008).
83 "Cartoons Row Hits Danish Exports", *BBC News* (September 9, 2006).
84 Luke Harding, "How One of the Biggest Rows of Modern Times Helped Danish Exports to Prosper", *Guardian* (September 30, 2006).
85 Aaron Goldstein, "Muslims Get Animated, Denmark Becomes the New Israel", *American Daily* (May 2, 2006).
86 *Anholt Nation Brand Index: Denmark* (2006) Internet: www.nationbrandindex.com/
87 Uffe Andreasen, "Reflections on Public Diplomacy After the Danish Cartoon Crises: From Crisis Management to Normal Public Diplomacy Work", *The Hague Journal of Diplomacy*, vol. 3, no. 2 (September 2008).
88 Andreasen, "Reflections on Public Diplomacy After the Danish Cartoon Crises", p. 204.
89 Klein, *No Logo*, p. 7.
90 Peter M. Daly, Hans Walter Frischkopf, Trudis E. Goldsmith-Reber, and Horst Richer (eds.), *Images of Germany: Perceptions and Conceptions* (New York: Peter Lang, 2000).
91 Peter York, "Branded", *Times* (October 14, 2000).
92 David McCrone, *The Sociology of Nationalism: Tomorrow's Ancestors* (London and New York: Routledge, 1998), p. 45.
93 Internet: www.interbrand.com/

8 Conclusions

1 Joan Hoff, *A Faustian Foreign Policy: From Woodrow Wilson to George W. Bush: Dreams of Perfectibility* (Cambridge: Cambridge University Press, 2008), and Seymour Lipset, *American Exceptionalism: A Double-Edged Sword* (New York: W.W. Norton, 1997).
2 Darrow Schechter, *Beyond Hegemony: Towards a New Philosophy of Political Legitimacy* (Manchester: Manchester University Press, 2005), and Martha Finnemore and Stephen J. Toope, "Alternatives to 'Legalization': Richer Views of Law and Politics", *International Organization*, vol. 55, no. 3 (Summer 2001).
3 Mahbubani, "The Case Against the West".
4 Laura Neack, *The New Foreign Policy: Power Seeking In a Globalized Era* (Lanham, MD: Rowman & Littlefield, 2008); Andrew Kohut and Richard Wike, "All the World's a Stage", *The National Interest*, no. 95 (May/June 2008); Colin Wight, *Agents, Structures and International Relations* (Cambridge: Cambridge University Press, 2006); and Kate O'Neill, Jörg Balisger, and Stacy D. VanDeveer, "Actors, Norms, and Impact: Recent International Cooperation Theory and the Influence of the Agent-Structure Debate", *Annual Review of Political Science*, vol. 7 (2004).
5 Drezner, *All Politics Is Global*.
6 Robert W. McChesney, "Global Media, Neoliberalism, and Imperialism", *Monthly Review*, vol. 52, no. 10 (March 2001), pp. 17–18. See also Jon Alterman, *New Media,*

New Politics: From Satellite Television to the Internet in the Arab World (Washington DC: Washington Institute for Near East Policy, 1998).
7 Martti Koskenniemi, "The Lady Doth Protest Too Much: Kosovo, and the Turn to Ethics in International Law", *Modern Law Review*, vol. 65, no. 2 (March 2002), and Karen E. Smith and Margot Light (eds.), *Ethics and Foreign Policy* (Cambridge: Cambridge University Press, 2001).
8 Jeroen van der Kris and Elske Schouten, "EU Wordt de Regelgever van de Wereld", *NRC Handelsblad* (October 21, 2007).
9 Mann, *The Sources of Social Power*.
10 U.S. Advisory Commission on Public Diplomacy, *Building America's Public Diplomacy*.
11 Olson, "The Globalization of Hollywood", p. 10. See also Blumenberg, *Work on Myth*.
12 Stefano Guzzini, "Structural Power: The Limits of Neorealist Power Analysis", *International Organization*, vol. 47, no. 3 (Summer 1993).
13 Volker Rittberger and Bernard Zangl, *International Organization: Polity, Politics and Policies* (New York: Palgrave Macmillan, 2006).
14 Kees van Kersbergen and Bertjan Verbeek, "The Politics of International Norms: Subsidiarity and the Imperfect Competence Regime of the European Union", *European Journal of International Affairs*, vol. 13, no. 2 (June 2007).
15 "Brussels Rules OK", *The Economist* (September 22, 2007), p. 42.
16 Mandelson, "Openness, Trade and the European Union".
17 Mattli and Büthe, "Setting International Standards", p. 27. Emphasis added.

Bibliography

Aaker, David A., and Alexander L. Biel. *Brand Equity and Advertising: Adevertising's Role in Building Strong Brands* (Hillsdale, NJ: Lawrence Erlbaum Associates, 1993).

Abbott, Kenneth W., Robert O. Keohane, Andrew Moravcsik, Anne-Marie Slaughter, and Duncan Snidal. "The Concept of Legalization", *International Organization*, vol. 54, no. 3 (Summer 2000).

Acharya, Amitav. "How Ideas Spread: Whose Norms Matter? Norm Localization and Institutional Change in Asian Regionalism", *International Organization*, vol. 58, no. 2 (Spring 2004).

Acheson, Keith, and Christopher Maule. "Convention on Cultural Diversity", *Journal of Cultural Economics*, vol. 28, no. 4 (November 2004).

Adcock, Robert, and David Collier. "Measurement Validity: A Shared Standard for Qualitative and Quantitative Research", *American Political Science Review*, vol. 95, no. 3 (September 2001).

Adler, Emanuel. "Seizing the Middle Ground: Constructivism in World Politics", *European Journal of International Relations*, vol. 3, no. 3 (September 1997).

—. (and Michael Barnett, eds.). *Security Communities* (Cambridge: Cambridge University Press, 1998).

Alden, Chris. *China in Africa: Competitor or Hegemon?* (London: Zed Books, 2007).

Alexander, Michele G., Marilynn B. Brewer, and Richard K. Herrmann. "Images and Affect: A Functional Analysis of Out-Group Stereotypes", *Journal of Personality and Social Psychology*, vol. 77, no. 1 (July 1999).

Alexander, Michele G., Shana Levin, and P.J. Henry. "Image Theory, Social Identity, and Social Dominance: Structural Characteristics and Individual Motives Underlying International Images", *Political Psychology*, vol. 26, no. 1 (February 2005).

Alleyne, Mark D. "The United Nations' Celebrity Diplomacy", *SAIS Journal*, vol. 25, no. 1 (Winter/Spring 2005).

Alpher, Yossi. "Bitterlemons.org and the Lebanon War", *Foreign Service Journal*, vol. 83, no. 12 (December 2006).

Alterman, Jon B. "The Middle East's Information Revolution", *Current History*, vol. 99, no. 633 (January 2000).

—. *New Media, New Politics: From Satellite Television to the Internet in the Arab World* (Washington DC: Washington Institute for Near East Policy, 1998).

Altheide, David L. "Consuming Terrorism", *Symbolic Interaction*, vol. 27, no. 3 (Summer 2004).

—. *Creating Fear: News and the Construction of Crisis* (New York: Aldine de Gruyter, 2002).

Bibliography

Anderson, Benedict. *Imagined Communities* (London: Verso, 1991).
Andoni, Lamis. "Deeds Speak Louder Than Words", *The Washington Quarterly*, vol. 25, no. 2 (Spring 2002).
Andreasen, Uffe. "Reflections on Public Diplomacy After the Danish Cartoon Crises: From Crisis Management to Normal Public Diplomacy Work", *The Hague Journal of Diplomacy*, vol. 3, no. 2 (September 2008).
Anholt, Simon. *Competitive Identity: The New Brand Management for Nations, Cities and Regions* (New York: Palgrave Macmillan, 2007).
—. (and Jeremy Hildreth). *Brand America: The Mother of All Brands* (London: Cyan Books, 2004).
—. *Brand New Justice: The Upside of Global Branding* (Oxford: Butterworth-Heinemann, 2003).
—. "Foreword", *The Journal of Brand Management*, vol. 9, no. 4–5 (April 2002).
Anholt Nation Brand Index: Denmark (2006) Internet: www.nationbrandindex.com/
Arango, Tim. "U.S. Media Thrive Worldwide, But Not U.S. Image", *International Herald Tribune* (December 1, 2008).
Archer, Candace. "Hegemony and Las Vegas", *International Studies Perspectives*, vol. 5, no. 2 (May 2004).
Arndt, Richard T. *The First Resort of Kings: American Cultural Diplomacy in the Twentieth Century* (Washington DC: Potomac Books, 2005).
Arnoldy, Ben. "Cyberspace: New Frontier in Conflicts", *The Christian Science Monitor* (August 13, 2008).
Aronowitz, Stanley, Barbara Martinsons, and Michael Menser (eds.) *Technoscience and Cyberculture* (London: Routledge, 1996).
Arquilla, John, and David Ronfeld. *The Emergence of Noopolitik* (Santa Monica, CA: RAND, 1999).
Arts, Bas, and Jan van Tatenhove. "Policy and Power: A Conceptual Framework Between the 'Old' and 'New' Policy Idioms", *Policy Sciences*, vol. 37, no. 3 (December 2004).
Aslan, Reza. "He Could Care Less About Obama's Story", *Washington Post* (December 30, 2007).
Auerbach, Jeffrey. "Art, Advertising, and the Legacy of Empire", *Journal of Popular Culture*, vol. 35, no. 4 (Spring 2002).
Babst, Stefanie. *Reinventing NATO's Public Diplomacy* (Rome: NATO Defence College Research Paper, 2008).
Bacevich, Andrew J. *The New American Militarism: How Americans are Seduced by War* (New York: Oxford University Press, 2006).
—. *American Empire: The Realities and Consequences of U.S. Diplomacy* (Cambridge, MA: Harvard University Press, 2004).
—. "New Rome, New Jerusalem", *The Wilson Quarterly*, vol. 26, no. 3 (Summer 2002).
Bailes, Alyson J.K. "The EU and a 'Better World': What Role for the European Security and Defence Policy?", *International Affairs*, vol. 84, no. 1 (January 2008).
Baker, Nicholson. "The Charms of Wikipedia", *The New York Review of Books*, vol. 55, no. 4 (March 20, 2008).
Baldwin, David A. "Power and International Relations", in Walter Carlsnaes, Thomas Risse, and Beth A. Simmons (eds.) *Handbook of International Relations* (London: Sage, 2002).
—. *Paradoxes of Power* (Oxford: Blackwell, 1989).
—. *Economic Statecraft* (Princeton, NJ: Princeton University Press, 1985).
—. "Power Analysis and World Politics: New Trends Versus Old Tendencies", *World Politics*, vol. 31, no. 1 (October 1978).

Barber, Benjamin R. "Shrunken Sovereign: Consumerism, Globalization, and American Emptiness", *World Affairs*, vol. 170, no. 4 (Spring 2008).
—. "Imperial Emporium", *Raritan*, vol. 26, no. 3 (Winter 2007).
—. *Consume: How Markets Corrupt Children, Infantilize Adults and Swallow Citizens Whole* (New York: W.W. Norton, 2007).
—. *Jihad vs. McWorld: How Globalism and Tribalism are Reshaping the World* (New York: Ballantine Books, 1995).
Bardos, Arthur A. "'Public Diplomacy': An Old Art, A New Profession", *The Virginia Quarterly Review*, vol. 77, no. 3 (Summer 2001).
Barnett, Michael. "Culture, Strategy, and Foreign Policy Change: Israel's Road to Oslo", *European Journal of International Relations*, vol. 5, no. 1 (March 1999).
—. (and Martha Finnemore). *Rules for the World: International Organizations in Global Politics* (Ithaca, NY: Cornell University Press, 2004).
—. (and Raymond Duvall, eds.). *Power in Global Governance* (Cambridge: Cambridge University Press, 2005).
—. (and Raymond Duvall). "Power in International Politics", *International Organization*, vol. 59, no. 1 (Winter 2005).
Barroso, José Manuel. "How Can European Culture Promote European Integration? – Speech for the European Cultural Parliament", Lisbon (December 3, 2005).
Barstow, David. "Behind TV Analysts, Pentagon's Hidden Hand", *International Herald Tribune* (April 20, 2008).
Baum, Matthew A. *Soft News Goes to War: Public Opinion and American Foreign Policy in the New Media Age* (Princeton, NJ: Princeton University Press, 2003).
—. "Sex, Lies, and War: How Soft News Brings Foreign Policy to the Inattentive Public", *American Political Science Review*, vol. 96, no. 1 (March 2002).
Bauman, Zygmunt. *Liquid Times: Living in an Age of Uncertainty* (Cambridge: Polity Press, 2007).
—. *Liquid Modernity* (Cambridge: Polity Press, 2000).
BBC News. "Cartoons Row Hits Danish Exports" (September 9, 2006).
—. "Muslim Cartoon Row Timeline" (February 19, 2006).
BDA Connect. "China Surpasses the US to Become the World's Largest Internet Population" (March 13, 2008).
Beck, Ulrich. *Macht und Gegenmacht im Globalen Zeitalter* (Frankfurt a/M: Suhrkamp, 2002).
Beers, Charlotte L. "Prepared Testimony Before the Committee on Foreign Relations of the United States Senate on American Public Diplomacy and Islam", Washington DC (February 27, 2003).
Beetham, David. *The Legitimation of Power* (Basingstoke: Palgrave, 1991).
Behr, Hartmut. "The European Union in the Legacies of Imperial Rule? EU Accession Politics Viewed from a Historical Comparative Perspective", *European Journal of International Affairs*, vol. 13, no. 2 (June 2007).
Behreandt, Dennis. "Satellite Wars", *The New American*, vol. 23, no. 7 (April 2007).
Belknap, Margaret H. "The CNN Effect: Strategic Enabler or Operational Risk?", *Parameters*, vol. 32. no. 3 (Autumn, 2002).
Bellamy, Carol, and Adam Weinberg. "Educational and Cultural Exchanges to Restore America's Image", *The Washington Quarterly*, vol. 31, no. 3 (Summer 2008).
Benford, Robert D., and David A. Snow. "Framing Processes and Social Movements: An Overview and Assessment, *Annual Review of Sociology*, vol. 26 (2000).

Benner, Thorsten, Wolfgang H. Reinicke, and Jan Martin Witte. "Multisectoral Networks in Global Governance: Towards a Pluralistic System of Accountability", *Government and Opposition*, vol. 39, no. 2 (Spring 2004).

Bennett, W. Lance, Regina G. Lawrence, and Steven Livingston. *When the Press Fails: Political Power and the News Media from Iraq to Katrina* (Chicago: University of Chicago Press, 2008).

Bennie, Lyn, Patrick Bernhagen, and Neil J. Mitchell. "The Logic of Transnational Action: The Good Corporation and the Global Compact", *Political Studies*, vol. 55, no. 4 (December 2007).

Berenskoetter, Felix. "Mapping the Mind Gap: A Comparison of US and European Security Strategies", *Security Dialogue*, vol. 36, no. 1 (March 2005).

Berlin, Isaiah. "The Bent Twig: A Note on Nationalism", *Foreign Affairs*, vol. 51, no. 1 (October 1972).

Bernhard, Nancy E. *US Television News and Cold War Propaganda, 1947–1960* (Cambridge: Cambridge University Press, 1999).

Bieler, Andreas, and Adam David Morton. "A Critical Theory Route to Hegemony, World Order and Historical Change", *Capital and Class*, vol. 85 (Spring 2004).

Biernacki, Richard. "Language and the Shift from Signs to Practices in Cultural Inquiry", *History and Theory*, vol. 39, no. 3 (October 2000).

Bignell, Jonathan. *Big Brother: Reality TV in the Twenty-First Century* (New York: Palgrave Macmillan, 2006).

Billig, Michael. *Banal Nationalism* (London: Sage, 1995).

Billig, Michael S. "Institutions and Culture: Neo-Weberian Economic Anthropology", *Journal of Economic Issues*, vol. 34, no. 4 (December 2000).

Bimber, Bruce. *Information and American Diplomacy: Technology in the Evolution of Political Power* (Cambridge: Cambridge University Press, 2003).

Bin Wong, R. "Asian Values: In Search of Possibilities", *Korea Journal*, vol. 42, no. 2 (Summer 2002).

Bishai, Linda S. "Liberal Empire", *Journal of International Relations and Development*, vol. 7, no. 1 (April 2004).

Bittman, Ladislav. *The KGB and Soviet Disinformation: An Insider's View* (Washington DC: Potomac Books, 1985).

Bjola, Corneliu. "Legitimating the Use of Force in International Politics: A Communicative Action Perspective", *European Journal of International Relations*, vol. 11, no. 2 (June 2005).

Björkdahl, Annika. "Norm Advocacy: A Small State Strategy to Influence the EU", *Journal of European Public Policy*, vol. 15, no. 1 (January 2008).

Blair, David. "UK Using Public Opinion to Change US Climate Policy", *Daily Telegraph* (July 20, 2008).

Blakley, Johanna. "Entertainment, Politics and Cultural Diplomacy", *Public Diplomacy Blog* (October 23, 2008).

Blankley, Tony, and Oliver Horn. "Strategizing Strategic Communication", *The Heritage Foundation WebMemo*, no. 1939 (May 29, 2008).

Blechman, Barry M. "Book Review of Nye's *Soft Power*", *Political Science Quarterly*, vol. 119, no. 4 (Winter 2004/5).

Bleifuss, Joel. "Selling the War", *In These Times* (November 25, 2002).

Blomgren Bingham, Lisa, Tina Nabatchi, and Rosemanry O'Leary. "The New Governance: Practices and Processes for Stakeholder and Citizen Participation in the Work of Government", *Public Administration Review*, vol. 65, no. 5 (September/October 2005).

Blumenberg, Hans. *Work on Myth* (Cambridge, MA: The MIT Press, 1985).
Blumenfeld, Samuel. "Hollywood et le Pentagone, frères d'armes contre Al-Qaida", *Le Monde* (September 11, 2002).
Boas, Taylor C. "Weaving the Authoritarian Web", *Current History*, vol. 103, no. 677 (December 2004).
Boix, Carles, and Daniel N. Posner. "Social Capital: Explaining Its Origins and Effects on Goverment Performance", *British Journal of Political Science*, vol. 28, no. 4 (October 1998).
Bolin, Göran. "Visions of Europe—Cultural Technologies of Nation-States", *International Journal of Cultural Studies*, vol. 9, no. 2 (2006).
Boot, Max. *The Savage Wars of Peace: Small Wars and the Rise of American Power* (New York: Basic Books, 2003).
Börzel, Tanja A. "Pace-Setting, Foot-Dragging, and Fence-Sitting: Member States Responses to Europeanization", *Journal of Common Market Studies*, vol. 40, no. 2 (June 2002).
Boulding, Kenneth E. "National Images and International Stereotypes", *Journal of Conflict Resolution*, vol. 3, no. 2 (June 1959).
—. *The Image* (Ann Arbor: University of Michigan Press, 1956).
Bounds, Andrew. "Brand Experts Study EU Identity Crisis", *Financial Times* (May 1, 2006).
Bourdieu, Pierre. *Language and Symbolic Power* (Cambridge: Polity Press, 1991).
Brady, Henry E., and David Collier (eds.) *Rethinking Social Inquiry: Diverse Tools, Shared Standards* (Lanham, MD: Rowman & Littlefield, 2004).
Braithwaite, John, and Peter Drahos. *Global Business Regulation* (Cambridge: Cambridge University Press, 2000).
Brodesser, Claude. "Feds Seek H'wood Help", *Variety* (October 7, 2001).
Broe, Dennis. "Fox and Its Friends: Global Commodification and the New Cold War", *Cinema Journal*, vol. 43, no. 4 (Summer 2004).
Brown, John. "Why Uncle Ben Hasn't Sold Uncle Sam", *Counterpunch* (April 8, 2003).
Bruno, Greg. "The Soft Power Surge", *Daily Analysis – Council on Foreign Relations* (July 21, 2008).
Buchanan, Allen. "Political Legitimacy and Democracy", *Ethics*, vol. 112, no. 4 (July 2002).
—. (and Robert O. Keohane). "The Legitimacy of Global Governance Institutions", *Ethics & International Affairs*, vol. 20, no. 4 (Winter 2006).
Buck, Tobias. "Brussels Plan for 'Made in EU' Label Could End Marks of National Origin", *Financial Times* (January 12, 2003).
Bukovansky, Mlada. *Legitimacy and Power Politics: The American and French Revolutions in International Political Culture* (Princeton, NJ: Princeton University Press, 2002).
Bull, Benedicte, and Desmond McNeill. *Development Issues in Global Governance: Public-Private Partnerships and Market Multilateralism* (London: Routledge, 2007).
Bull, Hedley. "Civilian Power Europe: A Contradiction in Terms?", *Journal of Common Market Studies*, vol. 21, nos. 1–2 (September/December 1982).
Burden, Matthew Currier. *The Blog of War: Frontline Dispatches from Soldiers in Iraq and Afghanistan* (New York: Simon & Schuster, 2006).
Burkhart, Grey E., and Susan Older, *The Information Revolution in the Middle East and North Africa* (Santa Monica, CA: RAND, 2003).
Buruma, Ian. "Ghosts", *The New York Review of Books*, vol. 55, no. 11 (June 26, 2008).
Bush, George W. *National Strategy for Combating Terrorism* (Washington DC, 2006).

—. "Freedom in Iraq and the Middle East – Remarks at the 20th Anniversary of the National Endowment for Democracy, United States Chamber of Commerce", Washington DC (November 6, 2003).
—. *The National Security Strategy of the United States of America* (Washington DC, September 2002).
Buxbaum, Peter A. "Winning the World's Hearts and Minds", *ISN Security Watch* (July 28, 2008).
Buzan, Barry, and Gerald Segal. "The Rise of 'Lite' Powers: A Strategy for the Postmodern State", *World Policy Journal*, vol. 13, no. 3 (Fall 1996).
Callaghan, Karen, and Frauke Schnell (eds.) *Framing American Politics* (Pittsburgh, PA: University of Pittsburgh Press, 2005).
Campbell, David. "The Biopolitics of Security: Oil, Empire, and the Sports Utility Vehicle", *American Quarterly*, vol. 57, no. 3 (September 2005).
Campbell, Duncan. "Bush Tars Drug Takers with Aiding Terrorists", *Guardian* (August 8, 2002).
Campbell, Kurt M., and Jonathon Price (eds.) *The Global Politics of Energy* (Washington DC: The Aspen Institute, 2008).
Carlson, Margaret. "Can Charlotte Beers Sell Uncle Sam?", *Time* (November 14, 2001).
Carpenter, Ted Galen. *Smart Power: Toward a Prudent Foreign Policy for America* (Washington DC: Cato Institute, 2008).
Carr, E.H. *The Twenty Years' Crisis* (New York: HarperCollins, 2001/1939).
Carroll, Conn. "Once Upon a Time, Hollywood Helped U.S. Image Abroad", *Heritage Foundation Blog* (July 7, 2008).
Carter, Ashton B., and William J. Perry, "China on the March", *The National Interest*, no. 88 (March/April 2007).
Cashore, Ben, Graeme Auld, and Deanne Newsom. *Governing Through Markets: Forest Certification and the Emergence of Non-State Authority* (New Haven: Yale University Press, 2004).
Cassidy, John. "Me Media", *The New Yorker* (May 15, 2006).
Castle, Stephen. "NATO Hires a Coke Executive to Retool Its Brand", *New York Times* (July 16, 2008).
Castonguay, James. "Conglomeration, New Media, and the Cultural Production of the 'War on Terror'", *Cinema Journal*, vol. 43, no. 4 (Summer 2004).
Cetindamar, Dilek, and Kristoffer Husoy. "Corporate Social Responsibility Practices and Environmentally Responsible Behavior: The Case of the United Nations Global Compact", *Journal of Business Ethics*, vol. 76, no. 2 (December 2007).
Chaban, Natalia, Ole Elgström, and Martin Holland. "The European Union as Others See It", *European Foreign Affairs Review*, vol. 11, no. 2 (Summer 2006).
Chase, Michael, and James Mulvenon. *You've Got Dissent: Chinese Dissident Use of the Internet and Beijing's Counter-Strategies* (Santa Monica, CA: RAND, 2002).
Chayes, Abram, and Antonia Handler Chayes. *The New Sovereignty: Compliance with International Regulatory Agreements* (Cambridge, MA: Harvard University Press, 1995).
Checkel, Jeffrey T. "Social Constructivisms in Global and European Politics: A Review Essay", *Review of International Studies*, vol. 30, no. 2 (April 2004).
—. "Why Comply? Social Learning and European Identity Change", *International Organization*, vol. 55, no. 2 (Summer 2001).
—. "The Constructivist Turn in International Relations Theory", *World Politics*, vol. 50, no. 2 (January 1998).
Chicago Council on Global Affairs, *Global Views 2008* (Chicago, 2008).

Chiti, Edoardo. "Regulation Through Agencies in the EU: A New Paradigm of European Governance", *Common Market Law Review*, vol. 44, no. 2 (April 2007).
Cho, Young Nam, and Jong Ho Jeong, "China's Soft Power: Discussions, Resources, and Prospects", *Asian Survey*, vol. 48, no. 3 (June 2008).
Chong, Dennis, and James N. Druckman, "Framing Public Opinion in Competitive Democracies", *The American Political Science Review*, vol. 101, no. 4 (November 2007).
Chouliaraki, Lilie. *The Soft Power of War* (Amsterdam: John Benjamins Publishing, 2003).
Chriss, James J. "Habermas, Goffman, and Communicative Action: Implications for Professional Practice", *American Sociological Review*, vol. 60, no. 4 (August 1995).
Christiansen, Thomas, Knud-Erik Jørgensen, and Antje Wiener (eds.) *The Social Construction of Europe* (London: Sage, 2001).
Chua, Amy. *Day of Empire: How Hyperpowers Rise to Global Dominance—And Why They Fall* (New York: Doubleday, 2008).
Chwieroth, Jeffrey M. "Testing and Measuring the Role of Ideas: The Case of Neoliberalism in the International Monetary Fund", *International Studies Quarterly*, vol. 51, no. 1 (March 2007).
Clark, Ian. *Legitimacy in International Society* (Oxford: Oxford University Press, 2005).
Clemetson, Lynette, and Nazila Fathi. "U.S.'s Powerful Weapon in Iran: TV", *New York Times* (December 7, 2002).
Cohen, Lizabeth. *A Consumers' Republic: The Politics of Mass Consumption in Postwar America* (New York: Knopf, 2003).
Cohen, Michael A., and Maria Figueroa Küpçü, "Privatizing Foreign Policy", *World Policy Journal*, vol. 22, no. 3 (Fall 2005).
Cohen, Michael. "What We Say, Goes! How Bush Sr. Sold the Bombing of Iraq", *Counterpunch* (December 28, 2002).
Cohen, Roger. "Democracy as a Brand: Wooing Hearts, European or Muslim", *New York Times* (October 16, 2004).
Coker, Christopher. "NATO's Unbearable Lightness of Being", *RUSI Journal*, vol. 149, no. 3 (June 2004).
Coleman, James S. "Social Capital in the Creation of Human Capital", *American Journal of Sociology*, vol. 94, no. 1 (January 1988).
Colombani, Jean-Marie. "Nous Sommes Tous Américains", *Le Monde* (September 12, 2001).
Colonomos, Ariel. "Non-State Actors as Moral Entrepreneurs: A Transnational Perspective on Ethics Networks", in Daphne Josselin and William Wallace (eds.) *Non-State Actors in World Politics* (London: Palgrave, 2001).
Cooper Ramo, Joshua. *The Beijing Consensus* (London: The Foreign Policy Centre, 2004).
Cooper, Andrew F. "Beyond One Image Fits All: Bono and the Complexity of Celebrity Diplomacy", *Global Governance*, vol. 14, no. 3 (July/September 2008).
—. "Beyond Hollywood and the Boardroom: Celebrity Diplomacy", *Georgetown Journal of International Affairs*, vol. 8, no. 2 (Summer/Fall 2007).
—. *Celebrity Diplomacy* (Boulder, CO: Paradigm Publishers, 2007).
Cooper, Robert. *The Breaking of Nations: Order and Chaos in the Twenty-First Century* (London: Atlantic Books, 2003).
—. "The New Liberal Imperialism", *Observer* (April 7, 2002).
—. *The Post-Modern State and the World Order* (London: Demos, 1996).
Cooper, Stephen D. *Watching the Watchdog: Bloggers as the Fifth Estate* (Spokan, WA: Marquette Books, 2006).

Corman, Steven R., Angela Trethewey, and Bud Goodall, *A 21st Century Model for Communication in the Global War of Ideas: From Simplistic Influence to Pragmatic Complexity* (Tempe, AZ: Arizona State Consortium for Strategic Communication, 2007).

Cornish, Paul, and Geoffrey Edwards. "The Strategic Culture of the European Union: A Progress Report", *International Affairs*, vol. 81, no. 4 (July 2005).

Cortell, Andrew P., and James W. Davis. "When Norms Clash: International Norms, Domestic Practices, and Japan's Internalisation of the GATT/WTO", *Review of International Studies*, vol. 31, no. 1 (January 2005).

Cox, Michael, and Adam Quinn, "Hard Times for Soft Power? America and the Atlantic Community", in David Held and Henrietta L. Moore (eds.) *Cultural Politics in a Global Age: Uncertainty, Solidarity and Innovation* (Oxford: Oneworld Publications, 2007).

Cox, Robert W. *Production, Power and World Order: Social Forces in the Making of History* (New York: Columbia University Press, 1987).

—. "Social Forces, States and World Orders: Beyond International Relations Theory", *Millennium*, vol. 10, no. 2 (June 1981).

Cram, Laura. "Governance 'To Go': Domestic Actors, Institutions and the Boundaries of the Possible", *Journal of Common Market Studies*, vol. 39, no. 4 (November 2001).

Crawford, Neta C. *Argument and Change in World Politics* (Cambridge: Cambridge University Press, 2002).

—. "Decolonization as an International Norm: The Evolution of Practices, Arguments, and Beliefs", in Laura W. Reed and Carl Kaysen (eds.) *Emerging Norms of Justified Intervention* (Cambridge, MA: American Academy of Arts and Sciences, 1993).

Crossley, Pamela Kyle, Helen F. Siu, and Donald S. Sutton (eds.) *Empire at the Margins: Culture, Ethnicity, and Frontier in Early Modern China* (Berkeley: University of California Press, 2006).

Cruz, Consuelo. "Identity and Persuasion: How Nations Remember Their Pasts and Make Their Futures", *World Politics*, vol. 52, no. 3 (April 2000).

Cukier, Kenneth Neil. "No Joke", *Foreignaffairs.org* (December 28, 2005).

Cull, Nicholas J. "Public Diplomacy: Lessons from the Past" (April 2007), unpublished report.

—. *Public Diplomacy Before Gullion: The Evolution of a Phrase* (Los Angeles: USC Center on Public Diplomacy, April 2006).

—. (and David Culbert and David Welch, eds.). *Propaganda and Mass Persuasion: A Historical Encyclopedia, 1500 to the Present* (Santa Barbara, CA:ABC-Clio, 2003).

Culpepper, Pepper D. "The Politics of Common Knowledge: Ideas and Institutional Change in Wage Bargaining", *International Organization*, vol. 62, no. 1 (Winter 2008).

Curry, Wendie. *The Global Information Society: A New Paradigm for the 21st Century* (Chichester: John Wiley & Sons, 2000).

Cutler, A. Claire. *Private Power and Global Authority: Transnational Merchant Law in the Global Political Economy* (Cambridge: Cambridge University Press, 2003).

—. (and Virginia Haufler and Tony Porter, eds.). *Private Authority and International Affairs* (Albany: SUNY Press, 1999).

d'Hooghe, Ingrid. *The Rise of China's Public Diplomacy* (The Hague: Clingendael Diplomacy Paper 12, 2007).

—. "Public Diplomacy in the People's Republic of China", in Jan Melissen (ed.) *The New Public Diplomacy: Soft Power in International Relations* (New York: Palgrave Macmillan, 2005).

Dahl, Robert A. *Democracy and Its Critics* (New Haven: Yale University Press, 1989).

Daily Mail, "Bush to Hold Talks on Ali G Creator After Diplomatic Row" (September 12, 2006).

Daley, Suzanne. "France Upbraids U.S. as 'Simplistic'", *International Herald Tribune* (February 7, 2002).

Dalrymple, Theodore. *In Praise of Prejudice: The Necessity of Preconceived Ideas* (New York: Encounter Books, 2006).

Daly, Peter M., Hans Walter Frischkopf, Trudis E. Goldsmith-Reber, and Horst Richer (eds.) *Images of Germany: Perceptions and Conceptions* (New York: Peter Lang, 2000).

Daniel, Lillian. "Doubting Tom", *The Christian Century*, vol. 120, no. 17 (August 23, 2003).

Daugbjerk, Carsten, and Alan Swinbank. "The Politics of CAP Reform: Trade Negotiations, Institutional Settings and Blame Avoidance", *Journal of Common Market Studies*, vol. 45, no. 1 (March 2007).

Davies, Paul J., Joanna Chung, and Gillian Tett. "Reputations to Restore", *Financial Times* (July 22, 2008).

Day, Julia. "Swiss Move to Ban Bin Laden Fashion Line", *Guardian* (January 18, 2002).

de Gouveia, Philip Fiske, and Hester Plumridge. *European Infopolitik: Developing EU Public Diplomacy Strategy* (London: The Foreign Policy Centre, 2005).

de Grazia, Victoria. *Irresistible Empire: America's Advance Through Twentieth-Century Europe* (Cambridge, MA: Harvard University Press, 2006).

de Hoop Scheffer, Jaap. "Speech at the Seminar on Public Diplomacy in NATO-led Operations", Copenhagen (October 8, 2007).

De Nevers, Renée. "Imposing International Norms: Great Powers and Norm Enforcement", *International Studies Review*, vol. 9, no. 1 (Spring 2007).

de Sola Pool, Ithiel. *Technologies of Freedom: On Free Speech in an Electronic Age* (Cambridge, MA: Belknap Press, 1983).

De Vey Mestdagh, Cees N.J., and Rudolf W. Rijgersberg, "Rethinking Accountability in Cyberspace: A New Perspective on ICANN", *International Review of Law, Computers & Technology*, vol. 21, no. 1 (March 2007).

De Vincente, J. *State Branding in the 21st Century* (Medford, Mass.: Tufts University, Fletcher School of Diplomacy MA Thesis, 2004).

Debrix, François. *Tabloid Terror: War, Culture, and Geopolitics* (London: Routledge, 2008).

Dedaic, Mirjana N., and Daniel N. Nelson (eds.) *At War With Words* (Berlin/New York: Mouton de Gruyter, 2003).

DeFleur, Margaret H., and Melvin L. DeFleur. *The Next Generation's Image of Americans: Attitudes and Beliefs Held by Teen-Agers in Twelve Countries* (Boston: Boston University College of Communication, 2002).

Delmas, Magali, and Ivan Montiel. "The Diffusion of Voluntary International Management Standards: Responsible Care, ISO 9000, and ISO 14001 in the Chemical Industry", *Policy Studies Journal*, vol. 36, no. 1 (February 2008).

DeMars, William E. *NGOs and Transnational Networks: Wild Cards in World Politics* (London: Pluto Press, 2005).

Deng, Yong. (and Fei-ling Wang, eds.) *China Rising: Power and Motivation in Chinese Foreign Policy* (Lanham, MD: Rowman & Littlefield, 2005).

—. "Hegemon on the Offensive: Chinese Perspectives on U.S. Global Strategy", *Political Science Quarterly*, vol. 116, no. 3 (Fall 2001).

—. "The Asianization of East Asian Security and the United States' Role", *East Asia*, vol. 16, nos. 3/4 (Autumn 1998).

Der Derian, James. *Virtuous War: Mapping the Military-Industrial-Medial-Entertainment Network* (Boulder, CO: Westview, 2001).

Detomasi, David Antony. "The Multinational Corporation and Global Governance: Modelling Global Public Policy Networks", *Journal of Business Ethics*, vol. 71, no. 3 (March 2007).

DeWinter, Rebecca. "The Anti-Sweatshop Movement: Constructing Corporate Moral Agency in the Global Apparel Industry", *Ethics & International Affairs*, vol. 15, no. 2 (December 2001).

Dieter, Heribert, and Rajiv Kumar. "The Downside of Celebrity Diplomacy: The Neglected Complexity of Development", *Global Governance*, vol. 14, no. 3 (July/September 2008).

Diez, Thomas. "Constructing the Self and Changing Others: Reconsidering 'Normative Power Europe' ", *Millennium*, vol. 33, no. 3 (June 2005).

—. (and Jill Steans). "A Useful Dialogue? Habermas and International Relations", *Review of International Studies*, vol. 31, no. 1 (January 2005).

—. "Europe as a Discursive Battleground: Discourse Analysis and European Integration Studies", *Cooperation and Conflict*, vol. 36, no. 1 (March 2001).

Dingwerth, Klaus. *The New Transnationalism: Transnational Governance and Democratic Legitimacy* (New York: Palgrave Macmillan, 2007).

—. "The Democratic Legitimacy of Public-Private Rule Making: What Can We Learn from the World Commission on Dams?", *Global Governance*, vol. 11, no. 1 (January/March 2005).

Dinnie, Keith. *Nation Branding: Concepts, Issues, Practice* (Oxford: Butterworth-Heinemann, 2008).

Dobbins, James. *Europe's Role in Nation-Building: From the Balkans to the Congo* (Santa Monica CA: RAND, 2008).

Doh, Jonathan P., and Hildy Teegen (eds.) *Globalization and NGOs: Transforming Business, Government and Society* (Westport CT: Praeger, 2003).

Dombrey, Daniel. "Transatlantic Climate Shift", *Financial Times* (June 4, 2007).

Douglas, Susan J. "The Turn Within: The Irony of Technology in a Globalized World", *American Quarterly*, vol. 58, no. 3 (September 2006).

Dowell, William Thatcher. "The Internet, Censorship, and China", *Georgetown Journal of International Affairs*, vol. 7, no. 2 (Summer 2006).

Drache, Daniel (ed.) *The Market or the Public Domain?* (London: Routledge, 2001).

Drezner, Daniel W. *All Politics Is Global: Explaining International Regulatory Regimes* (Princeton, NJ: Princeton University Press, 2007).

Duchêne, François. *Jean Monnet: The First Statesman of Interdependence* (London: W.W. Norton, 1994).

—. "Europe's Role in World Politics", in Richard Mayne (ed.) *Europe Tomorrow: Sixteen Europeans Look Ahead* (London: Fontana, 1972).

Dufresne, Jacques. "Soft Opposition to Soft Domination", *Technology in Society*, vol. 20, no 3 (August 1998).

Dumenco, Simon. "Stopping Spin Laden", *New York Magazine* (November 12, 2001).

Dunn Cavelty, Myriam. *Cyber-Security and Threat Politics: US Efforts to Secure the Information Age* (London: Routledge, 2008).

Duong, Thanh, *Hegemonic Globalisation: U.S. Centrality and Global Strategy in the Emerging World Order* (New York: Ashgate, 2002).

Easterly, William. "Foreign Aid Goes Military!", *The New York Review of Books*, vol. 55, no. 19 (December 4, 2008).

Edwards, Lee. *Mediapolitik: How the Mass Media Have Transformed World Politics* (Washington DC: Catholic University of America Press, 2001).

Eisenman, Joshua, and Joshua Kurlantzick, "China's Africa Strategy", *Current History*, vol. 105, no. 691 (May 2006).

Eisenman, Joshua, Eric Heginbotham, and Derek Mitchell (eds.) *China and the Developing World: Beijing's Strategy for the Twenty-First Century* (Armonk, NY: M.E. Sharpe, 2007).

Elgström, Ole. "Do Images Matter? The Making of Swedish Neutrality: 1834 and 1856", *Cooperation and Conflict*, vol. 35, no. 3 (September 2000).

Elias, Norbert. *The Society of Individuals* (Oxford: Blackwell, 1991).

Enloe, Cynthia. "Margins, Silences, and Bottom Rungs: How to Overcome the Underestimation of Power in the Study of International Relations", in Steve Smith, Ken Booth, and Marysia Zalewski (eds.) *International Relations Theory: Positivism and Beyond* (Cambridge: Cambridge University Press, 1996).

Entman, Robert M. "Framing Bias: Media in the Distribution of Power", *Journal of Communication*, vol. 57, no. 1 (March 2007).

—. *Projections of Power: Framing News, Public Opinion, and U.S. Foreign Policy* (Chicago: University of Chicago Press, 2004).

—. "Framing: Towards Clarification of a Fractured Paradigm", *Journal of Communication*, vol. 43, no. 4 (Autumn 1993).

—. "How the Media Affect What People Think: An Information Processing Approach", *The Journal of Politics*, vol. 51, no. 2 (May 1989).

Esbenshade, Jill. *Monitoring Sweatshops: Workers, Consumers, and the Global Apparel Industry* (Philadelphia: Temple University Press, 2004).

Esty, Daniel C. "What Stakeholders Demand", *Harvard Business Review*, vol. 85, no. 10 (October 2007).

—. "Good Governance at the Supranational Scale: Globalizing Administrative Law", *The Yale Law Journal*, vol. 115, no. 7 (May 2006).

EurActiv.com. "EU to Challenge Hollywood Rule" (June 11, 2008).

—. "Sarkozy Defends 'Offensive' Francophony Concept" (March 21, 2008).

European Commission. *Eighth Communication on the Application of Articles 4 and 5 of Directive 89/552/EEC "Television Without Frontiers"*, Brussels (July 22, 2008).

—. *Communication from the Commission to the European Parliament, the Council, the European Economic and Social Committee and the Committee of the Regions on a European Agenda for Culture in a Globalizing World*, Brussels (COM(2007) 242 final, May 25, 2007).

—. *A Single Market for Citizens: Interim Report to the 2007 Spring European Council*, Brussels (COM(2007) 60 final, February 21, 2007).

—. *Communicating About Europe via the Internet: Engaging the Citizens* (Brussels, December 21, 2007).

—. *Unifying Europe Through Culture*, Brussels (November 17, 2006). Internet: http://ec.europa.eu/news/culture/061117_1_en.htm

—. *The Trade and Development Aspects of EPA Negotiations: Commission Staff Working Report*, Brussels (SEC(2005) 1459, November 9, 2005).

—. *Action Plan to Improve Communicating Europe by the Commission*, Brussels (SEC(2005) 985 final, July 2005).

—. *Information and Communication Strategy 2005–2009* (Brussels, 2005). Internet: http://ec.europa.eu/development/body/tmp_docs/external_strategy_en.pdf

—. *Shaping the New Europe: Strategic Objectives 2000–2005*, Brussels (COM(2000) 154 final, 2000).

—. *First Report on the Consideration of Cultural Aspects in European Community Action* (Luxembourg: Office for Official Publications of the European Communities, April 17, 1996).

European Council, *Council Resolution of 21 January 2002 on the Role of Culture in the Development of the European Union*, Brussels (2002/C 32/02, January 21, 2002).
Evans, Gareth. "The Responsibility to Protect: When It's Right to Fight", *Progressive Politics*, vol. 2, no. 2 (July 2003).
Everard, Jerry. *Virtual States: The Internet and the Boundaries of the Nation-State* (London: Routledge, 2000).
Farrell, Henry. "Constructing the International Foundations of E-Commerce: The EU-U.S. Safe Harbor Arrangement", *International Organization*, vol. 57, no. 2 (Spring 2003).
Farrell, Theo. "Strategic Culture and American Empire", *SAIS Review*, vol. 25, no. 2 (Summer 2005).
—. "Transnational Norms and Military Development: Constructing Ireland's Professional Army", *European Journal of International Relations*, vol. 7, no. 1 (March 2001).
Feinstein, Lee, and Anne-Marie Slaughter, "A Duty to Prevent", *Foreign Affairs*, vol. 83, no. 1 (January/February 2004).
Ferguson, Charles D., and Peter van Ham. "Beyond the NRA Doctrine", *The National Interest*, no. 87 (January/February 2007).
Ferguson, Niall. "A World Without Power", *Foreign Policy*, no. 143 (July/August 2004).
—. *Colossus: The Price of America's Empire* (New York: Penguin, 2004).
—. "An Empire in Denial", *Harvard International Review*, vol. 25, no. 3 (Fall 2003).
Ferguson, Yale H. "Approaches to Defining 'Empire' and Characterizing United States Influence in the Contemporary World", *International Studies Perspectives*, vol. 9, no. 3 (August 2008).
Ferree, Myra Marx, William A. Gamson, Jürgen Gerhards, and Dieter Ruchs. *Shaping Abortion Discourse: Democracy and the Public Sphere in Germany and the United States* (Cambridge: Cambridge University Press, 2002).
Financial Times. "Nationalise to Save the Free Market" (October 14, 2008).
Finnemore, Martha (and Kathryn Sikkink). "International Norm Dynamics and Political Change", *International Organization*, vol. 52, no. 4 (Autumn 1998).
—. (and Stephen J. Toope). "Alternatives to 'Legalization': Richer Views of Law and Politics", *International Organization*, vol. 55, no. 3 (Summer 2001).
Fitzpatrick, Kathy. "Advancing the New Public Diplomacy: A Public Relations Perspective", *The Hague Journal of Diplomacy*, vol. 2, no. 3 (October 2007).
Florida, Richard. *Who's Your City? How the Creative Economy is Making Where You Live the Most Important Decision in Your Life* (New York: Basic Books, 2008).
Florini, Ann. "The Evolution of International Norms", *International Studies Quarterly*, vol. 40, no. 3 (September 1996).
Foer, Franklin. "Flacks Americana: John Rendon's Shallow PR War on Terrorism", *The New Republic* (May 20, 2002).
Foley, Conor. *The Thin Blue Line: How Humanitarianism Went to War* (London: Verso, 2008).
Ford, Peter. "China Blocks YouTube, Reporters Over Tibet News", *The Christian Science Monitor* (March 18, 2008).
Fordham, Benjamin O., and Victor Asal. "Billiard Balls or Snowflakes? Major Power Prestige and the International Diffusion of Institutions and Practices", *International Studies Quarterly*, vol. 51, no. 1 (March 2007).
Foreign Policy, "Pop Anti-Americanism", no. 134 (January/February 2003).
—. "Brand U.S.A.", no. 127 (November/December 2001).
Forman, Shepard, and Derk Segaar. "New Coalitions for Global Governance: The Changing Dynamics of Multilateralism", *Global Governance*, vol. 12, no. 2 (April/June 2006).

Bibliography

Foucault, Michel. "Governmentality", in Graham Burchell, Colin Cordon, and Peter Miller (eds.) *The Foucault Effect: Studies in Governmentality* (Chicago: University of Chicago Press, 1991).

Franchino, Fabio. *The Powers of the Union: Delegation in the EU* (Cambridge: Cambridge University Press, 2007).

Franck, Thomas M. "The Power of Legitimacy and the Legitimacy of Power: International Law in an Age of Power Disequilibrium", *The American Journal of International Law*, vol. 100, no. 1 (June 2006).

—. *The Power of Legitimacy Among Nations* (New York: Oxford University Press, 1990).

Frederick, H. *Global Communication and International Relations* (Belmont, CA: Wadsworth Publishing, 1993).

Freedland, Jonathan. "Patten Lays into Bush's America", *Guardian* (February 9, 2002).

French, Howard W. "Will the Great Firewall Stand?", *New York Times Upfront*, vol. 140, no. 11 (March 10, 2008).

Friedman, Thomas L. *The World is Flat: A Brief History of the Twenty-First Century* (New York: Farrar, Straus, and Giroux, 2006).

—. "Global Village Idiocy", *New York Times* (May 12, 2002).

—. "Glasnost in the Gulf", *New York Times* (February 27, 2001).

Fuchs, Doris, *Business Power in Global Governance* (Boulder, CO: Lynne Rienner, 2007).

—. "Commanding Heights? The Strength and Fragility of Business Power in Global Politics", *Millennium*, vol. 33, no. 3 (June 2005).

Fukuyama, Francis. "The Damage to Brand USA Needs Urgent Repair", *Times* (October 14, 2008).

—. "US Must Balance Hard Power with Soft Power", *New Perspectives Quarterly*, vol. 21, no. 3 (Summer 2004).

—. "We Remain at the End of History", *The Independent* (October 11, 2001).

—. *The Great Disruption: Human Nature and the Reconstitution of Social Order* (New York: The Free Press, 1999).

—. *Trust: The Social Virtues and the Creation of Prosperity* (New York: The Free Press, 1996).

—. "Social Capital and the Global Economy", *Foreign Affairs*, vol. 74, no. 5 (September/October 1995).

Fullerton, Jami, Alice Kendrick, and Courtney Wallis. "Brand Borat? Americans' Reactions to a Kazakhstani Place Branding Campaign", *Place Branding and Public Diplomacy*, vol. 4, no. 2 (May 2008).

Gabler, Neal. *Life: The Movie. How Entertainment Conquered Reality* (New York: Vintage Books, 2000).

Gaddis, John Lewis. *The Cold War: A New History* (New York: Penguin, 2006).

Gans, Herbert. *Deciding What's News* (New York: Vintage Books, 1979).

Garton Ash, Timothy. "Europe Needs a Bold New Story—And to Invent New Ways to Tell It", *Guardian* (March 22, 2007).

Gat, Azar. "The Return of Authoritarian Great Powers", *Foreign Affairs*, vol. 86, no. 4 (July/August 2007).

Gates, Robert M. "Landon Lecture – Kansas State University", Manhattan, Kansas (November 26, 2007).

Geertz, Clifford. *The Interpretation of Cultures* (New York: Basic Books, 1973).

Gelner, Ernest. *Nations and Nationalism* (Oxford: Blackwell, 1983).

Ger, Güliz, and Russell W. Belk. "I'd Like to Buy the World a Coke: Consumptionscapes of the 'Less Affluent World'", *Journal of Consumer Policy*, vol. 19, no. 3 (September 1996).

Ghareeb, Edmund. "New Media and the Information Revolution in the Arab World: an Assessment", *The Middle East Journal*, vol. 54, no. 3 (Summer 2000).

Giannini, Curzio. "Promoting Financial Stability in Emerging-Market Countries: The Soft Law Approach and Beyond", *Comparative Economic Studies*, vol. 44, nos. 2/3 (Summer 2002).

Gilboa, Eytan. "Searching for a Theory of Public Diplomacy", *The Annals of the American Academcy of Political and Social Science*, vol. 616 (March 2008).

—. "Global Television News and Foreign Policy: Debating the CNN Effect", *International Studies Perspectives*, vol. 6, no. 3 (August 2005).

—. (ed.). *Media and Conflict: Framing Issues, Making Policy, Shaping Opinions* (Ardsley, NY: Transnational Publishers, 2002).

—. "Global Communication and Foreign Policy", *Journal of Communication*, vol. 52, no. 4 (December 2002).

—. "Mass Communication and Diplomacy: A Theoretical Framework", *Communication Theory*, vol. 10, no. 3 (August 2000).

Giles, Chris. "Time to Stop the Dominoes Falling", *Financial Times* (October 10, 2008).

Gill, Bates, and Yanzhong Huang, "Sources and Limits of Chinese 'Soft Power'", *Survival*, vol. 48, no. 2 (Summer 2006).

Gillespie, Nick, and Matt Welch. "How 'Dallas' Won the Cold War", *Washington Post* (April 27, 2008).

Glassman, James K. "Winning the War of Ideas", *The New York Sun* (July 23, 2008).

—. "Foreign Press Center Briefing", Washington DC (July 15, 2008).

—. "Lecture at the Council on Foreign Relations", Washington DC (June 30, 2008).

Goffman, Erving. *Frame Analysis: An Essay on the Organization of Experience* (New York: Harper & Row, 1974).

Goldsmith, Jack, and Tim Wu. *Who Controls the Internet? Illusions of a Borderless World* (New York: Oxford University Press, 2006).

Goldstein, Aaron. "Muslims Get Animated, Denmark Becomes the New Israel", *American Daily* (May 2, 2006).

Goldstein, Avery. *Rising to the Challenge: China's Grand Strategy and International Security* (Stanford: Stanford University Press, 2005).

Grantham, Bill. "America the Menace: France's Feud with Hollywood", *World Policy Journal*, vol. 15, no. 2 (Summer 1998).

Gray, Colin S. "Strategy in the Nuclear Age: The United States, 1945–91", in Williamson Murray, MacGregor Knox, and Alvin Bernstein (ed.) *The Making of Strategy: Rulers, States, and War* (Cambridge: Cambridge University Press, 1994).

Gray, Jonathan. "Imagining America: The Simpsons Go Global", *Popular Communication*, vol. 5, no. 2 (March 2007).

Graz, Jean-Christophe, and Andreas Nölke (eds.) *Transnational Private Governance and Its Limits* (London: Routledge, 2008).

Greene, Richard, and Peter Vernezze (eds.) *The Sopranos and Philosophy: I Kill Therefore I Am* (Chicago and La Salle, IL: Open Court, 2004).

Gregory, Bruce. "Public Diplomacy and National Security: Lessons from the U.S. Experience", *Smallwarsjournal.com* (2008).

Grossberg, Josh. "Kazakhstan on Borat: Not Nice", *E! News* (November 14, 2005).

Grossman, Lev. "Blogs Have Their Day", *Time* (December 27, 2004).

Guéhenno, Jean-Marie. *The End of the Nation-State* (Minneapolis: University of Minnesota Press, 2003).

Guoguang, Wu. "The Peaceful Emergence of a Great Power?", *Social Research*, vol. 73, no. 1 (Spring 2006).

Guzzini, Stefano (and Anna Leander, eds.) *Constructivism and International Relations: Alexander Wendt and His Critics* (London: Routledge, 2006).
—. "The Concept of Power: A Constructivist Analysis", *Millennium*, vol. 33, no. 3 (June 2005).
—. "The Use and Misuse of Power Analysis in International Theory", in Ronen Palan (ed.) *Global Political Economy: Contemporary Analysis* (London: Routledge, 2000).
—. "Structural Power: The Limits of Neorealist Power Analysis", *International Organization*, vol. 47, no. 3 (Summer 1993).
Ha, Michael. "Samsung Shapes Korea's Image", *Korea Times* (June 23, 2008).
Haass, Richard N. *The Reluctant Sheriff: The United States After the Cold War* (New York: Council on Foreign Relations Press, 1997).
Hables Gray, Chris. *Peace, War, and Computers* (London: Routledge, 2005).
Hajer, Maarten A. *The Politics of Environmental Discourse: Ecological Modernization and the Policy Process* (Oxford: Oxford University Press, 1995).
—. (and Hendrik Wagenaar, eds.). *Deliberative Policy Analysis: Understanding Governance in the Network Society* (Cambridge: Cambridge University Press, 2003).
Hale, John. "The Renaissance Idea of Europe", in Soledad Garcia (ed.) *European Identity and the Search for Legitimacy* (London: Pinter, 1993).
Hall, Rodney Bruce. "Private Authority: Non-State Actors and Global Governance", *Harvard International Review*, vol. 27, no. 2 (Summer 2005).
—. (and Thomas J. Biersteker, eds.). *The Emergence of Private Authority in Global Governance* (Cambridge: Cambridge University Press, 2003).
—. (and Thomas J. Biersteker). "The Emergence of Private Authority in the International System", in Rodney Bruce Hall and Thomas J. Biersteker (eds.) *The Emergence of Private Authority in Global Governance* (Cambridge: Cambridge University Press, 2003).
Hankinson, Graham. "Relational Network Branding: Towards a Conceptual Model of Place Brands", *Journal of Vacation Marketing*, vol. 10, no. 2 (April 2004).
Hanks, William F. "Pierre Bourdieu and the Practices of Language", *Annual Review of Anthropology*, vol. 34, no. 1 (October 2005).
Hansen, Hans Krause, and Dorte Salskov-Iversen (eds.) *Critical Perspectives on Private Authority in Global Politics* (New York: Palgrave Macmillan, 2008).
Harden, Craig. "Arguing Public Diplomacy: The Role of Argument Formation in US Foreign Policy Rhetoric", *The Hague Journal of Diplomacy*, vol. 2, no. 3 (October 2007).
Harding, Luke. "How One of the Biggest Rows of Modern Times Helped Danish Exports to Prosper", *Guardian* (September 30, 2006).
Hardt, Michael, and Antonio Negri. *Empire* (Cambridge, MA: Harvard University Press, 2000).
Harlow, Carol. "Global Administrative Law: The Quest for Principles and Values", *European Journal of International Law*, vol. 17, no. 1 (February 2006).
Harrison, Brigid C., and Thomas R. Dye, *Power and Society: An Introduction to the Social Sciences* (Florence KY: Wadsworth Publishing, 2007).
Haselberger, Stephan, and Nikolaus Blome. "Wir sind keine Satelliten", *Die Welt* (February 12, 2002).
Haufler, Virginia, "International Diplomacy and the Privatization of Conflict Prevention", *International Studies Perspectives*, vol. 5, no. 2 (May 2004).
—. *A Public Role for the Private Sector* (Washington DC: Carnegie Endowment for International Peace, 2001).
Held, David (and Henrietta L. Moore, eds.). *Cultural Politics in a Global Age: Uncertainty, Solidarity and Innovation* (Oxford: Oneworld Publications, 2007).

—. (and Antony McGrew, David Goldblatt, and Jonathan Perraton). *Global Transformations: Politics, Economics and Culture* (Oxford: Blackwell, 1999).
Hemelrijk Donald, Stephanie, Eleonore Kofman, and Catherine Kevin (eds.) *Branding Cities: Cosmopolitanism, Parochialism, and Social Change* (London: Routledge, 2008).
Henry, Neil. *American Carnival: Journalism Under Siege in an Age of New Media* (Berkeley: University of California Press, 2007).
Herman, Edward S., and Noam Chomsky, *Manufacturing Consent: The Political Economy of the Mass Media* (New York: Pantheon Books, 1988).
Herrmann, Richard K. "Image Theory and Strategic Interaction in International Relations", in David O. Sears, Leonie Huddy, and Robert Jervis (eds.) *Oxford Handbook of Political Psychology* (New York: Oxford University Press, 2003).
Hertel, Shareen. "New Moves in Transnational Advocacy: Getting Labor and Economic Rights on the Agenda in Unexpected Ways," *Global Governance*, vol. 12, no. 3 (July/September 2006).
—. *Unexpected Power: Conflict and Change Among Transnational Activists* (Ithaca, NY: Cornell University Press, 2006).
—. "The Private Side of Global Governance," *Journal of International Affairs*, vol. 57, no. 1 (Fall 2003).
Hewson, Martin, and Timothy J. Sinclair (eds.) *Approaches to Global Governance Theory* (Albany, NY: State University of New York Press, 1999).
Hilderbrand, Lucas. "YouTube: Where Cultural Memory and Copyright Converge", *Film Quarterly*, vol. 61, no. 1 (Fall 2007).
Hill, Christopher. "The Geopolitical Implications of Enlargement", in Jan Zielonka (ed.) *Europe Unbound: Enlarging and Reshaping the Boundaries of the European Union* (London: Routledge, 2002).
Hillgenberg, Hartmut. "A Fresh Look at Soft Law", *European Journal of International Law*, vol. 10, no. 3 (June 1999).
Hindess, Barry. *Discourses of Power: From Hobbes to Foucault* (Oxford: Blackwell, 1996).
Hobsbawm, Eric. *On Empire: America, War, and Global Supremacy* (New York: Pantheon, 2008).
Hochschild, Arlie Russell. *The Time Bind: When Work Becomes Home and Home Becomes Work* (Berkeley: University of California Press, 1997).
Hoff, Joan. *A Faustian Foreign Policy: From Woodrow Wilson to George W. Bush: Dreams of Perfectibility* (Cambridge: Cambridge University Press, 2008).
Holbrooke, Richard. "Get the Message Out", *Washington Post* (October 28, 2001).
Holm, Hans-Henrik, and Georg Sørensen (eds.) *Whose World Order? Uneven Globalization and the End of the Cold War* (Boulder, CO: Westview Press, 1995).
Holmes, Stanley. "Nike Goes for the Green", *Business Week* (September 25, 2006).
Holt, Douglas B. *How Brands Become Icons: The Principles of Cultural Branding* (Boston: Harvard Business School Publishing, 2004).
Holzinger, Katharina, and Christoph Knill. "Causes and Conditions of Cross-National Policy Convergence", *Journal of European Public Policy*, vol. 12, no. 5 (October 2005).
Holzscheiter, Anna. "Discourse as Capability: Non-State Actors' Capital in Global Governance", *Millennium*, vol. 33, no. 3 (June 2005).
Hongju Koh, Harold. "Why Do Nations Obey International Law?", *The Yale Law Journal*, vol. 106, no. 8 (June 1997).
Hooghe, Liesbet, and Gary Marks. *Multi-Level Governance and European Integration* (Lanham, MD: Rowman & Littlefield, 2001).

Hopf, Ted. "The Promise of Constructivism in International Relations Theory", *International Security*, vol. 23, no. 1 (Summer 1998).
Howland, Douglas, and Luise White (eds.) *The State of Sovereignty: Territories, Laws, Populations* (Bloomington, IN: Indiana University Press, 2008).
Howorth, Jolyon. "European Defence and the Changing Politics of the European Union: Hanging Together or Hanging Separately?", *Journal of Common Market Studies*, vol. 39, no. 4 (November 2001).
Hudson, Dermott, and Imelda Mahler. "The Open Method as a New Mode of Governance: The Case of Soft Economic Policy Co-Ordination", *Journal of Common Market Studies*, vol. 39, no. 4 (November 2001).
Hughes, John. "The Key to a Better U.S. Image", *The Christian Science Monitor* (June 26, 2008).
Hunter, James Davison. *Culture Wars: The Struggle to Define America* (New York: Basic Books, 1991).
Huntington, Samuel P. "The Lonely Superpower" *Foreign Affairs*, vol. 78, no. 2 (March/April 1999).
—. *The Clash of Civilizations and the Remaking of World Order* (New York: Simon & Schuster, 1996).
Hurd, Ian. *After Anarchy: Legitimacy and Power in the United Nations Security Council* (Princeton, NJ: Princeton University Press, 2007).
—. "Legitimacy, Power, and the Symbolic Life of the UN Security Council", *Global Governance*, vol. 8, no. 1 (January/March 2002).
—. "Legitimacy and Authority in International Politics", *International Organization*, vol. 53, no. 2 (Spring 1999).
Hurrell, Andrew. *On Global Order: Power, Values, and the Constitution of International Society* (Oxford: Oxford University Press, 2007).
—. "Legitimacy and the Use of Force: Can the Circle Be Squared?", *Review of International Studies*, vol. 31, Special Issue (December 2005).
Hvistendahl, Mara. "China Moves Up to Fifth as Importer of Students", *The Chronicle of Higher Education*, vol. 55, no. 4 (September 19, 2008).
Hyde, Henry J. *The Message is America: Rethinking U.S. Public Diplomacy*, Hearing before the Committee on International Relations, House of Representatives, Washington DC (14 November 2002).
Hyde-Price, Adrian. "'Normative' Power Europe: A Realist Critique", *Journal of European Public Policy*, vol. 13, no. 2 (March 2006).
Ignatius, David. "From 'Connectedness' to Conflict", *Washington Post* (February 22, 2006).
Ikenberry, G. John, *After Victory: Institutions, Strategic Restraint, and the Rebuilding of Order After Major Wars* (Princeton, NJ: Princeton University Press, 2001).
—. (and Charles A. Kupchan). "Socialization and Hegemonic Power", *International Organization*, vol. 44, no. 3 (Summer 1990).
Independent Task Force Sponsored by the Council on Foreign Relations. *Finding America's Voice: A Strategy for Reinvigorating U.S. Public Diplomacy* (Washington DC: Council on Foreign Relations, 2003).
Innes, Judith E., and David E. Booher. "Collaborative Policymaking: Governance Through Dialogue", in Maarten A. Hajer and Hendrik Wagenaar (eds.) *Deliberative Policy Analysis: Understanding Governance in the Network Society* (Cambridge: Cambridge University Press, 2003).
International Herald Tribune, "Sarkozy to Go to North Africa to Sell Proposal for Mediterranean Union" (July 9, 2007).

—. "Kazakh Anger Has Yet to Subside Over Borat" (October 21, 2006).
Jackman, Robert W., and Ross A. Miller. "Social Capital and Politics", *Annual Review of Political Science*, vol. 1 (June 1998).
Jaffe, Eugene D., and Israel D. Nebenzahl. *National Image and Competitive Advantage: The Theory and Practice of Place Branding* (Copenhagen: Copenhagen Business School Press, 2001).
Jansen, Sue Curry. "Designer Nations: Neo-Liberal Nation Branding—Brand Estonia", *Social Identities*, vol. 14, no. 1 (January 2008).
Jepperson, Ronald L., Alexander Wendt, and Peter J. Katzenstein, "Norms, Identity, and Culture in National Security", in Peter J. Katzenstein (ed.). *The Culture of National Security: Norms and Identity in World Politics* (New York: Columbia University Press, 1996).
Jervis, Robert. *Perception and Misperception in International Politics* (Princeton, NJ: Princeton University Press, 1976).
—. *The Logic of Images in International Relations* (Princeton, NJ: Princeton University Press, 1970).
Joachim, Jutta. *Agenda Setting, the UN and NGOs: Gender Violence and Reproductive Rights* (Washington DC: Georgetown University Press, 2007).
—. "Framing Issues and Seizing Opportunities: The UN, NGOs and Women's Rights", *International Studies Quarterly*, vol. 47, no. 2 (June 2003).
Joffe, Josef. "Who's Afraid of Mr. Big?", *The National Interest*, no. 64 (Summer 2001).
Johnstone, Ian. "Security Council Deliberations: The Power of the Better Argument", *European Journal of International Law*, vol. 14, no. 3 (June 2003).
Jones, Seth G., and Martin C. Libicki, *How Terrorist Groups End: Lessons for Countering Al Qa'ida* (Santa Monica, CA: RAND, 2008).
Jost, John T., and Brenda Major (eds.) *The Psychology of Legitimacy: Emerging Perspectives on Ideology, Justice, and Intergroup Relations* (Cambridge: Cambridge University Press, 2001).
Judge, Clark S. "Hegemony of the Heart", *Policy Review*, no. 110 (January 2002).
Kagan, Robert. *The Return of History and the End of Dreams* (New York: Knopf, 2008).
—. "Power and Weakness", *Policy Review*, no.113 (June/July 2002).
Kahle, Lynne R., and Chung-Hyun Kim (ed.) *Creating Images and the Psychology of Marketing Communication* (Mahwah, NJ: Lawrence Erlbaum Associates, 2006).
Kahler, Miles. (and David A. Lake, eds.) *Governance in a Global Economy: Political Authority in Transition* (Princeton, NJ: Princeton University Press, 2003).
Kahn, Joseph. "China Disputes Defense Assessment", *New York Times* (May 28, 2007).
Kalathil, Shanthi, and Taylor C. Boas. *Open Networks, Closed Regimes: The Impact of the Internet on Authoritarian Rule* (Washington DC: Carnegie Endowment for International Peace, 2003).
Kalb, Marvin. *The Israeli-Hezbollah War of 2006: The Media as a Weapon in Asymmetrical Conflict* (Cambridge, MA: Harvard University Shorenstein Center Working Paper, 2007).
Kalicki, Jan H., and David L. Goldwyn (eds.) *Energy and Security: Toward a New Foreign Policy Strategy* (Washington DC: Woodrow Wilson Center Press, 2005).
Kaplan, Amy. *The Anarchy of Empire in the Making of U.S. Culture* (Cambridge, MA: Harvard University Press, 2002).
Kaplan, David E. "Hearts, Minds, and Dollars: In an Unseen Front in the War on Terrorism, America is Spending Millions… To Change the Very Face of Islam", *US News and World Report* (April 17, 2005).
Kapuscinski, Ryszard. *The Other* (London: Verso, 2008).

Katzenstein, Peter J. "Introduction: Alternative Perspectives on National Security", in Peter J. Katzenstein (ed.) *The Culture of National Security: Norms and Identity in World Politics* (New York: Columbia University Press, 1996).

—. (ed.) *The Culture of National Security: Norms and Identity in World Politics* (New York: Columbia University Press, 1996).

—. (and Robert O. Keohane). "Anti-Americanisms", *Policy Review*, no. 139 (October/November, 2006).

Keck, Margaret E., and Kathryn Sikkink. *Activists Beyond Borders: Advocacy Networks in International Politics* (Ithaca, NY: Cornell University Press, 1998).

Kelemen, R. Daniel, and Eric C. Sibbitt. "The Globalization of American Law", *International Organization*, vol. 58, no. 1 (Winter 2004).

Kell, Georg, Anne-Marie Slaughter, and Thomas Hale. "Silent Reform Through the Global Compact", *UN Chronicle*, vol. 44, no. 1 (March 2007).

Kelman, Herbert C. "Reflections on Social and Psychological Processes of Legitimization and Delegitimization", in John T. Jost and Brenda Major (eds.) *The Psychology of Legitimacy: Emerging Perspectives on Ideology, Justice, and Intergroup Relations* (Cambridge: Cambridge University Press, 2001).

Keohane, Robert O. "International Relations and International Law: Two Optics", *Harvard International Law Journal*, vol. 38, no. 2 (Spring 1997).

—. (and Joseph S. Nye, Jr.). "Redefining Accountability for Global Governance", in Miles Kahler and David A. Lake (eds.) *Governance in a Global Economy: Political Authority in Transition* (Princeton, NJ: Princeton University Press, 2003).

—. (and Joseph S. Nye, Jr.). "Power and Interdependence in the Information Age", *Foreign Affairs*, vol. 77, no. 5 (September/October 1998).

—. (and Joseph S. Nye, Jr.). *Transnational Relations and World Politics* (Cambridge, MA: Harvard University Press, 1972).

Khagram, Sanjeev, James V. Riker, and Kathryn Sikkink (eds.) *Restructuring World Politics: Transnational Social Movements* (Minneapolis: University of Minnesota Press, 2002).

Khanna, Parag. *The Second World: Empires and Influence in the New Global Order* (New York: Random House, 2008).

—. "America in the Age of Geodiplomacy", *Georgetown Journal of International Affairs*, vol. 4, no. 1 (Winter/Spring 2003).

King, Andrew, and Michael Lenox, "Industry Self-Regulation Without Sanctions", *Academy of Management Journal*, vol. 43, no. 4 (August 2000).

Kirste, Knut, and Hanns W. Maull, "Zivilmacht und Rollentheorie", *Zeitschrift für Internationale Beziehungen*, vol. 3, no. 2 (1996).

Kirtley, Jane. "News or Propaganda?", *American Journalism Review*, vol. 23, no. 10 (December 2001).

Klein, Naomi. "China's All-Seeing Eye", *Rolling Stone*, no. 1053 (May 29, 2008).

—. "America is Not a Hamburger", *Guardian* (March 14, 2002).

—. *No Logo: Taking Aim at the Brand Bullies* (New York: Picador, 1999).

Klotz, Audie. *Norms in International Relations: The Struggle Against Apartheid* (Ithaca, NY: Cornell University Press, 1995).

Knudson, Jerry W. "Rebellion in Chiapas: Insurrection by Internet and Public Relations", *Media, Culture & Society*, vol. 20, no. 3 (July 1998).

Koenig-Archibugi, Mathias. "Transnational Corporations and Public Accountability", *Government and Opposition*, vol. 39, no. 2 (Spring 2004).

Kohut, Andrew, and Richard Wike. "All the World's a Stage", *The National Interest*, no. 95 (May/June 2008).

Kolk, Ans. "Corporate Social Responsibility in the Coffee Sector: The Dynamics of MNC Responses and Code Development", *European Management Journal*, vol. 23, no. 2 (April 2005).

—. (and Rob van Tulder). "Setting New Global Rules? TNCs and Codes of Conduct", *Transnational Corporations*, vol. 14, no. 3 (December 2005).

Kollman, Kelly. "The Regulatory Power of Business Norms: A Call for a New Research Agenda", *International Studies Review*, vol. 10, no. 3 (September 2008).

Koskenniemi, Martti. "The Lady Doth Protest Too Much: Kosovo, and the Turn to Ethics in International Law", *Modern Law Review*, vol. 65, no. 2 (March 2002).

Kotler, Philip, Somkid Jatusripitak, and Suvit Mausincee, *The Marketing of Nations: A Strategic Approach to Building National Wealth* (New York: The Free Press, 1997).

Krasner, Stephen D. "Structural Causes and Regime Consequences: Regimes as Intervening Variables", *International Organization*, vol. 36, no. 2 (Spring 1982).

Kratochwil, Friedrich, "Of False Promises and Good Bets: A Plea for a Pragmatic Approach to Theory Building (The Tartu Lecture)", *Journal of International Relations and Development*, vol. 10, no. 1 (March 2007).

—. "On Legitimacy", *International Relations*, vol. 20, no. 3 (September 2006).

—. (and Yosef Lapid, eds.). *The Return of Culture and Identity in IR Theory* (Boulder, CO.: Lynne Rienner Publishers, 1996).

—. "Is the Ship of Culture at Sea or Returning?", in Friedrich Kratochwil and Yosef Lapid (eds.) *Nationalism, Citizenship and Identity* (Boulder, CO: Lynne Rienner, 1995).

Krause, Elliott A. *Death of the Guilds: Professions, States, and the Advance of Capitalism, 1930s to the Present* (New Haven: Yale University Press, 1996).

Krauthammer, Charles. "The New Unilateralism", *Washington Post* (June 8, 2001).

—. "America Rules, Thank God", *Time* (August 4, 1997).

Krisch, Nico. "The Pluralism of Global Administrative Law", *European Journal of International Law*, vol. 17, no. 1 (February 2006).

—. (and Benedict Kingbury). "Introduction: Global Governance and Global Administrative Law in the International Legal Order", *European Journal of International Law*, vol. 17, no. 1 (February 2006).

—. "International Law in Times of Hegemony: Unequal Power and the Shaping of the International Legal Order", *European Journal of International Law*, vol. 16, no. 3 (June 2005).

Kristof, Nicholas D. "Make Diplomacy, Not War", *New York Times* (August 10, 2008).

Küchler, Teresa. "Europe Has Forgotten Its Emigration Past, Says EU Cultural Ambassador", *EUObserver.com* (February 2, 2008).

Kühnhardt, Ludger. *The Global Proliferation of Regional Integration: European Experience and Worldwide Trends* (Bonn: ZEI Discussion Paper, 2004).

Kunczik, Michael. *Images of Nations and International Public Relations* (Mahwah, NJ: Lawrence Erlbaum Associates, 1997).

Kupchan, Charles A. *The Vulnerability of Empire* (Ithaca, NY: Cornell University Press, 1994).

Kurlantzick, Joshua. *Charm Offensive: How China's Soft Power Is Transforming the World* (New Haven: Yale University Press, 2008).

—. *China's Charm: Implications of Chinese Soft Power* (Washington DC: Carnegie Endowment Policy Brief 47, 2006).

LaFeber, Walter. "The Post-September 11 Debate Over Empire, Globalization, and Fragmentation", *Political Science Quarterly*, vol. 117, no. 1 (Spring 2002).

—. *Michael Jordan and the New Global Capitalism* (New York: W.W. Norton, 1999).

Bibliography

Laïdi, Zaki. "The Normative Empire: The Unintended Consequences of European Power", *Les Essays de Telos* (Paris: Telos, 2008).

—. "Are European Preferences Shared by Others? – Keynote speech at SciencesPo", Paris (June 23–24, 2006).

Lake, David A. "The New American Empire?", *International Studies Perspectives*, vol. 9, no. 3 (August 2008).

Lakoff, George. *Don't Think of an Elephant: Know Your Values and Frame the Debate* (White River Jct.: Chelsea Green Publishers, 2004).

—. *Moral Politics: How Liberals and Conservatives Think* (Chicago: University of Chicago Press, 2002).

Lal, Deepak. *In Praise of Empires: Globalization and Order* (New York: Palgrave Macmillan, 2004).

Lamy, Pascal, and Zaki Laïdi. "A European Approach to Global Governance", *Progressive Politics*, vol. 1, no. 1 (September 2002).

Lapid, Yosef, and Friedrich Kratochwil (eds.) *The Return of Culture and Identity in IR Theory* (Boulder, CO: Lynne Rienner, 1996).

Laqueur, Walter. "Save Public Diplomacy: Broadcasting America's Message Matters", *Foreign Affairs*, vol. 73, no. 5 (September/October 1994).

Larsen, Henrik. "The EU: A Global Military Actor?", *Cooperation and Conflict*, vol. 37, no. 3 (September 2002).

Lasn, Kalle. *Culture Jam: The Uncooling of America™* (New York: HarperCollins, 2000).

Lasswell, Harold. *Politics: Who Gets What, When, How* (Cleveland: Meridian Books, 1958).

Lavery, David (ed.) *Reading the Sopranos* (London: I.B. Tauris, 2006).

Lebow, Richard Ned. *A Cultural Theory of International Relations* (Cambridge: Cambridge University Press, 2008).

—. "Reason, Emotion and Cooperation", *International Politics*, vol. 42, no. 3 (September 2005).

—. "Power, Persuasion and Justice", *Millennium*, vol. 33, no. 3 (June 2005).

—. *The Tragic Vision of Politics: Ethics, Interests and Orders* (Cambridge: Cambridge University Press, 2003).

—. (and Robert Kelly). "Thucydides and Hegemony: Athens and the United States", *Review of International Studies*, vol. 27, no. 4 (October 2001).

Legro, Jeffrey W. "Which Norms Matter? Revisiting the 'Failure' of Internationalism", *International Organization*, vol. 51, no. 1 (Winter 1997).

Leigh Brown, Patricia. "Among California's S.U.V. Owners, Only a Bit of Guilt in a New 'Anti' Effort", *New York Times* (February 8, 2003).

Leonard, Mark. "The Road Obscured: New Left or 'Neo-Comm'?", *Financial Times* (July 8, 2005).

—. "Ascent of Europe", *Prospect*, no. 108 (March 2005).

—. (and Conrad Smewing). *Public Diplomacy and the Middle East* (London: The Foreign Policy Centre, 2003).

—. "Diplomacy by Other Means", *Foreign Policy*, no. 132 (September/October 2002).

—. "Velvet Fist in the Iron Glove", *Observer* (June 16, 2002).

—. (and Vidhya Alakeson). *Going Public: Diplomacy for the Information Society* (London: The Foreign Policy Centre, 2000).

Levin, Carl, and Jack Reed. "Toward a More Responsible Nuclear Nonproliferation Strategy", *Arms Control Today*, vol. 34, no. 2 (January/February 2004).

Levy, David, and Daniel Egan. "Corporate Political Action in the Global Polity", in Richard Higgott, Geoffrey Underhill, and Andreas Bieler (eds.) *Non-State Actors and Authority in the Global System* (London: Routledge, 2000).
Lewis, Elen. "Branding War and Peace", *Brand Strategy*, no. 167 (January 2, 2003).
Lieberman, Sarah, and Tim Gray. "GMOs and the Developing World: A Precautionary Interpretation of Biotechnology", *British Journal of Politics & International Relations*, vol. 10, no. 3 (August 2008).
Lin, Nan. "Building a Network Theory of Social Capital", *Connections*, vol. 22, no. 1 (1999).
Lindley-French, Julian. *A Chronology of European Security and Defence, 1945–2006* (Oxford: Oxford University Press, 2007).
Lindsay, Marsha. "The Brand Called Wisconsin™: Can We Make It Relevant and Different for Competitive Advantage?", *Economic Summit White Paper 2000* (October 2000).
Linklater, Andrew. "Dialogic Politics and the Civilising Process", *Review of International Studies*, vol. 31, no. 1 (January 2005).
—. (and Matthew Paterson, Christian Reus-Smit, and Jacqui True, eds.). *Theories of International Relations* (New York: Palgrave, 2001).
—. *The Transformation of Political Community* (Cambridge: Polity Press, 1998).
Lipschutz, Ronnie D. "Power, Politics and Global Civil Society", *Millennium*, vol. 33, no. 3 (June 2005).
—. (and James K. Rowe, eds.). *Globalization, Governmentality, and Global Politics: Regulation for the Rest of Us?* (London: Routledge, 2005).
Lipset, Seymour. *American Exceptionalism: A Double-Edged Sword* (New York: W.W. Norton, 1997).
Litowitz, Douglas. "Gramsci, Hegemony, and the Law", *Brigham Young University Law Review*, vol. 2000, no. 2 (2000).
Little, Richard, and Steve Smith (eds.) *Belief Systems and International Relations* (Oxford: Blackwell, 1988).
Liu, Lydia H. *The Clash of Empires: The Invention of China in Modern World Making* (Cambridge, MA: Harvard University Press, 2006).
Livingston, Steven. "Diplomacy in the New Information Environment", *Georgetown Journal of International Affairs*, vol. 4, no. 2 (Summer 2003).
Lopez-Santana, Mariely. "The Domestic Implications of European Soft Law: Framing and Transmitting Change in Employment Policy", *Journal of European Public Policy*, vol. 13, no. 4 (June 2006).
Lord, Kristin M. "Public Diplomacy and the New Transatlantic Agenda", *Brookings US-Europe Analysis* (August 15, 2008).
Los Angeles Times, "Food Diplomacy Works" (June 9, 2008).
—. "Cheney Exhorts Europe to Promote Diplomacy" (January 25, 2004).
Loveman, Mara. "The Modern State and the Primitive Accumulation of Symbolic Power", *The American Journal of Sociology*, vol. 110, no. 6 (May 2005).
Lukes, Steven. "Power and the Battle for Hearts and Minds", *Millennium*, vol. 33, no. 3 (June 2005).
—. *Power: A Radical View* (London: Macmillan, 1974).
Lull, James. *Media, Communication, Culture: A Global Approach* (New York: Columbia University Press, 2000).
Lundestad, Geir. *The United States and Western Europe Since 1945: From "Empire" by Invitation to Transatlantic Drift* (Oxford: Oxford University Press, 2003).
Lury, C. *Brands: The Logos of the Global Economy* (New York: Routledge, 2004).

Lutz, Ellen, and Kathryn Sikkink. "The Justice Cascade: The Evolution and Impact of Foreign Human Rights Trials in Latin America", *Chicago Journal of International Law*, vol. 2, no. 1 (Spring 2001).

McChesney, Robert W. "Global Media, Neoliberalism, and Imperialism", *Monthly Review*, vol. 52, no. 10 (March 2001).

McCrone, David. *The Sociology of Nationalism: Tomorrow's Ancestors* (New York: Routledge, 1998).

McLuhan, Marshall. *Understanding Media: The Extensions of Man* (New York: Signet, 1964).

McNamara, Kathleen R. *Constructing Authority in the European Union* (Washington DC: Georgetown University Mortara Center for International Studies Working Paper, 2007).

Madden, Thomas F. *Empires of Trust: How Rome Built—And America Is Building—A New World* (New York: Dutton, 2008).

Mahbubani, Kishore. "The Case Against the West", *Foreign Affairs*, vol. 87, no. 3 (May/June 2008).

—. *The New Asian Hemisphere: The Irresistible Shift of Global Power to the East* (New York: PublicAffairs, 2008).

Mahony, Honor. "Barroso Says EU is an 'Empire' ", *EUObserver.com* (July 11, 2007).

Malone, Gifford D. *Political Advocacy and Cultural Communication: Organizing the Nation's Public Diplomacy* (Lanham, MD: University Press of America, 1988).

Mandelson, Peter. "Biotech and the EU – Speech at the European Biotechnology Info Day, Bavarian Representation", Brussels (June 14, 2007).

—. "Openness, Trade and the European Union – Speech at the Chambre de Commerce et de l'Industrie de Paris", Paris (June 30, 2007).

Manheim, Jarol B. *Strategic Public Diplomacy and American Foreign Policy: The Evolution of Influence* (Oxford: Oxford University Press, 1994).

Manly, Lorne. "In Wars, Quest for Media Balance is Also a Battlefield", *New York Times* (August 14, 2006).

Mann, Michael. *The Sources of Social Power: A History of Power from the Beginning to A.D. 1760* (Cambridge: Cambridge University Press, 1986).

Manners, Ian. "Normative Power Europe Reconsidered – Paper Presented at the CIDEL Workshop", Oslo (October 22–23, 2004).

—. "Normative Power Europe: A Contradiction in Terms?", *Journal of Common Market Studies*, vol. 40, no. 2 (June 2002).

Manning, Philip. "Credibility, Agency, and the Interaction Order", *Symbolic Interaction*, vol. 23, no. 3 (August 2000).

Maratea, Ray. "The E-Rise and Fall of Social Problems: The Blogosphere as a Public Arena", *Social Problems*, vol. 55, no. 1 (February 2008).

Mark Tremayne (eds.) *Blogging, Citizenship, and the Future of the Media* (London: Routledge, 2007).

Marks, Alexandra. "Rethinking the Post-9/11 Strategy", *The Christian Science Monitor* (August 1, 2008).

Marshall, P. David. *Celebrity and Power: Fame in Contemporary Culture* (Minneapolis: University of Minnesota Press, 1997).

Martin, Lisa. *Global Governance* (Farnham: Ashgate, 2008).

—. "Interests, Power, and Multilateralism", *International Organization*, vol. 46, no. 4 (Autumn 1992).

Mathews, Jessica T. "Power Shift", *Foreign Affairs*, vol. 76, no.1 (January/February 1997).

Mattern, Janice Bially. "Why 'Soft Power' Isn't So Soft: Representational Force and the Sociolinguistic Construction of Attraction in World Politics", *Millennium*, vol. 33, no. 3 (June 2005).
Mattli, Walter, and Tim Büthe. "Setting International Standards: Technological Rationality or Primacy of Power?", *World Politics*, vol. 56, no. 1 (October 2003).
Mazey, Sonja, and Jeremy Richardson. "Policy Framing: Interest Groups and the Lead Up to the 1996 Inter-Governmental Conference", *West European Politics*, vol. 20. no. 3 (June 1997).
Mead, Walter Russell. *Power, Terror, Peace, and War: America's Grand Strategy in a World at Risk* (New York: Vintage Books, 2005).
—. "America's Sticky Power", *Foreign Policy*, no. 141 (March/April 2004).
Mearsheimer, John J. *The Tragedy of Great Power Politics* (New York: W.W. Norton, 2001).
—. "The False Promise of International Institutions", *International Security*, vol. 19, no. 3 (Winter 1994).
Meidinger, Errol. "The Administrative Law of Global Private-Public Regulation: The Case of Forestry", *European Journal of International Law*, vol. 17, no. 1 (February 2006).
Melissen, Jan. "The New Public Diplomacy: Between Theory and Practice", in Jan Melissen (ed.) *The New Public Diplomacy: Soft Power in International Relations* (New York: Palgrave Macmillan, 2005).
—. (ed.) *The New Public Diplomacy: Soft Power in International Relations* (New York: Palgrave Macmillan, 2005).
Menon, Rajan. *The End of Alliances* (Oxford: Oxford University Press, 2007).
Merkel, Angela. "Germany's Foreign and Security Policy in the Face of Global Challenges – Speech at the 41st Munich Conference on Security Policy", Munich (4 February 2006).
Meyer, Christoph O. *The Quest for a European Strategic Culture: Changing Norms on Security and Defence in the European Union* (London: Palgrave Macmillan, 2007).
Miles, Hugh. *Al-Jazeera: The Inside Story of the Arab News Channel That is Challenging the West* (New York: Grove Press, 2006).
Miller, John D. B. *Norman Angell and the Futility of War: Peace and the Public Mind* (London: Palgrave Macmillan, 1986).
Miller, M. Rex. "The Digital Dynamic: How Communications Media Shape Our World", *The Futurist*, vol. 39, no. 3 (May/June 2005).
Miller, Toby, Nitin Govil, John McMurrian, and Richard Maxwell. *Global Hollywood* (Berkeley: University of California Press, 2002).
Milliken, Jennifer. "The Study of Discourse in International Relations", *European Journal of International Relations*, vol. 5, no. 2 (June 1999).
Monten, Jonathan. "Thucydides and Modern Realism", *International Studies Quarterly*, vol. 50, no. 1 (March 2006).
Montoya, Celeste. "The European Union, Capacity Building, and Transnational Networks: Combating Violence Against Women Through the Daphne Program", *International Organization*, vol. 62, no. 2 (April 2008).
Mor, Gal. "The First Photoshop War", *Ynetnews.com* (August 17, 2006).
Moran, Michael. "Losing the Cold Peace", *Op-Ed – Council on Foreign Relations* (July 20, 2008).
Morano, Lou. "Propaganda: Remember the Kuwaiti Babies?" *United Press International* (February 26, 2002).
Morçöl, Göktuğ. *A New Mind for Policy Analysis: Toward a Post-Newtonian and Postpositivist Epistemology and Methodology* (Westport, CT: Praeger Publishers, 2002).

Morey, David E., and Ted Dalen Carpenter. "Should the United States Invest Heavily in New Efforts to Advance Public Diplomacy?", *Insight on the News* (September 30, 2002).
Morgenthau, Hans J. *Politics Among Nations: The Struggle for Power and Peace* (New York: Knopf, 1978/1948).
Morriss, Peter. *Power: A Philosophical Analysis* (Manchester: Manchester University Press, 2002).
Motyl, Alexander K. "Empire Falls: Washington May Be Imperious But It Is Not Imperial", *Foreign Affairs*, vol. 85, no. 4 (July/August 2006).
Mouffe, Chantal. "Hegemony and Ideology in Gramsci", in Chantal Mouffe (ed.) *Gramsci and Marxist Theory* (London: Routledge, 1979).
Mulcahy, Kevin V. "Cultural Imperialism and Cultural Sovereignty: U.S.–Canadian Cultural Relations", *Journal of Arts Management, Law, and Society*, vol. 31. no. 4 (Winter 2002).
Mulligan, Shane P. "The Uses of Legitimacy in International Relations", *Millennium*, vol. 34, no. 2 (February 2006).
—. "Questioning (the Question of) Legitimacy in IR: A Reply to Jens Steffek", *European Journal of International Relations*, vol. 10, no. 3 (September 2004).
Mulvenon, James. "Golden Shields and Panopticons: Beijing's Internet Control Policies", *Georgetown Journal of International Affairs*, vol. 9, no. 2 (Summer 2008).
Mumby, Dennis K. "The Problem of Hegemony: Rereading Gramsci for Organizational Communication Studies", *Western Journal of Communication*, vol. 61, no. 4 (Fall 1997).
Muravchik, Joshua. "America Loses Its Voice", *The Weekly Standard* (June 9, 2003).
—. "Hearts, Minds, and the War Against Terror", *Commentary*, vol. 113, no. 5 (May 2002).
Murdock, Graham. "Notes From the Number One Country: Herbert Schiller on Culture, Commerce and American Power", *International Journal of Cultural Policy*, vol. 12, no. 2 (July 2006).
Murphy, Joe. "Blair Tells BBC to Censor Bin Laden", *Daily Telegraph* (October 14, 2001).
Murray, Susan (ed.) *Reality TV: Remaking Television Culture* (New York: New York University Press, 2004).
Nadvi, Khalid. "Global Standards, Global Governance and the Organization of Global Value Chains", *Journal of Economic Geography*, vol. 8, no. 3 (May 2008).
Nakamura, Lisa. *Cybertypes: Race, Ethnicity, and Identity on the Internet* (London: Routledge, 2002).
Neack, Laura. *The New Foreign Policy: Power Seeking in a Globalized Era* (Lanham, MD: Rowman & Littlefield, 2008).
Neier, Aryeh. "Warring Against Modernity", *Washington Post* (October 9, 2001).
Nelson, Daniel N. "Conclusion: Word Peace", in Mirjana N. Dedaic and Daniel N. Nelson (eds.) *At War With Words* (Berlin/New York: Mouton de Gruyter, 2003).
Nelson, Michael. *Wars of the Black Heavens: The Battles of Western Broadcasting in the Cold War* (Syracuse, NY: Syracuse University Press, 1997).
Neuhold, Hanspeter. "The Legal Dimension of Transatlantic Relations: Basic Positions and Some Key Issues", in Hanspeter Neuhold (ed.) *Transatlantic Legal Issues – European Views* (Vienna: Favorita Papers, 2005).
Neumann, Iver B. "Returning Practice to the Linguistic Turn: The Case of Diplomacy", *Millennium*, vol. 31, no. 3 (July 2002).
—. *Russia and the Idea of Europe: A Study in Identity and International Relations* (New York: Routledge, 1996).
Nossel, Suzanne. "Smart Power", *Foreign Affairs*, vol. 83, no. 2 (March/April 2004).

Novitz, Tonia. "Legal Power and Normative Sources in the Field of Social Policy: Normative Power Europe at Work?", in Jan Orbie (ed.) *Europe's Global Role: External Policies of the European Union* (Aldershot: Ashgate, 2008).
Nye, Joseph S. Jr. "Beware an October Surprise From Bin Laden", *Financial Times* (October 16, 2008).
—. "Barack Obama and Soft Power", *Huffington Post* (June 12, 2008).
—. "Squandering the U.S. 'Soft Power' Edge", *International Educator*, vol. 16, no. 1 (January/February 2007).
—. "The Decline of America's Soft Power", *Foreign Affairs*, vol. 83, no. 3 (May/June 2004).
—. "Soft Power and American Foreign Policy", *Political Science Quarterly*, vol. 119, no. 2 (Summer 2004).
—. "When Hard Power Undermines Soft Power", *New Perspectives Quarterly*, vol. 21, no. 3 (Summer 2004).
—. *Soft Power: The Means to Success in World Politics* (New York: PublicAffairs, 2004).
—. "Propaganda Isn't the Way: Soft Power", *International Herald Tribune* (January 10, 2003).
—. (and William Owens). "America's Information Edge", *Foreign Affairs*, vol. 75, no. 2 (March/April 1996).
—. *Bound to Lead: The Changing Nature of American Power* (New York: Basic Books, 1990).
O'Kane, Rosemary H.T., and David Beetham. "Against Legitimacy – Comment/Reply", *Political Studies*, vol. 41, no. 3 (September 1993).
O'Neill, Kate, Jörg Balisger, and Stacy D. VanDeveer. "Actors, Norms, and Impact: Recent International Cooperation Theory and the Influence of the Agent-Structure Debate", *Annual Review of Political Science*, vol. 7 (2004).
O'Shaughnessy, John, and Nicholas Jackson O'Shaughnessy. "Treating the Nation as a Brand: Some Neglected Issues", *Journal of Macromarketing*, vol. 20, no. 1 (June 2000).
Obama, Barack. *Remarks by the President on a New Beginning* (Cairo, June 4, 2009). Internet: whitehouse.gov
Ohmea, Kenichi. *The End of the Nation State: The Rise of Regional Economies* (New York: The Free Press, 1996).
Olins, Wally. *On Brand* (New York: Thames & Hudson, 2003).
—. "Branding the Nation – The Historical Context", *The Journal of Brand Management*, vol. 9, nos. 4–5 (April 2002).
—. *Trading Identities: Why Countries and Companies are Taking on Each Others' Roles* (London: The Foreign Policy Centre, 1999).
Olson, Scott R. "The Globalization of Hollywood", *International Journal on World Peace*, vol. 17, no. 4 (December 2000).
Onuf, Nicholas G. *The World of Our Making: Rules and Rule in Social Theory and International Relations* (Columbia, SC: University of South Carolina Press, 1989).
Ortega, Martin (ed.) *Global Views on the European Union* (Paris: European Union Institute for Security Studies, 2004).
Osgood, Kenneth A. "Hearts and Minds: The Unconventional Cold War", *Journal of Cold War Studies*, vol. 4, no. 2 (Spring 2002).
Ougaard, Morten. *Political Globalization: State, Power and Social Forces* (New York: Palgrave Macmillan, 2004).
Owen, David. *Balkan Odyssey* (London: Victor Gollancz, 1995).
Pace, Michelle. "The Construction of EU Normative Power", *Journal of Common Market Studies*, vol. 45, no. 5 (December 2007).
Packard, Vance. *The Hidden Persuaders* (New York: Mackay & Co, 1957).

Padoa-Schioppa, Tommaso. *Europe, a Civilian Power: Lessons from EU Experience* (London: The Federal Trust, 2004).
Pagden, Anthony. *Lords of All the Worlds: Ideologies of Empire in Spain, Britain and France c. 1500–c. 1800* (New Haven: Yale University Press, 1998).
Pahlavi, Pierre C. "Evaluating Public Diplomacy Programmes", *The Hague Journal of Diplomacy*, vol. 2, no. 3 (October 2007).
Pappas, Charles. "Should American Values Be Marketed to Muslim Nations?", *AdAge.com* (December 17, 2001).
Parsons, Craig. "Showing Ideas as Causes: The Origins of the European Union", *International Organization*, vol. 56, no. 1 (Winter 2002).
Paschke, Karl Theodor. *Report on the Special Inspection of 14 German Embassies in the Countries of the European Union* (Berlin: Auswärtiges Amt, 2002).
Pattberg, Philipp H. *Private Institutions and Global Governance: The New Politics of Environmental Sustainability* (Northhampton, MA: Edward Elgar, 2007).
Pauly, Nancy. "Abu Ghraib (Un)becoming Photographs: How Can Art Educators Address Current Images From Visual Culture Perspectives?", *The Journal of Social Theory in Art Education*, vol. 25 (2005).
Payne, Rodger A. "Persuasion, Frames, and Norm Construction", *European Journal of International Relations*, vol. 7, no. 1 (March 2001).
Peerenboom, Randall. *China Modernizes: Threat to the West or Model for the Rest?* (Oxford: Oxford University Press, 2008).
Perry, Tom. "Critics Accuse Hollywood of Vilifying Arabs", *Reuters.com* (May 1, 2008).
Peterson, Mark Allen. "American Warriors Speaking American: The Metapragmatics of Performance in the Nation State", in Mirjana N. Dedaic and Daniel N. Nelson (eds.) *At War With Words* (Berlin/New York: Mouton de Gruyter, 2003).
Pew Global Attitudes Project, *A Year After Iraq: A Nine-Country Survey* (Washington DC: Pew, 2004).
Philpott, Daniel. *Revolutions in Sovereignty: How Ideas Shaped Modern International Relations* (Princeton, NJ: Princeton University Press, 2001).
—. "Ideas and the Evolution of Sovereignty", in Sohail H. Hashmi (ed.) *State Sovereignty: Change and Persistence in International Relations* (University Park: The Pennsylvania State University Press, 1997).
Pincus, Walter. "New Pentagon Media Agency Seeks to Fill Top Job", *Washington Post* (August 25, 2008).
Pollack, Mark. *The Engines of European Integration: Delegation, Agency and Agenda-Setting in the EU* (Oxford: Oxford University Press, 2003).
Porter, Michael E. *The Competitive Advantage of Nations* (New York: The Free Press, 1990).
Porter, Tony, and Karsten Ronit. "Self-Regulation as Policy Process: The Multiple and Criss-Crossing Stages of Private Rule-Making", *Policy Sciences*, vol. 39, no. 1 (March 2006).
Portes, Alejandro. "Social Capital: Its Origins and Application in Modern Sociology", *American Review of Sociology*, vol. 24 (August 1998).
Postman, Neil. *Amusing Ourselves to Death: Public Discourse in the Age of Show Business* (London: Penguin, 1985).
Potter, Evan H. *Cyber-Diplomacy: Managing Foreign Policy in the Twenty-First Century* (Montreal: McGill-Queen's University Press, 2003).
Powell, Colin. *My American Journey* (New York: Random House, 1995).
Pretorius, Joelien. "The Security Imaginary: Explaining Military Isomorphism", *Security Dialogue*, vol. 39, no. 1 (March 2008).

Prevots, Naima. *Dance for Export: Cultural Diplomacy in the Cold War* (Middletown, CT: Wesleyan University Press, 1998).
Price, Monroe E. *Media and Sovereignty: The Global Information Revolution and Its Challenge to State Power* (Cambridge, MA: The MIT Press, 2002).
—. *Television: The Public Sphere and National Identity* (Oxford: Clarendon Press, 1995).
Price, Richard. "Reversing the Gun Sights: Transnational Civil Society Targets Land Mines", *International Organization*, vol. 52, no. 3 (Summer 1998).
Prodi, Romano. "2000–2005: Shaping the New Europe – Speech at the European Parliament", Strasbourg (February 15, 2000).
—. *Europe as I See It* (Cambridge: Polity Press, 2000).
Puttnam, David. *Movies and Money: The Undeclared War Between Europe and America* (New York: David McKay Company, 1998).
Qiang, Xiao. "The Rising Tide of Internet Opinion in China", *Nieman Reports*, vol. 58, no. 2 (Summer 2004).
Radosh, Daniel. "The Borat Doctrine", *The New Yorker* (September 20, 2004).
Rajiva, Lila. *The Language of Empire: Abu Ghraib and the American Media* (New York: Monthly Review Press, 2005).
Rampton, Sheldon, and John Stauber. *Weapons of Mass Deception: The Uses of Propaganda in Bush's War on Iraq* (London: Constable & Robinson, 2003).
Rasler, Karen A., and William R. Thompson. *War and State Making: The Shaping of the Global Powers* (Boston: Unwin Hyman, 1989).
Rauch, Jonathan. "In Arabic, 'Internet' Means 'Freedom'", *National Journal*, vol. 38, no. 9 (March 4, 2006).
Raustiala, Kal. "Form and Substance in International Agreements", *The American Journal of International Law*, vol. 99, no. 3 (July 2005).
—. "The Architecture of International Cooperation: Transgovernmental Networks and the Future of International Law", *Virginia Journal of International Law*, vol. 43, no. 1 (Fall 2002).
—. "Governance in World Affairs", *The American Journal of International Law*, vol. 94, no. 4 (October 2000).
Rawls, John. *Political Liberalism* (New York: Columbia University Press, 1993).
Reimann, Kim D. "A View From the Top: International Politics, Norms and the Worldwide Growth of NGOs", *International Studies Quarterly*, vol. 50, no. 1 (March 2006).
Reinhard, Wolfgang (ed.) *Power Elites and State Building* (Oxford: Oxford University Press, 1996).
Reinicke, Wolfgang H. "The Other World Wide Web: Global Public Policy Networks", *Foreign Policy*, no. 117 (Winter 1999).
—. *Global Public Policy: Governing Without Government?* (Washington DC: Brookings Institution Press, 1998).
Rengger, Nicholas. "The Ethics of Trust in World Politics", *International Affairs*, vol. 73, no. 3 (July 1997).
Reus-Smith, Christian. *American Power and World Order* (London: Polity, 2004).
—. (ed.) *The Politics of International Law* (Cambridge: Cambridge University Press, 2004).
Rheingold, Howard. *Smart Mobs: The Next Social Revolution* (New York: Basic Books, 2003).
—. *Virtual Reality: The Revolutionary Technology of Computer-Generated Artificial Worlds – And How It Promises to Transform Society* (New York: Simon & Schuster, 1992).
Richmond, Yale. *Practicing Public Diplomacy: A Cold War Odyssey* (New York: Berghahn Books, 2008).

Rifkin, Jeremy. *The European Dream: How Europe's Vision of the Future is Quietly Eclipsing the American Dream* (Oxford: Blackwell, 2004).
Ringmar, Erik. *Identity, Interest and Action: A Cultural Explanation of Sweden's Intervention in the Thirty Years' War* (Cambridge: Cambridge University Press, 1996).
Rinnawi, Khalil. *Instant Nationalism: McArabism, Al-Jazeera, and Transnational Media in the Arab World* (Lanham, MD: University Press of America, 2006).
Risse, Thomas. "Global Governance and Communicative Action", *Government and Opposition*, vol. 39, no. 2 (Spring 2004).
—. " 'Let's Argue!', Communicative Action in World Politics", *International Organization*, vol. 54, no. 1 (Winter 2000).
—. (and Kathryn Sikkink). "The Socialization of International Human Rights Norms into Domestic Practices", in Thomas Risse, Stephen C. Ropp, and Kathryn Sikkink (eds.) *The Power of Human Rights: International Norms and Domestic Change* (Cambridge: Cambridge University Press, 1999).
—. (and Stephen C. Ropp, and Kathryn Sikkink, eds.). *The Power of Human Rights: International Norms and Domestic Change* (Cambridge: Cambridge University Press, 1999).
Rittberger, Volker, and Bernard Zangl. *International Organization: Polity, Politics and Policies* (New York: Palgrave Macmillan, 2006).
Robb, David L. *Operation Hollywood: How the Pentagon Shapes and Censors the Movies* (Amherst, NY: Prometheus Books, 2004).
Roberts, Carla Anne. "The U.N.: Searching for Relevance", *Wall Street Journal* (October 21, 2003).
Robinson, William I. "Gramsci and Globalisation: From Nation-State to Transnational Hegemony", *Critical Review of Social and Political Philosophy*, vol. 8, no. 4 (December 2005).
Roll, Martin. *Asian Brand Strategy: How Asia Builds Strong Brands* (New York: Palgrave Macmillan, 2006).
Rosamond, Ben. "Conceptualizing the EU Model of Governance in World Politics", *European Foreign Policy Review*, vol. 10, no. 4 (Winter 2005).
Rosecrance, Richard. *The Rise of the Virtual State: Wealth and Power in the Coming Century* (New York: Basic Books, 1999).
—. *The Rise of the Trading State* (New York: HarperCollins, 1985).
Rosenau, James N. *People Count! The Networked Individual in World Politics* (Boulder, CO: Paradigm Publishers, 2007).
—. "Governance, Order, and Change in World Politics", in James N. Rosenau and Ernst-Otto Czempiel (eds.) *Governance Without Government: Order and Change in World Politics* (Cambridge: Cambridge University Press, 1992).
Rosenberg, Tina. *The Haunted Land: Facing Europe's Ghosts After Communism* (New York: Vintage Books, 1995).
Rosendorf, Neal M. "Social and Cultural Globalization: Concepts, History, and America's Role", in Joseph S. Nye, Jr. and John D. Donahue (eds.) *Governance in a Globalizing World* (Washington DC: Brookings Institution Press, 2000).
Rothkopf, David J. "Cyberpolitik: The Changing Nature of Power in the Information Age", *Journal of International Affairs*, vol. 51, no. 2 (Spring 1998).
Roy, Ishita Sinha. "Worlds Apart: Nation-Branding on the National Geographic Channel", *Media, Culture & Society*, vol. 29, no. 4 (July 2007).
Rubin, Barry, and Judith Colp Rubin. *Anti-American Terrorism and the Middle East: A Documentary Reader* (Oxford: Oxford University Press, 2002).

Rudderham, Melissa A. *Middle Power Pull: Can Middle Powers Use Public Diplomacy to Ameliorate the Image of the West?* (Toronto: York University YCISS Working Paper 46, 2008).
Ruggie, John G. "Reconstituting the Global Public Domain: Issues, Actors, and Practices", *European Journal of International Relations*, vol. 10, no. 4 (2004).
—. "Multilateralism: The Anatomy of an Institution", *International Organization*, vol. 46, no. 3 (Summer 1992).
—. "International Regimes, Transactions, and Change: Embedded Liberalism in the Postwar Economic Order", in Stephen D. Krasner (ed.) *International Regimes* (Ithaca, NY: Cornell University Press, 1983).
Rushdie, Salman. "Anti-Americanism Has Taken the World by Storm", *Guardian* (February 6, 2002).
Rushkoff, Douglas. *Cyberia: Life in the Trenches of Hyperspace* (London: HarperCollins, 1994).
Rutenberg, Jim. "In Farewell, Rumsfeld Warns Weakness is 'Provocative'", *New York Times* (December 16, 2006).
—. "Hollywood Seeks Role in the War, *New York Times* (October 20, 2002).
Ryan, Alan. "What Happened to the American Empire?" *The New York Review of Books*, vol. 55, no. 16 (October 23, 2008).
Ryan, Henry C., and Edward C. Peartree (eds.) *Information Revolution and International Security* (Washington DC: Center for Strategic and International Studies, 1998).
SACD, *L'AMI: l'Ennemi* (Paris: pamphlet, 1998). Internet: www.sacd.fr
Sagafi-nejad, Tagi. *The UN and Transnational Corporations: From Code of Conduct to Global Compact* (Bloomington, IN: Indiana University Press, 2008).
Said, Edward W. *Power, Politics, and Culture* (New York: Vintage Books, 2002).
Sain, Peter. "In Search of a European Brand", *EuropaWorld* (May 4, 2006).
Sandvoss, Cornel. "On the Couch With Europe: The Eurovision Song Contest, the European Broadcast Union and Belonging on the Old Continent", *Popular Communication*, vol. 6, no. 3 (July 2008).
Sarantakes, Nicholas Evan. "Cold War Pop Culture and the Image of U.S. Foreign Policy: The Perspective of the Original Star Trek Series", *Journal of Cold War Studies*, vol. 7, no. 4 (Fall 2005).
Sarotte, Mary Elise. *Dealing With the Devil: East Germany, Détente, and Ostpolitik, 1969–1973* (Chapel Hill: The University of North Carolina Press, 2000).
Sartori, Anne E. "The Might of the Pen: A Reputational Theory of Communication in International Disputes", *International Organization*, vol. 56, no. 1 (Winter 2002).
Sassen, Saskia. *Global Networks, Linked Cities* (London: Routledge, 2002).
—. *The Global City: New York, London, Tokyo* (Princeton, NJ: Princeton University Press, 1991).
Sauer, Abram. "Borat vs. Kazakhstan – Identity Crisis?", *Brandchannel.com* (October 30, 2006).
Saunders, Robert A. "Buying into Brand Borat: Kazakhstan's Cautious Embrace of Its Unwanted 'Son'", *Slavic Review*, vol. 67, no. 1 (Spring 2008).
Schäferhoff, Marco, Sabine Campe, and Christopher Kaan. *Transnational Public-Private Partnerships in International Relations: Making Sense of Concepts, Research Frameworks and Results* (Berlin: SFB-Governance Working Papers 6, 2007).
Schapiro, Mark. *Exposed: The Toxic Chemistry of Everyday Products and What's at Stake for American Power* (White River Jct., VT: Chelsea Green Publishing, 2007).

240 Bibliography

Scharpf, Fritz W. *Regieren in Europa: Effectiv und Demokratisch?* (Frankfurt a/M: Campus Verlag, 1999).

Schatz, Edward. "Transnational Image Making and Soft Authoritarian Kazakhstan", *Slavic Review*, vol. 67, no. 1 (Spring 2008).

Schechter, Darrow. *Beyond Hegemony: Towards a New Philosophy of Political Legitimacy* (Manchester: Manchester University Press, 2005).

Schell, Orville. "China's Quest for Moral Authority", *The Nation*, vol. 287, no. 12 (October 20, 2008).

Schelling, Thomas C. *Arms and Influence* (New Haven: Yale University Press, 1966).

Schlesinger, Philip R. "Europe's Contradictory Communicative Space", *Daedalus*, vol. 123, no. 2 (Spring 1994).

Schimmelpfennig, Frank. "The Community Trap: Liberal Norms, Rhetorical Action, and the Eastern Enlargement of the European Union", *International Organization*, vol. 55, no. 1 (Winter 2001).

Schirm, Stefan (ed.) *New Rules for Global Markets: Public and Private Governance in the World Economy* (New York: Palgrave Macmillan, 2004).

Schneider, Cynthia P. "Culture Communicates: US Diplomacy That Works", in Jan Melissen (ed.) *The New Public Diplomacy: Soft Power in International* Relations (New York: Palgrave Macmillan, 2005).

Scholte, Jan Aart. "Civil Society and Democratically Accountable Global Governance", *Government and Opposition*, vol. 39, no. 2 (Spring 2004).

Schön, Donald A., and Martin Rein. *Frame Reflection: Toward the Resolution of Intractable Policy Controversies* (New York: Basic Books, 1994).

Schoppa, Leonard J. "The Social Context in Coercive International Bargaining", *International Organization*, vol. 53, no. 2 (Spring 1999).

Schwartau, Winn. *Information Warfare: Chaos on the Electronic Superhighway* (New York: Thunder's Mouth Press, 1994).

Schwartz, Barry. *The Costs of Living: How Market Freedom Erodes the Best Things in Life* (New York: W.W. Norton, 1994).

Scott, Catherine. "Americans Aren't Consumers Who Have to be Sold on War', *Atlanta Journal-Constitution* (January 22, 2003).

Scott, John. *Power* (Cambridge: Polity Press, 2001).

Searle, John R. *The Construction of Social Reality* (New York: The Free Press, 1995).

Secunda, Eugene, and Terence P. Moran. *Selling War to America: From the Spanish American War to the Global War on Terror* (Westport, CT: Praeger, 2007).

Segal, Gerald. " 'Asianism' and Asian Security", *The National Interest*, no. 42 (Winter 1995).

Seib, Philip. *The Al Jazeera Effect: How the New Global Media are Reshaping World Politics* (Washington DC: Potomac Books, 2008).

—. "Hegemonic No More: Western Media, the Rise of Al-Jazeera, and the Influence of Diverse Voices", *International Studies Review*, vol. 7, no. 4 (December 2005).

Semati, M. Mehdi, and Patty J. Sotirin, "Hollywood's Transnational Appeal: Hegemony and Democratic Potential?", *Journal of Popular Film & Television*, vol. 29, no. 4 (Winter 1999).

Sending, Ole Jacob, and Iver B. Neumann. "Governance to Governmentality: Analyzing NGOs, States, and Power", *International Studies Quarterly*, vol. 50, no. 3 (September 2006).

Sennett, Richard. *The Corrosion of Character: The Personal Consequences of Work in the New Capitalism* (New York: W.W. Norton, 1998).

Service, Robert. *Stalin: A Biography* (Cambridge, MA: Belknap Press, 2006).

Shaheen, Jack G. *Guilty—Hollywood's Verdict on Arabs After 9/11* (Northampton, MA: Interlink Publishing, 2008).
Shambaugh, David. "China's Propaganda System: Institutions, Processes and Efficacy", *The China Journal*, no. 57 (January 2007).
Shen, Dingli. "Why China Sees the EU as a Counterweight to America", *Europe's World*, no. 10 (Autumn 2008).
Shore, Cris. "'In Uno Plures' (?) EU Cultural Policy and the Governance of Europe", *Cultural Analysis*, vol. 5 (2006).
Short, Nicola. "A Review of the Ottawa Process to Ban Landmines", *ISIS Briefing Paper*, no. 15 (November 1997).
Sikkink, Kathryn. "Restructuring World Politics: The Limits and Asymmetries of Soft Power", in Sanjeev Khagram, James V. Riker, and Kathryn Sikkink (eds.) *Restructuring World Politics: Transnational Social Movements* (Minneapolis: University of Minnesota Press, 2002).
—. "Transnational Politics, International Relations Theory, and Human Rights", *PS, Political Science & Politics*, vol. 31, no. 3 (September 1998).
Simes, Dimitri K. "America's Imperial Dilemma", *Foreign Affairs*, vol. 82, no. 6 (November/December 2003).
Sjursen, Helene. "What Kind of Power?", *Journal of European Public Policy*, vol. 13, no. 2 (March 2006).
Slaughter, Anne-Marie. *A New World Order* (Princeton, NJ: Princeton University Press, 2004).
—. "Courting the World", *Foreign Policy*, no. 141 (March/April 2004).
—. "Everyday Global Governance", *Daedalus*, vol. 132, no. 1 (Winter 2003).
—. "Leading Through Law", *The Wilson Quarterly*, vol. 27, no. 4 (Autumn 2003).
Smiers, Joost. *Arts Under Pressure: Promoting Cultural Diversity in the Age of Globalisation* (London: Zed Books, 2003).
Smith, Karen E., and Margot Light (eds.). *Ethics and Foreign Policy* (Cambridge: Cambridge University Press, 2001).
Smith, Mitchell P. "Soft Power Rising: Romantic Europe in the Service of Practical Europe", *World Literature Today*, vol. 80, no. 1 (January/February 2006).
Smith, Steve. "The Increasing Insecurity of Security Studies: Conceptualizing Security in the Last Twenty Years", *Contemporary Security Studies*, vol. 20, no. 3 (December 1999).
Smyth, Rosaleen. "Mapping US Public Diplomacy in the 21st Century", *Australian Journal of International Affairs*, vol. 55, no. 3 (November 2001).
Snow, Nancy (and Philip N. Taylor, eds.). *Routledge Handbook of Public Diplomacy* (New York: Routledge, 2008).
—. *Information War: American Propaganda, Free Speech, and Opinion Control After 9/11* (New York: Seven Stories Press, 2003).
—. *Propaganda Inc.: Selling America's Culture to the World* (New York: Seven Stories Press, 2002).
Snyder, Alvin. *Warriors of Disinformation: American Propaganda, Soviet Lies, and the Winning of the Cold War* (New York: Arcade Publishing, 1995).
Solana Madariaga, Javier. "The New Paradigm of Cooperation in Europe", *Hampton Roads International Security Quarterly*, vol. 8, no. 2 (April 2008).
—. "Mars and Venus Reconciled: A New Era for Transatlantic Relations". Albert H. Gordon Lecture at the Kennedy School of Government, Harvard University (April 3, 2003).
Sperandei, Maria. "Bridging Deterrence and Compellence: An Alternative Approach to the Study of Coercive Diplomacy", *International Studies Review*, vol. 8, no. 2 (June 2006).

242 Bibliography

Spielvogel, Christian. "'You Know Where I Stand': Moral Framing of the War on Terrorism and the Iraq War in the 2004 Presidential Campaign", *Rhetoric & Public Affairs*, vol. 8, no. 4 (Winter 2005).

Spongenberg, Helena. "EU Considers Going Virtual", *EUObserver.com* (March 2, 2007).

Steensland, Brian. "Why Do Policy Frames Change? Actor-Idea Coevolution in Debates Over Welfare Reform", *Social Forces*, vol. 86, no. 3 (March 2008).

Steffek, Jens. *Embedded Liberalism and Its Critics: Justifying Global Governance in the American Century* (New York: Palgrave Macmillan, 2006).

—. "The Legitimacy of International Governance: A Discourse Approach", *European Journal of International Relations*, vol. 9, no. 2 (June 2003).

Steinbock, Dan. "Mobile Service Revolution: CNN Effect Goes Mobile", *Georgetown Journal of International Affairs*, vol. 6, no. 2 (Summer 2005).

Stelzer, Irwin. "Bush Turns Away from the Weaklings of Europe", *Times* (February 19, 2002).

Stephens, Bret. "A President, Not a Symbol", *The Wall Street Journal* (March 11, 2008).

Sterling-Folker, Jennifer. "The Emperor Wore Cowboy Boots", *International Studies Perspectives*, vol. 9, no. 3 (August 2008).

—. (and Rosemary E. Shinko). "Discourses of Power: Traversing the Realist-Postmodern Divide", *Millennium*, vol. 33, no. 3 (June 2005).

Stevens, Philip. "Hollywood's Geopolitics Lesson for China", *Financial Times* (February 14, 2008).

Stobart, Paul. *Brand Power* (New York: New York University Press, 1994).

Stokman, Frans, Rolf Ziegler, and John Scott. *Networks of Corporate Power* (Cambridge: Cambridge University Press, 1985).

Stolte, John F., and Shanon Fender, "Framing Social Values: An Experimental Study of Culture and Cognition", *Social Psychology Quarterly*, vol. 70, no. 1 (March 2007).

Stoppard, Tom, and Derek Walcott. *Cultural Power: A Conversation* (New York: The City University of New York, November 10, 2008). Internet: www.greatissuesforum.org

Strange, Susan. "Finance, Information and Power", *Review of International Studies*, vol. 16, no. 3 (July 1990).

Styan, David. "Tony Blair and Africa: Old Images, New Realities", *OpenDemocracy.net* (May 25, 2005).

Sullivan, Andrew. "Andrew Sullivan on America: An Honest Blogger Will Never Make a Quick Buck", *The Sunday Times* (October 13, 2002).

Swartz, David. *Culture and Power: The Sociology of Pierre Bourdieu* (Chicago: University of Chicago Press, 1998).

Szondi, Gyorgy. *Public Diplomacy and Nation Branding: Conceptual Similarities and Differences* (The Hague: Clingendael Discussion Paper in Diplomacy, 2008).

Tapscott, Don, and Anthony D. Williams. *Wikinomics: How Mass Collaboration Changes Everything* (New York: Portfolio/Penguin, 2006).

Taylor, Philip M. *Munitions of the Mind: A History of Propaganda from the Ancient World to the Present Day* (Manchester: Manchester University Press, 1995).

Teicholz, Nina. "Privatizing Propaganda", *Washington Monthly*, vol. 34, no. 12 (December 2002).

Telhami, Shibley. "History and Humiliation", *Washington Post* (March 28, 2003).

Teubner, Gunther (ed.) *Global Law Without a State* (Aldershot: Dartmouth, 1997).

The Chronicle of Higher Education, "Philantropists Take a Closer Look at Second Life" (June 22, 2007).

The Economist. "Brussels Rules OK" (September 22, 2007).

—. "Europe: Euro Visions" (May 14, 2005).
—. "Watch Out, Arabs and the Internet" (July 10, 2004).
—. "Ronald Reagan, Surprising Victor of the Cold War" (June 10, 2004).
—. "The Case for Brands" (September 6, 2001).
Thomas, Daniel C. "Human Rights Ideas, The Demise of Communism and the End of the Cold War", *Journal of Cold War Studies*, vol. 7, no. 2 (Spring 2005).
Thussu, Daya Kishan, and Des Freedman (eds.) *War and the Media: Reporting Conflict 24/7* (Thousand Oaks, CA: Sage, 2003).
Tilly, Charles. "War Making and State Making as Organized Crime," in Peter B. Evans, Dietrich Rueschmeyer, and Theda Skocpol (eds.) *Bringing the State Back In* (Cambridge: Cambridge University Press, 1985).
TimesOnline, "70,000 Gather for Violent Pakistan Cartoons Protest" (February 15, 2008).
Tindall, Karen, and Paul 't Hart. "Leadership by the Famous: Celebrity as Political Capital", in John Kane, Haig Patapan, and Paul 't Hart (eds.) *Dispersed Leadership in Democracies* (Oxford: Oxford University Press, 2009).
Toennies, Ferdinand. *Community and Association* (London: Routledge, 1974).
Toffler, Alvin, and Heidi Toffler, *War and Anti-War* (Boston: Little, Brown, 1993).
Tomlinson, John. *Cultural Imperialism: A Critical Introduction* (London: Pinter, 1991).
Touraine, Alain. *Return of the Actor* (Minneapolis: University of Minnesota Press, 1988).
Traub, James. "The Celebrity Solution", *New York Times* (March 9, 2008).
—. "The New Hard-Soft Power", *New York Times Magazine* (January 30, 2005).
Tremayne, Mark (ed.) *Blogging, Citizenship, and the Future of the Media* (London: Routledge, 2007).
True, Michael. *People Power: Fifty Peacemakers and Their Communities* (Jaipur: Rawat, 2007).
Tsu, Jing. *Failure, Nationalism, and Literature: The Making of Modern Chinese Identity* (Stanford: Stanford University Press, 2005).
Tuch, Hans N. *Communicating With the World: U.S. Public Diplomacy Overseas* (New York: St. Martin's Press, 1990).
Tucker, Robert W., and David C. Hendrickson. "The Sources of American Legitimacy", *Foreign Affairs*, vol. 83, no. 6 (November/December 2004).
U.S. Advisory Commission on Public Diplomacy, *Building America's Public Diplomacy Through a Reformed Structure and Additional Resources* (Washington DC: U.S. Department of State, 2002).
Ullmann-Margalit, Edna. *The Emergence of Norms* (Oxford: Clarendon Press, 1977).
Urbina, Ian. "This War Brought to You by Rendon Group", *Asia Times* (November 13, 2002).
Vaida, Bara. "Blogging On", *National Journal*, vol. 39, no. 40 (October 6, 2007).
Van der Kris, Jeroen, and Elske Schouten, "EU Wordt de Regelgever van de Wereld", *NRC Handelsblad* (October 21, 2007).
Van Elteren, Mel. "U.S. Cultural Imperialism Today: Only a Chimera?", *SAIS Review*, vol. 23, no. 2 (Summer 2003).
—. "GATT and Beyond: World Trade, the Arts and American Popular Culture in Western Europe", *Journal of American Culture*, vol. 19, no. 3 (Fall 1996).
Van Gelder, Sicco. "A View on the Future of Branding", unpublished paper (April 2002).
Van Ham, Peter (and Jon Coaffee). "Guest Editorial – Security Branding: The Role of Security in Marketing the City, Region or State", *Place Branding and Public Diplomacy*, vol. 4, no. 3 (August 2008).
—. "Place Branding Within a Security Paradigm – Concepts and Cases", *Place Branding and Public Diplomacy*, vol. 4, no. 3 (August 2008).

—. "Europe, War, and Territory", in Michael Burgess and Hans Vollaard (eds.) *State Territoriality and European Integration* (London: Routledge, 2006).

—. "Branding European Power", *Journal of Place Branding*, vol. 1, no. 2 (March 2005).

—. "Branding European Territory: Inside the Wonderful Worlds of PR and IR Theory", *Millennium*, vol. 31, no. 2 (March 2002).

—. "The Rise of the Brand State: The Postmodern Politics of Image and Reputation", *Foreign Affairs*, vol. 80, no. 5 (September/October 2001).

—. *European Integration and the Postmodern Condition: Governance, Democracy, Identity* (London: Routledge, 2001).

—. *Identity Beyond the State: The Case of the European Union* (Copenhagen: COPRI Working Paper 15, 2000).

Van Kersbergen, Kees, and Bertjan Verbeek. "The Politics of International Norms: Subsidiarity and the Imperfect Competence Regime of the European Union", *European Journal of International Affairs*, vol. 13, no. 2 (June 2007).

Van Lit, Erik, "Osama Bin Laden Als Popidool", *ZemZem*, vol. 4, no. 2 (2008).

Vanden Brande, Edith. "Green Civilain Power Europe", in Jan Orbie (ed.) *Europe's Global Role: External Policies of the European Union* (Aldershot: Ashgate, 2008).

Volcic, Zala. "Former Yugoslavia on the World Wide Web: Commercialization and Branding of Nation-States", *The International Communication Gazette*, vol. 70, no. 5 (October 2008).

Von Eschen, Penny M. *Satchmo Blows Up the World: Jazz Ambassadors Play the Cold War* (Cambridge, MA: Harvard University Press, 2004).

Wagnleiter, Reinhold. *Coca-Colonization and the Cold War: The Cultural Mission of the United States in Austria After the Second World War* (Chapel Hill: University of North Carolina Press, 1994).

Walker, Martin. "Globalization 3.0", *The Wilson Quarterly*, vol. 31, no. 4 (Autumn 2007).

Wall Street Journal. "The New Multilateralism" (January 8, 2004).

Wallace, Dickie. "Hyperrealizing 'Borat' With the Map of the European 'Other' ", *Slavic Review*, vol. 67, no. 1 (Spring 2008).

Waller, J. Michael. *The Public Diplomacy Reader* (Washington DC: Institute of World Politics Press, 2007).

Walt, Stephen M. *Taming American Power: The Global Response to U.S. Primacy* (New York: W.W. Norton, 2006).

Wang, Shaoguang. "Changing Models of China's Policy Agenda Setting", *Modern China*, vol. 34, no. 1 (January 2008).

Wanta, Wayne, Guy Golan, and Cheolhan Lee. "Agenda Setting and International News: Media Influence on Public Perceptions of Foreign Policy", *Journalism and Mass Communication Quarterly*, vol. 81, no. 2 (Summer 2004).

Wasko, Janet. "Can Hollywood Still Rule the Word?", in David Held and Henrietta L. Moore (eds.) *Cultural Politics in a Global Age: Uncertainty, Solidarity and Innovation* (Oxford: Oneworld Publications, 2007).

Waterfield, Bruno. "Barroso Hails the European 'Empire' ", *Daily Telegraph* (July 12, 2007).

Weber, Cynthia (ed.) *International Relations Theory: A Critical Introduction* (New York: Routledge, 2001).

—. *Simulating Sovereignty: Intervention, the State and Symbolic Exchange* (Cambridge: Cambridge University Press, 1995).

Webster, Frank. *Theories of the Information Society* (New York: Routledge, 2006).

Weigel, David. "An Army of Bloggers", *Reason*, vol. 38, no. 3 (July 2006).
Weigel, George. *Witness to Hope: The Biography of Pope John Paul II* (New York: Harper Perennial, 1999).
Weinraub, Bernard. "Islamic Nations Move to Keep Out 'Schindler's List' ", *New York Times* (April 7, 1994).
Weintraub, Sidney. *U.S.-Latin American Attitudes: Mistrust and Indifference* (Washington DC: CSIS Issues in International Political Economy 41, 2003).
Welsh, Jolyon, and Daniel Fearn (eds.) *Engagement: Public Diplomacy in a Globalised World* (London: Foreign and Commonwealth Office, 2008).
Wendt, Alexander. *Social Theory of International Politics* (Cambridge: Cambridge University Press, 1999).
—. "Anarchy is What States Make of It: The Social Construction of Power Politics", *International Organization*, vol. 46, no. 2 (Spring 1992).
Western, Jon. "The War Over Iraq: Selling War to the American Public", *Security Studies*, vol. 14, no. 1 (January/March 2005).
Whitfield, Stephen J. *The Culture of the Cold War* (Baltimore: The Johns Hopkins University Press, 1991).
Whitfield, Teresa. *A Crowded Field: Groups of Friends, the UN, and the Resolution of Conflict* (New York: New York University CIC Occasional Paper, 2005).
Wight, Colin. *Agents, Structures and International Relations* (Cambridge: Cambridge University Press, 2006).
Williams, Michael C. *Culture and Security: Symbolic Power and the Politics of International Security* (London: Routledge, 2007).
Williamson, John. "Putting the Fizz Back into the Tory Party" (October 7, 2001). Internet: www.wallyolins.com
Wilson Lewis, John, and Xue Litai. *Imagined Enemies: China Prepares for Uncertain War* (Stanford: Stanford University Press, 2006).
Wohlforth, William C. "The Stability of a Unipolar World", *International Security*, vol. 24, no. 1 (Summer 1999).
Wolff, Larry. *Inventing Eastern Europe: The Map of Civilization on the Mind of the Enlightenment* (Stanford: Stanford University Press, 1994).
Wolfowitz, Paul D. "Speech at the 38th Munich Conference on Security Policy", Munich (February 2, 2002).
Wolin, Sheldon S. *Democracy Incorporated: Managed Democracy and the Specter of Inverted Totalitarianism* (Princeton, NJ: Princeton University Press, 2008).
—. "Fugitive Democracy", in Seyla Benhabib (ed.) *Democracy and Difference* (Princeton, NJ: Princeton University Press, 1996).
Wolozin, Benjamin. "The Art of Persuasion in Politics (and Science)", *The Skeptical Inquirer*, vol. 31, no. 1 (January/February 2007).
Woodward, Gary C. *Center Stage: Media and the Performance of American Politics* (Lanham, MD: Rowman & Littlefield, 2007).
Woolley, Benjamin. *Virtual Worlds: A Journey in Hype and Hyperreality* (Harmondsworth: Penguin, 1993).
World Information Access. *Blogger Arrests* (Seattle: University of Washington, 2008).
York, Peter. "Branded", *Times* (October 14, 2000).
Young, Oran R. *International Governance: Protecting the Environment in a Stateless Society* (Ithaca, NY: Cornell University Press, 1994).
Youngs, Richard. "Normative Dynamics and Strategic Interests in the EU's External Identity", *Journal of Common Market Studies*, vol. 42, no. 2 (June 2004).

Zaharna, R.S. "The Soft Power Differential: Network Communication and Mass Communication in Public Diplomacy", *The Hague Journal of Diplomacy*, vol. 2, no. 3 (October 2007).

—. "American Public Diplomacy in the Arab and Muslim Worlds: A Strategic Communication Analysis", *Foreign Policy in Focus* (November 2001).

—. "Intercultural Communication and International Public Relations: Exploring Parallels", *Communication Quarterly*, vol. 48, no. 1 (Winter 2000).

Zakaria, Fareed. *The Post-American World* (New York: W.W. Norton, 2008).

—. *From Wealth to Power: The Unusual Origins of America's World Role* (Princeton, NJ: Princeton University Press, 1998).

Zald, Mayer N. "Culture, Ideology, and Strategic Framing", in Doug McAdam, John D. McCarthy, and Mayer N. Zald (eds.) *Comparative Perspectives on Social Movements: Political Opportunities, Mobilizing Structures, and Cultural Framings* (Cambridge: Cambridge University Press, 1996).

Zehfuss, Maja. *Constructivism in International Relations: The Politics of Reality* (Cambridge: Cambridge University Press, 2002).

Zelditch, Morris, Jr. "Theories of Legitimacy", in John T. Jost and Brenda Major (eds.) *The Psychology of Legitimacy: Emerging Perspectives on Ideology, Justice, and Intergroup Relations* (Cambridge: Cambridge University Press, 2001).

Zetterholm, Staffan (ed.) *National Cultures and European Integration* (Oxford: Berg, 1994).

Zielonka, Jan. *Europe as Empire: The Nature of the Enlarged European Union* (Oxford: Oxford University Press, 2006).

Zürn, Mathias. "Global Governance and Legitimacy Problems", *Government and Opposition*, vol. 39, no. 2 (Spring 2004).

Zwiebel, Michael J. "Why We Need to Reestablish the USIA", *Military Review*, vol. 86, no. 6 (November/December 2006).

Index

24 (TV series) 53, 109

Abu Ghraib 32, 107, 110, 150, 164
accountability 15, 85
Acharya, Amitav 13
acquis communautaire (EU) 37, 165
Adonnino Report (EU) 63
advertising 48, 111, 119, 144, 150
Afghanistan 9, 37, 98, 126, 131–2, 155; invasion 59; war 6, 24, 33, 95, 121, 162
Africa 24, 36–7, 55, 65, 93, 109, 131, 147, 161; China policy 41–3; poverty 88–9, 117
African Economic Community 36
African Union (AU) 36, 161
agency 2, 4, 13, 20, 96, 99, 136
agenda-setting 4, 8, 10, 28, 62, 81, 93–4, 99
Akel, Pierre 104
Alakeson, Vidhya 116, 118
Al-Arabiya 94–5
Albania 143
Al Jazeera 92, 94–5, 103–4, 124, 165
Al Qaeda 92, 104, 109, 126–7, 131
Alterman, Jon 103
Al-Zawahiri, Ayman 92
Amazon.com 98
americanization 50, 54, 56, 59, 62, 68
Amnesty International 117, 128, 138
anarchy 1–2, 14, 35, 67, 147
Anderson, Benedict 91
Andreasen, Uffe 156
Angell, Norman 6
Anholt, Simon 144, 148–50, 152, 156
An Inconvenient Truth (movie) 117
anti-Americanism 18, 32–3, 54, 119–20
Anti-Ballistic Missile Treaty (ABM) 31
Apple 28

arkhe (control) 26
Asal, Victor 27
Asia 4, 14, 24–5, 32, 34, 43, 55, 68, 80, 109, 123–4, 126, 128, 131, 145, 147, 153; hemisphere 38–41; values 39
attraction 16–17, 25, 41–2, 49, 54–5, 58–9, 76, 115–17, 140, 147, 149, 152, 161, 163; soft power 6, 8, 19, 128, 159
authority 1–2, 4–5, 8, 13, 15–17, 24–6, 44, 47, 52, 63, 69, 71, 87–8, 93–4, 100, 109, 117, 137–9, 145, 160, 167; global 9; moral 28, 80; *see also* private authority
Axis of Evil 4, 140, 153, 155; *see also* George W. Bush

Bacevich, Andrew J. 30
Baker, Nicholson 98
Baldwin, David A. 3, 22, 123
Balkans 110, 121, 143, 148
Baltic states 157
Barber, Benjamin 5, 51, 55–6, 60, 67, 89
Barnett, Michael 22
Barroso, José Manuel 24, 63–4
Basle Committee on Banking 77
Baum, Matthew A. 110–11
Bauman, Zygmunt 72
Baywatch (TV series) 52
Beatles 51
Beers, Charlotte 119, 124, 151
Beijing consensus 41–2, 160
Belarus 37
belief system 27
benchmarking 2, 13, 72, 165
Berlin, Isaiah 33
Berlin Wall 11, 55
best practices 72, 77, 116, 165
Biersteker, Thomas J. 81–2

Billig, Michael S. 47
bin Laden, Osama 92, 95, 104, 119, 126–7
Biological Weapons Convention 31
biopolitical 49–50, 56
Bishai, Linda 19
Björkdahl, Annika 28
Blair, Tony 29, 117, 126
blog 34, 92–4, 96–100, 104, 106–8, 111–12, 156, 163; blogosphere 97, 112; China policy 102; Lebanon war 106; public diplomacy 116, 130, 132–3
Blumenberg, Hans 53, 164
Boas, Taylor C. 101
Bono 88–9, 117
Borat (movie) 141, 153–6
Börzel, Tanja 27–8, 72
Bosnia 37, 92, 110
Bourdieu, Pierre 48, 87–9
Braithwaite, John 75–6
Brazil 42, 54, 80, 94
Bretton Woods institutions 9, 70; *see also* IMF; World Bank
bricolage 67
British Council 133
British Empire 24–5
Bulgaria 143, 157
Bureau, Jean-François 145
Bush, George W. 4, 19, 32, 53, 57, 70, 89, 95, 98, 105, 117–18, 120, 122, 126–7, 140–1, 151–3, 155; disregard for social power 33–4, 120, 151; doctrine 31; Iraq invasion 12
Büthe, Tim 74, 165
Buzan, Barry 29, 52

Campbell, David 57
Capra, Frank 51
Cardoso, Henrique 80–1
Carr, E.H. 2, 7
Carroll, Conn 54
cartoon crisis 141, 155–6
celebrity 29, 95, 108, 110, 148
celebrity diplomacy 43, 66, 88–90, 110, 115, 148
censorship 101–3, 106, 126
Central Europe 5, 25, 37, 65, 142, 145, 163; US social power 18, 51–3, 55, 121, 161
Centre for Humanitarian Dialogue 71
Chechnya 143
Checkel, Jeffrey T. 13, 20
Cheers (TV series) 108
Cheney, Dick 31, 53

China 57, 89, 93–4, 99, 104, 114, 116, 138, 157, 160, 164, 167; Great Firewall 101, 163; Olympics, Beijing (summer 2008) 42–3, 101, 128; public diplomacy 117–18, 128–9, 144; rising power 1, 25, 39–45, 116; social power 9, 30, 39–45; *Wangluo Yulun* (internet opinion) 102–3
Cho, Young Nam 40
Christendom 146; *see also* religion
Churchill, Winston 32
Cisco Systems 98, 101
citizens 10, 35, 49, 62–4, 66, 96, 115, 124, 130, 146, 148–9, 161; citizen-consumer 13, 56–7, 79–80, 111, 139–40, 144, 151, 166
civilian power 30, 65, 145, 148
civil society 25, 78–81, 84, 88, 135
clash of civilizations 25, 50, 122; *see also* Samuel P. Huntington
Clerc, Beatrice 60
climate change 9, 80, 117, 145
Clooney, George 89
CNN 52, 92, 101, 104, 109, 126, 142, 154–5; effect/factor 105, 111
Coalition Information Center (CIC) 125
coercion 3–4, 6, 13, 17–20, 27–8, 32, 39, 44, 76–7, 85–6, 90, 104, 116, 159–60; definition 8; *dolos* 26; *see also* force; hard power
cognitive framing 11, 47; *see also* framing
Cohen, Lizabeth 56
Cohen, Roger 104
Cohen, Sasha Baron 154–5; *see also* Borat
Cold War 1, 8, 12, 18, 26, 30–1, 37, 42, 63, 105, 121, 131, 142; popular culture 5, 49–53, 55, 119, 161, 163
colonialism 25, 143, 150, 160
comitology 73, 165
Committee on Public Information 119
Common Agricultural Policy (CAP-EU) 38
Common Foreign and Security Policy (CFSP-EU) 28
Common Market for Eastern and Southern Africa 37
communication 3, 8, 19, 33, 65, 93–4, 97–8, 108, 112, 115–8, 138, 142–3, 148, 151, 164; Hollywood 53; public diplomacy 121–34; symbolic 144; technology 61–2, 68, 93, 99, 102–6, 116
communicative rationality 19
Communism 18, 25, 55, 142, 145, 161
compliance 14, 17, 19, 28, 75, 86, 90, 145, 162; voluntary 9, 48, 70

Comprehensive Test Ban Treaty
  (CTBT) 31
conflict prevention 28, 65
Confucianism 39; see also religion
Congo, Democratic Republic 42, 51, 148
constructivism 7, 17, 20, 48, 50, 52, 69,
  90, 136; power 8, 21–2, 46–7
Consultative Group on International
  Agricultural Research 78
consumption 48, 50, 56–8, 62, 67, 80,
  96, 163; sovereignty 80
Cooper, Andrew F. 88
Cooper, Robert 29–30
corporate social responsibility (CSR) 79,
  83, 90, 163, 166
Cox, Robert 27
Crawford, Neta C. 19
credibility 13, 21, 33, 41, 44, 87, 95, 121,
  124, 133, 137–8, 140, 144–5, 151,
  157–62, 164–6; EU policy 38, 66,
  146–7, 149, 153; NGOs 9, 80, 84, 89,
  97, 100, 158; US policy 18, 34, 141,
  153; see also trust
Croatia 37
Cronkite, Walter 94
Crusades 14
Cull, Nicholas 115
Culpepper, Pepper D. 11
culture 6, 10, 13–15, 23, 26, 34–7, 41, 44,
  48–68, 74, 91, 93, 95–6, 105, 110–113,
  128, 136–8, 146, 149–50, 153, 158–9,
  162–5, 167; constructivism 17, 46–7;
  corporate 68; diplomacy 88, 115,
  122–3, 125, 127–8, 133–4; hegemony
  39–40, 59–60, 67, 101, 122; legitimacy
  25, 60–1; strategic 35, 50, 60, 62–7;
  see also entertainment; Hollywood;
  popular culture
cyberdiplomacy 135; see also virtual
  diplomacy
cyberpolitik 112–13, 135
cyberspace 102–3
Czechoslovakia 163

Dahl, Robert 15–16, 22, 71
Dallas (TV series) 52, 55
Debrix, François 110
debt 42, 88–9, 117
de Charette, Hervé 61
DeFleur, Margaret and Melvin 54
de Gaulle, Charles 158
de Gouveia, Philip Fiske 131
de Grazia, Victoria 56
de Hoop Scheffer, Jaap 132

De Nevers, Renée 18
Denmark 141, 153, 155–6
Desperate Housewives (TV series) 164
deterrence 8
development aid 37, 42, 89, 117,
  131, 148
d'Hooghe, Ingrid 129
Diderot, Denis 142
Die Hard (movie) 164
digitalization 61
disciplinary power 49, 55
discourse 19, 22, 31, 39, 47, 57–8, 60, 69,
  82–3, 86, 89, 92–4, 102, 11, 121, 132;
  coalition 10; linguistic turn 7; social
  power 3, 26, 48, 76
disinformatia 114
dolos (deceit, coercion) 26, 30, 33
Douglas, Susan J. 92, 95
Drahos, Peter 75–6
Drezner, Daniel W. 82
Duchêne, François 36
dunamis (resources) 26
Duvall, Raymond 22

eBay 98, 100
e-commerce 74, 76, 93, 102
Economic Partnership Agreement
  (EPA-EU) 37
e-democracy 82, 93
Egypt 25, 99, 126
Ellington, Duke 50–1
embeddedness 2, 10, 17, 27, 46, 56, 69,
  70, 76, 83, 90, 100, 108, 112, 150, 160,
  162; John G. Ruggie and 49, 72, 76, 85;
  social power 4, 6, 10, 23, 100, 105;
  symbolic power 84–6
empire 14, 26, 29–31, 33–4, 42, 44, 49,
  52, 56, 58, 70, 92, 115, 143, 150, 160;
  China 39; EU 24–5, 34, 64;
  postmodern 27, 29; see also British
  Empire; Evil Empire; Pax Americana;
  Pax Romana
emulation 12
England, Lynddie R. 107–8, 110
English School (IR) 7
entertainment 48, 50, 52–3, 92, 95,
  108–11, 122, 163–4
Entman, Robert M. 12, 91
environment 12, 57–8, 66, 73, 75–7,
  79–80, 90, 117, 161, 166
Eritrea 37
Estonia 65
Esty, Daniel C. 14–16
Ethiopia 37, 43

250 Index

Euro-Mediterranean Partnership (Euromed-EU) 130
European Automobile Manufacturers Association (ACEA) 74
European Commission (EU) 24, 36–7, 62–6, 73, 75, 129–31, 146, 148–9, 165
European Community Humanitarian Aid Office (ECHO) 131
European Council (EU) 28–9, 63, 148
European Film Academy 59–60
europeanization 27, 63
European Neighbourhood Policy (ENP-EU) 130
European Parliament (EU) 37
European Security and Defence Policy (ESDP-EU) 30, 161
European Union (EU): credibility 38, 66, 146–7, 149, 153; empire 24–5, 34, 64; enlargement 37, 63, 157; hard power 37–8; identity 28, 30, 34–5, 62–5, 141, 145–6, 148–9; image 24, 63, 65, 72, 141, 145–50; integration 12, 35–7, 50, 62–4, 73, 138, 146, 165; model 35–9, 41, 44, 63, 66, 76, 121, 145–7, 158, 161; norm entrepreneur 44, 62, 72, 74–6, 129, 146–8, 165; place branding 145–9; public diplomacy 36, 65, 114, 129–31; reputation 129, 145; standards 37–8, 63, 67–8, 73–5, 129, 145, 147, 149, 153, 162; symbols 63, 65; *see also* European Commission; European Council; European Parliament; Lisbon Treaty
European Year of Intercultural Dialogue (EU) 65–6, 149
Eurovision Song Contest 65, 146
Evil Empire 5, 153; *see also* Ronald Reagan
exchange diplomacy 41, 65, 115, 119, 121–2, 127, 130, 133–4
expertise 9, 16, 71, 77–8, 80, 84, 109, 125

Fahrenheit 9/11 (movie) 54
Farrell, Theo 25
Farrow, Mia 43
Fascism 51, 144
fashion 10, 50, 54, 56, 158, 162
Felix (film award) 60
Ferguson, Yale H. 3
financial crisis 1, 11, 34, 38, 58, 84–5
Finland 65, 138, 142
Finnemore, Martha 10–11, 28, 38
Fondacaro, Steve 106

force 3–6, 8–10, 13–14, 18–20, 25, 28–30, 32–3, 35, 37–8, 43–4, 77, 85, 91, 104, 106, 110, 157, 159, 161; *see also* coercion; *dolos*; hard power; representational force
Fordham, Benjamin O. 27
Foucault, Michel 35, 48–9
framing 7–9, 12–13, 28, 48, 53, 110–11, 127, 138, 151; NGOs 16, 20, 62, 80, 94, 99, 101, 106–7, 111, 134; social power 4, 8, 11, 19, 90; *see also* cognitive framing; grafting
France 32, 36, 42, 59–61, 70–1, 143, 147, 158
Franck, Thomas M. 14
Free Aceh Movement 71
Freedom House 128
free trade 9, 16, 50, 60–1
Friedman, Thomas L. 1, 95, 100, 161
Friend, David 106
Friends (TV series) 53
Fuchs, Doris 20, 84
fugitive democracy 80
Fukuyama, Francis 15, 122

gatekeepers 1, 62, 93, 96, 99–100, 111, 135, 144, 153, 163
Gates, Bill and Melinda 88–9; *see also* Microsoft
Gates, Robert M. 6, 32
Gaza 104–5
Geertz, Clifford 46–7, 49
Geldof, Bob 117
Gellner, Ernest 64
Gemeinschaft 15, 62
General Agreement on Tariffs and Trade (GATT) 60
genetically modified organisms (GMOs) 58, 75
genocide 12, 107
geopolitics 9–10, 24, 26, 36, 38, 40, 43–5, 148, 157
Germany 14, 16, 32, 53, 57, 114, 116, 138, 142–3, 146–7, 157; Cold War 11, 52, 55, 163; unification 71; *see also* Berlin Wall
Gershwin, George 50
Gesellschaft 15, 62
Ghana 143
Ghandi, Mahatma 25
Giddens, Anthony 67
Gill, Bates 41–2
Gitlin, Todd 57
Glassman, James K. 45, 51, 127

Index 251

Global Compact (UN) 78–9, 166
global governance 2, 8–10, 17, 26, 30, 44, 64,71–3, 76–9, 81, 84–90, 96, 146, 153, 158–60, 165–7; legitimacy 16, 85–6; models 25, 36–7; social power 9, 88; *see also* soft law
globalization 1, 12, 31, 36–7, 45, 47, 50, 53, 61, 67, 75–9, 83, 89, 96, 116, 135, 138, 147, 163; media 68, 93, 100, 137, 156; social power 5, 38
global public policy network (GPPN) 78–82, 85, 89–90, 135, 166
Global Water Partnership 78
Goffman, Erving 13
goodwill 32, 41, 164
Google 96, 100–2, 142
Gorbachev, Mikhail S. 25, 55
Gore, Al 117
Göring, Hermann 46
governmentality 35, 45, 55, 150
grafting 11, 13, 65; *see also* framing
Gramsci, Antonio 27, 48–9, 76
Gray, Colin S. 35
Greenpeace 80, 153
Gregory, Bruce 115, 127
Grossman, Lev 97
Guantanamo Bay 32, 107, 152, 164
Gullion, Edmund 115

Haass, Richard 1
Habermas, Jürgen 16, 19–20, 65, 71, 121
Hagman, Larry 52
Hale, John 146
Hall, Rodney Bruce 81–2
hard power 5–6, 8–9, 11, 17–20, 26, 29, 33, 39–40, 43–5, 86, 118, 152, 159; EU policy 37–8; US policy 5, 6, 18, 32, 44, 120–1, 161; *see also* coercion; *dolos*; force
Hardt, Michael 49, 56
hegemonic socialization 27, 43, 68; *see also* Antonio Gramsci
hegemony 1, 9, 24–8, 30–1, 43, 53, 68, 70, 118, 132, 166; culture 40, 50, 55, 59, 62, 67, 122, 150, 164, 167; legitimacy 13–14, 26, 33, 48; *see also* British Empire; empire; hegemonic socialization; *Pax Americana*; *Pax Romana*
Held, David 2
Henkin, Louis 86
Hezbollah 103, 105–6
Holbrooke, Richard 118, 151
Hollywood 26, 51–5, 59, 61–2, 67, 108–9, 119, 123, 150, 163; mythotypos 53, 164

Holocaust 146
Holzinger, Katharina 12
Holzscheiter, Anna 10
honest broker 10, 71
Hong Kong 54
Hongju Koh, Harold 86
Hopf, Ted 47
Huang, Yanzhong 41–2
humanitarian aid 37, 127, 131, 148
humanitarian intervention 5, 37, 45, 105, 131
human rights 10, 35, 37, 78–80, 86, 88, 90, 103, 107, 147, 152, 156; China 39, 43, 128
Huntington, Samuel P. 50, 122
Hurd, Ian 13
Hussein, Saddam 30, 120, 125

ideal speech situation 19
identity 7, 14–15, 21, 29, 36, 46–7, 56–8, 92, 111–12, 116, 123, 137, 140–3, 156, 158; Asian 39, 49; bubble of 49–50, 64, 91–3, 100, 142, 163; EU 28, 30, 34–5, 62–5, 141, 145–6, 148–9; national 53, 57, 119, 124; US 53, 57, 119, 124
image 5, 11, 20–1, 27, 35, 43, 49, 58, 61, 67, 76, 80, 91, 93, 95–6, 106, 111–12, 116, 136–8, 156–8; China 39, 42–3, 128–9, 163; Denmark 155–6; EU 24, 63, 65, 72, 141, 145–50; Kazakhstan 154–5; US 18, 32, 35, 44, 52–4, 59–60, 107, 118–19, 122–5, 141, 149–53, 164; place branding 140–53
India 1, 94, 118, 147
Indonesia 33, 71, 92, 148
industry code of conduct 56
information dominance 94, 113, 117, 133
information technology (IT) 1, 34, 55, 66, 68, 93, 102, 116
intellectual property 48, 77
International Association of Insurance Supervisors (IAIS) 77
International Campaign to Ban Landmines (ICBL) 80, 134
international community 9, 34, 121, 159; *see also* international society
International Criminal Court (ICC) 31
International Crisis Group (ICG) 89
International Electrotechnical Commission (IEC) 83
International Labour Organisation (ILO) 145
international law 18, 31, 44, 69–70, 79, 86, 161

International Monetary Fund (IMF) 9, 15, 31, 72
International Organization for Standardization (ISO) 77, 83
International Organization of Securities Commissioners (IOSCO) 77
International Relations (IR) 2, 7–8, 21–2, 27, 46–7, 51, 90, 142, 159, 162, 167
International Security Assistance Force (ISAF) 132; *see also* NATO
international society 10, 28–9, 46, 49, 69, 86–7, 165; *see also* international community
internet 1, 48, 59, 66, 68, 72, 77, 83, 114, 116–17, 134, 142, 144; Arab world 101, 103–4, 123, 126; China 43, 94, 101–2, 128; diplomacy 114, 116–17, 129–31, 148; freedom 55, 92–4, 96–7, 112, 163; Lebanon war 105–6; *see also* e-commerce; e-democracy
Internet Corporation for Assigned Names and Numbers (ICANN) 83, 85
Iran 9, 30, 42, 92, 99, 101, 126, 152, 156; image 4, 140, 155
Iraq 9, 24, 30, 51, 54, 59, 94, 98, 104, 107, 125–6, 141, 151–2, 159, 162, 164; war 5–6, 12, 20, 33, 43, 70, 80, 95, 106, 120–1
Islam 14, 59, 94, 103–4, 122, 125–6, 155, 162; *see also* religion
Israel 24, 95, 105–6, 114, 133, 135, 147
Ivan IV (Russian czar) 142

Japan 14, 39, 41–2, 138
jazz 26, 50–1, 163
Jeong, Jong Ho 40
jihad (holy war) 14, 97, 127
Jintao, Hu 41, 89
Joffe, Joseph 34
John Paul II, Pope 5
Jolie, Angelina 89
Judge, Clark S. 150

Kalathil, Shanthi 101
Kalb, Malvin 106
Kammer, Raymond 74
Kant, Immanuel 6, 35, 146
Katzenstein, Peter J. 46, 54–5
Kazakhstan 141, 153–6
Kelly, Robert 25–6
Keohane, Robert O. 6, 54–5, 137
Khamenei, Ayatollah Ali 42
Khrushchev, Nikita S. 51
Kidman, Nicole 89

Kissinger, Henry 50
Klein, Naomi 144
Knill, Christoph 12
Kosovo 5, 24, 105, 131, 143, 159
Krasner, Stephen D. 7
Kratochwil, Friedrich 2, 46, 49
Krauthammer, Charles 30
Kühnhardt, Ludger 37
Kurlantzick, Joshua 42
Kuwait 155
Kyoto Protocol 31

LaFeber, Walter 50, 59
Laïdi, Zaki 38, 104, 162
Lake, David A. 24
Lake, Ricki 89
Lapid, Yosef 46
Latin America 33, 41–3, 54
Latvia 65
law 1, 23, 28, 36–7, 47, 49, 53, 72–3, 78–9, 81, 88–9, 112, 123, 145, 147, 162; lawfare 29; natural 10; power 14, 25, 36, 69–70; Roman 25; *see also* international law; soft law
Lebanon 103, 105–6, 155
Lebow, Richard Ned 25–6
legitimacy 3, 9, 18–19, 21–2, 28, 41, 45, 47, 58, 63, 65, 69–71, 75, 77, 87–90, 104, 116, 121, 137, 139–40, 145, 153, 157–66; governance 13–17, 80–5, 135, 146; hegemony 25, 33, 50, 149; power 4, 6, 13, 26, 69, 87, 89, 105, 120, 152, 159
Legro, Jeffrey W. 13
Leonard, Mark 42, 116, 118
liberal democracy 4–5, 14, 34, 41, 121–2
liberal institutionalism 7, 22
Libya 95, 155
lifestyle 48, 52, 55–6, 62, 108, 110–11, 139, 163
Linux (software) 28
liquid modernity 72, 88, 131, 166; *see also* Zygmunt Bauman
Lisbon Strategy (EU) 66
Lisbon Treaty (EU) 147
Lite Powers 27, 29, 36, 44
Lott, Trent 97
loyalty 2, 10, 32, 88, 135, 137–41, 145, 149, 158, 161
Lukes, Steven 3, 18, 48
Lula da Silva, Luiz Inacio 42
Luther, Martin 92

McCain, John 121
Machiavelli, Niccolo 2, 151

McLean, Charles M. 104
McLuhan, Marshall 95–6, 108, 142
Mad Men (TV series) 164
Mahbubani, Kishore 38–9, 94
mainstream media 91–4, 96–7, 107; *see also* radio; television
Mali 37
Mandelson, Peter 75, 165
manipulation 13, 19, 48, 105, 115, 163
Mankell, Henning 66
Mann, Michael 69, 162
Manners, Ian 35–8, 161
Marshall aid 51
Martin, Lisa L. 70
Marxism-Leninism 14
mass media 49, 57, 91, 96, 111, 123, 134, 164; *see also* mainstream media
Mattern, Janice Bially 19
Mattli, Walter 74, 165
Mead, Walter Russell 6, 8–9
Mearsheimer, John J. 7
mediapolitik 135
Melissen, Jan 133
me-media 96, 99–100, 156, 163; *see also* blog; Twitter
Merkel, Angela 16
Microsoft 28, 89, 101, 119, 138
Miller, M. Rex 106–7, 112
Milosevic, Slobodan 119
Minsk Group (OSCE) 71
mission civilisatrice 160
modeling 76
modernity 25, 67, 78, 122
Moïsi, Dominique 152
Mongol (movie) 155
Monnet, Jean 36, 50, 64
Moran, Terence P. 52
Morgenthau, Hans J. 2, 27, 114
Morocco 95
MTV 51, 110, 126
Multilateral Agreement on Investments (MAI) 60
multilateralism 31, 35, 44, 66, 70–2, 84, 117–18, 132
multipolarity 40, 44
Mumby, Dennis 27
Murphy, Jim 114
Muslim world 20, 33, 118–19, 121–4, 127, 133, 144, 155–6, 164
mutual assured destruction (MAD) 8

Nagorno-Karabach 71
naming-and-shaming 20, 165
nationalism 56, 91, 106, 137, 140, 157–8

NATO 10, 16, 31–2, 37, 39, 70–2, 105, 110, 128, 156–7, 167; Cold War 5; reputation 131–2, 136, 145–6
Nazism 14, 25, 46, 143
Negri, Antonio 49, 56
Nelson, Michael 51
neoliberalism 8, 68, 83–5, 89
Neumann, Iver B. 142
new media 34, 92, 95–108, 111, 132, 134, 142, 151, 153, 156, 165; democratization 96, 98, 101–4, 107, 112; diplomacy 114, 116–17, 129–31, 148; social power 93, 95, 100, 104, 116; *see also* blog; information technology (IT); me-media
new public diplomacy 114, 116, 130, 133–5, 151; *see also* public diplomacy
Niger 37
Nigeria 33, 94, 155
Nike 4, 59, 80, 153, 157
Nixon, Richard 51
non-governmental organization (NGO) 1, 7, 10–11, 17, 58, 71, 88–90, 101, 103, 125, 130–1, 133, 136, 138–9, 160, 165–6; influence 16, 20, 28, 62, 73, 75, 78–81, 83–4, 86, 115, 134, 158
noopolitik 135
norm advocacy 8, 10, 28
normative power 35–6, 38, 62, 79, 104, 141, 145, 147, 161
norm entrepreneur 10, 13, 19–20, 28, 30, 34, 70, 80, 115, 123, 138, 141, 153; EU 44, 62, 72, 74–6, 129, 146–8, 165; social power 11, 84, 148; US 141, 153, 165
norms cascade 28
North Korea 4, 140
Norway 156
Nossel, Suzanne 150
Nye, Joseph S. 6, 8, 34, 44, 120, 137, 159; information dominance 94, 113

Obama, Barack 34, 44, 71, 98, 141, 152
Office of Global Communications (OGC) 124
Office of Public Diplomacy 119
Office of Strategic Information (OSI) 124
Office of War Information 119
O'Grady, Scott 110
Olins, Wally 140–1, 143
Olsen, Scott R. 53, 164
Onuf, Nicholas G. 46
Oprah Winfrey 111
Organisation of African Unity 36

Organization for Economic Co-operation and Development (OECD) 60, 79
Organization for Security and Co-operation in Europe (OSCE) 71
Ostpolitik 18
Owens, William 94, 113

Packard, Vance 144
Pakistan 118, 147, 155
Palestine Authorities 133, 135, 148
Parsons, Craig 20–1
Partnership and Cooperation Agreement (PCA-EU) 145
patriotism 57, 108–9, 112, 124, 137
Patten, Chris 34
Pax Americana 18, 24, 30, 33–4, 43–4, 58, 120
Pax Romana 24, 92
Pearl Harbour (movie) 109
peitho (friendship) 26, 29–30
persuasion 2, 6, 8–9, 11, 19–20, 26, 28, 32, 76, 80, 82, 86, 90, 159
Philpott, Daniel 10
piracy 12, 18
place branding 4, 22–3, 27, 50, 54, 58, 66, 92, 99, 116, 123, 135, 138; definition 136; EU 145–9; history 143–4, 158; IR 142, 158; negative 153–7; NGOs 139, 167; popular culture 65, 137; social power 8, 13, 136; US 149–53
Plumridge, Hester 131
policy convergence 12, 62
popular culture 25–6, 34–5, 53–5, 57, 61–2, 65, 88, 110, 112, 122, 163–4; Cold War 5, 49–53, 52, 55, 119, 161, 163; hegemony 49–50; social power 48, 50, 67–8
Portman, Natalie 89
Postman, Neil 91
postmodernism 21, 46, 48, 71, 88, 96, 110, 117–18, 133, 140, 146, 157–9, 165; empire, 27, 29
Powell, Colin 108, 119
prestige 13, 16, 18, 22, 27, 33–4, 39, 42, 116
Price, Monroe E. 49, 51, 91, 100
privacy 76
private authority 15, 72, 75, 77, 81–5, 89–90, 160, 166
private military company (PMC) 83
Prodi, Romano 36
propaganda 51, 53, 104, 114, 127, 129, 144; public diplomacy 14, 117, 130; US 67, 92, 105, 115, 120, 126, 151

protectionism 49, 61, 76, 161
Protestantism 92; *see also* religion
public administration 8, 162
public diplomacy 8–9, 13, 23, 27, 50, 99, 105, 114, 116–8, 156; blog 116, 130, 132–3; China 40, 116, 128–9, 144, 163; definition 115; EU 36, 65, 114, 129–31; NATO 131–2; social power 4, 14, 54, 92; US 12, 19, 45, 51, 109, 118–28, 151–2; *see also* new public diplomacy
public relations (PR) 9, 42, 65, 83, 119, 125, 128, 151, 153–4
Putin, Vladimir V. 41

Qatar 92, 94–5, 142
Qiang, Xiao 102

radio 48, 61, 91–2, 106, 116, 126, 128, 130, 142
Radio Free Europe/Radio Liberty 92
Radio Sawa 126
Rasmussen, Anders Fogh 155
Rather, Dan 97–8
Rauch, Jonathan 104
Raustiala, Kal 72
REACH program (EU) 73, 75–6
Reagan, Ronald 5, 18, 119, 153, 161
Realism 7, 14, 17
Realpolitik 37, 42, 49–50, 112, 118, 135, 147, 161, 165
reflexive thinking 107
regime change 15, 120
regime theory 7, 69
regulatory competition 13, 30, 73–4, 77
Reid, T.R. 65
Reimann, Kim D. 80
Rein, Martin 12
religion 10, 14–15, 25, 54, 103, 105, 124, 126, 157
Renan, Ernest 158
Reporters Without Borders 101
representational force 19–20, 121; *see also* image
reputation 7, 21, 58, 80, 90, 124, 136–8, 141–4, 153–8, 164; EU 129, 145; NATO 131; US 123, 145
respect 1, 9, 12, 29, 33, 42, 81, 100, 140, 146–7, 155; social capital 18, 41
Responsible Care Program 85
Reuters 106
Reynolds, Glenn 97, 99
Rice, Condoleezza 53, 155
Riefenstahl, Leni 143

Rifkin, Jeremy 35
Risse, Thomas 20
River Path Associates 133
Robertson, Roland 67
rock 'n' roll 26, 51, 88, 163
Rolling Stones 51
Roman Catholic Church 5, 117; *see also* religion
Roosevelt, Teddy 161
Rosamond, Ben 36, 147
Rosenau, James 16–17
Rosenberg, Tina 5
Rothkopf, David J. 112
Ruggie, John G. 49, 69, 72, 76, 85
Rumsfeld, Donald 31, 71
Russia 1, 30, 41, 45, 55, 70, 92–3, 118, 142, 145; place branding 143, 154, 164

Safe Harbor agreement 76
Sarkozy, Nicolas 36, 59
SARS 129
Saudi Arabia 101, 103, 155
Schapiro, Mark 75
Scharpf, Fritz W. 85
Schelling, Thomas 8
Schön, Donald A. 12
Second Life 134–5, 148
Secunda, Eugene 52
Segal, Gerald 29, 52
Seib, Philip 95
self-regulation 74, 77, 81–4, 96
Sennett, Richard 71
September 11, 2001 terrorist attacks (9/11) 9, 11–12, 19, 29–33, 41, 53–4, 57–9, 70, 95, 108–9, 112, 118–21, 123–4, 126–7, 144, 151, 163; *see also* terrorism
Serbia 65, 119, 143
Seton-Watson, Hugh 142
Shaheen, Jack 54
Sharp, Paul 115
sharp power 6, 8–9
Shea, Jamie 131
Shell (Royal Dutch) 80, 117, 153
Shore, Cris 63
Sikkink, Kathryn 10–11, 20, 28, 38, 86
Simes, Dimitri 33
slavery 12, 18, 76, 86
social capital 33, 44, 87, 90, 141, 149, 157, 160, 165, 167; definition 15; popular culture 26; social power 15, 18, 41, 86
social Darwinism 29

social isomorphism 12
social knowledge 3, 33, 116
social learning 3, 14, 90
social power: Central Europe 18, 51–3, 55, 121, 161; China 9, 30, 39–45; definition 8; embeddedness 4, 6, 10, 23, 100, 105; framing 4, 8, 11, 19, 90; global governance 9, 88; globalization 5, 38; new media 93, 95, 100, 104; norm entrepreneur 11, 84, 148; place branding 8, 13, 136; popular culture 48, 50, 67–8; public diplomacy 4, 14, 54, 92; social capital 15, 18, 41, 86; US disregard for 33–4
social-networking websites 92, 99
soft law 72, 76–7, 90
soft news 108, 110–11
soft power 8, 38, 40, 50, 67, 104, 137, 159, 167; China 42, 45, 128–9; definition 6; US 34, 44, 120, 152; *see also* Joseph S. Nye
Solana, Javier 70
Solidarity movement 51
Sopranos (TV series) 54, 123
South Korea 24
Soviet Union (USSR) 5, 18, 25, 40, 51–3, 55, 71, 114–15, 143–4, 157, 163
Spain 32, 70
Spielberg, Steven 43
spin-doctoring 2, 126–7, 144, 149
sport 50, 63, 88, 92, 122, 126, 128, 148, 150, 155
sports utility vehicle (SUV) 57–8
Sri Lanka 143
Stability Pact for South Eastern Europe 37
Stalin, Joseph 5
standards 8, 10–11, 28–31, 33, 36, 39, 44, 48, 55–6, 61, 69–79, 81–5, 88, 90, 94, 103–4, 112, 123, 126, 131, 133–6, 138–9, 141, 143–4, 158–9, 162–6; EU 37–8, 63, 67–8, 73–5, 129, 145, 147, 149, 153, 162; social 4, 79, 153, 162; US 55, 74, 153
Standards Developing Organization (SDO) 83
Steinberg, Donald 89
Stelzer, Irwin 32
Sterling-Folker, Jennifer 52
sticky power 2, 6–7, 9, 159
Stopford, Michael 145
Strategic Defense Initiative (SDI) 5
subsidiarity 62
Sudan 43

Sullivan, Andrew 93
Summers, Lawrence H. 24
Sutherland, Kiefer 109; *see also 24* (TV series)
sweatshops 4, 56, 80
Sweden 28, 66, 134, 156
symbolic interaction theory 49, 57, 65
symbolic power 84, 87–9
symbols 47–8, 87–8, 92, 107, 112, 137, 143; EU 63, 65; US 54–5, 57, 151
Syriana (movie) 54

tabloidization 110
Taiwan 39, 42–3, 128
Taliban 92, 126, 131–2
television 48, 52–4, 59, 61, 65, 67, 91, 93, 95, 103, 105–7, 109, 111–12, 123–4, 142, 144, 152, 159
territory 2, 4, 8, 24, 29, 48–9, 53, 61, 110–11, 116, 136–40, 157–8, 160
terrorism 12, 18, 29, 31–2, 34, 53–4, 57, 78, 95, 104–5, 107–10, 112, 117–20, 124, 126–7, 141, 151, 159; *see also* September 11, 2001 terrorist attacks (9/11)
Thucydides 2, 26
Tibet 92, 101, 128
Titanic (movie) 53
torture 32, 107, 109, 150, 152, 164
Touraine, Alain 3
tourism 4, 41–2, 66, 136, 138, 144, 150
tradition 10, 13, 15, 36, 40, 47, 51, 56, 66, 73, 77, 121, 128, 137, 157, 162
transatlantic cooperation 16, 29, 76, 117, 131–2
transgovernmental policy network 72, 77–8, 139, 160, 166
transnational advocacy coalition 10, 79, 166
Traud, James 89
trust 9, 40, 81, 83, 88, 97, 100, 108, 126, 131, 134, 137–40, 147, 158, 160; Asia 14; social capital 14–15, 18, 33, 165; US 31, 33, 70, 76, 119, 164; *see also* credibility
Tuch, Hans 115
Tunisia 95
Turkey 32, 37, 63, 65, 143, 155
Twitter 92, 116

Ukraine 37, 65
UNESCO 61
unilateralism 32, 34–5, 82, 121, 145, 151
Union for the Mediterranean 36

United Kingdom 24–5, 29, 32, 57, 66, 70–1, 114, 117, 126, 133
United Nations (UN) 15, 70–2, 78–9, 87–8, 136; Arab Human Development Report 103; Commission on Human Rights 43; Security Council 14, 31, 121; *see also* Global Compact
United States: credibility 18, 34, 141, 153; hard power 5, 6, 18, 32, 44, 120–1, 161; identity 53, 57, 119, 124; image 18, 32, 35, 44, 52–4, 59–60, 107, 118–19, 122–5, 141, 149–53, 164; norm entrepreneur 141, 153, 165; propaganda 67, 92, 105, 115, 120, 126, 151; public diplomacy 12, 19, 45, 51, 109, 118–28, 151–2; place branding 149–53; reputation 123, 145; social power 18, 51–3, 55, 121, 161; soft power 34, 44, 120, 152; standards 55, 74, 153; symbols 54–5, 57, 151; trust 31, 33, 70, 76, 119, 164
United States Information Agency (USIA) 51, 53, 115, 119, 121
US Ad Council 53, 124
US Advisory Commission on Public Diplomacy 122, 163
USAID 131
US National Institute of Standards and Technology (NIST) 74
US National Security Strategy 31, 122
US Office of National Drug Control Policy (ONDCP) 57

Valenti, Jack 109
verbal fighting 19–20, 40, 121, 132
Vietnam 12, 120
violence 8, 18, 20, 28, 52, 54, 57, 104–5, 110, 121, 127, 146
virtual diplomacy 134–5, 148; *see also* cyberdiplomacy
virtual reality 105, 108
Voice of America (VoA) 51, 92, 121, 126
Voice of China/China Radio International 128
Voltaire 142

Walker, Martin 94
Wallström, Margot 129, 148
Waltz, Kenneth 2
War on Terror 12, 31–2, 34, 57, 105, 108–9, 112, 118–19, 124, 127, 141, 151
Washington consensus 41
weapons of mass destruction (WMD) 120, 146

web 2.0 127
Weber, Max 16, 47, 71, 139
Weeds (TV series) 123
Wenders, Wim 59
Wendt, Alexander 46
Westphalia, system of 36, 44, 147
wielding problem 21–2, 54, 63, 67, 118, 149, 151, 153, 162
wiki 93, 96, 98–9, 163
Wikipedia 96, 98–100
Wolff, Larry 142
Wolff, R.P. 4
Wolfowitz, Paul 70
Wolin, Sheldon 80, 87
World Bank 9, 31, 133
World Commission on Dams 78
World Health Organization (WHO) 88
World of Warcraft 134

Word Trade Organization (WTO) 15–16, 31, 38, 61, 70
World War I 1, 119
World War II 9, 14, 18, 51, 53, 57, 115, 119, 150, 155

Yahoo! 101
Yard Birds 51
Yeats, W.B. 1
York, Peter 157
Young, Oran R. 49, 69
YouTube 96, 99–101, 116, 132, 135
Yugoslavia 37, 71
Yushenko, Viktor 37

Zelditch, Morris 13
Zetterholm, Staffan 64
Zimbabwe 42, 143

Lightning Source UK Ltd.
Milton Keynes UK
21 December 2010

164703UK00001B/28/P